A DIFFERENT DRUMMER

The History of
Columbia College Chicago
by Mike Alexandroff

ACKNOWLEDGMENTS

I am grateful to Dr. John Duff, my successor as Columbia College's president, who first urged me to write the college's history, and to his successor, Dr. Warrick Carter, who graciously agreed to publish the book through the Columbia College Press. The encouragement, support, criticism, and management of all publishing arrangements, by my son, Norman Alexandroff, was indispensible. Indeed, without him there wouldn't have been a book. My great appreciation also goes to Patricia DeWitt, who patiently produced all of the book's early drafts from my confusing and poorly typed copy; to Tony Neuhoff, Linda Naslund, and Deborah Roberts who provided copy editing; to Paula Epstein, who provided essential research and searched scattered files for pictures and other documentation; to Andrea Lather, the book's designer; Anita Strejc who provided production support and to my talented and diligent editor, Dr. Charles Gold, who gave order and effect to my text.

Published by
COLUMBIA COLLEGE CHICAGO
600 South Michigan / Chicago, Illinois 60605-1996

Copyright 2003
Columbia College Chicago
All Rights Reserved

No part of this book may be reproduced in any form or by any means without the prior, written permission of the publisher, excepting brief quotes used in connection with reviews, written specifically for inclusion in a magazine or newspaper.

Library of Congress Catalog Number: 2003094242
ISBN: 0-932026-65-6

Printed by *Consolidated Carqueville Printing Co.* (United States of America)

If a man does not keep pace with his companions,

        perhaps it is because he hears a different drummer.

Let him step to the music which he hears,

     however measured or far away.

— *Thoreau*

CONTENTS

In the mid 1970s, George Bonham, then editor of *Change* magazine, sent me into America to explore three institutions of higher learning that he found to be remarkable. My trips took me to rural Indiana to experience the world of Earlham College, southern Colorado to visit Adams State College, and, providentially, to my hometown, my beloved Chicago, to encounter a world of education at the same time radical and traditional, inclusive and distinctive. In retrospect, there is a trace of irony that I embarked from Boston, my present home, as it is this great New England city that first sent Miss Blood to Chicago and then, for a while, hosted Columbia College's present president, Dr. Duff.

But that first journey to Columbia College, known to me only as an open enrollment school that employed Chicago's outstanding professionals on its faculty and quietly assumed that its campus could rightly be the entire city, was utterly life changing. Met by a thin, almost frail-looking young man, Bert Gall, whose long hair and general appearance made me believe he was a rock star, I was taken to a Lake Shore Drive building, a warehouse it seemed, where I met a man so huge and robust, so full of life and vision for this educational experiment he was undertaking, that I was mesmerized. Within hours I was involved with a man named Schultz and a form of teaching creative writing that was utterly remarkable. And then there was a television cameraman named Lyman who was putting young people, steeped in knowledge, smack dab in the middle of the city's television industry. There was a gentleman named Russo who they said played for Stan Kenton's band, and a woman named Mordine who convinced students of the greatness that is theater. And the artist Harry Bouras and the scientist Zafra Lerman and others, gifted women and men, all of whom were as committed to the young people they taught as they were to their fields, their disciplines, their art. But all roads, as they say, led back to the huge one, the radical one, the generator of an educational power plant that underwrote one of America's most extraordinary chapters of learning.

Mike Alexandroff probably won me over with some reference to baseball, or to Bouras, or Mike Fish's restaurant. Or perhaps it was his constant allusion to some place on the Near West Side called Deni's Den that inevitably would have to be part of my Columbia College experience. As I look back almost twenty-five years later, I see Columbia College as a Field of Dreams, a place with rare ability to attract unusually gifted and caring people, all with superlative credentials. But the players in this Field of Dreams were not famous ghosts of the past. More precisely, they were quite often the unseen, forgotten children of America whose futures were born on the sacred grass of this unusual field.

Perhaps that is the point of this remarkable chronicle of a single institution. Yes, we must learn of its population growth, its financial woes and successes, the changes in faculty and board constitution. We must know the honorary-degree recipients, the Harbourgs, Fallacis, Russells, Halberstams, and Terkels. But all of this pales next to the world of the young men and women who discovered, learned, and established their futures at Columbia.

Only a great writer could begin to describe Mike Alexandroff, although his own description of his father, apart from the physical characteristics, would do quite nicely.

And therein lies another irony, a metaphor perhaps, of what Columbia College means to so many people. I was struck by the passages of Norman Alexandroff's developing cancer, of him losing his entire voice box only to teach himself to speak again. It might have been a hoarse sound that came out at first, but his voice returned. In this same way, I think Mike Alexandroff and his faculty have always been in the business of giving students back their voices—or is it that they made it possible for students to discover their inimitable voices in the first place? Through the media, arts, sciences, and writing, young people were becoming knowledgeable, educated. They were valued and honored. They discovered the grand rewards of knowing oneself to be competent. They were leaving Columbia, many of them, with jobs, dignity, and a sense of themselves and the world.

Entire generations of people can be altered by education; it may be the only thing that allows for this form of transformation in which social mobility, civic responsibility, and an abiding morality emerge as prominent features. The great educators Dewey, Mann, Parker, and Alexandroff knew this going into their respective experiments. They knew, too, as Parker intoned, that schools must be model homes, complete communities, and embryonic democracies.

Mike Alexandroff knew something else as well, something he learned from his parents, his city, and his country. It is that even at its best, education cannot escape the political realities of the moment. Some of these realities moved education forward. Others forever obstructed even the most elementary forms of progress. The great educators inevitably seem able to handle education and the politics, and this is

essential for at least two reasons: First, their experiments cannot last without this brand of sophistication. Second, without this skill, their experiments would die when they do. Charisma, Weber taught, lasts only so long before it becomes routinized. Mike Alexandroff may have proved him wrong. Columbia College has flourished, and will continue to do so. As I carry on because of two unusual people, Chicagoans now long dead, so will Columbia College carry on without Mike in his office, in the halls, in the classrooms, in the meetings, in the ether waves, everywhere.

Years ago, well after I became a convert—a "Miker"—and had committed myself to commuting to Chicago to teach part-time at the college, Mike put his arm around me and uttered these words: "Speak the radical slogans but go first class." At first, I misconstrued his words. Surely this man could not have meant that one should utter various political slogans of the left only to lead the life of the very people who held one back. Then I finally got it, and I think when I did, I got Columbia College. I take his words to mean that America cannot possibly accept the reality that presently constitutes its formidable educational institutions. A very radical vision is required because people's lives are at stake. But the vision for these people, as well as for the people who will educate and counsel and befriend them, must be first class. Their lives, their training, the quality of their friendships, and their sense of moral rectitude must all be first class.

The philosopher John Rawls is correct, I believe: None of us deserves anything! But in choreographing our culture, indeed in drawing our most utopian visions, we remind ourselves that none of us knows where we might end up in the dance.

Knowing this, that huge and robust dynamo I met a quarter of a century ago clearly decided he would draw it up first class for all of us, or kill himself trying. The last pitch at Comiskey Park may have sailed ten feet from the plate, but those of us who have watched this powerhouse of an educational hurler for several decades know his complete games, his strikeouts, and his earned run average to be of Cooperstown dimensions.

Big lives push us in directions we never imagined, or ever imagined possible. Little lives, unfortunately, seem to keep us where we are, if in fact they even let us know where we are, or who we are. We are stirred by reading this volume, just as we who knew Mike have been profoundly changed by his presence—and what a mountainous presence! My own change is not that I was moved to write an encomium for my editor at *Change* magazine, nor that I was so taken by the school that I chose to teach there. No, the epiphany occurred at Deni's Den, where, amid friends and strangers, I actually danced. For several hours, it as all Greek to me, as the old expression goes, and I was Greek, and I loved it, as I do the man who took me to the Den in the first place.

Thomas J. Cottle
Professor of Education
Boston University

Columbia College Chicago is a prosperous, independent college institution identified by its distinctive urban mission and comprehensive focus on the arts, public information, and entertainment media within a context of enlightened liberal education. Columbia has 9600 undergraduate and graduate students (6500 full-time) and is the fifth largest private college or university in Illinois; more than nine hundred full- and part-time faculty members; five hundred staff members; fourteen big buildings in Chicago's South Loop, including a 350-resident dormitory, three theaters, a large variety of public performance spaces, studios, and laboratories, and a number of satellite locations—in all, more than one million square feet of educational space; a wealth of state-of-the-art professional facilities and technology to serve every subject of instruction; and a modern college library incorporating the most contemporary information systems. Columbia College Chicago has an annual operating budget exceeding $100 million, and endowment and reserve funds of more than $50 million.

These are unremarkable figures when compared to familiar wealthy and influential colleges and universities. Nonetheless, Columbia is a remarkable institution, particularly so when it is understood that in 1964, after seventy-four years of halting and hesitant history, Columbia was a virtually failed, unaccredited institution with fewer than two hundred students in a rented warehouse building, with twenty-five part-time faculty, no library, severely limited facilities, and very minimal and undependable finances. Columbia then was orphaned and penniless, with small visibility and doubtful collegiate respectability, without patrons, endowment, or public constituency.

But what Columbia had then was a small band of supremely loyal and talented individuals, myself—a college president surely by default, and the beginnings of an unorthodox idea of creating a contemporary college focused on the arts, media, and liberal education. That a "new Columbia" would arise from the rubble of resources and vague themes of its past to become a successful institution is surely the stuff of miracles. To the best of my knowledge, Columbia College Chicago is the only private urban college begun, in effect, as an alternative to mainstream higher education that was to survive and prosper.

Apart from the reference to Columbia College's current state in 2000 and the College's episodic history from 1890 to 1934, this record is mainly concerned with the years after 1964, when Columbia was reinvented, until my retirement in 1992. The span of fifty-seven years, beginning in 1935, is linked intimately with my father, Norman Alexandroff, who served as president from 1935 to 1960, and myself as his successor from 1960 to 1992. This narrative is inescapably personal because of my family's ties to Columbia's history, and because I am the only close witness of nearly sixty years of Columbia's life, though much of this is only a memory of stories my father told me and fragments dimmed by the passing of time.

In writing this history of Columbia College, I've tried to create a record that will give a sense of Columbia and the events that contributed to its unusual success. It was not my intention to write an autobiography, except inclusions that relate closely to Columbia's life or explain what I had in mind in relevant instances. Nor, in describing Columbia's individuals, have I attempted anything but an estimate of the distinctive personal qualities that inspired their influential contribution to the college's course. With this, I offer the reservation that I may be unusually susceptible to personal charm and goodness in individuals. Thus, as my narrative tells of many individuals I dearly love and respect, my sentiment for them may seem without boundary.

While my arbitrary division of Columbia's history, particularly after 1964, into year-to-year accounts may be tedious, I found such separations the only way to report the events that constituted the college's life. For many years after 1964, when Columbia's survival was a year-to-year proposition, every year stood by itself. Indeed, until the 1980s, the college's existence remained precarious, at least in the sense that Columbia was critically dependent on year-to-year results, and all efforts to improve the institution's condition and quality had threatening financial risks that could only have been relieved by a succession of "good years." This peculiarity of Columbia's life exaggerates the significance of every year.

There is only sketchy documentation of the college's early years until 1944. What is known stems from a small number of early catalogs, general bulletins, and, admirably, from perfectly intact student records. Crucially valuable in reconstituting Columbia's early history is the research accomplished by Theodore Kundrat, an alumnus (B.S.'36; M.S.'39), a talented teacher, and for many years the principal member of Columbia's speech-arts faculty. The college's more recent history (since 1945), is informed by accessible documentation, though much remains dependent on my memory and interpretation.

* Kundrat's 1985 series, "Columbia College in Retrospect," published in Columbia College Alumni Bulletins

Columbia College traces an irregular line from a conservatory founded in 1890 as a private enterprise, the Columbia School of Oratory, the title having had some identity with the Columbian Exposition, the world's fair held in Chicago in 1893. An early pioneer in speech-arts education and oral expression, the Columbia School of Oratory became the Columbia College of Expression, a private and nonprofit institution, in 1907. By 1928, this Columbia was bankrupt, though it survived as the ward of the Pestalozzi-Froebel Teachers College until 1939, when it regained its independence as the Columbia College of Drama and Radio. Finally, in 1944, Columbia became, then and forever, Columbia College.

The Columbia School of Oratory was founded by Mary A. Blood and her colleague, Ida Morey Riley. Apparently of New England origin if not authentically Bostonian, Ms. Blood had been a faculty member of the Boston Conservatory of Elocution, Oratory and Dramatic Arts, at the time a leading college of education in speech, theater, and the arts of expression, and the forerunner of Boston's venerable Emerson College (now Emerson University). Ida Morey Riley was Blood's student and a conservatory graduate (O.B., 1889 and M.A., 1890), and Blood was the first recipient of the conservatory's honorary master of arts award in 1889. Regrettably, little more is known about the earlier personal history of Blood and Riley, not even why they chose Chicago as the school's first place or what resources these intrepid women had to start.

Their Columbia undertaking was a daunting challenge in the late nineteenth century. Much of America then was still frontier, and women were distinctly second-class citizens. Women would not win the right to vote for another thirty years. Few women had the opportunity of college education, and fewer still could aspire to a professional career other than teaching. And certainly, few young women (or women of any age) started colleges. Columbia's bloodline was surely begun by eminently brave and intelligent souls.

Blood and Riley, eager to establish a school in the pattern of the Boston Conservatory, rented Columbia's first place in the Stevens Arts building. That it was a South Loop Chicago location is all that is now known. Similarly uncertain is the year when the school moved to Steinway Hall at 17 Van Buren Street (later 64 East Van Buren). The school's 1905 catalog shows the Steinway building as its address and makes no mention of a recent move, so it may be assumed to have moved earlier. The floor plans of the Steinway location indicate a comfortably spacious two floors (sixth and seventh), which the school occupied until 1916 when it secured a mansion at 3358 South Michigan Avenue.

Kundrat's account describes the mansion as having "a first floor used as a reception room, principal's office, library, and student lounge. The second and third floors were occupied by classrooms, the upper floor serving as living quarters for Blood and her sister, and a ground floor used as an assembly hall with a stage for presentation events." While the size and levels of the mansion and grounds are unknown, the neighborhood did include a number of impressive large homes and grounds and, presumably, the school's place was of similar character. The mansion's property included a back building that was used for physical education. Also, it provided a site

1

(in 1918) across the boulevard for a dormitory building, Colledge Hall, named for William A. Colledge, for many years president of the college's board of directors.

The School of Oratory and its successor, the Columbia College of Expression, consistently retained a statement of mission that guided the institutions during Blood's long tenure:

This is a College of Expression for ladies and gentlemen, professional or nonprofessional. It is a school for character building and preparation for life. The physical, mental and moral nature of each pupil is carefully studied and training adapted not only to the individual's mental and expressional development, but to his character development as well. Nowhere can the precept, 'know thyself,' be so fully realized as in a school of true expression.

The mission statement was expanded by Blood and Riley in 1893 and 1894:

Expression has to do with the whole man. In this art, thoughts, emotions and purposes form the content, while the body and voice present the form. . . . In order that the student may reach his greatest possibilities in expression, besides having a voice and body cultivated to the highest perfection, he must have a mind enriched by all its departments and strengthened in all its processes. . . . The three departments of the mind—intellectual, emotional and volitional—must be developed through experience. The stringent training afforded within the "School's" widely varied curriculum enables the students to achieve and fulfill that "experience."

And subsequently by Ms. Blood's remarks in 1916:

The Columbia College of Expression is singularly unfettered by preconceived ideas and ancient methods, yet it is strongly conservative in that it occupies the medium ground between the Emotional or Impulsive School on the one extreme and the Mechanical or Imitative on the other. It (Columbia) recognizes that expression is concerned with a subjective content which must be apprehended, comprehended and experienced, and an objective form which must be strengthened, beautified and made effective. It agrees with the pedagogic principle that growth must be from within and by organic change, not be mere accretion. It believes that speakers and readers must be thinkers, but realizes that many of our best thinkers and writers are our poorest speakers and readers. Genuine literary training is made the basis of all the work in interpretation. Its classroom mottoes are: "Cooperation," "Learn to do by doing," "Theory never made an artist." Its business precepts are: "Secure good pupils by all honorable means, deal with them according to the Golden Rule while they remain, and, if possible, secure positions for them after they graduate." "The Faculty are original in their methods and are among the most advanced teachers of expression in the profession. They are open to the truth, however presented, and are generous with their knowledge, time and sympathy. They pay particular attention to the individual growth of each pupil." There is an atmosphere of sunshine, encouragement and helpfulness about the whole institution. That greatest principle of the new pedagogy and the new sociology, that old fashioned Christian principle of "Service" underlies the business, social and educational relations of teacher and pupil, pupil and pupil, teacher and teacher. Columbia graduates are successful.

While the language of Columbia's early mission may be a bit dated, the intent of its message is contemporary, moral, and not inconsistent with the essence of enlightened instruction in the expressive arts.

In spite of what must have been great difficulty in starting the school in an unfamiliar city, without an extant constituency and with only small resources, the fledgling institution prospered quickly. By 1900, the school offered a comprehensive curriculum including physical education, anatomy, physiology, and dance. Its Saturday and evening extensions enrolled a large number of clergy, many in business and other professions, and many adults from the city and suburbs in the various forms of public speaking. Also, a great number of children were enrolled in dramatic instruction. In fact, inspired by Mary Blood, children's theater in Chicago had its origin at Columbia. In 1911 an alumni bulletin lists 538 graduates (between 1892 and 1910) of regular degree and diploma programs exclusive of the many hundreds of students who had been enrolled in extension courses.

During its first decade, the Columbia School was led by its cofounders and principals. But in March 1901, apparently very suddenly, Ida Morey Riley died, a sad and untimely event widely mourned by all who were associated with the school. After Riley's death, Mary Blood remained the sole figure and dominant influence on Columbia's life until her death in 1927. Almost irreplaceable, Riley was succeeded by Blood's sister, Hattie, who joined the school as Blood's principal aide and companion until her retirement at the time of her sister's death.

In 1905, in response to great enrollment growth and Mary Blood's unique vision, the School of Oratory became the Columbia College of Expression. The most immediate reason for a new identity and new corporate form was a recognition by Blood that if she were to die or become disabled, the school might pass on to others'

hands and no longer represent the ideas and purposes of its founders. Blood and others concluded that the school's proper course was to give up its proprietary character and become a permanent not-for-profit corporation. Accordingly, on May 5, 1905, the Columbia School of Oratory was reincorporated as the Columbia College of Expession, and as Illinois law required, a board of directors was formed with authority to manage the college's affairs and to give continuity to its life and purposes. Also, Illinois statutes had strict guides for the disposition of an institution's assets in the event of a cessation of its business activity (such as bankruptcy) and/or corporate purposes. Such regulations remain in force to the present day. After 1905, a listing of the college's board of directors is shown prominently in a succession of the college's general catalogs, and these boards included a number of Chicago's civic, business, education and ministerial leaders. While presidents of colleges report to their boards and serve at their pleasure, Mary Blood was unquestionably the college's dominating decision-maker during her lifetime. What role and degree of influence and control was exercised by early Columbia boards is unknown; though as a general rule, if presidents are not successful and persuasive, boards will not long retain them.

Columbia's first board consisted of nine individuals chosen for their civic prominence and familiarity with the college. Three of these, including the board's president, Frank W. Gunsaulus, were clergymen, and one was Blood herself.

Another motive for a change in the institution's title was Blood's perception that "oratory was an overly narrow description of the School's more comprehensive intents," and that a new title as a "college" was more accurate and allowed much greater opportunity to lead an influential life and attract a larger student audience. "Oratory," said Blood, "while certainly not obsolete was merely passé in its application to Columbia's new approach to its purposes and major objectives. It connotes an oratorical display of artificial mannerisms, bombastic elocution and mechanical gesticulation." It was a pretty astute observation that did not have wide acceptance for many years.

In 1905, teacher education became a prominent emphasis, as did a practice teaching exchange (a relatively new concept in teacher training). Successfully organized, too, were a writer's laboratory, interscholastic activities such as declamation and debating contests, dramatic recitals, an emphasis on storytelling in children's classrooms, and Chicago's first speaker's bureau, which served many city and suburban communities with Columbia-trained speakers and lecturers on a variety of subjects in the pattern of the ubiquitous Chautauqua circuit that then served the whole country. Indeed, many Columbia graduates enjoyed profitable employment as Chautauqua and Redpath speakers.

The curricular patterns and degree and diploma expectations established by Blood and her colleagues prevailed to the mid-1930s, though the absence of catalogs for a number of these years and the often archaic academic language employed make a detailed description difficult. The core of the college's educational offering was a two-year (six terms/forty-five courses) curriculum of professional studies in the expressive arts with varying emphases leading to a "graduate's diploma" in teaching (expressive arts), public reading, and public speaking. A "personal culture diploma" could be earned by mastery of forty courses. It seems that a bachelor's or master's degree could only be earned by those who had already graduated from another college. Qualification for the bachelor's degree in expression (B.E.) required prior college graduation plus four terms of Columbia study; the master's degree, prior college graduation plus three years (nine terms) of Columbia study.

The Columbia School, and College subsequently, had a professional rather than conventional collegiate emphasis, though undoubtedly a number of Columbia students qualified for bachelor's and master's degrees. In 1916, a new two- or three-year diploma in teaching and a two-year diploma in physical education were added.

The college had always included an emphasis on the physical qualities of expression, and in the years up to 1916 a full complement of physical education subjects was an important part of the curriculum. This intent was given a distinct life in the Columbia Normal School of Physical Education, formally introduced in 1916. The normal school's curriculum was based on a pattern of physical education initiated in Danish and Swedish gymnastic training ideas and techniques that earned quick acceptance among gymnasts, dancers, and physical education teachers, and wide influence in the progressive education movement. Practices included an emphasis on styles of folk dancing and expressions of various ethnic cultures, which gave international vitality to the normal school's project.

From 1890 to the 1930s, the curriculum offered practice opportunities in professional settings, as well as outstanding faculty in all the principal disciplines of the liberal arts and sciences. These cultural subjects were a required part of every study emphasis. In 1915–16, the college reported a library of 3,000 volumes and reference books—particularly literature—and a large collection of texts on oral expression.

All catalogs after 1905 carry the imprimatur: "The Columbia College of Expression is recognized by the Illinois State Examining Board for Teacher Certification. Men and women holding Columbia diplomas were qualified to teach any branch of English vocal expression and physical training in the schools of this state and in all states having reciprocity with Illinois without examination. Courses of Columbia College of Expression are accredited by the Chicago Board of Education for salary promotion of both grade and high school teachers."

Unfortunately, Mary Blood is known mostly as Columbia's founder, director, and inspiration. As a teacher and administrator she was, unquestionably, a preeminent figure. It is evident that she had an impressive, comprehensive intelligence and that she was a progressive modern educator, foresightedly so. Little is known about her as an individual. Kundrat describes Blood only from having seen a portrait and a few blurry pictures of her in early catalogs and having heard some description of her by Anne Larkin, who was a Columbia teacher of long tenure (from the times of the School of Oratory to the 1930s). Kundrat wrote from such scant evidence that Mary Blood "was auburn haired, darkly complexioned with a turned-up nose and firm mouth. She was stately and regal in appearance with a poised manner and a very expressive face. When speaking, she always carried conviction and had the ability to captivate an audience and hold its rapt attention. Her personality was scintillating and effervescent."

I seldom, if ever, thought about Mary Blood, and then only that her name was familiar as someone who had started a distant episode in Columbia's life, which had meaning to me only in that I occasionally referred to the ancestral Columbia to give a venerable cast to advertisements of the contemporary Columbia of my personal experience. My father hardly mentioned the old Columbia at all, except a bit unpleasantly after some controversy with a few old faculty and alumni when he was asked to take Columbia's rusty helm in the mid-1930s.

For the most part, Columbia's records from 1927 are buried in a Pestalozzi-Froebel Teachers College (PFTC) basement or in the far reaches of scattered files (PFTC no longer exists independently), or are lost entirely. It was only with recent effort to narrate Columbia's history and to assemble the documentation of it that I began to know and appreciate the progressive educational themes and mutuality of educational focus common to the Columbias of now and then, though I suspect that such connections are more coincidental than deliberate and that whatever lessons the past may have held, these, mostly unknown, gave little if any guide to the contemporary college.

In the late nineteenth and early twentieth century, the forms and technologies of communication as we know them were scarcely imagined, and the spoken word was the principal currency of everyday life. Political platforms, lectures, forums, debates, theatricals, and all sorts of speech-making occasions were immensely popular. Elocution lessons had life in nearly every American community, and schools and colleges gave attention to speech subjects; and while perhaps not on a par with reading, writing, and arithmetic, schools expected their students to be well spoken. If anything, it is surprising that only a few collegiate institutions included the teaching of speech and the varieties of oral expression in their pedagogical design. Thus, the special effort of such institutions as the Boston Conservatory and the Columbia school(s) answered a very genuine and neglected need in the common schools and in higher education.

Although mainstream higher education ultimately took over the expressive arts and related subjects that had been taught by special colleges, over time education in the expressive arts (specifically, personal speech) has all but disappeared as a study requirement (except as an emphasis of theater arts). Given the present indifferent and deteriorated state of American speech, one can only wish that personal speech training had not been abandoned so prematurely.

The early 1900s were lively and liberating times in American intellectual, political, and civic life. Among the many signal events, issues, and inventions that reshaped the national society were the accelerated democratization of the American polity fueled by the influence of vast numbers of new immigrants and the opportunity of attending public schools; the industrialization of the national economy; the quick growth of urban society and the corresponding development of social service agencies; the growing literacy of the American population, who were the audience for an exploding proliferation of newspapers, magazines, and intellectual and political journals; the ready accessibility of the telephone and electricity, and just ahead, automobiles, radio, and movies; the dynamic movement for women's suffrage; and the cataclysm of World War I.

Similarly, the changing nature of education was an integral part of all the great changes occurring in American life. The ideas of John Dewey and the "new educators" provoked wide discussion. Many experimental schools, such as New York's Little Red Schoolhouse, Bank Street, and the Neighborhood School, were influential advocates of progressive education. While educational innovation had been pioneered independently in a small number of colleges and normal schools in previous decades, their experimentation was coopted, often in diluted form, in the 1920s and after by more prominent colleges and universities. What was radical at first became fashionably mainstream, and genuine innovation was often more rhetorical than real.

The Columbia College of Expression would ultimately lose its popularity as a place of focused, innovative educational practice in the expressive arts, and its identity would be lost among more comprehensive universities and marginalized by new forms of communication. In the early 1920s such a fate could only be vaguely sensed. However clouded its horizons, Columbia continued to prosper until 1925. There are no financial records from 1890 to nearly 1940, and there is no mention whatsoever of financial subjects in any existing publications.

In 1923 recruitment of students was recognized as an insistent problem, though a safe level of enrollment had been sustained for a number of years. Despite this, Columbia remained a healthy institution. If it had a pressing problem, it was the growing insufficiency and inconvenience of its South Michigan Avenue location. In 1915, two distinguished women had joined the faculty. Alice Gerstenberg was a prominent playwright and novelist who had staged and directed a successful New

York run of *Alice in Wonderland*. She was the founder of Chicago's Playwrights' Theater, president of the Chicago Women's Club, and a doyen of Chicago's high society. Her new colleague, Marie Merrill, was a dramatist, lecturer, and pioneer in children's theater. Later they headed a search committee for a new Columbia home, a project aided by Ms. Gerstenberg's wealthy connections, which included such rich and powerful families as the Fields, Piries, Bordens, and McGanns. Mrs. Robert McGann was the daughter of U.S. Senator Charles B. Farwell and the niece of John W. Farwell. The Farwell brothers had built two mansions side-by-side on East Pearson and Pine Streets (later North Michigan Avenue) after the Chicago Fire in 1872. They were two of Chicago's finest mansions, and their owners were among the city's wealthiest and best-known citizens.

After Senator Farwell's death, Ms. McGann bought her family home at 120 East Pearson, opposite the Water Tower, a venerable Chicago monument. The mansion had remained vacant until spring 1925 when Ms. McGann, in a great act of generosity, rented it to the college. The mansion was an imposing building with a mansard roof and a French-style red brick façade, dark and time-stained. Its three stories had twenty-two rooms, seven baths, an extensive library, a large dining room, and a spacious oak-paneled reception hall. The college's administrative offices, library, and dining hall occupied the first floor. The second floor was used for classrooms and the third floor served as a dormitory and study hall. A Queen Anne style carriage house stood behind the mansion. It had been large enough for eight carriages. As at the college's Michigan Avenue site, its upper floor, formerly servants' quarters, was used as an apartment for Blood and her sister. The ground floor housed the college's department of physical education, and provided an arena with four rows of bleachers and a large performing space used for dance and physical education activities. The mansion's splendid reception hall, with its decorative grand staircase, oak beam ceilings, huge fireplace of Italian marble, and glistening cut-glass chandeliers, became the assembly hall. Once a week, the students, faculty, and staff gathered for Blood's address. The staircase's first landing became her rostrum, where she would deliver the Lord's Prayer in a mellifluous resonant voice followed by announcements and a discussion of the week's proceedings. Hanging on the wall behind her was her portrait, an oil painting by New England artist Don Galloway. The society columns of the day commented that "the unusual new tenant of the Farwell mansion, the Columbia College of Expression, adds a certain prestige to the area."

The college advertised itself as coeducational, but its students were mainly women. Only a very small number of male students were evident in a span of more than thirty years, though there is an occasional statement that increasing male numbers was an important objective. Presumably, most of the female students enjoyed privileged social and economic station, since few women of ordinary and lower means attended college in the late nineteenth and early twentieth centuries. Records showing religious affiliation are sketchy. Apparently, a Christian persuasion was simply assumed. There are frequent Christian references in records of the college's life, and some ministerial presence is evident. All students were expected to attend religious services regularly and apparently this was subject to some monitoring, but there is nothing to suggest a particular denominational preference.

The number of students is difficult to know, too. There were perhaps 125 students in 1895, though in subsequent years there are a variety of categories of enrollment, including graduate students, upper classmen, juniors, special students, summer session, and children. There were 457 students enrolled in 1915–16; of these, forty-three were students of the normal school and 107 were enrolled in the summer session, including seventy-seven from out of state and foreign countries. In general, about 20 percent of Columbia's students were not residents of Chicago or Illinois. All students enjoyed a lively campus life. There were frequent field trips, museum visits, and a wealth of cultural events and student organizations, a glee club, drama society, and storytelling league among these. There were counseling and support services (academic and personal) and the college stressed its deliberate family atmosphere. Columbia was, as far as one can tell, a distinctly sunny place, an idea fostered by the college's principals.

Blood was the college's principal teacher of Bible classes. She recorded her Bible readings on phonograph records, and the college maintained a Bible literature department associated with its general library collection. At the annual national convention of the Women's Christian Temperance Union held at Saint Louis in the autumn of 1896, the Columbia School of Oratory was endorsed as the Central Training School for W.C.T.U. workers, an endorsement that continued when the School became a College. Also, a regular catalog inclusion was that "a tuition discount of 50 percent will be granted to all clergymen, theological students, or W.C.T.U. Workers who are making Christian work or the temperance cause their

life's business." The W.C.T.U. endorsement and tuition-discount entitlement confirms that at least in the matter of temperance, Columbia took a partisan position on a raging social issue.

Consistent with the racially segregated character of American life and the then customary exclusion of national and religious minorities from higher education (a state of the nation that would prevail for at least another half century), Columbia was hardly a less enlightened place than virtually the whole of the American college and university community. Possessing humane values and a natural interest in audiences integral to theater and platform performance and cultural exhibit, the college's focus on the venues and techniques of oral expression was set within a context of intense respect for the traditional cultural arts, although these were mostly the property then of a literate, educated, and privileged elite, which was Columbia's constituency. Columbia's available publications rarely mention a contemporary world swirling about just outside its classrooms. Even World War I went unmentioned. While after 1915 the college enjoyed a campus environment, it was essentially an urban institution. Except for its dormitory residents, most of its students were commuters, and all students and faculty had the unparalleled pleasurable and cultural opportunities that central location in a great city provides.

By other measures, the Columbia College of Expression was undoubtedly outside higher education's traditional mainstream and evidenced significant progressive vitality, which reflected the general ongoing ferment in education and American society. Columbia was from its beginnings an alternative institution, inspired and managed by women who were in tune with the evolution and social implications of their subjects.

The earlier Columbia had a strong occupational bent and an immediate relation to the contemporary real world. It sought to prepare students as professionals in various venues of expression and had successful graduates and professionally qualified faculty members. Thus, it may be misleading to charge Columbia with unusual cultural elitism, as that could be an imaginary fault stemming from an absence of information, which might give a fairer and more comprehensive sense of the college's mind. Such a view is evidenced by the instructive observations of Daisy Beard Nettleton, a senior faculty member at the twentieth anniversary of Columbia's founding. The following is excerpted from her remarks on "The Reading Department's Relation to the Other Departments of the School":

Today there is universal recognition of the value of scientific teaching. Teachers' colleges have been organized in connection with universities and colleges. Junior and Senior normal schools have increased in number and in attendance. Quite a different situation from that of nearly a century ago, when the first school for the training of teachers was established. This school was born in an atmosphere of contention and criticism and for several years had a real struggle for life. Only a few educators then believed the systematic training of teachers a requisite. Now all believe it to be essential. Charles Dickens was England's greatest educational reformer because he gave Froebel's theory of play its educational wings. . . . James Carter, Cyrus Pierce and Edmond Dwight gave the idea of technical training to the people of Massachusetts; but it was the courage, heroism and zeal of Horace Mann that made an institution for this training a real-

ity. We are indebted to Horace Mann, the "Father of Normals," for our present Normal School courses and for the elevation of the public school system also. The transformation from the idea that the public schools were patronized only by the lower classes, to the uniform democracy which we have now in matters of education, was accomplished in large measure through the normal or teachers colleges. If these schools stand back of the great public school system, which Horace Mann said "is the greatest discovery made by man," they must have the best methods and equipment and the most perfect system possible. In every school of this kind there is a department of reading or expression. Those who have charge of this department have received their training in the schools of expression. The schools of expression determine the reading methods of the normal, secondary and public schools. The recent inauguration of departments of expression and public speaking in the public schools of the middle west, where previously they had been reluctant to acknowledge the value of the subject, is sufficient proof that our best schools of expression are getting impressive results.

These serve as cautionary words for those today who would diminish or abandon support of the public schools to elitist and sectarian alternatives—or recast them mainly to serve the lower classes.

As the college's catalogs make little distinction between full- and part-time faculty, lecturers, and other classifications, faculty numbers can only be estimated for specific years; similarly for administrators. A fair estimate might be five faculty in 1895, a few part-time faculty, and four or five administrators. There was at least double that number of faculty in 1910 and as many as fifteen to eighteen in 1915–16. By the early 1920s, the number of administrators must have also grown considerably, too, to staff a number of student activities, community programs, and dormitories. And after 1916, the newly formed Columbia Normal School of Physical Education would have required an increase in faculty. In all of the college's early years, faculty members were eminently qualified; indeed, many had impressive reputations. In the 1920s, for a time, everything about Columbia grew. And then suddenly it all ended.

There is much evidence that the Columbia College of Expression enjoyed renewed prosperity in the Farwell mansion, unquestionably a prestige location. Grandly elegant, perfectly convenient, comfortably spacious, and entirely affordable, Columbia's new home quickly resulted in more students, an affluent constituency, a prominent presence in the civic community, and a very reasonable promise of a secure and rewarding future. Impressed by Ms. Blood's well-bred Bostonian origins and the opportunity to attend swank social and cultural events in the senator's mansion, many moneyed benefactors were attracted. Columbia's enrollment grew most encouragingly, and the registrar's records read like a blue book of high society.

High spirits prevailed until 1927, and then the deluge came. The other Farwell mansion had gone to the widening of Michigan Avenue in 1924. The Columbia mansion remained until, in early 1927, the college's great benefactor, Ms. Robert McGann, died and the college's rights to use the mansion evaporated. Big real estate interests quickly controlled the property. The college was given six months to get out.

Utterly unforeseen, the very existence of Columbia was at stake. It had been believed, albeit naively, that the college would have the mansion in reasonable per-petuity. Now there was nowhere to go and not enough time or money to find and furnish a new location. Two months before the get-out deadline, Mary Blood died, a sudden and tragic end undoubtedly hastened by her college's dispossession. The worry, strain, and anxiety were just too much. According to Kundrat, Hattie Blood, overwhelmed by her sister's death, just gave up and went back to her home in New Hampshire, bequeathing management and control of the homeless college to five remaining faculty members: Anne Larkin, Irene Antoinette Skinner, Bertha Martin, Alice Gerstenberg, and Marie Merrill. This was a questionable bequest if then, as now, the board is the owner of a not-for-profit institution, and there are strict rules for disposition of any nonprofit corporation. The faculty five almost immediately after became two, Larkin and Skinner. Both had been students and then faculty members since the early 1900s when the college was the Columbia School of Oratory. Perhaps they were the only two survivors when the Columbia ship went down in official bankruptcy in late 1927, and it was they who effected Columbia's rescue by Pestalozzi-Froebel Teachers College (PFTC).

No records, documents, or testimony can be found to describe the Columbia College of Expression's last two years (1925-27), and the end of Mary Blood's Columbia time except for a few Kundrat notes. Certainly these were dramatic years. That the college left its South Michigan Boulevard location in the summer of 1925 and opened the 1925-26 college year at 120 East Pearson is confirmed by the 1925 catalog and the bulletin of the 1925 summer session. The 1925-26 catalog, which might have told more, has simply not been found, and there is no up-to-date historical summary in the remnants of the 1927 catalog, though such histories had regularly appeared in catalogs of previous times. Unexplained are the circumstances of the move from the South Michigan Boulevard campus to East Pearson Street. What happened to the old campus and its buildings? Were the properties sold? The answers are all unknown. Similarly unknown is what happened to the board and what its role and legal obligations were when the College's Pearson Street tenancy ended in 1927 and the institution's subsequent bankruptcy. What happened to the students who presumably were enrolled in the spring 1927 session? What were the college's financial resources and holdings at the time of the fateful eviction notice? And what were its financial obligations at the time of bankruptcy? It is reasonably likely that some students and faculty followed Larkin and Skinner after Columbia merged with the PFTC. Presumably, some facilities, and library holdings, traveled to PFTC's location at 616 South Michigan Avenue (coincidentally next door to Columbia College's present central building). Such details, however, are also unknown. Only the sketchiest information about the merger is known, and it is unsatisfyingly obscure. The best that can be discerned is that the assets of Columbia were purchased by PFTC in the bankruptcy proceedings for a minimum amount, which suggests that Columbia College had very limited possessions.

The Pestalozzi-Froebel Teachers College was closely associated with Columbia's life from 1927 to 1963. It was named in recognition of the celebrated Swiss educator, Pestalozzi, and Froebel, a German leader in the field of early childhood education. Both had international reputations as pioneering educators in the late nineteenth century. PFTC was founded by a visionary elementary school principal, Bertha Hegner, and her minister husband, Herman Hofer Hegner, as a college specializing in teacher training for kindergarten and the primary grades. This educational focus remained for all of PFTC's years.

Though Columbia College had some independent life under PFTC's aegis and authority, PFTC owned Columbia's name, assets, records, and student files (which are carefully preserved even today). What lively alumni interest was retained by a hobbled Columbia is uncertain, except that after a controversy in 1935 between the alumni, Larkin, Skinner, PFTC's President Herman H. Hegner, and Norman Alexandroff, the old alumni virtually disappeared, and to my memory had no contact with the college after the mid-1930s, except for occasional transcript requests. The controversy apparently resulted in the separation of Anne Larkin, possibly Irene Antoinette Skinner, and other faculty (the terms of settlement are unknown) and the end of all ties between the old Columbia and its successor(s). During the times of Columbia's embrace by PFTC (1927-1936 and to some extent even to 1944), Columbia continued to publish a catalog of courses and faculty listings, though by the early 1930s there were few signs of life at Columbia.

In 1934 both the Columbia College of Expression and the Pestalozzi-Froebel Teachers College were failing institutions. In what was a clutch at straws, I suppose, Herman Hegner Jr., then Pestalozzi's president, asked Norman Alexandroff, who headed a small radio-production company, to develop a radio curriculum for the teachers college and its ward Columbia. Norman told me years later that he knew the job was a bit of a lark which paid something, and that at least it was an opportunity, however oblique, to test his conviction that radio broadcasting would soon become a major industry with great influence on American society, as well as an important agency of education.

Norman's main interest in 1935 was, first, to rescue PFTC, which was the stronger of the two institutions and owned Columbia. His initial concern was to modernize PFTC's curriculum by giving its subjects greater contemporaneity and more attractive titles. He wanted to recruit expert part-time faculty, who were currently teachers in progressive schools or colleges. The idea was to give PFTC greater public visibility and educational credentials, and to recruit students to a teacher education program focused on pre-school, kindergarten, and primary grades.

PFTC was then located at 616 South Michigan Avenue, and radio classes were held two blocks away in Alexandroff's studios in the Fine Arts building. In 1937 the colleges consolidated entirely in the Fine Arts building. It soon became evident, however, that neither institution had a realistic prospect of surviving, irrespective of whatever benefit could be realized from the radio project. Columbia College of Expression had fewer than twenty students, mostly on some cockamamie scholarship arrangement, and PFTC had at most forty students. Hegner had no remedy for what would be the institutions' inevitable failure. I've no explanation why Norman chose to move into this hopeless void, but within months he became the de facto manager of both Columbia and PFTC, a role which occupied him full time.

Norman Alexandroff was a talented, interesting, genuinely humane man. He was complex and not easily described. Many of my impressions of him remain unsorted, incomplete, and unresolved. A bit of an impresario, charming, funny, loving, and a devoted friend, he was intensely self-disciplined, strong willed, authoritarian on occasion, and deliberately dramatic when the effect served him. Nonetheless, he was a thoroughly engaging personality: open and accessible, infinitely kind, sympathetic, forgiving, and very generous. He was an elegant and impressive man, seen typically with his camel's hair coat draped like an opera cloak on his shoulders; a tilted Borsalino on his head, and a Corona-Corona cigar like a cannon in his square jaw. Though he stood only five feet three inches, no one had any sense that he was a small man.

His life was primarily a "here and now" engagement. When he was satisfied that he had made something happen, that it worked, he had less interest in furnishing its permanence. In personal profit, regrettably, he had no interest at all. He seldom mentioned his life before America, not to repress his memories, but simply to express his indifference toward the past, much like his disinterest in yesterday's projects. He was a consummate intellectual. He spoke and read a number of languages fluently (English, Russian, Polish, Ukrainian, Moldavian, German, and Yiddish), was mildly conversant in French and Spanish, could do a bit of Greek and Turkish, and had an entertaining talent for impersonating foreign accents. Self-taught, he was well read in history, economics, philosophy, political ideas, literature, drama, poetry, and music.

Norman was a serious scholar, in some part evidenced by having an assigned desk in the Library of Congress. He was an indefatigable reader and attentive listener, and he had a magical aesthetic and structural sense, and a prodigious memory in drama, art, music, and literature. He was a brilliant critic and interpreter of the arts ,and a compelling public speaker and debater. He said he had learned to speak on soapboxes in factory yards. His many projects were original, timely, skillfully promoted, and reflected a rare gift for publicity. He enjoyed a great range of friends, among them Jack London, William Dean Howells, John Philip Sousa, Clarence Darrow, Gregor Piatagorski, Moholy Nagy, Frederick Stock, Franz Allers, Paul Douglas, and scores of dramatists, writers, artists, academics, symphony conductors, and musicians. Many great pianists played for Norman on his rare Mason and Hamlin piano that stood at the far end of his office.

Norman was a political man, an unconventional radical who persistently preserved his independence. He was philosophically eclectic and insistently practical, and he had a passionate belief in democracy. He thought Kropotkin's and Proudhon's advocacy of anarchism was persuasive for its emphasis on an ideal of ultimate democracy and the perfectibility of man, though utterly impractical as political doctrine. While he respected Marxism's moral and economic analysis, he regarded Russia's Stalinists as gangsters. He rejected Jamesian pragmatism as an immoral philosophy and Aristotle as muddled. He was vehemently antifascist. In the 1920s he chaired, with Clarence Darrow, the Anticapital Punishment League, and was a passionate partisan of the worldwide campaign to save Sacco and Vanzetti from execution. In the 1930s, he was active in efforts to free the Scottsboro defendants and win antilynching legislation.

Norman was born in 1886 in Kishinev, a city in Russian Moldavia near the Black Sea in southern Ukraine. He never attended a school. An older brother, Alexander, who was a teacher in their Jewish community, tutored him. Mostly, Norman taught himself. He said he read well when he was five. In the late nineteenth and early twentieth centuries, Russia was a terribly hostile place for Jews. It is reported that 100,000 Jews were massacred in his city, Kishinev, during the Easter Pogrom in 1905. Young Jewish men were in constant danger of being taken by the police to serve in the tsar's army. Few survived the twenty-five-year military service. Indeed, fleeing army recruitment was the largest impetus to and motive for Jewish emigration to America. Literate and nonreligious Jews were often revolutionary-minded, putting them in acute jeopardy. Norman, in great danger, had to leave Russia quickly. He walked from Kishinev to Bremen in Germany, his trek taking months. In Bremen, he stowed away on a herring boat for Liverpool. There he got passage in steerage to America. He was sixteen years old.

Norman got to Ellis Island in 1903. His rightful name was Norman Kulchinski. He spoke no English, had no money, knew nobody, and had no idea where to go. The dock was empty except for him and a man carrying a sign hand printed with the name "Alexandrov," who apparently had missed the immigrant he was supposed to meet. Norman identified himself as Alexandrov, and the man, a representative of the "Jewish Immigrants Protective Association," took him to a family named Weiss in Philadelphia. There he substituted a couple of "f"s for the "v" and became, ever after, Norman Alexandroff. The Weiss family gave him a start in America. He got a factory job for three dollars a week. Each way to work was a five-mile walk. Thirty-seven years later, Norman met a man named Weiss. It was his family that had taken Norman in. They became intimate friends, and this was the A. C. Weiss who later served Columbia for many years as a board member and the college's treasurer. His son, Edward Weiss, became one of Columbia's most distinguished alumni.

In the next years, Norman worked in factories and machine shops in Philadelphia, Pittsburgh, New York, and Milwaukee. He quickly became fluent in English. He gave speeches, engaged in debates, and wrote articles. By 1908 he had become a master toolmaker and mechanic. He remained proud of his craft and made his own precision tools, even micrometers. He became a union organizer in the shops where he worked, and for a time was an IWW organizer in Colorado and an organizer of foreign-born workers for Daniel DeLeon's Socialist Labor Party–the only time in his life that he would be a member of a political party. He trained himself to get by on only three hours of sleep, a habit that gave him time to study. He spent large amounts of time in libraries, art museums, theaters, and symphony halls.

Together with the celebrated American writer William Dean Howells, Norman organized reading centers for the foreign-born in working-class neighborhoods in many American cities; and with Howells, David Starr Jordan, and Jack London, founded the Literary Association of America.

In 1911–12, Norman and Von Liebnicht, who had been a close colleague of the great Norwegian composer Edvard Grieg, became a lecture team: Von Liebnicht on music and Norman on drama and other arts. They were a popular feature on the national lecture circuit, which gave Norman a fair bit of cachet in leading cultural circles. He associated with many prominent artists and for the next years was occupied with various arts projects, mostly in New York. But intermittently, he returned to the shop. He was anxious not to lose his trade.

In 1917, America went to war and Norman was recruited as a supervisory toolmaker and designer in the Washington and Philadelphia naval shipyards. At the war's end, he invented a pleating machine—his first entrepreneurial venture. It sold wonderfully on the promise of its manufacture, except that in 1922 pleats went entirely out of fashion and the pleating machine business died abruptly. The only bright side of 1922 was that my father married my mother, Cherrie, in New York, and they moved to Chicago. In 1923, I joined the family. Norman got a job selling real estate. In a short time he became the sales and general manager of one of Chicago's most prominent real estate firms, where he developed a number of major Chicago suburbs. Then came the Great Depression. Real estate and everything else went bust!

In 1932 Norman began in radio. He developed an ingenious dramatic program, *Pages from Life*. For two years, it was broadcast daily in fifteen-minute episodes on WMAQ and briefly on the new NBC radio network. For a time, his program aired just after *Amos and Andy*. It involved the adventures of a Mr. Rubin and his "Hurry-up Substitute Company." It had a large cast of characters who spoke in a variety of ethnic dialects. Norman played all the parts. *Pages from Life* had a large audience and was about to become a network feature. But when Hitler came to power in 1933, Norman became deeply concerned that his show, centered on Mr. Rubin's Jewish character, would give currency to anti-Semitism and a fascist message, so he dropped the show. After this, he organized a radio production company, and developed a number of programs, among them, *The Rise of America*, which, as *Cavalcade of America*, became one of the most successful and long-running radio shows. The show was somehow lost to network producers and advertising agencies, as is not atypical of the fate of many independent productions.

In 1933, the Chicago public schools were in chaos. The system was politicized, and the teachers had not been paid for nearly a year, having to accept discounted script instead of money. Norman and my mother (who was a first-grade teacher at the Parker Practice Elementary School) organized a parent-teacher protest group that met first in the Hamilton Park fieldhouse, several blocks away from the city's public school campus, which associated the Chicago Normal School (later Chicago Teachers College), the Parker Practice Elementary School, Parker High School, and Wilson Junior College. The Hamilton Park group grew quickly into a city-wide movement demanding fair pay for teachers and a reorganization of the public school system. This coalition of citizens and teachers contributed importantly to the organization of the Chicago Teachers Union.

After *Pages from Life* had been abandoned, Norman organized the Peoples Opera Company (The Chicago Opera and Concert Company), which was meant to produce professional opera of highest quality for mass audiences, at affordable twenty-five- and fifty-cent prices. The opera company's casts employed a number of singers and musicians who had been stranded by the failure of the Civic Opera Company, resulting from the scandalous collapse of Samuel Insull's business empire, which had provided the opera's main financial support, and by the impoverished state of opera everywhere caused by the worldwide depression. The People's Opera Company performed a partial season at the Auditorium Theater, but financing was very difficult and singers and musicians ultimately drifted away, though some remained for the early years of the Grant Park Concerts.

Later, Norman would serve as a producer of several productions of the Federal Theater. Among these was Paul Green's *Hymn to the Rising Sun*, a rousing drama about African-American men in prison which was padlocked on opening night at the Selwyn Theater by city authorities, who charged that the play offended public morals. During the same period, Norman was a principal sponsor, together with Shirley Graham, the wife of W. E. B. DuBois, of the production of *Stevedore* at the Eleventh Street Theater, a powerful play about African-American workers on the Saint Louis docks. His role in the productions of *Hymn to the Rising Sun* and *Stevedore* was consistent with his lifelong advocacy of theater based on social realism and his interest in dramatizing the oppressive realities of African-American life. He was similarly concerned with giving opportunities and recognition to African-American and women artists of every age and discipline.

In 1933 Norman had the idea of a public summer music festival in Grant Park. He enlisted Frederick Stock, the celebrated conductor of the Chicago Symphony Orchestra, in the project. Together they went to Mayor Kelly with the idea. It was Kelly who enlisted the interest of Jimmy Petrillo, the head of the Musicians Union, who was persuaded by the mayor's promise that the festival would create jobs for a number of the union's unemployed musicians. This is contrary to the current belief that Petrillo founded the Grant Park Concerts. Norman produced a number of concerts over the first several years, including the now customary Fourth of July occasion that has Tchaikovsky's *1812 Overture* as its signature piece. Norman persuaded Fort Sheridan officers to provide an artillery company which would fire its cannons at the climax of the Overture's performance. Today, it's fireworks.

In 1936, after a two-year inquiry conducted with a respected educator, John DeBoer, Norman published a study, "Children and Radio," which provoked national discussion of the effect of radio on children. This project was the first significant effort to establish standards for children's radio entertainment. In support of the study's findings, J. W. Studebaker, then U.S. Commissioner of Education, said, "Successful use of radio in the service of education depends chiefly on having a corps of teachers and others competent to write and produce children's radio programs."

Norman's study was particularly timely, as radio was still in its infancy and viewed as an entertainment novelty, as was the earlier advent of talking motion pictures. The vast potential of radio and the movies was still to be fully appreciated, their role as sources of information and entertainment then only barely understood. Another important emphasis of the study was its demonstration that children's interest in a radio program was markedly stimulated by dramatic effects and lively music as reinforcement of a story line: in short, that tempo was a critical factor in enlisting children's attention. As a corollary, the study contended that drama enlists emotion and can thus be an essential component of successful learning, a thesis validated by Prescott in his classic work, *Emotion and the Educative Process*. "Children and Radio" enjoyed big-bang publicity, and Norman was offered a job by Niles Trammel, the president of NBC, if he would continue his project as head of NBC's department of children's radio. He refused because he believed that such corporate sponsorship would compromise the integrity of the study and appear to influence its conclusions.

In the long run, the study's effect on children's radio programming was transitory, though undoubtedly many of its issues are germane to current debate about the quality of children's television. And surely advertisers have discovered the value of drama and music in TV commercials.

In 1940 Norman initiated the National Artists Foundation. Supported by twenty-eight American universities, the foundation meant to secure performance opportunities and fund first-concert occasions for young American artists.

The foundation enjoyed a wealth of national publicity, in part because its announcement was accompanied by Norman's attack on child music prodigies. The extent of both positive and negative publicity that ensued was astounding, and indeed hilarious. (As I said earlier, Norman had a rare talent for publicity.)

Somehow, in 1938, Norman briefly managed the national tour of an ensemble of Mexican singers. With his usual flair he got the assistance of the U. S. Department of State with the appeal that the Mexicans' tour would strengthen U.S. ties with Latin America. He won the endorsement of Eleanor Roosevelt, and she agreed to speak at the tour's first event at Chicago's Orchestra Hall. Mayor Kelly introduced her. The whole bit was unmemorable except that the event occasioned a truly memorable *faux pas*. When Mayor Kelly spoke of the first lady, he said, "Mrs. Roosevelt knows our great president the best because she's been intimate with him," which only goes to prove that the elder Mayor Daley's occasional stumbles were not unprecedented.

When, in 1934, Herman Hegner Jr. asked Norman Alexandroff to help PFTC and Columbia, Norman had no idea he would have a career in education. In retrospect, while he may have been an eminently qualified educator waiting in the wings, this was, in actuality, simply accidental. He lacked the customary academic credentials, but he did have an abundant equivalent in his scholarly and cultural experiences. And he had the counsel and partnership of an extraordinarily talented educator, my mother, Cherrie.

Essentially nonpolitical, Cherrie Alexandroff had been an intensely engaged suffragette, was a prominent figure in the progressive education movement and a friend of John Dewey and other new educators. She had been an associate editor of Margaret Anderson's *Little Review*, a leading national literary journal; and had written a number of books, including an important treatise on children's health and education, and texts and teachers' manuals for teaching English and health in the primary grades. She was born in 1890 in Chicago's Bridgeport neighborhood (her mother was a heroine of the Chicago fire) and graduated at age nineteen from the Chicago Normal School (her master's degree was earned later). While teaching at an experimental school in New York, she was recruited to join the select faculty of Chicago's Parker Practice Elementary School, the city's showcase of progressive education, where she remained until her retirement in 1945. Cherrie never considered any career other than teaching. She was undoubtedly the guiding spirit of the Alexandroff family's engagement with education.

My mother was kind, gracious, patient, thoughtful, literate, and boundlessly affectionate. Teaching was an expression of her soul. She filled my childhood with stories, music, art, and the wonders of nature. With her I enjoyed a regular round of symphony concerts, the Art Institute, the Field Museum, the Shedd Aquarium, and the Lincoln Park Zoo. We spent summers at the Indiana Dunes State Park, spring vacations at Turkey Run State Park, and many nights studying the sky. By the time I was six, I could recognize most prominent stars and constellations, hundreds of plants and tree leaves, an array of bird species and bird calls, and had made a collection of crinoids—fossils whose remnants were scattered on Indiana Dunes' beaches. She had an inexhaustible store of games, which made learning great fun. She used states, capitol cities, countries, oceans, continents, rivers, lakes, and mountains everywhere as grist for my mill. If childhood is a significant life influence, as experts claim, I sure had the best of it.

Aided in some part by Norman's enhanced reputation in education resulting from publicity about his study "Children in Radio," and by Cherrie Alexandroff's reputation in progressive education, PFTC's faculty was strengthened significantly by a number of specialists with exceptional qualification as classroom teachers, including Francis Horwich (later Miss Francis of *Ding Dong Schoolhouse* TV fame), Saul Bellow, and Cherrie Alexandroff among these, and by association with a group of impressively credentialed university figures. Among these were Ralph Tyler, later an icon of American education; John Brumbaugh, Academic Dean of the University of Chicago; John Bartky, President of the Chicago Teachers College, who later became the dean of Stanford University's School of Education; John DeBoer, Norman's colleague in the preparation of "Children in Radio," and later, president of the National Council of Teachers of English; David Kopel, a brilliant young professor of educational psychology; and others.

Norman's study of the effects of radio and movies on young children and the learning process was incorporated into PFTC's curriculum, together with increased emphasis on methods of teaching, classroom management, children's health, and greater practice teaching opportunities. The result of Norman's reordering of PFTC's life was that in 1937 its enrollment had increased to 250 students. Though handicapped by the institutions' mixed identities and his murky authority, some confusions had been sorted out. Notably, the old Columbia folk were gone and with them, whatever existed of the commitments and traditions of prior Columbias.

While Norman was then, in effect, the manager of both institutions, he still lacked any real control, and Columbia's development was stunted by PFTC's primacy. He was certain that Columbia's potential could only be realized if it had an independent life; and, moreover, that he could never expect PFTC leadership as this was securely vested in the Hegner family, who, given Columbia's frailty, viewed it as dispensable.

Apparently in 1937 some sort of bargain was struck. Columbia's board then had three members: Rev. Herman H. Hegner, his son, Herman Hegner Jr., and his wife, Erme Rowe Hegner. At the director's meeting that year, Rev. Hegner resigned, and Herman Hegner and his wife were reelected, together with Norman and my mother, Cherrie; and the now four directors elected Herman Hegner as Columbia's president and Norman Alexandroff as vice president. At that meeting the Hegners also agreed to return all the rights and properties which had been purchased in Columbia's 1928 bankruptcy, and the directors authorized the use of "Columbia College of Speech and Drama" as the college's title. This became "Columbia College of Drama and Radio," which clearly represented the college's main educational interests in 1939.

In 1939 and for several years after, "Motion Pictures" became a subtitle to "Drama and Radio" in advertisements for the college. This happened after Norman had established a close relationship with Orsatti and Orsatti, then Hollywood's major talent agency, which led to Norman's representation of the Orsatti agency in the Midwest and to Columbia's appointment as the official training site for the Orsattis' screen actor clients. Among these was Adolph Kiefer, the United States swimming star in the 1936 Olympics, who was being considered for the Tarzan movie role.

Though Columbia had become a more independent institution, Herman Hegner, Jr., still remained president and chairman of the board, and ultimate control still rested mainly with the Hegners. It remained this way until 1942 when Norman and Hegner swapped titles. Norman became president and Hegner, vice president, and somehow, Rev. Hegner reappeared as a member of the Board of Directors. While in 1938 Norman would have preferred even greater independence for Columbia, given prevailing circumstances, achieving control and a more definite authority for himself was the best he could hope for at the time. Family control of a not-for-profit institution is not objectionable per se, if such control is meant to insure the continuity of a worthy purpose, particularly if the purpose is not a matter of excessive personal or family enrichment. Surely, back then, neither Columbia nor PFTC enjoyed more than what was at best the barest minimum of profitability. "Not-for-profit" was certainly an appropriate designation. Of course, a board whose members are able to provide a variety of talents, intelligence, counsel, and fund raising contacts, is necessary in institutions of greater size and complexity.

Columbia's name and structure changed substantially in 1944, initially in response to a revision in the Illinois not-for-profit law, and subsequently to adapt to new conditions generated by the GI Bill. With a new Illinois State charter, Columbia became once and for all Columbia College. While the newly named college retained the bits and pieces of its history, what might have been valuable traditions and lively alumni were mainly lost as a resource of the new Columbia. The new Columbia did inherit some prior credentials, including, most importantly, official identity as a degree-granting institution authorized by the Illinois State Examining Board for Teacher Education. In fact, it was this precious credential that qualified Columbia College to enroll GI Bill veterans, despite the lack of accreditation by the North Central Association (the regional accrediting agency).

In 1944, a new board of trustees (replacing the board of directors) was constituted of five members—three Hegners and Norman and Cherrie Alexandroff. Herman Hegner, Jr., remained as board chairman, Norman Alexandroff as president, and Cherrie Alexandroff as vice president. Erme Rowe Hegner resigned and was replaced by Norman's nominee, Dr. Clara Tigay, who was one of the first woman medical doctors in Illinois and a pioneer in treating women's medical problems. Rev. Hegner disappeared again (religion has its bits of mystery) and was replaced by Ralph Himmelhoch, the college's legal counsel. The reconstituted board retained family balance, got a first measure of board independence, and gave the college a permanent name.

With PFTC's rescue reasonably secure, Norman focused his efforts on the renewal of the Columbia College of Expression. Radio broadcasting quickly became Columbia's paramount educational identity, though "Expression" remained in the College's title for several years, and speech, theater, and a nominal program in teacher education remained. The radio faculty included a number of respected and popular radio names. It was advertised as a faculty of leading professionals who brought the realities of the job to the college's classrooms. Chicago's announcers, producers, directors, writers, production specialists, actors, and actresses were recruited to Columbia's faculty. Many were friends made during Norman's radio years and through his associations with theater people. Many of the faculty taught both radio and theater classes. Radio in those days was live, and the staffs of major radio stations were larger and employed a greater variety of talents than a network TV center would have today. Many of the bigger stations even had an in-house orchestra.

In 1937, a professional theater company was organized at Columbia. Its actors were experienced theater professionals and taught Columbia classes, too. Student-actors and other students who worked as production staff augmented the ensemble. The Company performed regular seasons of plays until 1942 at the Eleventh Street Theater, an excellent professional theater and even more so today as Columbia's impressive Getz Theater. The theater and radio curriculum stressed voice and diction competencies. In shared classes with PFTC, students enjoyed a valuable opportunity in the liberal arts.

Columbia's appeal was based on the popularity of radio as a career. At the time, theater-minded students looked more to radio drama than to the conventional stage. In 1938, Norman contrived a publicity ploy that conferred an honorary degree on the great comic actor Jimmy Durante, at some sort of trumped-up ceremony at the Congress Hotel. Hokey it might have been, but the story and the pictures made nearly every newspaper and magazine in the country.

While Columbia's enrollment reached two hundred students in 1939, this brought only temporary prosperity, particularly as American life continued to suffer the hardships of the Great Depression. The draft, however, begun in 1940, moved quickly after the bombing of Pearl Harbor, and swept up the majority of young American men. It followed, of course, that male students virtually disappeared from America's campuses, and Columbia was no exception. Though Columbia had some success in recruiting women students, they did not replace the number of men lost to the war. In effect, Columbia was on hold during the war years, albeit a precarious hold. Then in 1944, Norman published a timely and influential study, "The Occupational and Educational Adjustment of Veterans." Its audience was nation-wide, directly and indirectly involving leaders of government, the military (from grunts to generals), educators, employers, and ordinary citizens, particularly men and women in military service.

In 1943 and early 1944, newspaper articles, magazine and radio features, and expert opinions by psychologists, warned that returning servicemen who had endured the war's horrors would be so shocked psychologically by their war experiences that they would only with great difficulty, time, and patience be reincorporated into the nation's life. Norman, who ordinarily was suspicious of psychologists, countered with, "How do they know this will happen?" Moreover, he thought, that as only, at most, 15 or 20 percent of all servicemen were engaged in any combat at all, it was a pretty wide brush that painted all servicemen as "shell-shocked" misfits. So he began a study, with Dr. Daniel D. Howard's assistance, which involved business, industry, and educational institutions, assessing the psychological, occupational, and educational adjustments of what ultimately would number 240,000 servicemen, already discharged from the military services in 1944. The results were overwhelming. Most servicemen readily adjusted to civilian life. Indeed, they were usually better employees and students than those who had never been in service at all. Norman's study convincingly countered the doomsayers, and the discouraging picture of returning American servicemen was virtually erased. Of course, many servicemen were horribly wounded, physically and psychologically, but the overwhelming majority was comparatively unharmed, particularly in terms of their employability or competence as students.

"The Occupational and Educational Adjustment of Veterans" generated great enthusiasm and praise, particularly among the government and military leaders and veterans organizations, including General of the Armies Dwight D. Eisenhower, and General Omar Bradley, who had commanded the invasion of Europe and would become director of the Veterans Administration. In fact, it was General Bradley who was most influential in the selection of Columbia as one of fifteen national institutions of higher education to administer Veterans Guidance Centers, which would make available free comprehensive testing, educational and occupational counseling, and psychological services to veterans of World War II. This remarkably enlightened program was part of U.S. Public Laws 346 and 16, popularly known as the GI Bill, and represented the first time that educational and vocational counseling, and psychological services had ever been designated as an entitlement. With its designation as a Veterans Guidance Center, Columbia College gained substantial prestige, and Columbia's center became one of the busiest and, one of the best. Dr. Howard, a psychologist and the dean of both Columbia and PFTC, seconded Norman in the center's administration and was the director of its psychological and counseling services. He assembled an outstanding staff of psychologists and organized a uniquely enlightened counseling process, employing the most contemporary psychological techniques in which many hours (and in many instances weeks) were spent with individuals served by the Center.

At the beginning of 1945, Columbia had about 200 students, largely part-time and mostly women. By the end of 1945 the number had more than doubled and included mainly full-time students and many more men. Students numbered approximately 400 in 1946 and varied between 400 and 500 through the end of 1951. During much of that span, Columbia's greatest problem was retention of new students. This was because in 1947 the Federal Communications Commission authorized an increase in the number of radio stations from roughly 1000 to more than 3000. For Columbia this meant that even minimally qualified radio students (and radio was the predominant interest of Columbia's students) had exceptional job prospects and compelling reasons to leave college. Also, as very few local or national schools educated (or more accurately, trained) people for radio jobs, Columbia's quite singular radio concentration was, to cop a phrase, a double-edged sword. Students were easily lured in, but also easily led away. In Chicago and the Midwest, Columbia had only a small number of comparatively small trade school competitors in radio broadcasting, though a few, newly organized, did have a profitable number of students. No local colleges except Northwestern University offered Radio Broadcasting as a major, but Northwestern was hardly competitive with Columbia's student market.

Columbia and PFTC together occupied the second and fifth floors of the Wabash Annex of the Fine Arts building, which fronted Michigan Avenue. A ramp-type bridge on the fourth floor connected the two buildings. In September of 1945, anticipating a large number of new students (mostly veterans), and needing space for the Guidance Center, half of the fourth floor and other scattered spaces in the Fine Arts building were leased. The Piccadilly Tea Room, a proper old place where women wore gloves and hats at lunch and teatime, occupied the other side of the fourth floor. (The restaurant fled after two years of living closely with the Colleges.) The Fine Arts building was a beautiful turn-of-the-century building that occupied nearly one third of a city block (Michigan Avenue to Wabash and Van Buren to Congress).

At the southwest corner of Michigan Avenue and Van Buren Street was the Chicago Club, the city's premier men's club. Many of the city's biggest financial deals were done in the gilded rooms of the Chicago Club, whose membership then excluded women, Jews, and minorities of any sort. The south third of the block (to Congress Street) was occupied by the Auditorium Theater building and a famous old hotel on Michigan Avenue. Designed by Louis Sullivan, the Auditorium building, a national architectural landmark, was used during World War II as the city's central USO facility. After the war, the Fine Arts building and the Auditorium complex were acquired by attorney and speculator Abe Titlebaum, reputed to have been one of Al Capone's lawyers. In 1947, Roosevelt University purchased the Auditorium building (including the theater) as its principal site. The Fine Arts building was purchased several years later by a private family and became only a shabby reminder of its former grandeur. In its prime the Fine Arts building had two excellent theaters, the Studebaker and what became the Fine Arts Cinema, several large and impressive recital halls, art galleries, and floors of studios used by Chicago's leading music teach-

ers—and a bit of folklore: the building's penthouse was briefly used in Titlebaum's time as a horse-betting parlor. The building also had six ornate, manually operated elevators of nineteenth-century vintage that were often in disrepair but contributed to its venerable, if not quaint character. (Only one of the elevators went to the penthouse.) Ultimately, the colleges took over about a third of the Fine Arts building, including a 5,000-foot recital hall, which, in 1950, Columbia turned into its first TV studio.

After World War II, PFTC's enrollment prospered, too, though this had nothing to do with GI Bill veterans. Instead, the source of its gain was a new Illinois State requirement that all Illinois public school teachers get bachelor's degrees if they had only two or three-year normal school diplomas, which traditionally had been the usual qualification for teacher certification. While teachers were allowed a generous number of years to satisfy the new degree requirements, the expectation affected thousands of Illinois teachers, nearly all older women. Many kindergarten and primary grade teachers took advantage of PFTC's emphasis on these grades and its convenient summer school and Saturday class schedules. Indeed, as the largest number of Columbia classes were held during weekdays and evenings and PFTC's largest student traffic was Saturdays and summers, the colleges could enjoy a comfortable space-sharing arrangement.

Columbia's students, then mostly GI veterans, represented a fair cross section of American life, except that the majority of people would likely not have attended a college in prewar years. Similarly, few who became radio students would have chosen careers in radio, at that time, as these were beyond ordinary aspiration. But the war had encouraged millions of young men and women to think of themselves differently. A good and satisfying life was not beyond their hopes. America was a plentiful place. In the military services, they had seen a new world, and they wanted a fair share of its opportunities. Of course many failed, Columbia students among them. Many simply did not have the talent; others had chosen careers and schools wrongly or too quickly. Many did not work hard enough, and many, immediately after the war, were too distracted by compelling life problems to deal successfully with education and new career aspirations. Veterans had many difficulties: in renewing personal relationships after long absence in military service; in finding housing, an acute problem of early post-war years; in simply adjusting to civilian life and an unfamiliar economy; and in resolving individual psychological problems. New times, yeah! But rough times, too. For first-time college students or those who had been away from classrooms for a long time, adapting to study and practice disciplines was unfamiliar stuff. Many dropped out, but that so many more actually made it is remarkable.

The veterans gave an exceptional vitality to Columbia and to all of higher education. The sudden democratization of student populations by older students, often impatient with the dogmas and practices that had prevailed in higher education, was a culture shock to America's campuses. Traditional college students had been young people from comparatively elite stations, whose life expectations were certainly more assured than those held by ex-GIs, whose new presence in colleges and universities was hesitantly and sometimes reluctantly endorsed by conventional faculties and administrators. Nonetheless, it was a prosperous, exciting time for America's campuses. War vet students were eager learners, and their exploding numbers brought large new tuition revenues and vast governmental expenditures for buildings and created unprecedented opportunity for new faculty. The late 1940s were heady and rewarding times for college and university teachers and those who managed higher institutions.

Columbia knew some tumult, too. But in the absence of fixed practices and traditions, Columbia far more easily adjusted to new conditions imposed by the GI Bill than traditional colleges and universities, though the sheer number of new students created some difficulties. A much greater problem was a need to recruit a large number of new faculty, though this was eased by the fact that all Columbia teaching was performed by part-time teachers and that close counseling and careful teaching guides were readily accessible to new teachers. Hiring administrative staff was also a problem, particularly because all had to be trained in the intricacies of unfamiliar Veterans Administration paperwork. A brief assessment of the importance of the GI Bill is included in the appendix.

This chapter in Columbia's history is based on recovered sources and Theodore Kundrat's 1985 series "Columbia in Retrospect," published in Columbia College Alumni Bulletins.

While Columbia's curriculum was largely set, the number of class sections scheduled in many subjects multiplied quickly and many subjects that had been offered periodically were offered every semester. Where college and university catalogs usually have a bit of fluff and a proliferation of course titles offered only occasionally, virtually every course listing in Columbia's catalogs was in actual play during GI Bill times. This included a full program of liberal arts subjects, some new Columbia offerings, and some offerings jointly sponsored with PFTC. As early as 1939, Columbia offered courses in "Contemporary World Culture" and "American Minorities," the latter then a usually neglected subject. In professional subjects, again, particularly in radio and allied interests, Columbia offered a comprehensive assortment of subjects. Radio drama virtually replaced theater study, though speech and acting skills remained as prominent in the radio medium as in conventional theater. In fact, careful speech and accurate reading was strictly required of radio announcers and performers on network and local radio stations, an expectation far less stressed in television and radio today. Similarly, articulate public speaking has become a lost art.

Columbia's postwar faculty included many prominent Chicago radio broadcasters. Among them were Harry Christian, Alan Earl, Gilbert Fergeson, Eric Lord, Ben Park, John Bryson, Carl Greyson, and Dean Almquist—people probably little remembered today, but once very popular radio figures. Years later, several of us speculated that nearly everyone in Chicago radio and television had either taught or gone to school at Columbia.

Columbia's faculty taught part-time, and most taught one or two classes each week. A comparatively small number taught the equivalent of full-time: fifteen or sixteen class hours per week each semester. The ordinary pay rate for teachers in the 1940s was $4 per class hour, thus $64 per semester credit hour—undeniably low, though perhaps not unusually low by wage rates then. (Full-time public school teachers made $1,800 to $2,400 a year, and radio announcers, who had relatively prestigious jobs, made about $60 a week.) A few Columbia teachers also got an extra stipend if they were unusually prominent or acted as chairs of departments. I think the rate in the 1950s may have been about $5 a class hour.

The chairman of the Radio Department in the 1940s was Jack Reidy, a very versatile stage and radio actor and announcer who enjoyed leading roles in the Columbia Players stock company and the opportunity to freelance in radio and theater. In the early 1950s, Norman, concerned that Jack Reidy would have no pension (an unthinkable benefit in Columbia's salad days), persuaded the Chicago Park District to hire Reidy as a supervisor of the park district's theater program. The park district didn't know Reidy's age. He worked there for twenty-five years until his retirement and pension at age "sixty-five" in the late 1970s. He died a few years later, actually in his eighties, I think, while playing golf. After Reidy, Clyde Caswell, a genuine radio pioneer, chaired the Radio Department until 1957. Years later, I was invited to Nashville by the Country-Western Music Association, where on the stage of the Grand Ol' Opry, I accepted a special award honoring Clyde Caswell as the first nationally aired country-western disc jockey. (Clyde's plaque still has a place on the wall of Columbia's radio station.) Bert Gall accompanied me to Nashville, and I remember the event because neither of us had ever seen so many gorgeous women in designer evening gowns and cowboy boots.

In 1948, Columbia began a concentration in television, then an infant industry, which by the mid-1950s would become the College's most popular subject and remain so for twenty-five years, much as radio had been the predominant student interest in the years before. Television at Columbia began with wooden mockups of TV equipment meant to simulate actual studio facilities. Wooden boxes constructed to look like cameras with metal tubes set like lens turrets were perched on tripod dollies and pushed about under a makeshift light grid. Real equipment was prohibitively expensive. Authentic cameras, for example, cost upwards of $25,000 and image-orthicon tubes, the heart of the system, cost $1,000 each and had an active life measurable in hours. It was a primitive setup, but it was a start.

In the fall of 1949 I went on a vacation to Mexico. While there, I made a small effort to discover something about the state of Mexican radio with the thought that perhaps some student interest in Columbia could be developed. When I returned, I remarked to my father that Mexico seemed entirely unprepared for television, though there was a sophisticated radio and film industry throughout Latin America.

Norman's curiosity was enlisted, and he went to Mexico shortly afterward. What he discovered was a small group of authentic television pioneers who were working at developing a domestic TV industry. Their project was generously supported by Don Emilio Escaraga, the principal owner of the Mexican radio industry, who also controlled Azteca Films, the dominant film and movie theater company in the Spanish-speaking world, and by an association with the O'Ferrill family, a major part of the Mexican and Latin American newspaper and publishing industries. Typically, Norman became a good friend of Don Emilio, who had already launched a four-station TV system in Mexico City, Televicentro, and a particular friend of Guillermo Camarena, a young man who was Televicentro's chief engineer and an inventor who had independently designed a TV camera and studio system, which, in some respects, improved on equipment made in the United States. Camarena had even invented a system of color television. The result of Norman's inquiries was that Camarena agreed to provide a wholly professional TV camera and studio system for Columbia: cameras and the whole studio and control room shebang. It was all delivered in the spring of 1950, and Camarena, working with local TV engineers, came to supervise the equipment's installation.

It was a coup of sorts. For $30,000, Columbia got a professionally equipped TV facility and control room that gave authenticity to the college's TV instruction. While Camarena's equipment was not as sophisticated as on-the-air TV stations, it sufficiently replicated a professional TV environment and allowed realistic student engagement. Chicago's TV stations gave us their used image-orthicon tubes. The TV Department's first chairman was Hunton Downs, an unusually competent TV director, producer, and writer, though at the time, few people could claim to be experienced. I persuaded him to take the job with the contention that despite meager pay (a per-class fee plus a stipend) he would gain invaluable TV experience and reputation.

We had also hired an inventive local TV engineer, Arthur Shapiro, who later accompanied Norman to Los Angeles. Downs remained for nearly three years, which, I vaguely remember, was as an alternative to recall as an army officer in the Korean War. Ultimately he became the head of Armed Forces Radio in Southeast Asia, and later a very successful novelist.

Thaine Lyman, who remained for thirty years until his death in 1982, followed Downs in the chairman's job as the TV Department's head and propelling spirit. Lyman was truly remarkable. He was a conservative man and a serious Catholic whose moral instincts were perfectly compatible with Columbia's humane intents. He was exceptionally zealous in serving students and was an intense advocate of job opportunity in television and radio for African-American and women students. Lyman was indefatigable; apparently, he slept hardly at all. During his entire Columbia tenure, he also worked full-time as a WGN-TV cameraman. His experience went back to television's early beginnings and, arguably, his knowledge of television was unexcelled. He could have had a very successful career in commercial television, but in a personal sense, his engagement in TV education was an overriding and satisfying priority. He played an indispensable role in Columbia's success.

While radio broadcasting was still Columbia's leading interest in the late 1940s, the college had significant enrollment in journalism, business, teacher education, and advertising. Dr. Harold Lawrence, who had headed advertising studies at several universities, taught advertising. I remember him as a mature man with unusual energy and thorough knowledge of advertising and marketing. He had a scholarly mien and

was a sort of Mr. Chips, regarded by students with respect and affection. In the mid-1950s and early 1960s, Dorothy LeFold taught all of the college's advertising and marketing subjects. She was then a prominent advertising agency executive who simply liked teaching. Like Lawrence, she enjoyed the great affection of her students, many of whom she helped to get advertising agency jobs.

The comparatively large number of students, the diversity of their career and academic interests, and a comprehensive liberal arts program contributed to a genuine collegiate environment. Typical activities of campus life grew correspondingly. A student newspaper, *The Columbia Dial*, was published regularly. A choral society was organized. As the student body included a number of professional musicians, a big band was organized to play at the College's frequent dances and several proms held at downtown hotels. Sixteen-inch softball was a very popular sport in Chicago. Every neighborhood had leagues and uniformed players, and the best of the city's teams played regular seasons in stadium settings. Columbia's team won a city championship and for several years was the Grant Park League's champion. Columbia's basketball team was a marvel, albeit not quite legitimately collegiate. Columbia had a student named Ed Silver, who pre-war was a basketball coach and sports promoter. He set out to make a Columbia College basketball team. He recruited a team of surpassing talent and size from the ranks of not yet discharged soldiers and officers stationed at Fifth Army Headquarters in the old Chicago Beach Hotel. Some members of the team had been college stars and some professionals. All enrolled at Columbia in one or several evening courses. Silver negotiated resplendent uniforms for the team with "Columbia College" emblazoned on their jerseys and warm-up jackets. The team's opening game in 1946 was with a south suburban junior college that had won the national junior college championship the year before. Columbia won, the score something like fifty to seven, and similarly beat the tail off a number of small college and semiprofessional teams in the Chicago region. The team was unbeaten in the 1946–47 season. Newspaper sports sections took notice. Ed Silver left Columbia after his second year to work as a Roller Derby track announcer. In two years, he was the manager of the Roller Derby's national circuits. In the early days of television (to the mid-1950s), the Roller Derby was the most popular sport on TV. Silver hired all the Derby's announcers from Columbia, among them Howard Mendelsohn, who for a time was the busiest of all TV sports announcers. Later, Mendelsohn spent nearly twenty years as public affairs manager for WBBM-TV (CBS) and subsequently was head of a Chicago public relations firm. He is now a member of Columbia's Board of Trustees.

Quite literally hundreds of Columbia students after various lengths of study got radio jobs, and by the end of the 1940s, many were program directors, station managers, and successful entertainers. To name only a few, popular comedian Shecky Green; Oscar-winner Peter Berkos; Don Mann, who would become the radio industry's most successful time salesman; Norman Pellegrini, WFMT's dean of classical music programming; featured radio and television personality Jim Conway; Chicago radio station managers Bill Mack and Al Michael; noted DJ Mike Rapchack; Alan Rafalson, who heads a major Chicago public relations company; Will Darch, man-

ager of WSBT-TV in South Bend, Indiana, who began in TV as a weatherman after a special Columbia course in weather reporting in 1948; Lou Ciocci, who headed United Artists' Midwest regional office; Alan Sweetow, a major Chicago radio and TV producer; Ed Weiss, many times award-winning program director of the University of Iowa's educational radio and television stations; and many other radio and television success stories all over the United States.

African Americans constituted only five percent of Columbia's postwar student population, and women perhaps twenty percent. This was a time when racial exclusion was the universal practice of the broadcasting and entertainment industries. Similarly, professional opportunity in most sectors of the American economy was virtually closed to people of color. Even being a war veteran was no benefit. For minorities and women, even to aspire to a job in broadcasting or the theater was to confront an utterly discouraging prospect. This is not to imply that the current record of minority opportunity in the main agencies of communication, the arts, and entertainment is satisfying. There's still a rough row to hoe.

A remarkable group of African-American students came together at Columbia: Janice Kingslow, the lead actress in *Anna Lucasta*, a long-running hit play in Chicago, New York, and London, a role which she shared with Hilda Simms, Ruby Dee, and Isabelle Cooley and a star cast which included Ossie Davis and Fred O'Neal; the uncompromising Oscar Brown Jr.; Sid McCoy, later a successful radio performer; and Art McCoo. These and other African Americans championed African-American issues in broadcasting, the theater, and American society. Among the projects they organized was *Destination Freedom*, a dramatic radio series regularly broadcast on WMAQ-NBC radio. It was directed by Dick Durham, who later would produce and direct *Bird of the Iron Feather*, a serial about African-American life on WTTW and the public television network.

Despite great talent and devoted effort, these pioneers and their colleagues did not find significant professional opportunity, except Sid McCoy, who had a very prominent career in radio, and Oscar Brown Jr., who enjoys great respect as a creative theater and musical artist and advocate of African-American consciousness in the arts. Janice Kingslow, a simply glorious, star-quality actress was defeated by the bitter fact that there were no roles for African-American women (or men) in film, television, radio, or the theater. Jim Crow was an unrelenting foe, not even yet overcome, of course. While Latinos suffered similar exclusion, opportunities in the arts and media professions had only small priority among them, reflected in the comparatively small number of Latino students at Columbia in the 1950s, 1960s, and 1970s.

The story for women was much the same. Except as actresses, women were simply not hired in any professional categories in radio, television, or film. Such exclusion of minorities and women would prevail in these industries until the late 1970s. While getting job opportunities for minorities and women in the communication and entertainment industries was a consistent and conscious Columbia priority, it was largely an unsuccessful effort, particularly so in the 1940s, 1950s and 1960s. Despite the college's rigorous efforts at affirmative action long before there was even a name for it, I doubt that many Columbia students who suffered racial or gender discrimination in the professions of their education would give more than a hesitant compliment for our effort. I can offer only that America's racist and sexist traditions were more powerful than our isolated contest.

I came to Columbia in 1947. Obviously, I inherited the mantle of Columbia's presidency, though by the time I got it in 1960, it was pretty threadbare. I have few of my father's unique credentials, but much of his knowledge was passed down to me. Undoubtedly, my father and mother had cardinal influence on my life, and their gifts to me have been immensely gratifying and useful. I grew up with Columbia. It was a central interest in my family's life, and it became the focus of mine. For this history's purpose, I offer only a brief description of myself. I am more known, I think, by the record of my Columbia time.

I have little memory of my early impressions of Columbia, except that when I was twelve, it was a downtown place where my father worked that had something to do with schoolteachers and radio. Later, I unwillingly went to the college's radio and theater productions. In 1940 and 1941, I took a few Columbia speech and radio courses. I got a couple of minor gigs in radio "soaps" with the encouragement of my father, who had undoubtedly grown impatient with my lack of life direction. Certainly, then, whatever my modest talents, I had no serious aspirations in radio, and surely no expectations of ever having anything to do with Columbia. Life's choices, I suppose, are more accidental than deliberate. More recently, when Yale's President Bart Giamatti was chosen as baseball's high commissioner, I realized that was what I really wanted to be. Oh, if only I had thought to advertise myself by writing op-ed pieces in the *New York Times*, which helped make baseball America's metaphor for life.

Until I was fourteen and a sophomore in high school we lived in Englewood on the South Side, a neighborhood identified then as St. Bernard's or alternatively as Hamilton Park or Normal Park. The immediate neighborhood was mostly lower-middle and working class and predominantly Irish Catholic. It was a typical big-city neighborhood. There were a few apartment buildings on every block, though the majority of people lived in small family-owned homes. A number of people owned cars, but the Normal Park spur of the El and streetcars were the ways people usually got about. There was little cause to go out of the neighborhood, except to attend sports events and (rarely) go downtown. (In the early 1930s, our car was parked permanently on the street in front of our apartment building. My father couldn't afford to drive it.)

Sports were neighborhood preoccupations, at least among fathers and sons, but my father thought sports interests were senseless. The neighborhood's boys played every sport that was in season, and virtually everybody was a devoted White Sox fan. At fourteen I discovered to my utter dismay that I couldn't hit a curve ball. (Forty years later, my son made the same dismal discovery.) But I was, and remain, an inveterate sports fan with a particular passion for baseball, as everyone who knows me will confirm. Not atypically, the old neighborhood had little intellectual life. While decent, generous, hard-working folk, few adults had gone to college and many had not completed high school. Just making a living and taking care of their families, especially during Depression times, was the unavoidable preoccupation of most.

In 1937, we moved to Hyde Park. Moving to a new high school and a new neighborhood was a cultural shock to me, but it quickly became a new life. In retrospect, it became more interesting and enlisting. My new friends were assorted, but mostly bright, misfits who had sports interests like myself. Another group of my friends was intensely engaged in matters of "social significance." Many were stimulating and intelligent and came from families with intellectual interests, a variety of "left" persuasions, and college aspirations for their children. I was introduced to a range of social issues, such as racial discrimination and the CIO's campaigns to organize unions in the mass-production industries, as well as to various economic, antifascist, and antiwar ideas. All of these are certainly worthwhile, but social causes were hardly my preoccupying interests then. Later, tracings of these would influence my views. If high school itself had any memorable effect, it escapes me entirely.

My early college time was different, not so much because at sixteen I became a serious student, but simply, I suppose, because I could do more grownup things. I ultimately went to Wilson Junior College, the Institute of Design, the Chicago Academy of Art, the University of Chicago, Roosevelt University, and Columbia College. I got degrees from two of these schools. From all, I received some valuable skills and cultural information, occasionally inspired teaching, a more informed view of the world, and many ideas that would shape my later views of education. While formal education is important, what are most memorable and influential for me were informal out-of-school experiences: my parents, my neighborhoods, the army, my unusual opportunities in the immediate years after the war, and the lessons of my Columbia lifetime. I believe, surely not uniquely, that life itself is a powerful educator if one's life is rich in variety and human service. In truth, I think the best credential that I brought to my Columbia job was the aggregate of my informal education.

In January of 1943, I became an infantry soldier in the South Pacific. I didn't learn a lot, but I stayed alive. After a year and a half of mucking about in mud and war noise, I luckily got a job running a post-exchange store. In the strange ways of army job selection, I got the job because my service record showed that I had worked—briefly and insignificantly—in the offices of Libby McNeil and Libby, a big food processor. If the army had taken closer note of the fact that I'd worked in a machine shop, too, I might have been made an engineering officer. Whatever, I quickly graduated to a bigger job supervising a number of post exchanges and to managing a vast special-service entertainment operation. The learning opportunities couldn't have been greater. The post exchanges in my purview did millions of dollars of business, and the entertainment job involved managing the tours of star-studded USO companies, entertainments produced within a large theater of military operations, and large-scale civilian musical productions in the Philippines. In effect, I got a cram course in big business and the entertainment industry.

My first Columbia job as a psychologist (of sorts) in the college's guidance center lasted nearly two years. I had then no intention of making a career in psychology and, if anything, even less in education. Psychology had been my undergraduate major, chosen, I suspect, because at the time it seemed the most convenient route to a college degree (which my parents insisted on) and because a job in the guidance center was a reasonable probability. My pre-war dabblings had accumulated three plus years of miscellaneous college credit without revealing any serious career or educational commitment. But it was at least enough so I could finish college in a year and a summer term. With a new wife, Anna, still in college, I had to have a regular job. The guidance center was an attractive place, in part because its flexible work schedule would allow me time to devote to the volunteer organizations that enlisted my interest.

I think that I am, as my father was, a humanist, radical, and elemental democrat. I am also, I think, a quintessential Chicagoan. I remain fascinated with the city. I have never lived nor wanted to live anywhere else. My roots are in Chicago as my mother's were before me. I have a comprehensive knowledge of the city gathered over seventy-seven years, and I have supported Chicago's humane causes for my entire adult life. I went to opening day at White Sox Park in 1929 and at least fifty-five opening days thereafter. And I believe that my Columbia College service made a significant contribution to Chicago's welfare.

I believed strictly that educational institutions, by their very nature, permit no indoctrination, expectations of orthodoxy, or private persuasions. Columbia is what it says it is in its public mission statement and deliberately free of any ideological intent whatsoever. Columbia in the Alexandroff times and now is guided by its conviction to be a place where the fullest freedom of inquiry, expression, faculty initiative, individual conscience, and independent thinking by students or any member of the college community can be exercised unconditionally and protected from threat, test, approval, or intrusion from any other influence. An absolute prohibition of any impediments, qualification, or threat to the independence of teachers, students, and the educative process is a traditional tenet of the college's by-laws.

In 1948, my time was shared between the guidance center and the college's operation. My title then was administrative assistant, though I have little memory of the particular responsibilities of the job. Daniel D. Howard was appointed as the college's dean, duplicating his PFTC function, though Norman remained, at least by title, PFTC's dean. My mother, Cherrie, had suffered a crippling stroke in 1946 that left her with little ability to speak or walk, and Norman's ordinarily limitless work energy was reduced significantly by his need to attend to her. Then, in late 1948, cancer was discovered in Norman's vocal chords, which resulted in the removal of his speech apparatus. Any restoration of even minimal speech was discouragingly doubtful. He could communicate only through little notes. But by some miracle of will power and unique physiological insight, he trained himself to speak again, not the pitiful speech that a few similar victims were being taught, but ordinary speech troubled only by a minor hoarseness and lack of volume. His doctors, eminent specialists, had no explanation, and Norman's description of how he did it was virtually impossible for others to understand. Within a year Norman could speak almost comfortably. He could even give speeches nearly as well as before.

Somewhere in all this I became Columbia's acting vice president, mainly a title I never had occasion to exercise, though I did function as business manager.

Having recovered only recently, Norman began to think about establishing a Columbia branch in California and possibly, too, some sort of outpost in Mexico City: the latter after he had made the Mexican connection, which led to the college getting television equipment. He made some purely speculative inquiries in Los Angeles but decided that a California project would need a practical hook to hang it on, apart from his strong belief that television would increasingly be centered in New York and Los Angeles as the entertainment industry already was, and that Chicago would ultimately only have a small role and excite only small student interest.

For personal reasons, mostly my mother's health, he preferred living in southern California, though he had no inclination to retire there or anywhere, nor could he have afforded to. Increasingly, I took on greater authority and responsibility for the college's ordinary operations. The California break came in early 1950, after the college's board, at Norman's recommendation, authorized a vaguely described "Los Angeles Department" and he had negotiated a profitable contract with the film studio unions to train their members in the fundamentals of television. In effect, Columbia's Los Angeles Department began with roughly 5,000 short-course students, which supplied part of the investment necessary to establish a Los Angeles Division of Columbia College Chicago. In 1951, Norman moved to Los Angeles.

Meanwhile, 1950 was a waning time for the GI Bill, and the enrollment of veterans began to decline, at first moderately but soon quickly, except a brief moment of prosperity on July 25, 1951, the last day World War II veterans could enroll with GI Bill benefits, when we registered nearly 200 GIs. Columbia coincidentally had a new summer term beginning on July 25; we had classes going to midnight. Tardy veterans just wanted to get in on the GI Bill, and they didn't have time to choose colleges or courses of study. Understandably, a large number of enrollees were gone by the end of the summer. The cutoff date didn't affect continued benefits for already enrolled students, but no new GI Bill veterans could be enrolled after that day, and those leaving obviously would not be replaced. But the Korean War was beginning, and there was the prospect of a new GI Bill, which ultimately generated new GI students. Though these never approached the number of World War II veterans, they were a substantial percentage of Columbia's students to the late 1950s.

The year 1952 was an eventful one for Columbia. Columbia and PFTC had been in protracted negotiations seeking a new lease for the colleges' space in the Fine Arts building. The building's managers insisted on nearly double the previous rent. This amount was unaffordable, but getting a new place was a formidable task. We needed at least 40,000 square feet in a downtown location at a reasonable rent. Such space was not readily available. Then rescue came from Herb Harris, the husband of Dr. Clara Tigay, who for years had been a member of Columbia's board. Harris worked for a major real estate firm, Alfred Perlman and Company, and Perlman owned a building on the southeast corner of Wabash and Adams. It was an eight-story commercial building with two manual elevators, not as spacious or historic as the Fine Arts building, but a godsend in a moment of great need. The rent was manageable, and Perlman subscribed a part of the remodeling costs. We moved to 207 South Wabash Avenue during the summer of 1953. Moving and setting up anew was a daunting job, particularly because we had to be ready for the new school year. The building's ground floor had two restaurants and a cigar store, and the eighth floor had a mail-order advertising agency. Otherwise, it was the college's building. The library, mostly PFTC's, was on the second floor and Columbia's TV studio on the fifth. The studio had a sort of L shape and several diverting posts and, depending on how the studio was configured, it also served as a theater of sorts. Offices and the main radio studio were on the seventh floor, and classrooms everywhere else. Albeit cramped and a bit makeshift, we made the best of the only home we had.

At the same time, we were seriously troubled by an effort of the Illinois Bureau of Registration to reclassify Columbia as a trade school. We had traditionally been within the purview of the Illinois Examining Board for Teacher Certification. The attempt was outrageous, unwarranted, and a clear abuse of governmental power. Nonetheless, we had to marshal all of our strength to defend Columbia's precariously held college identity. We never knew what prompted the bureau's punitive proceeding, though we suspected it reflected some bumble-headed bureaucrat's effort to increase his domain or the improper influence of some radio-broadcasting school competitor. Corruption was not unknown in Illinois. To head our defense against the state's arbitrary ruling, we engaged former Cook County Assistant State's Attorney and influential Republican John Dickstein, who conveniently was an Elks Lodge brother of the college's board member and treasurer, A. C. Weiss. After a series of threatening sessions and exhausting testimony by Daniel Howard and me, the bureau's case simply collapsed.

Columbia Los Angeles was being readied to open in September 1954. My mother, Cherrie, died that June. It was a tragic end to the life of a woman whose life had been spent selflessly in devoted service to the highest ideals of education, to society's welfare, and to her husband and son. After her funeral service an ancient woman introduced herself as Mary Gallagher and said she was a friend of my father's from a long time ago. He had once told me a story about a meeting in Chicago held to protest the Palmer Raids, a government-sponsored witch-hunt which fell on American radicals in 1919. The meeting, he said, was raided by the Chicago police's "red squad" headed by a notorious sergeant named Mike Mills. Mills had gleefully grabbed the meeting's chairwoman, Mary Gallagher, saying, "Got you, you red-headed bitch," When she told me her name, I clumsily said, "You're the red-headed bitch my father told me about. How sweet it is of you to come to my mother's service."

With my mother's death and Los Angeles's approaching debut, Norman understandably had limited time for Chicago's operation. On his recommendation, a contract had been struck with Columbia Los Angeles to the effect that whatever its fortunes, it would become an entirely separate, independent institution in September 1959 at the latest and return to Chicago whatever surplus money Los Angeles might have then to compensate Chicago for its investment. The investment in Columbia Los Angeles ultimately exceeded $150,000, though after 1957, no further subsidy was necessary. Additionally, Columbia College Pan-Americano in Mexico City was scheduled to open in 1955. Altogether, it was a precarious balancing act, though Mexico would require little investment, and Los Angeles's enrollment and income prospects were very encouraging.

Columbia Chicago in the 1950s had serious financial strains, largely because enrollment had declined and because the college's expansion to Los Angeles and Mexico City had drained reserve funds that could have helped Chicago overcome its difficulties. Chicago's problems were probably inevitable. Norman was accurate in his prediction that the Chicago student market would be less and less able to sustain a specialized college of sufficient size and variety, which depended on a prosperous, popular entertainment industry that was fleeing Chicago for New York and Los Angeles. Obviously, the loss of GI Bill students and income would increasingly diminish the college's life. Privately, Norman believed that PFTC's comparative prosperity would increase strains between the institutions. Also, he wanted me to join him in Los Angeles, a move I strongly resisted. In fact, Columbia Chicago would hang by its fingertips well into the 1960s. It was increasingly evident that to be successful, Columbia had to shed its isolated state, which would require formal collegiate accreditation. That wouldn't happen until 1973.

Notwithstanding a host of problems, Columbia's quality improved significantly during the 1950s. Television had become, by far, Columbia's leading interest and we were beginning to enjoy deserved respect for a lively liberal arts program. This came about principally because we had begun to enlist a number of outstanding teachers. Among these were Mark Benny, British novelist, critic, and film writer (including Alec Guiness's *Kind Hearts and Coronets*); Harry Mark Petrakis, who would become a major American writer; Jack Conroy, formerly editor of the *Anvil*, author of *The Disinherited*, and spokesperson of American proletarian literature; the indomitable Studs Terkel, who first taught Columbia classes in jazz and folk music; and in 1954, William Russo, then winner of *Downbeat* magazine's award as best trombonist and arranger for the Stan Kenton orchestra. Russo returned to Columbia in 1965 as the college's first full-time faculty member. Russo was succeeded by a series of *Downbeat* magazine editors—Jack Tracy, Dom DeMichael, Les Brown (later the TV editor of the *New York Times*), and Don Gold, who became the editor of *Holiday* and *Chicago* magazines and a prominent American writer. He returned to Columbia in 1985 as a member of the college's Journalism faculty, and retired in 1995. Also, two distinguished young scientists, Alan Rovick and Ernest Sukowski, joined the faculty and began Columbia's interest in science. Sukowski has taught classes continuously since 1955 in addition to his impressive career in science research.

Hans Adler was among the brightest stars in Columbia's faculty constellation in the 1950s, and he continued to light up the college's classrooms for more than thirty years. He taught literature, philosophy, and a great range of humanities and social studies classes to a generation of Columbia students. A lively, cherubic little man, Adler was charming, literate, an extraordinary lecturer, and a raconteur nonpariel. A former editor of *Figaro*, an influential French publication, and a respected critic and writer, Adler was fluent in French, German, Russian, and English, and typical of the European antifascist and Jewish intelligentsia who came to America to escape Hitler's horrors and stayed to have major influence on post-war cultural life. Adler was also a remarkable source of outstanding Columbia faculty, and the intellectual elite, such as David Reisman and Ruell Denny, frequently visited his classrooms.

I add an anecdote about one of Adler's closest friends, who I often sought to recruit to Columbia's faculty. His name was simply "Axelrod." He had fled Austria after its annexation by Germany. For some years before, Axelrod had been Vienna's leading cabaret producer, and he was particularly distinguished as an originator of then wildly popular "blackout sketches": bang-bang dramatic briefs ended by a quick lights-out. A blackout sketch might go like this: A husband pecks his wife good-bye and leaves for work. (Short pause.) A janitor comes in and flies into a groping embrace with the housewife. They hear a key in the door. The janitor dives into a closet. The husband reenters and berates his wife for her slutty infidelities. She is tearfully repentant. The husband leaves again and as he goes out he raps on the closet door and says, "Hello, Kasperic." (Go to black.)

When Adler and Axelrod came to America, they were promptly put in the army and sent back to Europe as interpreters. (Two more unlikely soldiers couldn't be imagined.) During the Battle of the Bulge they were captured by an American platoon, set for execution as German spies, and rescued only at the last moment by an officer of their unit who happened by. When the war ended, Adler and Axelrod came to Chicago. Axelrod spent years after as the night clerk at a seedy North Side hotel. Despite still being enormously bright, interesting, and entertaining, he had strangely just given up.

Then there is Harry Bouras. I found this short, round, delightful young man in a droopy sweater working in Werner's Bookstore at Van Buren and Michigan. One had to notice Harry, as apart from his shape, he knew with astonishing accuracy where every book and title was among the thousands in the store. Harry had a competitor in the paperback section of Kroch's and Brentano's. He, too, knew where every title was. Their competition had the stuff of legend about it. Harry had no formal education. He had spent a brief time at the Eastman School of Music and dropped in at several other institutions. He was self-taught, including his prodigious artistic talents. A composer, a writer, an artist, and sculptor, who would later be represented in major museums and private art collections, he was an incredible teacher of the widest range of subjects. A consummate intellectual, he had an encyclopedic memory. Once my family and I visited the British Museum with Harry. One of my children asked him a question about the Rosetta Stone, one of the great relics of antiquity. Harry's answer began with a translation of the Rosetta Stone's ancient script and went on to a compendium of scholarly information cast in easily understandable terms. A number of people gathered around, and the audience quickly multiplied. Harry's answer became an entertaining and informative lecture. It was a great performance.

Harry was knowledgeable in art history, literature, poetry, music, history, medicine, and philosophy, and he had an uncanny ability to create associations among an array of subjects. He was the most enlisting lecturer, more perhaps a performer, and later his weekly (WFMT) radio show on art subjects and artists enjoyed a large audience and gave popularity to a great number of local, national, and world artists. Harry Bouras introduced thousands of people to fine art. He taught everything in his expert kit to thirty years of Columbia students, and he gave countless numbers of them the confidence to engage their own intellectuality and cultural pleasure. He was a tribune of enlightenment and inspiration, and surely no Columbia teacher, perhaps no teacher anywhere, has had more valuable effect on students than Harry

Bouras. And for many years he gave the college its largest public dimension and intellectual legitimacy.

Al Parker, whose Columbia tenure began in 1944 and continued until his death in 2000, returned to virtually full-time service in 1957 as the chair of the Radio Broadcasting Department. Like his colleague Thaine Lyman, Parker gave up sleeping. Until recently, in addition to his Columbia role, he worked full-time as a radio announcer for several Chicago radio stations and later more than twenty-five years as a principal announcer at Channel 7 (Chicago's ABC-TV), plus an exhausting schedule of freelance assignments. Among the most prominent Chicago radio and television personalities, Parker was a high-energy employment agency for many Columbia graduates in local and national radio and television. He was responsible for Columbia's exemplary radio broadcasting department. He was the inspiration and the guide of the college's very successful sound engineering program and its state of the art installation in a separate college building. He was similarly responsible for developing Columbia's popular radio station, WCRX. And he married the college's librarian, Jeanne Yager, fifty years ago. Parker has been an indispensable player in Columbia's success.

Among other 1950s faculty were sports columnist Ed Sachs; Harry Trigg, Channel 5's program manager and later station manager; Jack Jacobson, WGN-TV's baseball director and later president of Sports Channel; Charles Walsh, business manager of WBBM-TV; featured WBBM-TV directors Niles Swanson, Chuck Strothers, Chalmers Marquis, and Dinny Butts, who later at Field Enterprises would become an exemplar of corporate public relations; in TV news, Channel 5's Brace Pattou; in public relations, Ed Morris, who, after an illustrious career as a leading executive at WTTW and the National Public Television Corporation and manager of Channel 44, would in 1984 become chairman of Columbia's Television Department.

Film, too, became a study emphasis, beginning with Robert Edmonds, who had been a leading producer and director at the legendary Canadian Film Board. In 1966, he would become Columbia's second full-time faculty member as chairman of the Film Department.

Interest in theater was minimal in the late 1940s and early 1950s, having been mainly expressed in radio drama, which offered at least some prospect of professional employment. In 1955, theater interest among Columbia students was quite suddenly revived. The impetus was provided by the vitality of three young faculty members who had graduated from the Goodman Theater School in the late 1940s: Robert Borelek, Ted Zeigler, and Joe Hundley. Borelek was first hired as my assistant; Zeigler was "Uncle Bucky," a featured performer on WGN's very popular *Bozo's Circus*; and Hundley was working at some unrelated job. Their enthusiasm for the theater just caught on. A number of students must have been waiting in the wings for stage opportunities. Columbia's theater was the TV studio. The theater audience was divided with the stage in between, half of a theater-in-the-round. And yet, an extraordinary quality of theater was produced: weekend seasons of contemporary theater, which included such plays as O'Casey's *Plough and the Stars*, William Inge's

Picnic, Arthur Miller's *All My Sons*, and *Death of a Salesman*, as well as popular hits like *The Corn is Green, Mr. Roberts*, and *Detective Story*. The student acting company featured a number of exceptionally talented Korean War veterans, including: Henry Buonocore, Clarence Burton, Walter Topel, Gene Matoin, Robert Kasparian, and a young woman, Barbara Bayer, who had star quality. None of them had any prior theater experience or the strong sense of self that gives life to theater ambition; they were just naturals. Walter Topel became one of the most successful directors of TV commercials, which he abandoned to build the Briar Street Theater, where he planned to produce and direct. His death several years ago was an untimely end to a great talent. Clarence Burton was a splendid actor. A proud, young, black man and ex-light-heavy-weight fighter, he made it briefly on Broadway and spent many hard years in off-Broadway productions. Henry Buonocore, a creative stand-up comic, went away somewhere to work in his wife's family dairy business. Gene Matoin knocked about the theater in New York for a while, and Kasparian owned for some years one of New York's most successful restaurants. Barbara just vanished. Ted Zeigler went to Hollywood, successfully starring in a TV sitcom, and Borelek and Hundley went on to other things. But together they got theater running again at Columbia.

In 1957, Lucille Strauss and Al Peters came to Columbia. They began what would be thirteen years of extraordinary theater education. Lucille was an actress of impressive reputation who had retired to raise her family, though she kept a passionate interest in theater. She was a talented director and was deservedly regarded as a doyen of Chicago theater. She had strict regard for classical theater training. Al Peters had been a leading director in the Federal Theater and the Chicago Repertory Theater, sharing Lucille's commitment to the theater and to theater training. With uncommon zeal, uncompromising standards, and profound affection for their students, Al and Lucille created an exemplary theater education program for students, many of whom were without experience and had limited, if any, theater ambition.

Many students first elected to study theater only because they thought its subjects might benefit their career interests in radio, television, or film. A good number came to embrace the theater, and all at least had the opportunity of an exemplary life education. For several semesters, Al and Lucille were joined by Eugenie Leontovich, a great actress. In addition to creating a professional theater setting for students, Al and Lucille organized a resident professional company of outstanding Chicago actors, including Nick and Diane Rudall and Don Marsten. The student company included some remarkably talented young people who had an unexcelled opportunity to perform a great variety of the best plays in world theater, particularly in contemporary drama. The student company included: Fred Wroblewsky, Lorraine Zelmanski, Monchill Dakich, Bill Piletic, and John Hillbert, among other splendid young actors and actresses. The performances included such plays as Sartre's *No Exit*, Arthur Miller's *View from the Bridge* and *Memory of Two Mondays*, a whole cycle of Clifford Odets, Shaw, and O'Casey. Despite professional ability, few of Columbia's acting students made it to Broadway or Hollywood, and there was then no Chicago theater in which to make it. Perhaps these students suffered the same doubts and lack of perseverance that infected Columbia acting students before them, though many theater students did enjoy satisfying careers in college and community theaters.

The 1950s were difficult times. Enrollment ranged from 325 in 1952, little more than half of average 1946–1950 numbers, to roughly 225 at the end of the 1950s. While the majority of students in the 1950s were Korean War veterans, their numbers grew smaller each year. As Norman was preoccupied with the Los Angeles project and to some extent in Mexico, I became, by default, the manager of Chicago's Columbia. Such a newly independent role was aided by Daniel Howard, though he was mostly occupied with PFTC. My principal handicap, however, was not lack of advice, but lack of money for anything beyond a skeletal apparatus and a minimal operation dependent exclusively on immediate tuition revenues. Despite the restrictions of its penurious state, Columbia did enjoy significant improvement in faculty competence, instructional facilities, and educational quality. Nowhere was improvement more evident than in the quality of students enrolled, beginning in the mid-1950s and continuing in the years ahead. In retrospect, I think what may have spurred the quality of student ability and performance was not the result of an accidental gathering of better students, but more intentionally, the introduction in 1956 of a comprehensive "Learn/Earn" program of paid apprenticeships for Columbia students in the television, radio, film, newspaper, and advertising industries. These were not internships in the usual sense of providing an unfocused sampling of job experiences, but instead, were actual paying jobs (both full- and part-time), albeit initially in low positions, which gave students a foot in the door to their careers. Many, many students enjoyed quick on-the-job promotion from mail departments and the like to more professional jobs, which in many instances they retained and advanced from after graduation. At the very least, all gained the advantage of an actual work history and job experience and references to serve their career ambitions. The greatest number of Columbia students then and in the following years chose to combine college study with relevant paying jobs. A number of enthusiastic faculty and I spent many hours developing learn/earn opportunities for students in the major communication organizations. Indeed, there came a time when virtually every entry-level job in Chicago's television and radio stations was filled by a Columbia student: in several stations, Columbia had a practical monopoly on such positions.

Examples of "Learn/Earn"'s success abound. Bill Harder, who began in the shipping department at Kling Film Studios, became the vice president and production manager of Niles Films, then the leading Chicago film production studio. Jack Wartlieb, who started in the WBBM-TV mailroom, became WBBM-TV's production manager in what Irv Kupcinet called a real Horatio Alger story, and ultimately went on to an illustrious career as a top network and Hollywood producer. Frazer Head moved from WNBQ-NBC's mailroom to become chief financial officer of the ABC-TV network. Ron Clasky went from being a film gopher to a noted film editor. Walter Topel went from his first hack job at WGN-TV to achieve prominence as a producer-director of TV commercials. Howard Shapiro went from WBKB-TV's mailroom to work many years as a leading Channel 7 director.

In addition to the success of "Learn/Earn," Columbia's acceptance as a primary source of new talent by the communication and entertainment industries was signaled by a headline in the 1957 edition of the alumni newsletter, "1957 Class Plays Lead in Spectacular Success Story" subtitled, "Sixty-five New Alumni Now Have Business Addresses in TV-Radio-Film and Advertising."

The 1950s also saw an encouraging influx of students from foreign countries. In 1958, twenty-six foreign students representing seventeen countries were enrolled, including a number from Arab countries. The secretary of the Arab Students League in America, Sadoon El Rayis, was among them. He was to my vague memory the brother-in-law of the strongman of Iraq after the king was assassinated. I believe also that Rayis later became Iraq's Minister of Information. I remember, too, a rather dramatic occasion when Dan Howard and I gave a dinner for our foreign students. Most were Arabs except one bewildered young Irishman who, when the assembled Arabs took a blood oath of fidelity to Arab brotherhood, cut himself similarly and mumbled incomprehensibly whatever slogans were spoken by his unfamiliar new brothers. Columbia's Arab contingent also included Mohammed Abbas, who was later to be the editor of *Al Ahrem*, the most influential newspaper in the Arab world, and Cairo's Egal Farid, a young woman who gained a prominent position in Egyptian television. Also, there was Il Mung Chung, who had been a colonel in the South Korean Army. I had a nearly two-year friendship with him, or so I thought until he told me he was leaving college because he couldn't understand English and I realized he probably hadn't ever understood a word I said. But he smiled and bowed and nodded at my monologues most convincingly.

In the mid-1950s I organized a project that won the attention of the television industry and large national publicity. It was a Columbia survey of job prospects in television conducted with TV industry leaders. Participants in the survey included 172 top executives of 154 TV stations, fourteen network officials, TV directors of ten leading advertising agencies, and four especially qualified people in government service and education.

TV executives forecast a doubling of TV stations and related jobs within the next five years: 46,000 new jobs. Fifty percent of the respondents believed that the predicted job growth would include a significant increase in the number of TV jobs for women, but more than 80 percent doubted there would be similar opportunities for African Americans. In actuality, these estimates were conservative. In general, respondents observed that the looming shortage was an unfamiliar state of affairs for the TV industry and most believed that while glamour occupations usually have more young people wanting in than they have jobs to offer, a job bonanza was developing for creative young people who could meet the special requirements of aptitude and acquire the education necessary to the exciting business of telecasting. While results of the survey got great publicity, which undoubtedly increased student recruitment, it did not have a dramatic or lasting effect on Columbia's enrollment.

What did attract a large number of short-term students, however, was a special program in "Effective Speech." In a sense drawing on the phenomenal success of the Dale Carnegie speech courses which enrolled tens of thousands of people nationally and promised all sorts of riches and life rewards, Columbia's Effective Speaking program, which included speech mechanics (voice and diction) and training in a variety of public speaking and audience techniques, offered a far more authentic education than Carnegie.

In the 1950s, we also sponsored several packages of concentrated studies in communication specialties. Most noteworthy of these was a sequence in television art, graphics, and stagecrafts, "The Applied Arts in Television," whose teachers had outstanding professional reputation. These included Monte Fassnacht, who was the production supervisor of the Chicago Opera Company and a national authority on stage crafts; Curt Nations, the art director of WNBQ-NBC TV; and Ken Ponte, the award-winning art director of WBBM-TV. This project extended for several years until its main audience of professional artists finally ran out.

On several occasions, I attempted ventures that the college could have developed if the projects had had more funding. One was a contraption for drivers' education and pilot training that used a variety of film devices to simulate actual road and flying conditions. On paper, it was an intriguing invention, but it ended only as the forgotten ancestor of the simulators used today. I also developed an idea for local, low-power educational TV networks to serve isolated areas in developing countries titled "Bush Television." The U.S. Agency for International Development (AID) was enthusiastic, but it ultimately lost out to competing budget items.

I also initiated a competition for high school science and communication arts teachers to stimulate greater student interest in science through more effective communication of science themes. Entries were sought from more than 1,000 Midwest high school teachers, who were invited to submit science communication projects designed for television, radio, or film presentation or discussion formats for classroom instruction, school assemblies, or community settings. The effort was prompted by a Purdue University study which disclosed an appalling lack of understanding among high school students about the role of science and the personality and work environment of scientists. I gathered an impressive list of prominent scientists and leaders of major technology industries to serve as the competition's jury. Many exceptional ideas were submitted and the whole undertaking got lots of publicity. The project, however, failed to get significant interest from funding sources, educational associations, or government agencies, whose support was necessary to implement the ideas which the competition generated. Nor did Columbia have the funds and resources or enough collegiate respectability to follow up on the project. It was further evidence that Columbia's anonymity could not be overcome with a big publicity stunt. On a more personal note, my Columbia colleague, Richard Thorne, and I originated a game show, "Make the Grade." It seemed destined for network TV success, except at the moment of decision, it collided with the big quiz show scandals and our high-riding game show was abruptly dead in the water.

I did have one success, however; indeed, it was so successful it almost sent my co-inventor Ted Zeigler and me to the poorhouse. One fateful day, Ted was fiddling around in my office with a pair of pliers and a box of assorted wires and transistors. He bent this and that to look like some sort of electrical device. We decided that there might be a market for such an utterly useless product that boldly claimed to be good for nothing. This goofy idea became the ElTech Diminisher TK5W3. Lots of people wanted one of our samples. We even wrote senseless user instructions and antiadvertisements. Ted and I each put in five hundred dollars, and we became manufacturers. Jane Legnard was our production manager. She got about twenty students at one dollar an hour to make the dumb things on tables in the library, and she recruited a number of disabled veterans at the Hines Veterans Hospital to help. Each device went into a cute little plastic box with the instructions. We thought we would get rich selling the ElTechTK5W3 for a dollar. At this point, Ted got a network TV shot to plug our "pet rock," I think on Steve Allen's *Tonight Show*. We got literally thousands of orders. We also discovered that our little mess of wires, capacitors, and transistors really cost $1.17 to make and ship. We were broke in twenty-four hours— if that long. And on top of everything, we had to pony up more money to return dollars to buyers. He who lives on laughs perishes on them, too. It was mostly a fun time, though I don't think we laughed the whole time.

While this narrative has so far only told the story of Columbia's Los Angeles venture in bits and pieces, the establishment of a California division was obviously a major event in Columbia's history. Certainly, it was at the time an unorthodox project, though the development of distant locations by colleges and universities is more familiar today, particularly extensions within city and close suburban boundaries and, of course, the statewide extensions of public university systems. Establishing colonies of parent institutions in distant locations remains unusual, except for such models as Antioch University's effort to create a national university and for a variety of cultural reasons and marketing ploys, the common collegiate practice of locating branches in foreign countries. In most instances, however, efforts to establish institutional branches whether close or distant is done with far more ample and dependable resources than Columbia could marshal. Arguably, Norman's estimate of Columbia's shrinking student market relative to the growing concentration of related industries in California and its more familiar proximity to Latin American were valid perceptions. Whatever the persuasions, Columbia's spread largely removed Norman's talent and inspiration from Chicago, and diluted the college's small resources, though whether these were sufficient then to fund even Chicago's renewal is questionable.

Columbia College Los Angeles was successful. Late in 1953, Columbia L.A. rented an exceptionally good 40,000-square-foot building at 2328 West Seventh Street, across the street from *MacArthur Park*, a place given some notoriety by Jimmy Webb's hit song and as the site of Joseph Wambaugh's novel of cop debauch, *The New Centurions*. The building's rent was $450 a month, an astonishingly low figure even then, and the landlord paid the costs of satisfying Los Angeles's strict school building codes. A spacious TV studio was constructed on the building's first floor and equipped with state-of-the-art professional facilities, most contributed by Los Angeles TV stations, manufacturers of TV equipment, and by local companies that served the TV and motion picture industries. This elaborate studio installation was prompted by a plan to use the studio as a place to make economical pilots of TV productions by independent producers. Such pilots were then ordinarily shot expensively on 16mm or 35mm film, but it was believed that kinescope recording, a device that was the forerunner of today's videotape, could make a high quality "film." For a time, the project was a profitable enterprise for the college, both because of the economy of using kinescopes and because students could be used to perform some studio functions that otherwise would have required expensive production crews. The students in turn got on-the-job professional TV experience, an arrangement worked out amicably with TV and film unions. But unfortunately, kinescopes did not sufficiently duplicate requisite film quality, and the scheme dwindled away.

Organizing even a very small college from literally nothing was a daunting task which, given a need to be economical, Norman had to perform nearly single-handed. At the beginning of 1954, he was aided by David Slade, who he had hired in Chicago, where I introduced him to Columbia's routines, and by Art Shapiro, Columbia's TV studio engineer who brought his many skills to Los Angeles. A skeletal administrative staff was hired only weeks before beginning efforts to recruit students.

Despite all the turmoil of preparing for a September 1954 opening, Norman was able to assemble a faculty with splendid credentials. After all, this was Hollywood—where big names in film and television and associated arts were quite ordinary. Anywhere else, these people would have been big celebrities. Among these were Gail Bonney, Robert Clark, Russ Conway, Betty Lou Gerson, Alan Soule, leading TV sports producer Mike Kizzah, Ernest Lonner, TV and film director Melvin Wald, featured radio and TV writer David Nowinson, and Ludwig Donath, celebrated actor and Oscar winner for *The Jolson Story*, who was blacklisted for his progressive sentiments.

Columbia College Los Angeles's first class had 175 students—many full-time, a number of Korean War veterans, a large number of women, and a significant representation of African- and Mexican-American students. Los Angeles's academic arrangements pretty much mirrored Chicago's Columbia. Los Angeles's catalogs largely duplicated Chicago's, though while course listings were similar, there was great student interest in television and film subjects with a greater emphasis on technology than in Chicago. Tuition in Los Angeles for full-time enrollment (fifteen to sixteen credit hours) was $217.50 each quarter, $652.50 each college year (three quarters), slightly higher than in Chicago. During the next four years, Columbia L.A.'s enrollment averaged 200 to 250 students, not including a profitable in-service training program for NBC-TV executives in 1957. The enrollment figure in 1959 was approximately the same as Chicago's, though the scale and variety of Columbia's Chicago operation was considerably greater. Undoubtedly, the L.A. branch benefited significantly from its derivative possession of its parent's collegiate credentials and reputation, and by the fact that the State of California regarded Columbia Los Angeles as a legitimate branch of an established institution. The L.A. branch, albeit barely profitable, became self-sufficient in 1957 and required no further subsidy by Chicago. When it is considered how quickly Columbia's Los Angeles project became an independent college institution with enrollment resembling that of many small American colleges on an investment of not greater than $150,000, its speedy achievement seems quite unusual. The California project had, of course, the benefit of Norman's customary organizing and promotional skills and his ability to make helpful and influential associations.

Columbia College Pan-Americano was developed in 1955 at the invitation of the Mexican and Latin American Broadcasting Associations, who asked Columbia to establish a television training center in Mexico City to serve new TV industries in their countries. Don Emilio Escaraga, whom Norman had befriended several years before, inspired the invitation. Don Emilio was an impressive giant of a man who, despite his great wealth and international power, was a deeply patriotic Mexican who was entirely committed to the idea that Mexican television would be an exclusively Mexican industry. I remember a telling moment when Norman and I introduced the cultural attaché of the United States Embassy to Don Emilio, who had several priceless Siquieros paintings standing on chairs in his office. The Embassy official remarked that Siquieros was a Communist, to which Don Emilio replied with grand hauteur, "But he's Mexican." The interview ended abruptly.

The formal opening of Columbia's Mexico City project in 1955 was prefaced by a one-year program that introduced television to Mexican and Latin American radio personnel and gave those already working in TV an opportunity to refine and update their skills and familiarity with commercial TV. Forty individuals graduated from this program at a formal graduation ceremony. While all paid some tuition, the project was sponsored and mainly subsidized by Don Emilio Escaraga's Televicentro complex. The teachers were exclusively Mexican, and they were trained by Guillermo Camarena who had created Columbia's first authentic TV installation, and his colleague, Roberto Kenny, who was the manager of Televicentro's Channel 1. Both Camarena and Kenny had spent nearly four months in Chicago studying Columbia's teaching methods and TV curricula, though both had sophisticated knowledge of television in the United States and were among the founders of the TV industry in Mexico. Some members of the initial class of forty became the faculty of Columbia College Pan-Americano, which, apart from separate offices, used Televicentro as its place of instruction.

The first class enrolled nearly 400 students, the majority Mexican, but many came from other Latin American countries. Norman described the first registration. He said when he came to the scene, a large room in Televicentro, he saw several hundred people lined against all the walls with their hands up in the air. He thought he had wandered into a big robbery and he raised his hands, too, assuming that some gunmen out of his sight were commanding the room. It turned out that it was only that the new student recruits were all using the walls as a hard surface on which to fill out their registration forms.

It was one thing, however, to recruit surprising numbers of students and another thing entirely to manage an orderly, fulfilling educational process. When the initial euphoria had settled, the reality of running a school, especially for such an unanticipated number of students, simply overwhelmed the individual chosen as chief administrator, his minimal clerical staff, and co-directors Camarena and Kenny. Perhaps if Norman or I had been on-site for several months before opening day, many problems could have been avoided.

It quickly became clear that Columbia College Pan-Americano could not be administered from afar, nor done successfully without fluency in Spanish and a much greater understanding of Mexican culture and the complex customs and attitudes that determine the Mexican national character and way of life. So much that Americans take for granted is alien to Mexican practice. And certainly the Mexican educational system is unfamiliar. Talk about imperialist notions! Our carpetbags were surely full of them. But in spite of everything, we somehow muddled through the first term.

Actual classroom instruction followed an orderly plan, and Televicentro's wealth of facilities gave students very satisfying hands-on experience, though spotty and tardy attendance by faculty and students was a constant problem. Before the second term, I spent nearly two months in Mexico and brought some order to the insistent chaos, but building a competent administration that could function without immediate supervision remained a thorny problem. It was our initial plan to offer a one-year diploma program and only later to consider a more extended study plan. More than half of the original students did complete a year's study, which, we were assured, was an unusually good record. Most of these students promptly got jobs or were upgraded at Televicentro or at allied companies in the television industry. Only 150 students were accepted in the second-year class and, again, nearly half completed the year and had job search experiences similar to the first-year students.

By January 1957, we still had not sufficiently solved the school's management problems, and it had become apparent that we could not efficiently nor profitably supervise the project from Chicago or Los Angeles. So it was decided that responsibility for Columbia College Pan-Americano would be given to Camarena, Kenny, and Televicentro, though the institution's identity would remain the same. I believe that after another year Televicentro established an in-house TV training program and that some intentions of Columbia's Mexican project were absorbed in the curriculum of the University of Mexico. Gratifyingly, in 1963, Edward R. Murrow, who had become director of the U.S. Information Agency in the Kennedy Administration, said that Columbia College Pan-Americano was an outstanding example of inter-American cooperation. At the least, Columbia's Mexican institution had educated a large number of television professionals, many the first in Mexico and Latin America. And as the costs of Columbia's Mexican project had not been excessive, it was a worthwhile undertaking, despite the fact that it had not satisfied expectations of profitability.

The leadership and vision of Columbia's presidents has had paramount influence on the college's life from its beginnings. The faculty's and board's effects on the course of the institution are comparatively recent phenomena. While little is known about Columbia under Mary Blood, as its founder and president over a thirty-seven-year span, she was clearly the institution's dominant figure, as was Norman Alexandroff during his twenty-five-year tenure, and as I was during my thirty-two years as Columbia's president (my entire service extended over forty-five years). None of this is meant to suggest that our roles were performed alone. Others, of course, made indispensable contributions. Each of Columbia's presidents founded and led distinct Columbia epochs. Blood's Columbia, begun in 1890, ended with her death in 1927. In 1935 Norman Alexandroff became president, and though his leadership was not entirely consolidated for several years, his presidential tenure endured until 1960, when my time as Columbia's president began, extending until my retirement in 1992.

During my tenure, a qualitatively different Columbia came to be. Again, I have no knowledge of Mary Blood's closest colleagues, except co-founder Ida Morey Riley, who died in 1901. Nothing is known of the board's role during Mary Blood's reign, though the faculty of the School of Oratory and later the Columbia College of Expression seems to have had a lively presence in the college's life and direction. Norman had only minimal help during the early years of his tenure, outside of my mother's counsel and the active interest of his many talented friends and some new faculty. I do remember that he had a tireless secretary who could perform any executive or menial task. It was only in the early 1940s that he could afford any semblance of an executive staff. For several years, his majordomo was Fred Murrow, as I remember, an ex-actor. Murrow left in late 1945 after inheriting a restaurant "gold mine" in Texas. But by that time, the very capable Daniel Howard was there to share the college's management, which he did ably until Columbia and PFTC separated in 1962, though he was there for me, too, when Norman became occupied with Los Angeles.

After 1952 I had principal responsibility for Columbia Chicago, which, for the rest of the 1950s, had only two administrators, including me. A switchboard/receptionist, accounting, and building functions were shared with PFTC. The registrar was the other administrative employee, doing nearly everything that I didn't do, though we shared the tasks of student service, student recruiting, counseling students, and composing class schedules. I engaged teachers, designed subjects, arranged class schedules, and generally monitored what was happening. We had morning classes (to 1:00 P.M.) and evening classes (to 10:15 P.M.). My ordinary day ran from about 8:00 in the morning until 10:30 at night, with half days on Saturdays. That schedule went on for years, into the 1960s, at least.

In the mid-1950s Robert Borelek was the registrar and taught a couple of classes, too. He successor was Jane Ann Legnard, and at the same time I hired Richard Thorne to supervise night classes and manage the college's popular Learn/Earn program. Thorne was exceptionally competent and a loyal colleague. He was a talented writer, a very experienced radio and television announcer and producer, and an outstanding teacher. (And, I add, he had a great radio voice.) I remember, probably imprecisely, that he left Columbia to become the press secretary to the Governor of Illinois, a position that was a bit loftier than being my associate. Jane Ann Legnard had been the college's switchboard operator and receptionist, though she did many other things. She knew all the students and faculty, a good bit about Columbia's subjects, and was readily familiar with all the college's routines. She had great presence and rare enthusiasm. The right stuff for a student recruiter, which was the main expectation of the registrar. And she was a good writer as well and willingly worked nearly the same exhausting schedule as I did. Jane was genuinely invaluable and continued to be so for thirty-five years, though in an altered role as this narrative tells later.

With infrequent change, the board's membership and college's officers remained constant until 1956 when I resigned as a board member and as vice president; though as business manager my functions remained unchanged. Daniel Howard replaced me as vice president and as a board member. My reason for resigning from the two offices was my belief that if Columbia were to seek accreditation as a customary college institution, having two family members simultaneously holding board and officer titles might hurt us.

The subject of accreditation was frequently discussed in board meetings and between Norman and me. In 1958, Norman and John DeBoer met with Norman Burns, the director of the North Central Association to explore the prospect of Columbia's accreditation. It was a discouraging conversation. The North Central agency was a bastion of traditional collegiate respectability and, perforce, Burns viewed Columbia as beyond the pale. We didn't look at all like a typical college institution: our practices were impermissibly unorthodox; our students' quality doubtful; and our financial resources puny. In effect, Columbia was penalized for its unfamiliar state. We were surely not a trade or vocational school. We were legitimately a college, albeit a specialized one. We had perfectly valid four-year bachelor's and master's degree programs. We were a certified teacher's training institution. We offered a comprehensive program of liberal arts subjects. But none of this cut any ice with the moguls of accreditation. The club of proper college institutions just would not have us. My resignations turned out to be entirely irrelevant, though I did not return to the board or to any college office until 1959. The quest for accreditation persisted, though it would go unrealized for another fifteen years.

47

An eventful meeting of Columbia's board of trustees in November 1959 charted a new course for the college. The meeting's purpose was to separate Columbia College and its branch operation in Los Angeles as had been contracted in 1953. Norman reviewed the history of the Los Angeles enterprise: "It was established at a time when most of higher education was insensitive to the enormous educational potential of the television medium." The board of trustees had very accurately anticipated the concentration of television network operations on the West Coast and the marriage there of the television and motion picture industries. It was this prediction, now proven by events that motivated the board to establish the branch operation in Los Angeles. The board of trustees (mainly Norman, of course) sought to expand the educational purposes of Columbia College by providing the initial financing, support, and guidance necessary to establish a specialized college center for communication arts education in Los Angeles. The board of trustees (again, mainly Norman) had faith that such an educational endeavor would, within a few years, become capable of independent life, without requiring further assistance from its Chicago parent. He confirmed that the time had come when any further support was unnecessary. The Los Angeles branch had become an independent college institution on its own. It had graduated three classes that had begun as freshmen four years earlier. Its revenues appeared sufficient. In short, the child had come of age. Moreover, a separation was desirable at this time, as both institutions planned to seek regional accreditation during the next few years. Such accreditation may preclude dependent ties between two institutions at such great geographical distance, nor can the well-being of either be dependent on the success of the other.

The board voted to separate the two institutions. Norman stated that a board of trustees would be formed of individuals having interest in and immediacy to the now independent Los Angeles college, and that appropriate tax-exempt status would be sought for Columbia Los Angeles, which he expected would be granted without difficulty. Los Angeles made a payment of $31,000 to Chicago, per the terms of the 1953 agreement. The board also voted to maintain an active fraternal relationship between the two now separate Columbias, and a cooperative effort to maintain the high standards of communication arts education which identify both institutions.

While Norman believed that Columbia Chicago required an active administration headed by a chief executive, intending that I be the person, the board decided, in a moment of sentiment, that Norman was to continue as president, without compensation, with the obligation to devote only such time to the affairs of that office as he might deem necessary and practical in view of his Los Angeles duties and responsibilities. The board didn't change Norman's status as board chairman, but it did elect Daniel D. Howard as acting chairman of the board.

Within several months of that meeting a new board was formed in Los Angeles, and Norman, as expected, was named board chairman and president. At the same time, I was elected to the Los Angeles board. Notwithstanding the board's decisions, Columbia College Chicago was in actuality unchanged, except that while Norman's abdication was a matter of fact, the board's contradictory intentions left the institution both with and without an official president. This caused little immediate trouble, apart from some minor inconveniences. But the clock was winding down. If we had only known it.

In the spring of 1960, I was in the hospital with a bad back that resisted treatment for weeks. While I was there, Norman's doctors called to tell me that he had an inoperable cancer and only several weeks to live. I was trussed up in a barrel cast (the cast and I took up two airplane seats), and rushed to Los Angeles days before the end. In June, Norman Alexandroff died. A unique personal history ended too, as did his extraordinary human vitality and generating presence in Columbia's life.

In terms of all the events, ideas, and personalities of Columbia's history, the cardinal issue was simply surviving. Inescapably, the elemental substance of it was money. My father and I, and surely Mary Blood, too, knew countless days when we felt as the first line of B. Traven's novel *The Slave Ship* says, "Some days you've just got to have some cash money!" Indeed, I can't remember a time, until quite recently, when the wolf at the door wasn't a pervasive presence, whether real or imagined. For myself, at least, it was not that I was consumed by unnatural subjectivity, for in truth, Columbia's existence really was endangered during most of my tenure. As the college was dependent exclusively on uncertain tuition revenue, it lived on the edge of a scary abyss. As an old GI phrase goes, I "sweated out" every registration session.

I had many occasions to wonder, "Was it all much ado about nothing?" What could have gotten us, my whole family, to give so many years of our lives to the service of what was for most of those years a miniscule, insignificant institution not likely to realize its educational goals?

For all of Norman's time, Columbia truly was a mom-and-pop-sized enterprise. Even in its best year, Chicago, Los Angeles, and Mexico City combined served at most 800 students, generating less than $300,000 in total revenue, and ultimately lost money. Norman was a man with enough talent and creativity to have been successful at whatever he chose to do. It may well have been that he preferred control of a small stage, which gave him free opportunity to exercise his will, though the precariousness of Columbia must have given him discouraging pause. As observed earlier, he prospered personally in challenge and chase and much less when the fox was cornered. What's more elemental, however, is that he had an intense commitment to a purposeful life. I strongly shared this commitment, in part derivatively, of course. Undoubtedly, both of us were intensely task oriented and consumed by our occupations, even if getting the job had been accidental, which his involvement with Columbia was. However hesitant I was, my engagement was more deliberate. Norman was philosophical, which led him to strong personal convictions. His most emphatic conviction was, in the words of Norman's friend and tutor Jack London, to "make fair the world." Norman wanted to live by London's injunction spoken in his preface to Upton Sinclair's, *Cry for Justice*: "That for those who seek to overcome the harshness and villainies of the world, the remedy is so simple, merely human service." I shared this conviction. While I believe that we all have some deep-felt imperatives, none exists naturally. We learn the patterns by which we live. As educators and entrepreneurs, Norman and I did what we did because of who we were and what we wanted to do. We had the best reward: the opportunity to live interesting lives.

For myself, at least, I don't know that I sacrificed much to do what I did; though I wish sometimes it had all been easier. But I was blessed then with an uncommonly beautiful wife, Anna. Classically Greek in appearance, she looked like a younger edition of film star Irene Papas. Anna was small, slim, and surprisingly athletic, an exceptionally independent woman of strong character. While quiet and gentle, she was a quick foe of injustice and a gutsy organizer. She was a serious teacher and a skilled school principal with a great love of the wilderness. She was a devoted wife and mother of our two young daughters, Niki and Pam. Like their mother, they would become teachers. And God knows Anna had patience with my exhausting work schedule. If she hadn't, there couldn't have been a Columbia.

In retrospect, I think that Columbia was too small and obscure to be a setting that reflected the turmoil of the 1950s. Students concentrated on their careers, and as most also worked, there was little time for outside interests. As reported, the 1950s were unusually good years for graduates in Columbia's specialties. Personally, I was not hunkered down during a time when social advocacy was unpopular and suppressed, but I was simply preoccupied with the college's affairs and its customary struggle to stay afloat. It was a state of concern that would prevail long into the years ahead.

The 1950s were tough times for the college. During the period 1952–59, Columbia College Chicago lost three thousand dollars annually, in effect breaking even. Though it was cutting it close, the college nonetheless was able to fund a number of significant improvements. For example, in 1957 nearly $50,000 was invested in new television equipment and film gear, and part-time teaching rates increased by two dollars per class hour (though they were still pretty meager, of course). We must have thought we were pretty flush then, as we had changed from a semester to a quarter system and enjoyed a small tuition increase. Memorably, the Columbia and PFTC boards voted in 1958 to provide medical insurance for their key full-time employees. In Columbia's instance, this meant Norman, Jane Ann Legnard, and me. In 1959, when Chicago and Los Angeles were separated, I was given a questionably optimistic ten-year contract at $12,900 a year, with annual 5 percent increases for five years, and a minimal pension contribution. I never actually got that salary, let alone the raises, until ten years later. There just was never enough money. But then again, Norman's highest salary was only $15,000 a year, and I was close to age forty, making less than $10,000 a year. In 1959, whatever prosperity we may have imagined, Columbia had no reserve funds, nor would we have for years.

After Norman died in June 1960, I returned to Los Angeles in early August, still a bit uncertain whether I would take up his role at Columbia Los Angeles. I was, in effect, the acting chairman of its board and the president's job would certainly have been mine if I chose it. Columbia's enrollment in Los Angeles was roughly the same as in Chicago, its resources and reserves were minimal but not more strained, and it was convincingly evident that a Columbia College in Los Angeles would have greater student potential because of its proximity to the main location of the entertainment industries. Despite strong arguments for choosing Los Angeles, leaving Chicago was an impossible prospect. I knew I couldn't be president of both institutions.

My choice could only be Chicago. There was no alternative but to get myself out of Columbia Los Angeles.

Whatever my earlier hesitations about Columbia's Los Angeles project, it was hard to give away Norman's dream of a new Columbia and the result of his great labors. A meeting of the Los Angeles board was convened, at which I renounced a role as president, but I was elected board chairman, a title I believe I retained for two years, until an entirely new Los Angeles board was constituted. At the 1960 Board meeting, I nominated and the board elected Ernest Baumeister as President. While he had a graduate degree in electrical engineering and many years in senior technical capacities in television and film, he was not an experienced educator. But he was a competent manager and had great work energy, which was evident in his role as Norman's principal aide in Los Angeles after 1958.

Baumeister was a convenient choice, as the alternative was that I would have had to manage both the Chicago and Los Angeles Columbias, at least until a more ideal candidate was found and trained in the position. It was an impossible alternative. Baumeister remained as the president of Columbia College Los Angeles for more than twenty-five years, though the institution settled for a role more as a professional school than as a genuine college. It retained its not-for-profit status as a degree-granting institution, an enrollment of 250 to 300 students, and reasonable financial sufficiency. In a sense, it was in a state of arrested development. At some time during the late 1980s, Columbia College Los Angeles became an operation of the New York Institute of Technology, a large, successful New York institution, but after more than

twenty-five years of separation, I have no knowledge of the circumstances. At least there was a Columbia of sorts in a small building on La Brea Avenue in Los Angeles when Bert Gall and I visited briefly in 1988. The day was a Saturday, and only one person was about, a teacher, I think. He didn't know very much, but he vaguely told me that Ernie Baumeister was gone. There was a big portrait of Norman hanging in the lobby. It was a sad end to the promise of thirty years before. I've never tried to find out anything else. As Thomas Wolfe said, "You can't go home again."

Now independent of the Los Angeles branch, Columbia College's board of trustees met in August of 1960. It was the first board or college occasion in many years without Norman. The acting chairman, Daniel D. Howard, said, "It was impossible to adequately eulogize the service to the college performed by Norman Alexandroff. The institution's very existence can be attributed to the vigorous, imaginative, and selfless leadership of its departed president."

We went on to discuss the college's present state. Still business manager, I reported that in the preceding year expenses had been reduced significantly, largely by the separation of the Los Angeles branch, which took responsibility for some expenses, including Norman's salary. At the same time, tuition income was lower, because the college had lost almost its entire Korean War veteran population by the end of the 1959–60 year. While it was expected that enrollment would increase, in September of 1960 the numbers reflected the loss of veteran students. A strenuous student recruitment effort was in progress, and expenses were controlled, though cautiously to avoid damage to the considerable advances that had been made during the last few years.

Dr. Howard observed, "The recruitment of students of high caliber, the continued engagement of most expert faculty, and the necessary enlargement of the administrative staff made it clear that Columbia could no longer depend on tuition revenues alone. The college would have to raise independent funds to prosper and grow. Moreover, given the attitude increasingly held by the public and educational community that liberal arts accreditation is the only accepted evidence of the validity and reliability of a college, Columbia must actively move towards achieving accreditation." Unfortunately, it took money to buy the essentials necessary for accreditation, and it takes accreditation to raise the money. It was a dilemma. It was agreed that board membership should be reconstituted to better assist in developing community support for the institution. A new board slate was elected, including Daniel Howard; A. C. Weiss; Dr. Clara Tigay; and new members, William Russo; Erwin Salk, a prominent member of the business community; Lucille Strauss; and after a four-year absence, me.

Electing a president was hardly competitive. As a matter of record, I was elected to succeed Norman as Columbia College's president. Daniel Howard formally became the board's chairman and vice president; and Herman Hegner remained as corporate treasurer. While final financial statements for the 1959–60 year had not yet been prepared, Hegner reported that these would show a break-even year, even without any Los Angeles expense. My Columbia era had officially begun.

As anticipated, September 1960 enrollment was down. We still had roughly 250 full- and part-time students, though the year's expenses were expected to be greater. It would be, as customary, a difficult time. I couldn't have imagined how difficult it would actually be.

When I returned from settling things in Los Angeles, my wife Anna was hospitalized with what would be diagnosed as inoperable cancer. She lingered in an awful state until her death in February 1961. She was thirty-four years old. It was a tragedy with which I still have difficulty. Unavoidably, I became preoccupied with my children and unfamiliar household tasks. While there are accessible records of the 1960–61 year, my personal impression of the time is pretty foggy.

Despite the often highly rhetorical quality of board discussion, meetings had routinely followed Norman's lead, and independent thinking was infrequent, though this began to change when David Kopel and John DeBoer joined the board. By 1960, it had become clear that Columbia could not prosper or perhaps even survive without an involved, responsive, and independent-thinking board. These qualities were evident at the August 1960 meeting and continued at the regular annual meeting in November. The board believed uniformly that while the immediate members of Columbia's family knew and understood the college's mission, it was little known by the constituencies we needed to reach: prospective donors, the news media, and the educational community. While the board recognized that effective publicity required expert personnel and an investment that was then beyond Columbia's resources, it insisted that such emphasis had high priority in the college's future. It

was at this point that I introduced a projection of the college's state and goals over the next five-year term. I projected four hundred students in 1966, doubling present numbers and a greater proportion of full-time students; a much enlarged plant and facilities; more courses in our educational specialties; a larger and better-compensated faculty with some full-time members; more student services; smaller class sizes and a tutorial emphasis which supported students' creative independence; more scholarship aid; a larger effort to recruit foreign students; and some greater selectivity in student admissions, if such practices could be employed without serious damage to Columbia's commitment to open admissions. I have consistently believed this is a core principle of Columbia's mission. A current need, I continued, was sufficient administrative staff (then only Jane Legnard) and an all-purpose secretary in addition to myself. An unfamiliarly lively board discussion ensued which included a long-term commitment to fund-raising. While the current year's budget projected only a very small deficit, I believed it was an unreliable expectation as expenses would inevitably be greater than calculated.

Despite my family distractions, we got through the year only minimally harmed. It ended with a loss of $6,000. We took in $95,000 and spent $101,000, not much different from the year before. We'd had a small amount of aid from a new government initiative, the National Defense Student Loan program, which allowed us to make tuition loans to students. The government contributed $9,000 to our loan bank and the college put up $1,000. I record all these small potatoes so no one will mistake the college's "prosperity."

But all in all, it was hardly an encouraging way to begin a college presidency. Most satisfying that year was the performance of the faculty, many of whom had been teaching at Columbia for many years. There were several exceptional new faculty, too: Don Nathanson, president of North Advertising, a major national ad agency; Robert Dressler, program manager of WNBQ-TV (NBC); and three alumni, Bill Harder, Jack Wartlieb, and Jim Sheerin.

1961–1962

I had little reason for optimism about the new college year, but whatever hope I did have was quickly dashed by a new danger even more threatening than our usually precarious finances. From its earliest days, Columbia's claim of collegiate identity, even in the absence of customary accreditation, was its certification as a teacher training institution. It was this credential which qualified Columbia for collegiate benefit programs sponsored by the U.S. government and the state of Illinois, and correspondingly, collegiate recognition by all government agencies. The GI Bills were paramount examples of the indispensable value of such eligibility. But in the fall of 1961, the U.S. Office of Education changed the rules of institutional eligibility. Beginning in 1962, only colleges accredited by regional agencies or equivalent professional associations would be certified to participate in federal programs and be recognized by U.S. government agencies. Such exclusion would be the end of Columbia. While our Illinois State teaching certification credential would be undisturbed by the Federal ruling, its only benefit would be the minimal revenues we gained from a few education "majors." A few years later this teaching credential was Columbia's qualifying certification for inclusion in the Illinois state scholarship program, which gave (and gives) vast benefit to Columbia's students. If we could not somehow overcome the smothering effect of the new rulings, Columbia could not, for example, have qualified as a place for students seeking deferment from the impending military draft or the benefits of a Cold War GI Bill. The ruling allowed only the narrowest glimmer of hope. As an alternative to accreditation, an institution could qualify if it could secure the unequivocal statement of three accredited institutions that they would accept Columbia course credits without qualification on the same basis that they accepted transfer credits from accredited institutions.

We well understood the virtually insurmountable difficulty we would have in getting such statements. Though many institutions had regularly accepted Columbia College credits in transfer, this was done unofficially on an individual basis. It would be an unusual accredited college that would record its commitment to an unorthodox practice. Columbia had no dependable relationships with any other colleges. Indeed, few, if any, had ever heard of us. No institution had anything to gain by helping Columbia. We could only hope to find some rare official who had some sense of collegiality. I worked for several weeks at drafting a convincing letter to college presidents that solicited a statement of their institution's willingness to accept Columbia's credits.

We restricted our mailing to comparatively small colleges. It was our thinking that we'd get nowhere with big institutions, where our appeal would be discarded or bucked about fruitlessly. We sent our appeal to about seven hundred colleges. A small number replied with mostly polite refusals, and a few so hedged their statements that we knew it would not satisfy the U.S. Office of Education. We were still at zero. One of the statements, from Emerson College, came close, but maybe they could be persuaded. I went to Boston to see Emerson's president. I appealed to him on the basis that Emerson and Columbia were virtually sister institutions. Similar pioneers in speech and theater education founded both. I pulled out all the stops, and finally he agreed to give us a suitable letter. We had one. I went to other institutions whose initial responses suggested they might be persuaded by my personal visit. All insisted on qualifying language. Then I went to see Morris Keaton at Antioch College, a progressive, socially responsive place. Keaton was then, I believe, its dean. I had met him some years before at the Highlander Folk School in Tennessee, and he was that rare individual who had a strong sense of collegial fraternity. He got me Antioch's letter. Now there were two. I flailed about unsuccessfully for several months. The filing deadline was near. And then, one fine day, a satisfying letter came from Greenville College in southern Illinois. Its president even apologized for his late response. We had the requisite three letters. It was like paradise regained.

At about the same time, in January 1962, I'd gotten another sight of green pastures when I married Jane Ann Legnard. She would share the Columbia helm for thirty years. Such pleasures aside, the college continued to muck along.

1962–1963

In the fall of 1962, I hired a full-time dean, Wolfram Dochtermann, though Daniel Howard still held the office, with limited function. Dochtermann was entirely familiar with Columbia, as a faculty member and earlier as a master's degree graduate. He had an excellent professional record in film and television and had commanded a United States Air Force unit of television, film, and photography specialists. In view of Columbia's comparatively primitive technology, perhaps Wolf was overqualified for Columbia's job. Unfortunately, he was only the dean for four months, when he was recalled to active Air Force service, presumably in anticipation of the Berlin crisis and because of his fluency in German.

Knowing that Columbia could not continue to depend exclusively on tuition revenue, I hired Walter Robinson to assist in the college's administration with primary focus on publicity and fund-raising. I knew virtually nothing then about public relations and a bit less about fund-raising. Whatever publicity Columbia had enjoyed was mostly the result of Norman's remarkable nose for news and my occasional exploitations. Fund-raising had no Columbia precedents whatsoever. At best, there was nothing except a gambler's chance that either effort could succeed in the face of the college's handicaps. We simply didn't have enough collegiate respectability to enlist the regular interest of mainstream news agencies, and surely we had no constituency to solicit for funds. Worse, we had no money to support the effort either. We went forward on my naïve belief that it was at least barely possible that an ingenious individual could magically lead us across the Jordan. After issuing a ton of unrequited press releases and trying fruitlessly to develop media allies, Robinson sensibly discouraged a large publicity emphasis. It was obvious, too, that fund-raising, which expected significant returns, would meet a similarly discouraging fate.

With Dochtermann's abrupt departure, Robinson's role was uncertain. If nothing else, he was surely a court jester of Falstaffian proportion. He made hard times bearable. Les Brown, then the Chicago Bureau chief of the *Daily Variety*, recommended him to me. Robinson had most recently been the public relations director of BMI, a power in the entertainment industry, and before that, one of the brilliant team of young comedy writers of *The Show of Shows*, then the number-one program on network television, starring Sid Caesar and Imogene Coca. This unique group of writer-performers included Mel Brooks, Carl Reiner, Howie Morris, Woody Allen, and, briefly, Robinson, who for some reason had left the show. Wally, Brown told me, was a decent and entertaining fellow who was a masterful writer and speaker. If anyone could publicize and raise money for a maverick place like Columbia, Robinson was surely the right man. He charmed me at our first interview. He seemed instinctively to understand Columbia, and I hired him immediately. He really did little, but he was a deeply caring man and was a pleasure to have about. He taught a comedy class on Wednesday evenings to which his loyal showbiz colleagues were regular class visitors. Mel Brooks came often. A number of Robinson's students went on to successful careers in comedy and other roles in entertainment.

At year's end, we had lost $17,000. It would have been more, but we had netted nearly $20,000 in donations drummed up mostly by board members. We then owed PFTC $42,000, and the new college year began with $2,000 in the bank. We were light-years away from the previous year's ambitious projections, but Columbia was still afloat, buoyed, perhaps, by the miracle of never, even in the worst of times, having missed or shorted a payroll, except for my own salary. But I wasn't even there to help when the end of the year came.

In July 1962 I went for a routine physical examination. I had a spot on a lung. After interminable days of probing and waiting, a first diagnosis of cancer was replaced by one of tuberculosis, and I was sent away to a TB sanitarium in Winfield, Illinois, a distant West Chicago suburb. Presumably it was for a brief stay. It wasn't. My banishment lasted nearly four months. While my commitment was voluntary, once in, you could only get out legally when the sanitarium's director authorized your release. I used to imagine that the place got some sort of per capita subsidy, and I was too valuable to send home. I finally was home at Christmas. Jane was pregnant when I went away. Our son, Norman, was born while I was still in the sanitarium. Jane also had two new daughters, a new household to manage, and me to visit on weekends. It was all very tough on her, and for me a time of great anxiety, relieved only by occupying myself with writing a libretto in verse for a contemporary take on Mozart's opera *Don Giovanni*. It was an unsuccessful exercise. I never could find a composer, and ultimately, my opus was buried away and forgotten.

The college's board met in September 1962 to assess the damage. No one knew when I'd return. They appointed Wally Robinson acting president, and Jane was summoned from "retirement." The board pledged whatever fund-raising was necessary to keep the wolf at bay. A most urgent task was to get Dochtermann out of military service. In the meantime, as Wally was adrift in responsibility, the greatest burden of running the college fell on Jane. I don't know how she did it, but she did. College, family, everything. She had the lead role in a real life "perils of Pauline," a lousy role even for a secret actress-in-waiting.

Jane was a very attractive, articulate woman: tall, slim, and always fashionably dressed. She was a most democratic person and a fierce advocate of human dignity. Indeed, she never even seemed aware of color, religion, nationality, class, or sexual preference. She quickly responded to injustice and had immediate sympathy for individuals in need. To name only a few of her causes, Jane was active in the civil rights movement and the fight for woman's rights and equality. She passionately opposed the Vietnam War and discrimination against gays and lesbians, disabled people, AIDS sufferers, and Native Americans. She cared deeply about education, the arts, human welfare, and a more equitable economy.

An alumna of the University of Pittsburgh, all her earlier education was in parochial schools. She came from a strict Irish Catholic family in Anderson, Indiana, and later Pittsburgh, who despite being Democratic Party loyalists had no personal contact with African Americans, Latinos, Jews, gays, or radicals of any sort. At seventeen, when she graduated from high school, she left the Catholic Church, saying its premises and doctrine were unconvincing. Though the church's instruction on personal morality remained influential, Jane was strongly pro-choice and a partisan of women's issues within the Catholic Church.

When she first came to Columbia and for many years after, Jane knew everyone: hosts of students, alumni, faculty, college workers of all sorts, board members, and even cops on the beat. Jane was the college's mother, confidant, counsel, and cheerleader. She was a legendary cook and baker, a talented designer of women's clothing, and a gifted seamstress. She was an inexhaustible hostess who nearly every week for years had dinners at our home for Columbia folk. Her occasions always mixed faculty, staff, Board members, and maintenance workers–upstairs and downstairs together. She cooked everything for parties of twelve to eighty. She also served countless memorable dinners to celebrities and shakers of all sorts. These occasions were veritable salons of great talk. Jane loved parties, good drinkers, late nights, and fast cars (not together, of course). Her children often say, "Whatever else, Mom taught us enthusiasm!" She was a wise and attentive mother, an incomparable wife, and an indispensable partner in Columbia's life.

There's a tragic postscript to all this. Jane always enjoyed the best health and had no doubt that she'd live at least as long as her mother, who died at age 102. Jane and her sister Margaret (also married to a "Mike"), believed sadly that their family genes destined them to outlive their husbands, and that the sisters would live together ever after in an eighteenth-century New England house mysteriously transported to some village near San Diego. But Jane's life ended abruptly in 1996 when she died of breast cancer, that awful decimator of women. Our retirement was too brief. An empty year later, I began to sketch out this book. Perhaps it saved me from despair.

At the September 1962 board meeting, Daniel Howard resigned as chairman and as board member. Dr. Tigay also resigned. Philip Lewis, an old friend of mine and manager of a national garment firm, and Sam Victor, a Chicago manufacturer, filled their positions. At the same meeting the board also consolidated the various loans which PFTC had made to Columbia and partly secured this indebtedness by pledging securities held by Columbia–the end of our small reserves. The board met again in November. Everyone was bailing furiously. A. C. Weiss became board chairman, and Russo resigned from the board, as he expected to remain in Europe indefinitely. Dochtermann was scheduled for release from service in January; I had made an appeal to Senator Dirksen, asking his intercession with the air force, and it worked.

I went back to work just after the New Year 1993 holiday. The first thing that happened that day was that Hegner and Howard told me that the Teachers College would separate from Columbia at the end of 1963. They had the subtlety of an avalanche, but it would probably have been just as staggering if I had heard it a few weeks later. In retrospect, I should have been prepared. Obviously, Hegner and Howard had concluded, certainly not unwisely, that Columbia wouldn't make it, and its dying would be expensive for PFTC if the institutions were still joined. At the time I was in despair at the news and afterward often pondered whether Columbia's struggle was worth continuing. But at the moment, I had to get on with it, albeit with doubting heart.

The most immediate task was to counter a declining enrollment. We worked hard that January to sustain fall enrollment figures in the spring semester, when enrollment usually declined. It seems ridiculous today to have made such a to-do about twenty-five or so students, but then, the whole business was cheap change. Our brief effort was successful. We had 230 students in the spring term, but we were dangerously poor and needed money quickly.

In the next months I dug up nearly $15,000 from such family friends as I'd missed the year before. One gift, however, was noteworthy. Just before I went to the TB sanitarium, I had agreed to manage the congressional campaign of Professor Robert Cosbey, who was running as an independent Democrat in the Ninth District. While my stay in the sanitarium abruptly ended my political role, it at least gave me the opportunity to meet Lucy Montgomery. A beautiful southern belle turned high society North Shore lady, she was surely unlikely to become, as she did, an icon of American progressives, and with her husband, a major financial supporter of the civil rights movement. The Cosbey campaign was her first political engagement, and I had only briefly known her. But in the spring of 1963 when I was out grasping for straws, I had an idea that Columbia might attract some support from the arts division of the U.S. Office of Education, and I thought that Lucy Montgomery might give my Washington foray a glittering dimension. So one Sunday afternoon, I went to her house to try to enlist her. Her house and gardened estate were beyond anything I'd ever imagined. Indeed, many national publications described it as one of America's most beautiful homes. Lucy's husband, Kenneth Montgomery, met me at the door and, after brief introductions, gave me an envelope and said, "Lucy has told me about hard times with your college. Perhaps this will help." The envelope held a check for $5,000. Lucy did go to Washington with me and helped mightily to found a relationship with government arts agencies that served Columbia well for many, many years, and Ken Montgomery became Columbia's largest and most crucial benefactor. He was always there when I needed help most, as later Harle Montgomery was, too. She is splendidly generous and genuinely committed to human welfare.

Notwithstanding my all-consuming efforts to strengthen the college, the remedies I pursued were short-range and meant mostly to assure Columbia's immediate survival, though my doubts about the institution's longer-term viability persisted. I had made a friend of Sandy Liveright, at one time the director of the American Council on Race Relations and an old associate of my father. I had told him my doubts about Columbia and that finding another job might be a critical issue. I was, after all, forty years old, with a wife and now three children. My work history was mainly confined to Columbia, and I wanted any job I considered to promise that my life would be put to good purpose. All this hardly made for a convincing resume. Liveright had spoken with a friend at Syracuse University, who suggested I might be interested in an associate dean's position at the Syracuse School of Communication, then among the most prominent centers of education in communication subjects. I interviewed for the job, which I may or may not have gotten, but shortly after withdrew my name from consideration. Leaving Chicago seemed too wrenching a prospect for me.

Liveright had also spoken with Edward Sparling, the president of Roosevelt University, who had founded the institution in 1944 to democratize access to higher education and, in particular, to give long-denied college opportunity to African Americans. This was then a relatively unprecedented idea in higher education. Sparling and I met frequently that spring, on occasion joined by Dr. Horton Sheldon, Roosevelt's dean of faculty. I shared with them my ideas about education and particularly about the value and attraction of a college of the arts and communications within a university setting. It was an appealing notion, and over time, they decided that Roosevelt was a good place to give it a shot.

I don't remember what I had in mind, whether it was just talk or whether I meant to persuade them. I suppose my motives were mixed. What I certainly didn't know at the time was anything about Roosevelt's internal politics, how weighty decisions were made and who had power. Also, I didn't know that Sparling's authority was shaky, that Sheldon had a limited constituency, and that the principal deans and board members had the greatest influence on the university's course. I naively thought that university presidents made decisions and that was that. If this was generally true, Roosevelt was surely an exception. Sparling and Sheldon launched the whole idea of a school of the arts and communications and Roosevelt's embrace of Columbia at a meeting with the deans and me. I particularly remember Otto Wirth, dean of Liberal Arts and Sciences; Rolf Weil, dean of the School of Business; and Walter Weiskoph, chair of the Economics Department. They were a formidable bunch, and while they were unfailingly courteous, I couldn't shake the feeling of being a dumbstruck graduate student taking a crucial oral examination. I suspect that they hadn't even heard of the proposition before the meeting. They simply dismissed the idea. It was clear that they had little respect for me and regarded Columbia as a trade school. While they were undoubtedly cultured men, they expressed little esteem for practical education in the arts disciplines, which they believed were inappropriate to the more scholarly interests of universities and better consigned to conservatories. One even opined that the arts were more nearly vocations and such subjects as television, radio, photography, and film were simply outside the university pale. These were perplexing observations in view of the fact that some years before, Roosevelt had adopted the venerable Chicago Music College as its own music department and Roosevelt's curriculum already included an art major. And with all that, the plan might have been acceptable if Sparling and Sheldon had done their political homework.

Despite my great affection and respect for Sparling, it was clear to me that Roosevelt had missed an extraordinary, profitable opportunity. The Columbia miracle might have happened under the Roosevelt roof. Twenty-five years later, Roosevelt may wish it had. By the time I got out of Roosevelt's door, I realized that Columbia and I could never have lived at Roosevelt. My ideas about education and the arts and media were poles apart from theirs.

While walking back to Columbia's place, I had a sort of epiphany. I would put Columbia together and make it a sound vessel of progressive education. I didn't know how, only that I had to do it. Walking along, I met Harry Bouras. We went across the street to Miller's Pub, and I told him about my moment of resolve. He cheered me on, and I went back to work.

A special board meeting was convened in late March 1963 to consider the college's perilous state. It was commonly known that PFTC would separate from Columbia at the end of the year, an event with many threatening implications, the most prominent of which was an acute need to find a new location. I reported that at the moment we had no practical prospects. Moreover, the year's loss would likely be in a $25,000–30,000 range, which could only be offset by donated funds. This was the college's first problem, which if unsatisfied would make any question of a new location irrelevant. It was clear we couldn't continue to live by paying off last year's deficits with next year's receipts. While accountants might hedge appearances of our virtually bankrupt state, they couldn't conjure up the cash we needed to operate. I volunteered a "loan" of $4,000 from my father's estate, which he had bequeathed "for good causes." Phil Lewis generously offered to contribute $5,000, Bud Salk gave $3,000, and we expected some return on an art auction which Harry Bouras was planning for the college in late spring. We still had to raise the rest of the money promptly, but we had made a good start. Bud Perlman, Seymour Gale, and Harry Bouras agreed to become board members. Gale was elected as the board's chairman. Daniel Howard and Herman Hegner submitted their resignations. Wolf Dochtermann was named as the college's acting vice president; A. C. Weiss, who had briefly been the board chairman, resumed his former post as secretary-treasurer. All members pledged their help in finding a new place.

The loose end of all of this was that I had to get rid of Wally Robinson. Although questionably productive, he was a delightful man. Jane and I were intensely fond of him. But in the last analysis, we just couldn't afford to keep him when Wolf came back.

1963–1964: Defining Columbia

In actuality, the 1962–63 year ended somewhat better than anticipated. While student revenues were nearly $100,000, and expenses, as forecast, roughly $130,000, that loss was offset by $20,000 in donations. All told, we'd lost $10,000. Only an eye as myopic as mine would see this as encouraging. The fall enrollment was nearly the same as the year before—not a reassuring number, but not entirely bleak, either.

I had spent a good part of the winter of 1963 contemplating Columbia's and my future. I had put off coming to grips with the consequences of PFTC's decision to split away from Columbia at the end of the year. The most important issue was that if Columbia was to continue, it obviously had to get a new home somewhere. It was impossible to continue at the Wabash Avenue location, because Columbia's functions were scattered over five floors to suit the building's configurations and the college's space-sharing arrangements. Moreover, there was no way Columbia could afford to rent the space that PFTC would vacate, and it would be too expensive to remodel a smaller part of the building. We surely had no money, and there was little likelihood that we could find a sympathetic landlord who would lease us anything without far greater guarantees of solvency than we could provide.

I looked all over downtown Chicago and nearby and found nothing available and no willing landlords, either. We were within six months of the moving deadline. Then there was a last-minute rescue, once again by Bud Perlman, newly a board member. He owned a building at Lake Shore Drive and Ohio Street, across the Outer Drive from the University of Illinois at Chicago, which occupied Navy Pier until construction of its new campus was completed. Inexplicably, Perlman embraced Columbia's mission, and he had generous confidence in me. He gave us a seven-year lease for the seventh (top) floor on the Lake Shore Drive side of the building at a beginning year's rent of $20,000, with 10 percent increases for three years. While the new space would double what we'd paid at Wabash Avenue, the Lake Shore Drive location was a vastly more attractive and usable place than what we had shared with PFTC, and the new space had fewer pillars and abutments to interfere with a convenient configuration. On top of Perlman's astonishing largesse, he advanced us $25,000 for remodeling expenses to be repaid in small monthly installments. Without a doubt, there wouldn't have been a Columbia College after 1964 without Perlman's optimism that Columbia would make it.

Wolf Dochtermann was put to the job of designing the college's new space, and as we were doing everything cheaply, he also did the work of a general contractor. Wolf's plan had all of the college's offices overlooking the lake and the Outer Drive. A theater and television studio occupied the ninety-foot-wide west side of the building. The whole floor had sixteen-foot ceilings. A raised, glass-enclosed TV and theater control room was at one end of the theater/TV studio, and at floor level, five tiered rows of upholstered theater seats with drop tables to allow use of the space as a classroom. The "stage" with a lighting grid above it had approximately 1,200 square feet.

Outside the studio was a long room for storing scenery, props, and TV gear, part of which could also be used as a dressing room for stage and TV productions. The only difficult construction problem was removing a midfloor column that support-ed the roof, but removing the column and running a steel girder across the width of the studio solved this. We also had five other good-sized classrooms, a radio stu-dio and classroom, a place for a small library, and another space we would soon con-vert into a photography darkroom. The whole place was compact, convenient, and attractively decorated, and I would have a snazzy wood-paneled office on the floor's northeast corner that conveniently was already there. The whole place sure beat where we were.

Columbia and PFTC had been joined for thirty-five years. At least during the Alexandroffs' time, the relationship had been friendly, fraternal, and mutually sup-portive, even affectionate. Now that separation was at hand, an unfamiliar tension prevailed. Polite but vaguely suspicious, we seldom talked with one another, except about necessary matters. I knew nothing about where PFTC was moving, and I believe they knew nothing about Columbia's plans. All the affectionate staff rela-tions seemed to fall away. The last months were really strange, and sad, I think. As is said, I suppose, "business is business." I don't have any memory of what either of us did about shared classes. It was likely that students would travel back and forth in January. We had thoroughly briefed our students and faculty about the move, and had even hyped the great advantages everyone would enjoy. Students would attend classes at the Wabash location until the Christmas holiday recess, and when they returned after the New Year, they would be at a new place. Everyone had a new room schedule and information about transportation and parking.

PFTC moved a few days after we did. The moves were done at night, which is all the city would allow downtown. I vaguely remember that we moved the night after Christmas. There's nothing vague about my memory of the night. It was bit-ter, bitter cold. Jane stayed at the Wabash building to watch over everything. We had carefully assembled, packed, and labeled all the Columbia stuff. Making sure it got on the trucks was a bit touch and go. The movers were prone to drink, and the job supervisor worked hardest, I think, at preaching moderation, if not temperance. We had to move as cheaply as possible, so we didn't know if we had the most depend-able crew. While Jane was at Wabash, Wolf and I were mostly on the loading plat-form of the Lake Shore building (which, happily, had a large freight elevator). Wolf or I went up with every load to show the movers where to put things. This was important because we didn't have much labor to help us set things up for the begin-ning of classes. Going up with a load kept us from freezing on the loading dock. When everything was out of Wabash, Jane joined us on the Lake Shore dock so we all could freeze together. The move took almost all night. I remember that it was light out when we finished and went for breakfast. The next three or four days were intensely busy with getting ready to open on schedule. All the shared staff stayed with PFTC, so we had to hire someone to work at the information office, a book-keeper, and a general clerk. As they wouldn't start on the job until we reopened, breaking them in, even minimally, was a taxing undertaking. But that first staff were exceptionally loyal and hardworking people, despite, as expected, not being very well paid.

We opened on schedule and in reasonably good order. Inevitably, there was some confusion, but it was minor and usually subsumed by everyone's pleasure at being in a bright new place. Columbia had 194 fall students enrolled. In reality, a whole new Columbia era began the first days of January in 1964. I remember the morning after the night we moved was terribly cold, but bright and sunny. It was a good omen.

The whole moving project had cost $40,000. We bought new classroom furniture and fixtures, rented television gear and office equipment, remodeled (for which Perlman had advanced the money), and hired movers. We also had new staff salaries. Talk about running on empty.

Incidentally, PFTC moved to a building at Wabash and Lake Street. I didn't see it or even talk to any PFTC folk for nearly ten years, and shortly after that, PFTC was absorbed by the National College of Education and became National's downtown campus.

The college's board met again in February 1964 for the first time at Columbia's new place. It was a lively occasion that reflected an optimistic sense that we were out from under the Damoclean sword, though serious financial strains remained, particularly as a result of moving expenses and the costs of new personnel. We had fifty new students in February, an unprecedented number. We had a prosperous and efficient look that must have been influential. Prospects for the fall were encouraging. Among other attractions, the new television studio with its new TV cameras and control gear was as up-to-date as many on-the-air stations. Dochtermann had gotten General Electric TV equipment valued at more than $40,000 for only $20,000 with an edu-cational discount, and GE allowed a three-year payment period. The board also acknowledged Ken Montgomery's pledge of $20,000.

The newly reconstituted board of trustees was a big plus in the college's life. Bud Perlman's help was invaluable, of course. As chairman, Seymour Gale gave a responsible, businesslike cast to board functions. Phil Lewis was a very bright, infinitely kind and generous man who would serve the board and the college with distinction for many years. Sam Victor was impressively helpful. And Harry Bouras, unfamiliarly cast in a business setting, took his board responsibilities seriously, not least of which was his indefatigable effort to hold annual art auctions to benefit the college. I think he was the first to organize such art events in Chicago, though the practice is common today.

The earliest of Harry's Columbia auctions was in the spring of 1964. Harry got 117 Chicago artists to contribute work. I believe we had nearly 150 pieces to auction that year. We netted about $6,000. In following years, Harry's auctions included not only the works of Chicago artists but also the art of celebrated national and international artists, which major galleries gave us on consignment to sell at set minimum prices that were outrageous bargains. One year we had a beautiful Franz Kline piece at a $7,000 minimum bid, as well as a Robert Motherwell, a magnificent Ashil Gorky, and four Giorgio Morandi drawings that could have been had for $3,000. If somebody had bought the best of our auction pieces and held them for twenty years, their profits would have been staggering. Unfortunately for us, the best stuff went for little more than the galleries' minimums and our events were costly to mount; but for five or six years, we had a dependable income of $5,000-10,000.

Also, Seymour Gale had discovered some brief vagary in the tax laws that allowed companies some tax benefit when they contributed their surplus products to a non-profit organization, who then in turn could sell the goods at bargain prices. As we didn't have enough of an apparatus to engage in a large-scale solicitation and sale of such manufacturers' gifts, our benefits were comparatively small; though in one instance, Sam Victor's company gave us a great quantity of metal fasteners, nuts, bolts, and screws, which we did profitably resell. We made seven thousand dollars on the deal. In another instance, however, we expected a profit of as much as $25,000 from a gift which Phil Lewis got of tens of thousands of maternity girdles and brassieres with the manufacturers' requirement that the goods be sold only in a foreign country. Phil got them sold in Cuba, but the Justice Department nullified the sale because the elastic in the products was considered to be war material. The only way that could have been true is if the Cubans extracted the elastic and used it to build a giant sling-shot to rain God knows what on south Florida. So go fight City Hall.

When I was elected president in 1960, there was a general expression of concern that knowledge of Columbia's unique quality and educational ideas was mainly limited to the college's immediate family. What was needed was a more articulate restatement of Columbia's mission and a development plan meant to persuade the support of influential and prosperous constituencies. It was hard to argue with this, but as I pondered it, I realized that even the most skillful public relations effort couldn't change our copper coins to gold. In truth, my prior descriptions of the college and the words of its ideas and expectation were only bits and pieces of an inchoate perception. I realized that I didn't really know what Columbia was or what I wanted it to be, except more successful. I did know that the college had to be convincingly distinctive and represent a legitimate alternative to mainstream institutions. At the moment, Columbia was only a faint dot on a distant horizon and too insubstantial to pretend we were significant. We simply had to be bigger and stronger and better defined before we could expect public notice and support. And I didn't know at the time how even to get to such a preliminary state.

I am quite certain that my father never stopped to draw up a specific plan of Columbia's purpose and what he meant the college to be. He had a self-satisfying mindset and assumed that what he did was good and appropriate, which it was, though he was at first so preoccupied with survival and later with developing Columbia College Los Angeles that he had no time or patience to articulate his philosophy. I was similarly concentrated on the exigencies of survival, which took me to a time when it was unmistakably clear that the college could not live much longer, from crisis to deeper crisis. It was time, as Kant says, "to reweigh the valuables." The best hope lay in largely reinventing Columbia. That would take time and serious inquiry. It was not until the spring of 1964 when we had moved to Lake Shore Drive that I summoned up enough optimism to make a serious effort to plan Columbia's renewal.

This project was not my sole doing as it closely involved a number of colleagues, prominently: Wolf Dochtermann, Gene DeKovic, Harry Bouras, Hans Adler, and board members Seymour Gale and Phil Lewis. Over a period of several months, we engaged in constant discussions and interviewed many independent educators, representatives of the professions of the college's interests, faculty, students, and alumni. For the first time, conclusions about the college's life and future could be drawn. In effect, this was the beginning of a more participatory Columbia where mutual respect, affection, and unity of purpose created a company of believers and a strong sense of family within the Columbia community. This was to be a principal strength of the college for many years ahead.

Our earliest work was to envision Columbia in relation to the American higher education community, particularly in greater Chicago and the Midwest. The elemental question was what distinctive purpose Columbia could articulate that would fill an empty niche left by conventional colleges. Obviously, it would have to be a purpose familiar to the college, which meant a continuing emphasis on education in the communication arts and related specialties. We searched the catalogs of all the local collegiate institutions and discovered that while all offered some communication arts subjects, and some even had departments or schools of study in arts disciplines, such subjects seldom were prominent interests of these institutions. Significantly, no local college offered practical study in television, radio, film, or photography. Virtually all institutions had small theater programs and some journalism subjects, with Northwestern University having major schools of theater and journalism. Most had programs in fine arts, but graphic arts and related specialties were usually left to professional schools. The School of the Art Institute had highly regarded concentrations in fine arts, as did the Goodman School in theater. Otherwise, Columbia's subjects were pretty well ignored by local higher education. There was a better niche for us out there than we had first discerned.

But to exploit these opportunities required a far greater assortment of linked media arts and arts concentrations than Columbia was offering at the time. Though we had minimal programs in film and journalism and to a lesser extent in advertising, our principal interests were television and radio broadcasting. Indeed, we were identified publicly as a television-radio school, and it was only in these subjects that we had sophisticated facilities. This restricted focus at best appealed only to a finite number of students as compared to the potential audience for an array of well-furnished media and arts specialties. In other words, we had to have much more to offer prospective students if we hoped to prosper. Even our virtual monopoly in Chicago television and radio instruction could not attract enough students. We also had to have a real diversity of subject concentrations to be able to sell ourselves as a distinctive college of related media arts and arts subjects. At that time, in 1964, we offered nothing in graphic arts, photography (though we had reserved a limited space for a dark room), or literary arts. Our exceptional theater program was badly handicapped. Despite its historical importance at Columbia, speech was a neglected, sparsely enrolled subject, as was teacher training.

The whole idea of creating a comprehensive college of media and fine arts depended on our being able to become a legitimate college consistent with the public's definition of a college and the expectations of the general collegiate community, the news media, and local secondary schools. Accreditation was again a serious issue. While we did have high quality instruction in liberal arts subjects, the program was very small owing in great part to the loss of numbers of liberal arts courses whose expenses and enrollment had been shared previously with PFTC. It was generally recognized that we had many other handicaps, not the least of which was our endemic financial distress. Also, the absence of full-time faculty, an inadequate administrative staff, and virtually no advertising or publicity severely limited any significant response to the opportunities that our inquiry had revealed. Nonetheless, we were determined to press ahead. Indeed we were infected with an unfamiliar enthusiasm about the college's prospects.

In addition to our agreement to continue the college's media arts concentrations and to strengthen our identity by adding new specialties, we agreed on the value of emphasizing certain traditional Columbia qualities which, while not new discoveries, could advertise our uniqueness. We also agreed that the language we used to describe ourselves should be as distinctive as possible. Our plan emphasized learning-by-doing in a professionally equipped, on-the-job learning environment; that a college education must have an occupational consequence; that Columbia's teachers had leading contemporary credentials in the professions of the subjects they taught and that they brought the real professional world to Columbia's classrooms; that we would sustain the lowest possible tuition costs among Illinois private colleges; that we would seize every opportunity to recruit outstanding new faculty, particularly in arts and liberal arts subjects; that we would continue to depend mostly on part-time faculty recruited from the city's professionals in the college's subjects and leading participants in the community's literary, artistic, cultural, and social life (while we all recognized the value of having full-time faculty whenever we could afford them); and that the central element of Columbia's educational project was the college's policy of open admissions.

Columbia's new design was not cut from whole cloth. I did have in mind some models of what I wanted Columbia to be. While I didn't regard the college as a personal, private possession, I was charged with the college's life for many years. Managing its destiny was my shot.

In charting Columbia's course, I did attempt some amalgam of my views of the colleges I had attended and other institutions I had observed. My first college experience had been at Wilson Junior College, a comparatively small public institution whose talented faculty served an openly admitted student population that had no elite credentials in terms of class, race, or prior educational achievement. Tuition costs were minimal. At the University of Chicago I had the opportunity to witness a most accomplished faculty, among the best minds of their generation. I was a close observer of the Institute of Design, which Moholy Nagy had modeled after Europe's famed Bauhaus School. The Chicago version had a bold idea, a wonderfully talented and dedicated faculty, and a vital and accomplished student body. I drew on my knowledge of the City University of New York, which had an extraordinary faculty and intensely able and eager students who were mainly the sons and daughters of often impoverished Eastern European immigrants; and on New York's New School for Social Research, which had many enlightened representatives of the twentieth century's intellectual ferment. I also studied the innovative ideas of Antioch College, Berea College's unique work-study community-related plan, the experiments of Black Mountain College, and other bold educational alternatives. Such, in part, was the stuff of my educational plan, then still an unformed collection of ideas.

Roughly, what I had in mind was a low-cost specialized college that practiced open admissions, and assembled an accomplished faculty of sharing professionals and socially engaged thinkers and doers who could inspire students to liberate the best of themselves. My primary concern was for educating students to live more occupationally rewarding, socially useful, and humanely sensitive lives than if they had not gone to college or, indeed, if they had not gone to Columbia. This view does not ignore alumni, who won unusual success. Undoubtedly, some of these are superior people who may have made better-than-ordinary use of their education. But I emphasize that the far greater number of alumni who have been helped to live rewarding and productive lives is more satisfying than a list of prominent people who were once Columbia's students. While this narrative is obviously not the place for a directory of thousands of alumni in arts and media professions, a selected list of successful alumni is included in the appendix.

I neither wanted nor expected Columbia to become a highly selective institution like Northwestern University, nor did I think it could afford a full-time faculty of the quality of the University of Chicago—I had no illusion about being able to persuade such accomplished individuals to devote themselves to inspiring and educating students of unproven academic talent. I did hope to enlist outstanding individuals who worked outside customary academic settings.

I envisioned a college with no strictly fixed prerequisites to the subjects that may represent a student's main incentive for being in college in the first place. I do advocate prerequisites in reading and writing skills; speech, where performance is contemplated; and, today, computer literacy. In my scheme, a full complement of liberal arts studies required for graduation would be elective, to be taken when such studies have relevance to the student's life and career. (My experience is that students will, by themselves, create a sensible balance of liberal arts and professional subjects over time.) My curricular plan sequenced courses according to levels of difficulty and prerequisite knowledge.

This plan describes in general terms Columbia's ideas in the summer of 1964. We needed to describe what Columbia was about, to give it an identity recognizable in publications and publicity. We needed a consistent image and the vocabulary to communicate our unique qualities to others and to define the institution for ourselves. Imagine how terribly difficult it was to promote and sell an unsung, disrespected, unaccredited speck of a place without any credentials, collegiate appearance, or resources, to confront a nearly universal resistance to our contention that we were a serious, legitimate college.

What we needed quickly was a public image that set Columbia apart, but at the same time preserved a familiar collegiate identity. Our paramount identity and elemental appeal had to emphasize that Columbia is a specialized college focused on the communication and entertainment arts, within a strong context of liberal education. While I believed then that ultimately Columbia's purview should be enlarged to include the principal arts disciplines, I viewed such prospect as evolutionary and dependent on improved institutional resources. This would happen more quickly than I imagined.

Columbia was among the earliest institutions to assemble education in the major fields of communication under the common rubric "communication arts" and to give students the opportunity of interdisciplinary study in diverse but related disciplines. Despite the omnipresence of the entertainment and communication industries in American life, few colleges offered specific study in television, radio, photography, or film. Peculiarly, education in these profoundly influential professions was regarded indifferently by most of the collegiate community. We needed to elevate the prestige of communication arts occupations (and later, the arts) in relation to students' choices of college concentrations.

Our challenge was to present our subjects as having the intellectual and cultural value of traditional college courses and that the distinctive quality of Columbia's liberal arts subjects was relevant to careers and to intelligent, participatory citizenship. My words and themes reflected my anticipation of a developing ferment in American society, particularly among young people, who several years later would literally be in the streets. Great cultural and social change was a visible prospect. The civil rights movement had unprecedented vitality. Developing antiwar sentiment and draft resistance were about to burst on the American scene. Young people from all walks of life were beginning to embrace popular culture and lifestyles alien to older Americans. Strident

folk-rock was a common expression of young peoples' discontent. Radical advocacies were shouted everywhere. Students on America's largest campuses were mounting a sharp critique of established institutions, particularly their own universities.

The year 1964 was the beginning of a time of great dissonance and disorder in the national life. In the next years, its clamor would grow more intense. It was an appropriate time, perhaps uniquely so, for Columbia to deliver its message of being a different college institution. I tried to invest the college's publicity with themes that anticipated the contagious effect of the vague idealism, permissive lifestyles, cultural expressions, and humane commitment advocated by a small but influential minority of American young people. For the briefest moment in American history, the confluence of the spirit of the civil rights movement, antiwar sentiment, and an awakening of the American campus may have revealed a more just and peaceful nation. I continued to believe that however unrealistic and distorted the elemental idealism of that moment was, its messages were, in some part, adaptable to Columbia. But never did I think to commit Columbia to any course of advocacy or indoctrination that would violate or compromise the institution's political neutrality or impair its freedom of inquiry and expression. Undeniably, Columbia first came of age during the late 1960s and early 1970s. However interpreted, our words and deeds worked impressively well, and certainly created a strong sense among students and faculty of being in a distinctive contemporary college, though the themes we expressed then became in time less noticed and less influential.

Certainly Columbia's purpose helped to shape the faculty and staff's view of the college and to create the intense sense of family loyalty and common purpose which prevailed among them and among board members for many years. I often heard my own words returned in complimentary descriptions of Columbia by parents and others. Ultimately we earned good support by foundations and government funding agencies, which usually closely scrutinized institutional statements. While I was often viewed suspiciously by college and university officials, this may have been directed more at me than the college.

In recent years, almost nothing is regarded as original or daring, and the things most distinctive about Columbia have become its size, security, the continued success of its specialization, its diversity of activities, its publicity, and how quickly it got to such a happy state. The college's reputation as a successful experiment and place of innovative education is largely forgotten, though it may be that in maturity Columbia has become less experimental and more ready to dismiss earlier distinctions and the words and deeds of its bearded notions.

I am certain that Columbia would never have succeeded on a significant scale had we continued to depend solely on publicity that claimed only communication arts specialization, expert professional faculty, learning-by-doing methods, and engaging liberal arts studies. After all, the college had exercised these identities with questionable effect for many years. What was different about the new Columbia was a distinctive mystique, made of old themes recast in contemporary terms—stuff that was "blowin' in the wind."

While such expressions may have given Columbia some sense of coherence and public identity, the college's distinction was not rhetorical, however heady my phrase-making penchants. Despite prior public perceptions, the college's transcendent distinctiveness was based on its practices and environment. The ideas that gave form and substance to Columbia's renewal were not static assumptions. Many initial perceptions and expectations were altered, adapted, and discarded in response to immediate experiences and continuing assessment. While I believed, accurately I think, that higher education did not work successfully, either in accessibility or educational process, for great numbers of young Americans, I had no panaceas to propose, only informed speculations which might successfully guide Columbia's course.

It was clear that Columbia could not prosper as a mild alternative to customary institutions. What was necessary instead was that Columbia become genuinely experimental and innovative in all respects. Educational focus, curricular forms, subject content, methods of instruction, and emphasis on part-time faculty were closely linked elements of an experiment meant to serve an unfamiliarly diverse student body. Columbia was not engaged in some mindless, manipulative exercise in the delights of being unconventional. What we attempted was an earnest, disciplined search for better and more inclusive ways to educate and unusual ways to finance our project. In this sense, Columbia was sensibly and, I submit, successfully experimental.

For many years, I was almost exclusively responsible for the recruitment and retention of new faculty, except some of those whose specialties were beyond me. These individuals were ordinarily chosen by Wolf Dochtermann during his tenure as dean, or at the suggestion of other faculty or a department's senior members. We had

COLUMBIA COLLEGE

54 YEARS NATIONAL RECOGNITION

GENERAL BULLETIN
1944-1945

★

RADIO — DRAMA — SPEECH
AND ACADEMIC COURSES

★

DAY AND EVENING CLASSES

★

THIS BULLETIN INCLUDES
special professional speed-up courses in

RADIO BROADCASTING

for those who are planning to enter the radio profession in
the shortest possible time without the necessity of enrolling in
academic departments. Such students may enter at any time.

See pages 3, 4 and 5.

FINE ARTS BUILDING
MICHIGAN BOULEVARD NEAR CONGRESS STREET
CHICAGO 5, ILLINOIS
PHONE WABASH 6762

LIBRARY
OF
COLUMBIA COLLEGE
CHICAGO, ILLINOIS

LEFT: MARY A. BLOOD; TOP MIDDLE: COLUMBIA COLLEGE OF EXPRESSION/COLUMBIA NORMAL
SCHOOL OF PHYSICAL EDUCATION; MIDDLE: THE 1920s MIKE ALEXANDROFF (MA) AGE 7; BOTTOM
MIDDLE: THE DORMITORY, IDA MOREY-RILEY HALL (3358 SOUTH MICHIGAN); RIGHT: 1944-1945
COLUMBIA COLLEGE GENERAL BULLETIN.

LEFT: THE 1940s MA; RIGHT: COLUMBIA COLLEGE OF EXPRESSION 1927. FACING PAGE: LEFT: COLUMBIA COLLEGE OF EXPRESSION BULLETIN 1910. RIGHT: BULLETIN, COLUMBIA SCHOOL OF SPEECH AND DRAMA (1936-1937).

THE HOME OF
THE COLLEGE
IN CENTRAL
CHICAGO

On Michigan Boulevard, the World's Most Beautiful Thoroughfare

COLUMBIA
COLLEGE
OF
EXPRESSION
BULLETIN

ALUMNI NUMBER

VOL. III   JUNE 1910   NO. 1

Issued quarterly by the Columbia College of Expression,

Steinway Building, Chicago.

Entered as Second Class Matter August 26, '08 at Chicago.

under Act of July 16, 1894

1936-37

RADIO INSTITUTE

of

COLUMBIA SCHOOL of SPEECH

and

DRAMA

Complete training in RADIO
BROADCASTING, including Act-
ing, Announcing, Writing, Directing,
Producing and Station Managing.

410 South Michigan Blvd., Chicago, Ill.

A   M O D E R N   P R O F E S S I O N

building
effective
speech

for a better tomorrow

...for a brighter

business and social future

EFFECTIVE SPEECH COURSES FOR MEN AND WOMEN IN THE
EXECUTIVE, PROFESSIONAL, BUSINESS AND SOCIAL WORLDS

Day and Evening Classes

COLUMBIA COLLEGE

410 S. MICHIGAN BLVD. • CHICAGO 5, ILL. • PHONE WAbash 2-6761

A LEADER IN PROFESSIONAL EDUCATION SINCE 1890

TOP LEFT: BILL RUSSO. BOTTOM LEFT: THE 1930s MA; MIDDLE LEFT (TOP AND BOTTOM): 1?
PROMOTIONAL BROCHURES. RIGHT: MA AT 1960s GRADUATION CEREMONY. FACING PAGE: LEFT ?
COLUMBIA CATALOG. TOP RIGHT: MA AND JANE ALEXANDROFF (1950s). BOTTOM RIGHT: AL AND JE?
PARKER.

COLUMBIA COLLEGE

CATALOG ISSUE   1952 · 1953

FOUNDED 1890

G PAGE: TOP LEFT: MA AND JANE CELEBRATING THEIR MARRIAGE WITH DAUGHTERS PAM (LEFT) AND
BOTTOM LEFT: MA'S FATHER NORMAN ALEXANDROFF. RIGHT: COLUMBIA'S MAIN CAMPUS BUILDING,
OUTH MICHIGAN, RENAMED THE ALEXANDROFF CAMPUS CENTER. LEFT: POET GWENDOLYN BROOKS.
MIDDLE: THE 1950s MA; TOP RIGHT: NAT LERMAN. BOTTOM MIDDLE: ED MORRIS. BOTTOM RIGHT:
RT (BOB) EDMONDS.

LEFT TO RIGHT: JOHN FISCHETTI CARTOON OF MIKE ALEXANDROFF (MA); MA WITH FIRST WIFE, ABJURAN ALEXANDROFF.

no full-time department chairs until 1966 and few until 1970, though some part-time faculty functioned as chairs. In all instances, however, I closely interviewed all prospective teachers, introduced them to Columbia's purposes, and instructed them in what we expected of them as teachers. My orientation sessions stressed, "You are here exclusively to serve students and to contribute valuably to their lives. Teaching is a serious calling. Be the best person you are in the classroom and in your relationships with students. Identify what you hold as truths and honor the expression of other views. Be generous with your knowledge and always be carefully prepared."

Obviously, apart from the pleasure of teaching, Columbia had little to attract prospective teachers. The salaries were meager and benefits entirely absent. Moreover, we had no library, nor much in the way of support facilities except old spirit duplicators and a few movie and slide projectors. My ordinary recruitment message described Columbia in the most idealistic terms and followed with an invitation to join us in our crusade. My mention of pay was delivered *sotto voce*. I did, nonetheless, set out to recruit the most accomplished and notable intellectuals, individuals who were prominently engaged in social purpose, and those who had leading roles in the professions of Columbia's educational interests.

The usual setting for my recruitment effort was a good restaurant. In the early 1960s, I often had to tell my targets that they'd have to pay for their own meals and drinks. It was several years before I could consistently perform as a bountiful host. I had learned from my father that serious business was best conducted in a relaxed and disarming setting. It is only then that individuals have the opportunity to get to know one another as humans and to find mutual causes. I found the counsel eminently valuable. Food and drink gives comfortable amiability to persuasive intents. It was a bit unorthodox, I suppose, but I did lots of the college's important business in saloons and restaurants, including recruiting faculty, fund-raising, developing media relations, and generally promoting Columbia and making friends. Many college successes began at such unconventional sites.

As these were key places in Columbia's development, they deserve more than casual mention. I remember going to Riccardo's before I went to the army. An eclectic Italian restaurant (at Rush and Hubbard Streets), it was popular among theater and literary folk. Riccardo's had two distinctions: it was the only downtown restaurant that served African Americans, and its proprietor Ric was a piece of theater. Of indeterminate age, he was an immensely charming and expressive man, tall with saturnine features and a royal demeanor. He was at once actor, singer, and talented artist. Remarkably literate, he spoke a number of languages, was a liberal man, and was reputed to be a legendary lover. I became a regular patron of Riccardo's after the war and remained so for more than forty years, spanning the ownership of young Ric, who inherited the restaurant when his father died, and later Nick Angelos. For nearly all of those years my waiter was Bobby Estrada, a Mexican-American who fluently spoke at least twelve languages. For more than forty years he had worked both lunches and dinners and spent the hours in-between studying at the Chicago Public library.

Riccardo's was Chicago's most lively, stimulating, and democratic place, gathering people from the arts, the news media, broadcasting, and the liberal community. There was always music in the evening from several excellent Italian tenors who doubled as waiters, including Ric himself, his son, who was an excellent singer too, and a number of prominent performers who happened to be in the house. In the spring of 1946, I spent many memorable nights at Riccardo's with the cast of *Anna Lucasta* and with Jimmy Edwards, a splendid young African-American actor whose starring role in *Deep Are the Roots* was unprecedented, except for Paul Robeson's *Othello*. *Anna Lucasta* was the only time that a play featuring an African-American cast had ever played in a downtown theater, again except for *Stevedore* briefly in 1938. In the 1970s a tradition of Friday luncheons, begun by John Fischetti and me (though Fischetti was the big attraction), had a loyal following that included Lee Freeman, Nick Shuman, Lowell Sacknoff, Dominic DiFrisco, and often Mike Royko, Studs Terkel, Jim Hoge, and an assortment of media celebrities like Walter Cronkite, when he happened to be in the city. Riccardo's had a brilliant mix of people. Indeed, I could have skipped inviting anybody and just table-hopped for faculty prospects. It was also an ideal place to drum up media support for Columbia.

In the late 1950s, I also did Columbia's business at Angelo's, owned then by Alan Peters, the cochair of the college's Theater Department. It was at the site of the old Black Orchid nightclub at Ontario and Rush. There I first met the withering political satirist Mort Sahl when he was the opening act for the very popular singer, Felicia Sanders, who was the daughter of my father's great friend, the actor Ludwig Donath. When Angelo's failed (Chicago wasn't ready for sophisticated Italian fare),

the restaurant became Mike Fish's, and Al Peters continued to own it until Mike joined his brother at a new Mike Fish's on Ontario just east of Michigan Avenue. Mike's restaurant was a bit like Toots Shore's in New York, with a similar clientele of big media and entertainment names, sports figures, lawyers and judges, local businessmen, assorted hangers-on, and reputed Mafiosi, some of whom grew up with Mike Fish in the old, near-West Side Italian neighborhood. That many of Mike's customers shared an easy familiarity might suggest that Chicago (still) wasn't ready for reform. Fish's didn't need the mob dons to give the place a racy reputation. If anything, they were very private and their conversations soft, only slightly animated when they talked reverentially about their mothers and families. And they were perfectly courteous. I remember that Murray Humphrey (sobriquet, "the Camel") always said, "Good evening, little lady" to Jane. Whatever his old neighborhood friends might have become, Mike Fish was unsullied and a most honorable man. He was a great cook and host who had been a notable newspaper photographer in New York and Los Angeles and later the principal still-photographer for MGM Pictures. Most people thought being taken to Mike Fish's was a big treat, and it was a good place to go when I could afford to impress someone.

I know that my unbridled enthusiasm might be viewed with a bit of suspicion. Even so, my unqualified affection for Deni's Den deserves exception. Deni's had an incomparable excitement that went far beyond the reaches of entertainment. The only thing close was an evening I spent with Jack Wolfsohn nearly sixty years ago at the Rumboogie on Chicago's South Side, when the old blues singer Teabone Walker sang "Jelly Jelly."

Beginning in the early 1970s, and for fifteen years Deni's was Jane's and my place. For me, it was a return to the Greek culture I lost when Anna died. Studs Terkel took us to Deni's when it was a cramped little "caffenia" at Lawrence and Western. Later, at Clark and Wellington, it became a big beautiful place tiered like a classical Greek garden. Deni's had music of extraordinary quality. It was identified with Denis Dimitreas, an unusually attractive, magnetic man, who was a singer and musician of startling talent. Vassily Gaetano, a dramatic tenor and consummate entertainer, sang in a number of languages, and Penny, a fabulous woman singer, seconded him. They were backed by an exceptional band of Greek musicians, which included two bouzouki players who could make their instruments sound like a full orchestra. The food was good and the wine plentiful.

Jane and I took scores of people to Deni's, and all were as enchanted as us. Even when we entertained at our home, the evenings often ended at Deni's. For years, all of Columbia's after-graduation parties were at Deni's, which on those occasions seemed a part of the college, particularly so to our honored guests. Many of them stayed till dawn. Among them was Maya Angelou, who danced and sang Greek songs. When I asked her how she knew the words, she said, "What kind of name do you think 'Angelou' is? Greek, of course." George McGovern stayed the course happily, and even Pamela Harriman joined the fun.

The 1977 commencement party at Deni's was indelibly dramatic. That year, we had honored the international journalist and novelist Oriana Fallaci. She had also been the lover of Alexander Panagoulis, who was the symbol of popular resistance to the dictator George Papadopoulos and the military clique that ruled Greece in the 1960s and early 1970s. Panagoulis was a poet and the solitary revolutionary who was sentenced to death for attempting the assassination of Papadopoulos. Saved from execution, he suffered years of imprisonment and terrible torture until his release under a general amnesty. Tragically, in 1973, just after Greek democracy was restored, the agents of the deposed fascist regime assassinated Panagoulis. In 1979, when Jane and I were in Greece, we went to the place where Panagoulis was killed. It was next to a gas station in a suburb of Athens. There, a low wall carried the spray-painted words "HE LIVES." Only briefly celebrated in life, his death seemed shadowed in Greece. But he was still a hero to Chicago's progressive Greek community, and Oriana was his heir. Hundreds of people came to Deni's that evening to pay her homage. For nearly an hour they filed past her table, making the sign of the cross and murmuring their respects. Many women kneeled to kiss the hem of her skirt. The orchestra, singers, and waiters saluted her. Otherwise, Deni's had the hush of a cathedral. Once the solemn line had passed, the place burst in applause. It was an exalted evening, deeply spiritual and at the same time grandly operatic.

Oriana had been reluctant to come to a Greek place, but Jane prevailed. Oriana is a maturely beautiful woman, small and slender with jet black hair and penetrating eyes. That evening she wore a stunning white gown. Though she couldn't have anticipated her reception, she was ready for the role. When the big drama was done, Oriana danced for more than an hour with Gordon Parks, whom we had also honored at the commencement. I don't know if Parks knew beans about Greek dancing, but he sure learned quickly. To end the story of Deni's Den brightly, Deni later graduated from Columbia, and many years later his son Kostaki did, too.

While the 1963–64 college year signaled Columbia's renewal, it was a memorable time also because Gwendolyn Brooks joined the College's faculty. The beginning of her Columbia teaching experience is recalled in her autobiography, *Report From Part One:*

"Teaching."

In 1963 Mirron Alexandroff, president of Chicago's Columbia College, which features the comunication [sic] arts, asked me to start a poetry workshop there. "Do anything you want with it," he said bravely. "Take it outdoors. Take it to a restaurant—run it in a restaurant, a coffee shop. Do absolutely anything you want with it. Anything!"

In my new little professor's blue suit, I entered my first classroom. Twenty-one young souls were sitting there, awaiting the knowledge, the magic, the definitions that I was bringing them surely. I felt the need to spin automatically around and leave within the minute of my arrival. But I stayed, and discovered that it was possible to enjoy this thing that I had never done before. There had been a tiny teaching attempt in 1962 at the University of Chicago. Frank London Brown, author of Trumbull Park, *who had tried hard to get me into Roosevelt University as a teacher of English (Roosevelt thought about it, and thought about it, and allowed me to fill out forms, but finally told me that my lack of a degree stood in my way), employed me as a teacher of American Literature when he became director of the University of Chicago's Union Leadership program. My little course was a three and a half week thing. Several of my students had read more American Literature than had their teacher.*

But Columbia was exciting, because there I was free to experiment—insanely, if I chose. Later, I "taught" at Elmhurst College in Elmhurst, Illinois, and at Northeastern Illinois State College, and at the University of Wisconsin in Madison, as Rennebohm Professor of English. In these places, my subjects were Freshman English, Twentieth Century Poetry and Short Story, as well as poetry workshops, fiction workshops, creative writing workshops. But I went, fall and spring and sometimes in summer, once a week to Columbia until the winter of 1969, in June of which year I gave up teaching. I was cajoled back, briefly, by the City College of New York for a proposed year as Distinguished Professor of the Arts (!) in a special program with Joseph Heller and John Hawkes, novelists. I met fine people there, students, faculty, office staff, and LORA, and my work as a poetry workshop leader was challenging and stimulating, but a small heart attack on Christmas Day of 1971 forced me to give up the Monday–Tuesday commuting (for of course I had no intention of leaving Chicago to live in New York for the year) after the end of my first term. And, now, "teaching" and I have said a final Goodbye.

They called me—mirabile dictu—"a good teacher." Will any of my students write great books? I remember my first class. Leonard Bishop, Cary Brown, Jane Brust, Lynell Cain, Bernard Caputo, Marlene Dixon, Roselyn Fields, Peter Gregory, Richard Lubbers, John Pritzen, Richard Raffals, Janice Pajak, Douglas Stoker, Sally Ventresca, Gary Schubert, Rob Ferrero, ladylike Carol Zientek, fiercely serious Thomas Staker. Are stars here? Any "teacher" of creative writing is asked "Can you teach people to write? How can you teach people to write poems?"—A teacher cannot create a poet. But a teacher can explain the "wonders" of iambic pentameter, can explain how the Shakespearian sonnet differs from the Petrarchan. More important; a teacher can oblige the writing student to write. In all poetry workshops of mine, the principal requirement has been the writing of a book of twenty poems, ten of them in pre-scribed forms, the rest in any. In "creative writing workshops," there was a fiction requirement also: it consisted variously of a number of short stories, or a novella, or the beginning of a novel.

1964–1965

When the 1963–64 year ended, our revenues increased by 39 percent over the year preceding, a result that reflected a large jump in spring semester enrollment and an increase in contributions. Expenses had increased by 16 percent too. While we'd lost $22,000 on the year, this deficit included nearly $40,000 in moving and remodeling expenses. In the past, we'd managed our customary summer cash shortage by turning a deaf ear to the howls of creditors who would be paid ultimately with first fall tuition receipts. This year, however, and for a number of years afterwards, we borrowed our cash deficit from the Continental Illinois Bank by having individual board members personally guarantee the loans, which, of course, still had to be repaid from fall revenues. Such board confidence relieved us at least of the awful financial juggling act we had had to perform annually.

In the weeks that followed our plan's construction, I worked to get as much of it as I could into the college's 1964–65 catalog and other timely bulletins and publications which might influence enrollment in the fall 1964 term. And I vigorously pursued the plan's mandate to recruit new faculty.

The great effort paid off. For the first time, to my memory, we began a college year on a genuine high note. Though the proverbial wolf still hung about, we'd at least distracted him. We had a splendid complement of new faculty. Among many were Jack Behrend, film technology specialist; William Braden, featured *Chicago Sun-Times* writer and authority on contemporary religion; Rev. James Jones, dubbed by the media "The Prison Pastor" and director of St. Leonard's House, a halfway house for released prisoners; notable American historian, Ira Kipnis; Jay Levinson, chief copywriter, BBDO; sports writer, Robert Markus; speech specialist, Sue Ann Park; film director, Gordon Weisenborn; and Eugene Zeemans, executive director of the John Howard Association.

Dr. Abbas Kessel came to the faculty that year, too, and he stayed for more than ten years. I believe that Hans Adler recruited him. A slight man, lightly bronzed, distantly Iranian, with unusual grace, he was the most gentle and humane man I've ever known. He was quiet but remarkably articulate. Genuinely brilliant, learned in the social sciences, literature, and philosophy, a talented musician, artist, and calligrapher, Kessel, like Adler and Bouras, was an animated lecturer and teacher of rarest quality. Despite near penury, his little apartment was imaginatively furnished, and he was a legendary host and fabulous cook. He usually taught five classes a week for the meager amounts we paid, and finally, "just to earn a living," he left reluctantly for a faculty appointment at a Minnesota teachers college. Columbia just wasn't prosperous enough to keep him. Luckily, he married a lovely woman and had a job and a pension. He died in 1988.

Significantly, Columbia's fall 1964 enrollment was up more than 35 percent. We had 303 students and a much better full-time to part-time ratio. Tuition revenues were also improved by an increased tuition rate. Tuition for a full-time student was now $448 per semester ($896 per year) and for part-time students $30 per credit hour. One hundred twenty eight hours of study were now required for the bachelor's degree. Enrollment gains were beginning to reflect numbers of students seeking draft deferment, a straggle of Vietnam veterans and early beneficiaries of the Illinois state scholarship program. We would enroll greater numbers of such students in subsequent terms. In fact, in time, they would constitute the greatest part of the college's full-time enrollment. Later, with the government's introduction of Pell grants, a large percentage of college students everywhere would be aided by state and/or U.S. government programs.

In the spring of 1964, Wolf hired Hubert Davis, then a city junior college librarian, to begin the development of a Columbia College library. Hubert Davis would play an important role in Columbia's life for many years.

At the November 1964 board meeting, I reported that we could reasonably expect a full-time-equivalent enrollment of 280 or more students in fall 1965, with 400 total students. Such figures closely approximated my 1960 projection of 1965's enrollment, though I suspect my original projections were little more than unfounded hopes.

The board carefully considered the plan of the college's course which had been prepared during the spring and summer of 1964. There had been continuous informal discussion between committee and board members during the months of the plan's development. It was understood that the plan was meant as a flexible guide which would be responsive to actual experience and evolving ideas. The board approved the plan and my intention to recast the college's course and identity in contemporary terms, which fastened on the evident vitality of a large number of young Americans.

A noteworthy feature of the fall term was the introduction of a new emphasis in graphic design. The project had some history. During the mid-1950s, a plan was afoot to merge the Institute of Design (I.D.) with the vastly larger Illinois Institute of Technology. A number of I.D.'s faculty resisted the merger and sent a delegation to meet with me, in the hope that Columbia College would embrace the Institute of Design. I fervently wished it could happen, but given Columbia's precarious state, it was an utterly impossible venture. At any rate, years later, some members of that original I.D. delegation joined a number of prominent Chicago graphic artists and designers and came again to solicit Columbia's interest in starting a graphic arts, design and photography program. Coincidentally at the time Dochtermann, DeKovic, and I had had some discussion of beginning pilot programs in graphic arts and photography. These were certainly communication arts subjects which fit closely with our plan of an enlarged program of communication arts specialties. The result of all this was that we launched a new graphic arts program and a separate photography emphasis in the fall of 1964.

Ideally, both programs had the benefit of outstanding, experienced faculty who understood our limited resources and were entirely willing to begin their concentrations at the most elementary levels. This was part of a general sequence of mass communication studies and surveys of communication arts specialties, which we contemplated establishing as a foundation program for all Columbia students. So in one swoop, we got Irving Titel, William Rose, Herbert Pinzki, and Leo Tannenbaum in Graphic Design, and Joseph Sterling and Lyle Mayer in Photography. All had great

recognition and teaching experience in their fields. Gene DeKovic was eminently qualified to head the new programs, and Dochtermann, as always, would be a close counsel. A past president of the American Society of Typographical Arts, DeKovic was a broadly talented man, who in less than a year's time had become critically important to a number of college projects, despite being only a part-time faculty member. (I trust we paid him some premium for the great time he spent on a variety of our assignments.)

I reported also to the board that Columbia had been granted the highest rating possible for a nonaccredited institution by the National Association of Collegiate Registrars, and that I would make a new appeal to the North Central Association to get on a track toward eventual accreditation.

In 1965, we had been accepted as a member of the Council for the Advancement of Small Colleges (CASC), a national organization of fifty-eight mainly church-related colleges that had joined together to assist one another in achieving regional accreditation and to foster improved educational quality and greater institutional security among its members. CASC brought together a great diversity of small, mostly struggling colleges giving college opportunity to unserved rural communities and denominational divisions. The CASC colleges were headed by a remarkable group of men and women presidents. Uniformly serious, competent, and devoted educators, they welcomed a diversity of views and institutional characteristics, and exemplified the best ideals of educational service. Their generosity and sense of fraternity was striking. If any member was having difficulties, a phone call would bring an immediate visit by one or several CASC presidents to give experienced counsel. It was like Alcoholics Anonymous—just call your sponsor for help. In a personal sense, Columbia's CASC membership was a rare opportunity for me. To be among a group of institutions and presidents who represented such a diversity of institutional and individual commitments was entirely alien to my experience. Members included Duane Hurley of Salem College in rural Appalachia; Roger Voskul of Westmont College in southern California; the president of Eastern Mennonite College in Virginia; President Woodward of a denominational college in upstate New York; and others. I had never before so appreciated the great diversity of the private college and university sector of American higher education. Christian fundamentalists, a host of Protestant denominations, small Catholic orders, and a distinctly urban place like Columbia all worked together. What a rich coat of many colors CASC wore. Ultimately, virtually all CASC colleges got accreditation. Many CASC institutions and a number of new ones later reformed as the Council of Small Colleges. Columbia remained a member for many years until we simply got too big for the appellation "small."

At a board meeting in January 1965, I announced that I had persuaded Bill Russo to return to Columbia in the fall of that year. He would be the college's first full-time faculty member. It was my expectation, too, that every effort would be made to have five or six more full-time faculty in 1966 and 1967, who would teach classes and supervise departments of study. Hiring Russo was a bit of a gamble, and hiring others was wildly speculative, as was a plan to rent more space in the build-ing and hire more administrative staff. Chairman Gale offered the sobering observa-tion, "Any significantly greater expense would create a serious deficit which would be difficult to subscribe even with greater tuition revenues. In fact," he said, "we have yet to secure donations of at least $30,000 to support the current year's operations." He reminded everyone, "Columbia remains cash-poor and the college's momentary state of shaky prosperity gave no promise of a remedy for the college's endemic cash shortages, though undoubtedly, the present year's results are encouraging." The results were encouraging to the extent necessary to gain the board's agreement to subscribe the year's anticipated deficit. At the same meeting, A. C. Weiss, who had served the college for twenty years as a board member and as secretary-treasurer, resigned all his offices. Weiss had been critically valuable to Columbia, and all members of the board expressed sincerest gratitude for his years of devoted service and great regret at his resignation. He was my father's oldest friend, and he had given me and the college most resolute loyalty. The ubiquitous Mr. DeKovic was elected to the board.

While Columbia had depended exclusively on part-time faculty since the 1930s, both as a matter of economy and to fulfill the college's intent to bring the most experienced professionals to its classrooms, the total absence of full-time facul-ty supervision of departmental concentrations gave the college's whole educational project a hit-or-miss character and an unsatisfactory dependence on my initiatives and limited experience in many subjects. Moreover, it was impossible to expand the college's educational purview to include various arts disciplines without having knowledgeable leaders. The familiar practice of giving part-time teachers some small salary premiums to manage departments of study was simply unworkable if we expected competent educational service, continued enrollment growth, and a greater variety of educational concentrations. At the same time, continuing financial handicaps prevented any large-scale engagement of full-time faculty apart from hiring chairs of selected departments, and even this seemed cost-prohibitive. I worked to create job descriptions for the departmental chairpersons we would seek and the terms and expectations of their engagement.

We sought unusual persons with principal interests in Columbia's communication arts specialties, in other arts disciplines, in fundamental college subjects such as English and speech, and in subjects of liberal education. Applicants had to have established professional reputations or show a potential for quickly achieving significant reputation for their artistry, scholarly competence, inventive educational method, or record of social service; a capacity for inspiring teaching and managerial aptitude prominently evident and similarly displayed; a quality of personality that would lead students to commit the best of themselves; a willingness to articulate their association with the college in all their representations to professional and civic communities, and an expectation of fraternal participation with colleagues in the discussions and tasks of Columbia's undertaking. While no oaths of fealty were prescribed, the individual would need to agree with the college's educational and social missions and accept the guideposts of the institution's course and its financial limitations.

Individuals chosen as departmental chairs would enjoy independence in departmental decisions and initiatives, choice of faculty, and allocation of department budgets while observing only financial limitations and a need for consistency with the college's stated mission and customary process and practice. In short, the department would be theirs to run. None of these expressions contained unusual expectations or grants of authority, though in aggregate, they described superior persons responsive to Columbia's special needs.

Obviously, a college by its nature is a collective enterprise that requires numbers of competent individuals to perform its instruction. In Columbia's instance, its persons would have the added and indispensable expectation of being public exemplars of the college's excellence, distinctive mission, and innovative spirit. I knew clearly that the college could not continue successfully without a greater diversity of educational focus and leadership than if I were to remain its sole public representative. Thus, it followed that the few individuals I chose would constitute the critical cadre of Columbia's future. Individuals chosen would have to possess unusual abilities, energy, originality, loyalty, public presence, and entrepreneurial spirit, and be willing to fully exercise such qualities in an environment of severely limited resources and relative absence of public identity.

Given Columbia's traditional concentration on education for communication arts occupations and that music had been only a peripheral subject, hiring Bill Russo as the first of the college's full-time faculty might seem incongruous. Recruiting supervisory faculty in departments which represented the college's central interests and largest enrollment would seem to deserve highest priority. But in my view, the choice of a small number of new faculty was based on a complex set of priorities, not a single need. As professional sports teams often draft the best athlete without regard for the position he plays, Bill Russo was simply the most valuable person I could draft for Columbia. I had known him well during his more than ten-year association as a member of the faculty and the college's board and knew his lively intellect, artistic energy, and philosophical commitment to Columbia's ideals and intents. Moreover, he had great public reputation as a musician. His celebrity would confirm Columbia's collegiate stature and give legitimacy to an expansion of the college's educational and public interests to include conventional arts disciplines. In short, Russo would be Columbia's public ambassador, albeit without departmental portfolio.

It would take pages to record Russo's musical biography. Briefly, he was principal composer and arranger for the Stan Kenton Orchestra (1950–54); *Downbeat* magazine's best trombonist (1953); director and composer for the Russo Orchestra, New York (1958–60); director of the London Jazz Orchestra (1962–65); composer of three widely performed operas, *John Hooten*, *The Island*, and *Land of Milk and Honey*; composer of "The English Concerto for Violin and Orchestra," commissioned and performed by Yehudi Menuhin; composer of the "Second Symphony," performed by Leonard Bernstein and the New York Philharmonic Orchestra. He recorded six solo albums among many other recordings and held university degrees in philosophy and political science. The eminent composer and critic Gunther Shuller identified Russo as America's most versatile composer. This was all before 1965 when he became Columbia's premier faculty member. An array of musical accomplishments and recognitions were yet to come during his now more than

thirty-five and continuing years of distinguished Columbia service. In addition to being a composer, Russo is a respected lecturer, critic, and conductor, and a prolific writer who has published many important articles on a wide range of music topics. His seminal volume *Composing For the Jazz Orchestra* is recognized as the most authoritative instruction on the subject. Unquestionably, Russo has had a profoundly valuable influence on Columbia's life and on the course of contemporary American music.

1965–1966

We ended the 1964–65 year with a surplus of $1,403 and paid off nearly $25,000 in old debts. (More remained, of course.) But all in all, it represented a remarkable turnaround in the college's fortune, though the surplus was an accountant's figure that didn't relieve the yearly cash shortage. At least we weren't quite as poor as we'd been the year before.

Impressive progress continued in 1965–66. In September, we registered nearly 350 students (a full-time equivalent of 260). The year's budget projected a 100 percent revenue gain over the dismal realities of two years earlier.

We again had a sterling complement of new faculty, which included: Harry Barnard, the distinguished *Daily News* columnist and writer whose biography of John Peter Altgeld, *The Eagle Forgotten*, is a major literary achievement; Hoyt Fuller, managing editor of *The Negro Digest*, an important journal of African-American intellectual life; Hans Graff, president of the Cinegraphic Corporation; Sidney Lens, author, labor journalist, and lecturer; Hoke Norris, noted writer, critic, and literary editor of the *Chicago Sun-Times*; C. Sumner Stone, editor of the *Chicago Defender*; Nicholas Von Hoffman, *Chicago Daily News* columnist; Albert Weisman, vice president of Foote, Cone and Belding and the dean of Chicago's publicists; and other outstanding figures in the communication professions.

Gene O'Hara joined the faculty in 1965, too, and he continued to teach three or four courses every semester for ten years. An intensely private man without academic credentials, O'Hara was a literary scholar, artist, and music historian, and a simply fabulous teacher. O'Hara was representative of a number of outstanding and accomplished Columbia faculty, like Harry Bouras, Gwendolyn Brooks, Hans Adler, and Harry Barnard, whose lack of customary collegiate credentials, doctorates and such, disqualified their faculty engagement at other colleges and universities.

In 1966, O'Hara, Ira Kipnis, and Harry Bouras combined to teach an evening course on George Bernard Shaw. All were great classroom performers, consummate experts on Shaw, and had sharply divided points of view. Each class session was a brilliant dialogue between them. Indeed it was the best college class I ever saw. It began with twenty students and the number grew informally to more than one hundred. When it was repeated the next semester, nearly 150 students registered for the course.

Bill Russo hit the ground running. In quick time, he organized a Columbia College Center for New Music, recruited an orchestra of outstanding Chicago jazz musicians, scheduled a series of concerts, developed a constituency of influential and affluent supporters, and got the college unprecedented publicity.

In May 1965, we filed a preliminary application for candidate status, the first stage in the North Central Association's accrediting process. We hoped somehow to get on the accreditation track. In September, North Central rejected our application, citing in a brief letter the absence of full-time faculty as a disqualifying concern. In a subsequent conversation with a North Central official, I got the impression that the issue of full-time faculty was simply a summary way to dismiss our interest. However Columbia might view itself and describe its virtues, it was obvious that in the North Central's view we satisfied few of their criteria for accreditation.

At least we had initiated an official dialogue, which was more than could be said ten years before. It was evident in 1965 that the North Central Association was not inclined to entertain the notion of an "alternative" or "experimental" college as an appropriate candidate for accreditation; nor did North Central officials seem sensitive to the warning thunders of change which would crash down on American society and its system of education in the immediate years ahead. Despite discouragements, we agreed we would press ahead to the goal of accreditation, faintly assured that contemporary history was on our side.

In the meantime, we leased and remodeled two additional floors (the second and fifth), and our friendly landlord agreed to identify the Lake Shore Drive building with a sign reading "Columbia College," which we placed over the building's entrance. At its November 1965 meeting, the college's board approved a new omnibus lease for a ten-year term to 1975, with options for additional space, at an annual rental beginning at $42,000. The witless optimism of this is mind boggling. Our new rental obligation was three times what we had been hard put to pay at the college's Wabash Avenue location less than two years before; and to extend a lease term to 1975 was simply incomprehensible when only moments before we'd been barely alive.

At the same meeting, Wolf Dochtermann had signaled his intention to leave Columbia at the end of the 1965–66 year. Without a ready alternative, I set out to find a progressive-minded educator who could help shape Columbia's identity and guide the educational process. I knew it would be difficult to find an exceptionally qualified individual who would be willing to share leading responsibility for a hardly competitive salary. The only card I had to play was my shabby invitation to join Columbia's crusade. But once again, Columbia's stars were favorably aligned.

Enter Thaddeus Kawalek, the dean who barely was. I had known him fifteen years before when he had been the superintendent of south-suburban Hazelcrest's schools, and my wife, Anna, was a teacher and a principal in the district. Most recently he had served as director of the Peace Corp's project in Sierra Leone, Africa. Ted, who had just received his Ph.D. from the University of Chicago, was a talented school administrator. In Hazelcrest he assembled an exceptional faculty, incorporated foreign languages in to the elementary school curriculum, and boldly hired African-American teachers in a virtually all-white district and community—no small achievement in a time when racial exclusion was common. Later, he served as superintendent of the Brookfield School District and Gary, Indiana schools. He was chairman of Roosevelt University's Education Department and, briefly, dean of faculties. Ted was also a widely recognized authority on public school finance, teacher education, and school construction. Somehow, I convinced him that together we could build a singular college, me as President, him as dean, or the reverse. Title was not at issue. As a matter of great courtesy, I think, he chose to be dean. The board enthusiastically approved Kawalek's selection, with only a slight demur from Bud Perlman, who objected to Ted's salary being greater than mine. A friend is a friend, after all.

A bit of Kawalek lore: Ted came from a family of steelworkers, and I once saw him with his father and two brothers. Ted was the smallest among giants. Together they could have taken on the army of a small country. Columbia had a little gathering of weightlifters who foolishly challenged Ted to an arm-wrestling contest once. He dispatched them all in seconds. I had envisioned a professional lifetime with Ted, but its wonders lasted only to the 1966–67 year. At the recommendation of the University of Chicago's Education Department, he was offered the job as president of the Chicago Osteopathic Medical College, an institution which had a $50 million construction project and needed a chief executive to head its medical school and manage its building program. The offer at nearly three times his Columbia salary was simply too attractive to refuse. Besides, as Ted said, he wanted to be the first Polish college president. He had an exceptional twenty-five-year tenure as the medical college's president. Indeed, he far surpassed my expectations of him, except the rub was that his best was done somewhere else. Regrettably, Ted had only a one-year Columbia run, and I was back to the hustings in search of a new dean.

After 1960 the board of trustees became increasingly important in the college's life. The board's growing maturity was convincingly evident by 1966. It had taken time, accumulated experience, and public membership before the board could realize its independent role in the college's management and collective responsibility for the institution's welfare. The board's coming-of-age was reflected in a formal resolution by Chairman Gale that fixed the college's officers and faculty with exclusive responsibility for Columbia's educational affairs and day-to-day management, and defined the board's role as the initiator and monitor of college policy and responsible agency of the college's financial security, including fund-raising. This delineation of authority was incorporated in the minutes of the March 1966 board meeting, together with a statement of the board's collective intents: "We seek a distinguished academy in which study of communication arts and media, cultural arts, and contemporary society are joined, so each creates the environment for study of the others. Our attention is to the how of communication and to the artistic and humane value of what is communicated." We were all clearly on the same page.

In 1966, the board numbered nine. The number was expanded to eleven. Spring 1966 enrollment had fallen 5 percent below expectations, owing mainly to stricter government regulations for granting draft deferment. As a consequence, we would need $40,000 in donations to weather the current year. While the board accepted responsibility for raising the amount, their task would be lessened by a timely contribution of $25,000 from our fairy godfather, Ken Montgomery, and by unexpected revenues from Russo's Center for New Music. The trustees acknowledged the failure of their effort to create a "Columbia Associates" organization as a source of regular income, a failure stemming from an inability to enlist a prominent person to head the project. We simply had too little cachet to attract a notable figure. At the June 1966 meeting, tuition for the 1966–67 college year was fixed at $475 per semester for full-time students and $36 per semester hour for part-time enrollment, and a preliminary 1966–67 budget was set anticipating revenues of $378,000 and a like amount of expenses. More precise estimates would not be possible until actual fall 1966 enrollment figures were known. Kawalek would begin the dean's job September 1. At a dinner following the meeting, the board's membership and I joined in expressing our affection and gratitude for Wolf Dochtermann's dedicated service to the college during its most troubled years.

While the 1965–66 year ended with a small deficit, the scale of the college's financial operations was vastly greater in every dimension than the figures of two years before. Having constantly to juggle cash between payables was an exhausting preoccupation. The consequence of such a troubled state was that all advance commitments necessary to fund the college's improvement and even its ability to sufficiently serve year-to-year enrollment growth had to be made with questionable certainty that we'd have the money to pay for them. Indeed, for many years Columbia's before-the-fact commitments were fueled only by precarious optimism. Betting always "on the come" is a dumb way to shoot dice. And scary, too!

1966–1967

Fall 1966 enrollment was 13 percent greater than the preceding year, with 390 students despite a continuing reduction in draft-deferred students. Among many new faculty were: columnist Jon Anderson; theater director Paul Sills, whose innovative "Story Theater" productions and new methods of theater training had earned national prominence; Paul Carroll, editor and publisher of Big Table Books and an important American poet; and John Schultz, who would have a major Columbia role for thirty years ahead.

Schultz was nominated by Hoke Norris, literary editor of the *Chicago Sun-Times* and a member of Columbia's faculty. At a luncheon conversation at Riccardo's, I remember, Hoke told me about visiting a unique class in fiction writing that Schultz taught in the basement of a near-North Side building. Hoke reported that Schultz had invented a method of teaching called "Story Workshop" that resulted in an exceptional quality of student writing, despite the fact that there was nothing to suggest that Schultz's students were more than typical, vaguely aspiring writers. Hoke's enthusiasm led me to visit a Schultz session. I witnessed a circle of students fanned about Schultz, engaging in free associations according to a pattern of planned exercises. The language was noticeably uninhibited, and the session was intensely dramatic and enlisting. I later read some of the students' work, and as Hoke had said, the writing was unexpectedly good. Schultz agreed to teach two creative writing classes that would employ his Story Workshop methods and give me and others an opportunity to evaluate the value of his unusual instruction. At the end of the semester, reports on Story Workshop classes had been uniformly enthusiastic. It was a distinctly new and effective way to teach writing and English, and it clearly engaged students in the learning process. It was this perception and my belief that Story Workshop's inventive methods might prove more successful than familiar methods of teaching writing that interested me in bringing Schultz to Columbia. We meant, after all, to be a place for serious educational experiments and harbored hope that the validity of our example would be contagious.

In his first semester, Schultz taught creative writing classes. By the second semester, I proposed that he take over all of Columbia's first-year English instruction. Thus he became the second regular full-time faculty member, or maybe he was the third, as Robert Edmonds was hired almost simultaneously as chairman of the Film Department.

Edmonds was a very experienced filmmaker, a leading member of the world documentary film community, and most recently, the executive secretary of the National Guild of Motion Picture Directors. He was the ideal person to head Columbia's film project, which already had a part-time faculty of notable filmmakers, including Fred Lasse, Gordon Weisenborn, Robert Longini, Seymour Zolotaroff, Hans Graff, Stanley Lazan, and experts in film technology Jack Behrend and George Colburn.

Regrettably, not all of my faculty recruiting forays were successful. At about the same time I persuaded Edmonds, I tried mightily to interest William Murray, who then and for years afterward wrote the regular *New Yorker* feature "Letter from Rome." Murray was a novelist, a dramatist, an opera singer when it was his fancy, and a skillful racetrack handicapper. He was also Bill Russo's friend. I thought I had him, and he would have been smashing at Columbia but, then again, I don't think he would have liked Chicago winters.

During his abbreviated tenure as dean, Kawalek had initiated a study concentration in audio-visual materials and educational technology in association with a renewed emphasis on teacher education in speech, theater, and communication arts. It was an entirely valid project, but with Kawalek's unexpected departure, we had nobody with sufficient experience in teacher education and contact with the school community to successfully carry it out.

Fund-raising was always mainly a response to emergency situations that prompted scurrying about to scratch up bits of money. We had never had a development plan to guide our fund-raising efforts, and we needed expert counsel. I asked the advice of Council for the Advancement of Small Colleges (CASC). They recommended Richard Taft, who headed a Washington firm and was, to CASC's experience, the premier expert on foundations. It was Taft's estimate, after a thorough investigation, that Columbia had excellent potential for getting foundation support, particularly because of our atypicality, which would be in tune with many foundations that were beginning to recognize the growing ferment on America's campuses and in the society in general. I reported his observations to the board, who believed that Taft's engagement would be valuable if his costs were minimal and, at least at first, short term. Taft suggested that we also seek the advice of a Chicago fund-raising firm, John Grenzebach and Associates, who would help to assess the college's local fund-raising potentials. We engaged both services in the spring of 1966 despite our severely limited funds and the fact that, as customary, we needed to raise $20,000 to promptly satisfy current cash needs. There was no likelihood that either Taft or Grenzebach would create any quick solutions to our fund-raising and foundation problems. At best, even a beginning at either would require time, careful study, and more expense.

As a way to develop a giving constituency, Grenzebach urged that we make a new effort to assemble an organization of "Columbia Associates." Jim Conway, a popular TV and radio personality and a Columbia alumnus, agreed to head this campaign, which would require time, investment, and an unfamiliar intensity of board solicitation to be successful. An "Associates" membership of at least two hundred, each pledging $100 annually, would be needed to justify the effort. It was no small task.

At its May 1967 meeting, the board voted to increase tuition for the 1967–68 year to $500 per semester for full–time students and $40 per credit hour for part-time enrollment, and urged a continuing accreditation effort. Though the next year's budget had not been cast, the board authorized an expenditure of $25,000 in new equipment and facilities for the Film Department.

When the year's financial results were tallied, 1966–67 revenues were $10,000 greater than expenses. On paper, it was an encouraging result that typically had little to do with cash anguishes. Undoubtedly, the college had enjoyed a very profitable year in all respects except real money. A remedy for that plague remained elusive.

1967–1968

The year 1967–68 was an eventful one for the college and surely so for America. I had expected a long and difficult effort to replace Dr. Kawalek as Columbia's dean, but I lucked out quickly. In August, the main speaker at a CASC meeting was the chairman of the Fine Arts Department of the University of South Florida, Dr. William Wilkes. He was a professional musician and an experienced college administrator of arts disciplines who shared Columbia's educational and social views. Our foundation consultant, Richard Taft, was also a speaker at the CASC session and he, by happy coincidence, knew Wilkes. Taft told me that Wilkes was an outstanding educator and a splendid individual. I contrived a long conversation with him and discovered that he was seriously considering other job opportunities. I cranked up all my persuasive tactics. I had him pretty convinced, but he was not at the moment ready to succumb to my blandishments and I had yet to investigate his references, which I hurried to do when I got back to Chicago. Everybody I spoke to about Wilkes heartily endorsed him. When little more than a week had gone by, I called him and after a surprisingly brief conversation, he agreed to become Columbia's dean. A month later he was at the job. It was a great fit.

The fall 1967 enrollment of 484 students (full-time equivalent: 338) was nearly 30 percent greater than the year before. A college bookstore was opened. We had many new distinguished faculty. For the first time, the college had even a bare sufficiency of administrative staff. "Glorioski," said Little Orphan Annie. Dean Wilkes and I even shared a secretary. Faculty salaries went up 10 percent—still pretty poor, but better. We had a new photography lab, albeit too small, but professionally equipped. We had $25,000 in new film gear and much-improved television facilities. Board members and faculty had very successfully solicited equipment contributions from local TV stations, motion picture and photography studios, radio stations, and advertising agencies. These gifts represented a far greater value than the little we could afford to spend. We added a full floor of the building to the college's space and created an attractive and spacious (to our eyes) library reading room and book circulating section.

By fall 1967, Columbia had 10,000 books, a quite contemporary collection: not chaff and rarely circulated, obscure, and out-of-date volumes, but really usable books, relevant periodicals, and ample general reference materials. Hubert Davis was now Columbia's full-time librarian, and he had several student helpers. A year later, we had nearly 20,000 volumes.

The library was a notable achievement. Two years before, it was nothing. Whatever few books we'd been left when Columbia and PFTC split were useless, and if we'd had any books, we wouldn't have had any place to put them. Without Hubert Davis, we wouldn't have remotely known how to go about building a library. Surely, a good library is essential to a college's life. But to begin even a barely respectable college library from scratch with virtually no money would daunt the hardiest optimist. Even when the college's survival was a desperate issue, the board agreed with me to somehow set aside $5,000 as a library investment, and Hubert began to collect dictionaries, encyclopedias, general reference books, and elemental library stuff. We got five years of government library grants, nearly $25,000 in all. board members got contributions of current and expensive books on Columbia's subjects from many communication agencies. And the profits of Harry Bouras's art auctions went to the library fund.

Bill Russo's project was in high gear. His jazz orchestra performed regularly for large Chicago audiences. He was particularly benefited by the support of Dr. Deton Brooks, the director of the Chicago Commission for Urban Opportunity (CCUO), whom I had interested in Columbia's plan to extend the college's arts and cultural activities to city neighborhoods and schools. Brooks was an unusual public official. An African-American man having a prominent city role was unusual then. A genuinely enlightened man in a leading position was equally rare. Brooks believed that arts and culture would have valuable presence in his agency's projects, which intended greater economic opportunity and improved life quality for the impoverished and the schools that served them. In 1967 and 1968, Brooks's CCUO was the main funder of Russo's activities, which included performances of the jazz orchestra in many locations, elaborate renderings of Russo operas in city high schools, and a major orchestral performance conducted by the renowned conductor Seigi Ozawa in the amphitheater on the University of Illinois campus. As Columbia College was identified in all of Russo's performances, the college enjoyed invaluable publicity in the press and in all sections of the city.

That year I also developed a point of view about enrollment. The GI Bills, draft deferments, and state and federal student aid awards favored full-time students;

though part-time enrollment was not discouraged, it was not as well subsidized. As Columbia had many low-income students, unusual numbers were eligible for government-sponsored student aid. Though student draft deferment cut across all income levels, this was a comparatively brief phenomenon.

Big-city college institutions now make a great effort to recruit part-time students by various adult-education appeals. Such projects require an extensive and expensive administrative apparatus and very costly advertising. I reasoned that the profitability of a part-time student emphasis was questionable unless it could be practiced on a very large scale. However I calculated full-time to part-time numbers and whatever the variables, I couldn't escape the fact that the tuition of four part-time students enrolled for four credit hours each was roughly equal to the tuition of one full-time student; and it would be more economical to educate 250 full-time students than 1,000 part-timers, whose term-to-term retention was less dependable than regularly enrolled full-time students. I know this isn't a perfect equation. There are many financial justifications for encouraging part-time enrollment. Even apart from financial considerations, the extension of a college's service to adult learners, those who may have short-term learn-more-to-earn-more objectives, and young people who cannot attend college full-time is valuable. In Columbia's instance, however, our curricular offering was too limited to attract sufficient numbers of part-time students to constitute a profitable project; and under any circumstances, we could not have even remotely afforded the necessary institutional services and advertising and promotional costs. Thus, there was no sensible or economical alternative but to concentrate our efforts and resources on full-time students. While we certainly valued part-time enrollment, we knew that Columbia's main bread and butter came from full-time students. In the late 1960s, we anticipated that such emphasis could be sustained if student draft deferments, a Vietnam GI Bill, and U.S.-sponsored student aid continued to encourage full-time enrollment. At that time we could not have foreseen the dramatic growth of *need-based* federal student aid and state benefits, and ultimately a general entitlement to student loans, which together have become essential parts of American higher education. We did recognize, however, that the unintended consequence of Columbia's emphasis on serving students who were underrepresented in higher education and denied opportunity in media and arts occupations embraced large numbers of students with financial aid eligibility.

The vitality of the college's board continued. At a meeting in October 1967, Seymour Gale submitted his resignation as the board's chairman. While it was anticipated, it was no less regrettable. Gale had served admirably for nearly four years. His wise and patient counsel, exemplary leadership, and consistent ingenuity had been invaluable during the college's most difficult times. William Cobbs, a very respected publisher and president of Encyclopedia Britannica Films, was elected chairman. Four new board members were added also: Donald Mann, a faculty member, distinguished 1947 alumnus, president emeritus of the Academy of Radio Arts and Sciences, senior account executive of CBS Radio, and a leader of the broadcasting industry; Devorah Sherman, a prominent advocate of cultural and social welfare causes; Frank Anglin, an outspoken progressive advocate who headed a distinguished

African-American law firm; and Dwight W. Follett, chairman of the Follett Publishing Company and distinguished leader of the publishing industry, who was honored by the college in June 1967, as a Doctor of Humane Letters.

At the meeting, the board adopted new, comprehensive bylaws which codified the board's structure and corporate practice, and also closely reviewed the progress of our consultants on fund-raising and foundations. The Grenzebach representative offered a chart of board committees and assignments, which after discussion between the chairman and individual members, would be ratified at the board's November meeting. He proposed, too, that before any planning of a comprehensive fund-raising project, the board promptly initiate a preliminary campaign to raise $100,000 to relieve the college's endemic cash shortages and the lack of sufficient working capital. The Taft agency had already begun to solicit the interest of foundations and government agencies and had compiled a detailed directory of foundations having possible interest in Columbia and its activities. A Taft representative would visit Chicago later in the month to search board member associations with local foundations and their officers. Also, Harry Bouras described a project he had initiated to compile a portfolio of signed art prints of the donated works of ten leading Chicago artists. In an issue limited to 125, the portfolios could be sold by the college in a $100–150 range. Bouras had arranged a donation of woodcuts and printing as well. The year's budget was fixed, anticipating revenues of $375,000 and expenditures of $400,000. The disparity flew gently away on the wings of soaring confidence. As Holly Golightly said, "I'll think about it tomorrow."

As anticipated, the board ratified committee assignments at its November meeting. It established executive, development, finance, education, and physical plant committees. The Grenzebach representative, Nick Lotz, detailed the preliminary fund campaign, which would seek $100,000 during the current year and expected sources of support. The effort would require diligent board participation, and Mr. Lotz would work closely with the development committee.

Mr. Follett suggested an exploration of the possibility of forming a cooperative consortium of local arts and related colleges in the general pattern of California's Claremont College complex. I was instructed to initiate preliminary discussions. The School of the Art Institute was first in mind. It was a splendid idea, but I discovered quickly that such marshalling of resources and institutions of similar interests was utterly alien to the visions of local college mandarins. With the Taft agency's lead, the college was pursuing several projects with foundations and government agencies. These included a music center and creative writing programs to be sponsored by the Federal Model Cities Act, and a large proposal for a $4 million endowment to fund a new-age school of journalism, which undoubtedly was unrealistic. At the meeting, I also announced the gift of a complete library (more than 1,000 volumes) on African-American history by Trustee Erwin Salk. It was a most generous and valuable gift. The meeting's final business was the board's approval of an appointment of full-time faculty status to Lucille Strauss, Gene DeKovic, Thaine Lyman, Al Parker, and Harry Bouras. While this action was largely a formality, it did include increased compensation and official recognition of their faculty standing. We also awarded full-time rank to Betty Shiflett, who had joined John Schultz's creative writing and English projects, and Sue Ann Park, who would head the college's Speech Department. As "Story Workshop" was in English, speech was an important emphasis of Columbia's experiment in instructional method. Sue Ann Park was a principal advocate of the "Lessac Method" of teaching speech to actors and in treating speech disorders. It stressed the mechanics of oral production, not, as typically taught, a repetition of sounds, but through a systematic progression of oral exercises involving tongue placements, mouth formations, and breathing. It was an ingenious technique and unusually successful. So much so that in the next several years when Sue Ann Parks had trained other teachers in the intricacies of the Lessac Method, speech was added to English as required study for all Columbia students.

A World Youth Congress

Many things crowded the college's (and my) spring 1968 calendar. In late March, I was a guest at a dinner at Ken Montgomery's house. The occasion honored Albert DeSmale, a former prime minister of Belgium who was currently serving in a leading United Nation's capacity. I talked with DeSmale about contemporary youth culture and its rebellious presence worldwide. We played with the idea of a world youth congress sponsored by the United Nations. Montgomery observed that it was a compelling idea that should be explored. Both DeSmale and I hastened to say that even a preliminary exploration of such a project would undoubtedly get bogged down in the U.N.'s bureaucracy and take years to realize. But Ken persisted, finally saying that he would fund an exploration of the idea, and if it were validated, he would contribute to the funding of a world youth congress if the event had the support of major world powers.

DeSmale believed the most practical and prompt route would be to explore the proposition with leaders of European countries, and if they were in accord, to solicit the interest of the United States and other countries, and only after that seek United Nations sponsorship. Sensibly, of course, such lofty schemes expect a whole organizing apparatus, but we were not bound by sensible restraints. DeSmale was confident that he could quickly arrange meetings with leading government officials in the principal European countries. We'd try to get the ball rolling with them. There was one mighty catch, however. DeSmale's schedule for the next months would not allow him time to personally interview the people we needed to enlist. I would have to be the project's salesman. This was absurd, for I knew as much about international diplomacy as I knew about quantum physics. Talk about an innocent abroad. I was it. Nevertheless, in a matter of days, I was off for Europe, guided only by DeSmale's itinerary. Fortunately, DeSmale joined me in Paris, my tour's first stop. He booked me into an elegant suite in the Raphael Hotel and arranged a dinner with six ministers in France's cabinet, sans DeGaulle. The dinner occasion was held at the Tour d'Argent, then the world's premier restaurant. The ministers were accompanied by their parliamentary secretaries. Over the rarest of aperitifs, DeSmale and I described our scheme. DeSmale did it in French, of course, and I in English. If I had spoken in Icelandic, they'd all have spoken that, too. Everyone was politely interested, and all promised to promptly consult their colleagues. I mistook courtesy for commitment, but then again, what did I know? Then we got to the serious business of dining. It was an elegant meal with the finest and most expensive of wines and cognacs, and great Cuban cigars at the end. Endless toasts. There was the warmest fraternity, and doubtful result. DeSmale believed it had gone exceptionally well; he would follow up on our dinner foray. I paid the bill. The amount was staggering—thousands. I was scheduled to meet with a prestigious delegation in Rome two days later, and had similar meetings after in Brussels, The Hague, London, and Bonn. In all these places, except Belgium, I was on my own. I had encouraging audiences but no dependable commitments. As DeSmale had chosen the best of hotels and restaurants, I went luxuriously first class everywhere. When my tour was done, I conferred again with DeSmale, who shared my view that our project couldn't have any timely resolution. Governments were simply unprepared and unwilling to cooperate on such a world-scale project as we had naively proposed. Montgomery was disappointed at my report, though he accepted the practical sense of it. It certainly would have given Columbia impressive world recognition.

More than thirty years later, my memory of this improbable quest for a role on the world's stage is mostly of two events. The night after my dinner with the French ministers was the only unscheduled time on my whirlwind European tour. The only restaurant I knew of in Paris was the Tour d'Argent. So what else but to go there again? When I arrived I was treated regally, undoubtedly because of the size of the check and the rank of my guests the night before. I was ushered to a coveted window table overlooking the Seine and Notre Dame Cathedral. It was a poetic sight. I ordered an elaborate dinner: *fois gras*, caviar, poached turbot, a Grand Marnier soufflé, and the finest champagne, wines, and cognac. At its end I was delightfully bombed. As I puffed on a Cuban cigar, the maitre d' asked, "Anything else, monsieur?"

I responded heroically, "Do it again."

"From the beginning?" he questioned.

"Exactly so," I said. As the second round began, a band of waiters and the maitre d' gathered about my table and chorused, "Bravo, monsieur," and there was muted applause. I nodded modestly. Somehow I got through my encore, even to another cigar. I've no memory of what happened after that, only that I woke to a beautiful morning in my hotel room.

And then despair. The newspapers all bannered that Martin Luther King, Jr., had been murdered.

The Arts and the Inner City

Less than a month later, Columbia's conference on "The Arts and the Inner City" got a ton of national publicity. This project got its start in a conversation that the Taft agency had arranged for me with Vernon Eagle, who directed the New World Foundation. The occasion was meant only to introduce Columbia and its unusual qualities and contemporary ideas. I had nothing specific to propose, but in the course of our discussion, I emphasized the absence of mainstream interest in supporting or fostering arts activity in America's inner cities, particularly in African-

American and Latino communities. Somehow, out of my exchange with Mr. Eagle, I invented the idea of a national conference on art in the inner cities, which would invite the participation of leading artists, art educators, and representatives of arts projects in minority and working-class communities. Such a conference would embrace prominent individuals in all the arts—theater, literature, music, dance, fine and popular arts, etc.—and would also invite representatives of leading foundations and funding sources, in hopes that their conference participation would generate greater mainstream funding for excluded artists and arts projects. Mr. Eagle was enthusiastic about such a meeting and told me if I would quickly prepare a convincing proposal, he believed that New World would contribute as much as $25,000 to fund such a conference. I had a formal proposal back to him in a few days and, less than a week later, he committed $25,000 to fund the project. To sweeten it all, Dr. Deton Brooks gave me another $10,000. The conference would be Columbia's first major effort at national recognition and influence. The event was planned as a three-day occasion and each of the participants (excepting foundation observers and Columbia faculty) would be paid $200 for their attendance, plus travel costs and a daily per diem. In deciding whom to invite, I had the indispensable assistance of Junius Eddy who, as chief program officer of the arts division of the U.S. Office of Education and later as a Rockefeller Foundation arts executive, was unusually knowledgeable about the conference's subjects and the individuals who headed successful arts programs in America's inner cities and depressed communities.

We consulted with experts across the country and ultimately developed a roster of more than one hundred names, hoping that about forty would come to the conference. While our list included some of America's most prominent minority and progressive artists, most were organizers of leading minority arts projects and arts organizations in inner-city communities. Forty-six people accepted our invitation. Indeed, it would be a sparkling and articulate assembly, to include novelist John Killens; theater director Douglas Turner Ward; historian, novelist, and poet Vincent Harding; photographer Dan Lyon; cinematographer Haskell Wexler; Luis Valdez, director of the United Farm Worker's "Campesio Cultural"; John Neal, director of the Free Southern Theater; Vinette Carol, director of New York's inner city arts program; Enrique Vargas, director of the Gut Theater; Robert Macbeth, director of the New Lafayette Theater; artist Leon Golub; director of a major Washington, D.C. arts program, Topper Carew; writer Piri Thomas; and Chicago musician Phil Cohran. Poet Gwendolyn Brooks, novelist Ron Fair, Harry Bouras, William Russo, and John Schultz represented Columbia's faculty. In addition, leading executives of nine major foundations and government arts funding agencies would attend as observers. I hired a Chicago writer, Joe Sander, as the conference's coordinator.

We had engaged the auditorium of the American Dental Association on Chicago Avenue as the main site of the conference and carefully designed the conference's agenda and discussion guides, scheduled speeches, dinners, and entertainment, and issued an assortment of pre-conference press releases. We'd done everything to insure a model event.

And all our plans went for naught. The conference began perfectly with a comfortable sense of fraternity and purpose. I gave an opening address. Whatever else I said, it had one memorable line, "There is a gnawing suspicion about that something big's gone wrong with most everything." I didn't know the immediacy of such an observation.

Among a raft of national publicity, Norman Mark's insightful article in the *Chicago Daily News* provided the most comprehensive view of the conference's dramatic course. It was titled, "A Matter of Black and White: Chicago Conference on 'The Arts and the Inner City' Explodes in Dramatic Confrontation," and went on to say:

The conference was called by Columbia College, which is not yet among the city's educational movers and shakers. The college brought together about sixty people, many of them from outside the city, who were neither presidents nor chiefs, but who were the lower echelon toilers in the streets.

On chairs arranged in two large semicircles around the podium were the conferees. At the rear of the hall sat a dozen local black artists—uninvited, quiet, sullen, watching.

Then COBRA struck. The Coalition of Black Revolutionary Artists, the group sitting at the back, interrupted the proceedings to deliver a position paper agreeing to white cooperation but vehemently protesting white control of the arts. Their statement said that whites could not bring programs to black artists nor control or direct projects in black communities. "If whites have money and want to give it, do so and leave. To initiate programs for blacks is folly, stupidity, a crime and an emasculation. Stay away!"

The white liberals at the conference had great difficulty in confronting this demand for separateness. Black and white together, all those times joined in singing "We Shall Overcome," were ideas deeply ingrained in the whites.

Artist Jeff Donaldson, the tall, slim co-chairman of COBRA, shouted the black ultimatums. "The unfortunate thing when we get in these sessions is that the people who are here consider themselves our friends or they would not be here. But you are the only ones we can attack. We do not need any more overseers. We do not need anybody to dispense money to us. We have a program. We need the money. Send us the money. Don't give it to somebody to give to us. Give it to us! We are here. We are happening and we will continue to happen. Send the money to us in the mail. You know what Greek art is because you know what Greeks are. You know what Roman art is. You know what Jewish art is. If you don't know what black art is, that's your problem, because you had it under your thumb for 400 years. If you didn't learn anything then, don't expect anyone to hip you now.

It was to have been a tidy three-day conference, a place where artists and educators would get together to define art and grope toward a few "objective, useful insights" about the arts and ghetto life. But it did not turn out that way. Instead, this neatly packaged event took on a dramatic life of its own, mushrooming suddenly into a mini-American forum which ultimately confronted its impassioned and often confused participants with the one basic question of today: How are the races to deal with each other? Because of the intensity and truthfulness of its confrontations, this "first national meeting on the new arts" changed the life of every person who was there.

The conference spent two-and-a-half days in unimaginable debate. All the combatants attended the conference's closing event, a performance of Russo's prophetically titled rock opera *The Civil War* (the old one between the North and South). Piri Thomas and Luis Valdez made stirring speeches about African-American and white unity. The sentiment was unchallenged.

In retrospect, what did the conference accomplish? Most significantly, of course, it provided a public platform for legitimate African-American protest and artistic aspiration. Even though this had not been our original intent, the result was consistent with the spirit of the conference's call, though undoubtedly COBRA's invasion had been an unexpected emphasis. In final reckoning, the college's conference was the first nationally publicized black/white confrontation in the arts, and unquestionably Columbia's event set a pattern for similar occasions which, in aggregate, seriously alarmed the barons of America's arts establishment and forged a new respect for African-American artists and recognition of their right to determine the content and direction of their art and the character and management of arts projects performed in their communities.

While arts funding, as traditionally, remained firmly in the hands of a white (albeit frightened) establishment, at least the system had no defensible alternative to at least minimally democratizing access to funding sources. In this respect, the response of government arts agencies was more immediately generous. In inviting representatives of the major foundations, Columbia's conference spurred a significant reordering of funding priorities in these foundations and among agencies they influenced to give greater benefit to African-American artists and observe the terms of support dramatically expressed by COBRA and the conference's African-American caucus. After the conference, several of my Columbia colleagues and I worked comfortably with members of COBRA and other local African-American arts organizations to develop support from government agencies and foundation funding sources. The conference and the grave issues it confronted strongly influenced my subsequent thinking about black/white relations and the college's practice, and I think the conference valuably influenced my immediate Columbia colleagues as well, though to varying extents all of us were personally shaken by the conference's events. While none disputed the elemental truths revealed, the conference's combative tones later led some to avoid the risks of racial confrontation by embracing the safety of noninvolvement in African-American issues, a state of mind not unlike the reaction of many bravely engaged white students and young people to the expulsion of whites from Student Nonviolent Coordinating Committee (SNCC) after earlier civil rights battles. Regrettably, many white Americans of presumed good will were repelled by the separatist ideology and the black nationalist ideas expressed by African Americans individually and in their collective associations. Many well-intentioned whites were more hurt by their unfamiliar rejection than won to thoughtfull self-examination and consciousness of African-American reaction to four hundred years of slavery and white racism. Undoubtedly, the conference gave Columbia valuable local and national recognition as well as recognition by educational and foundation communities and government agencies. The Conference on Arts and the Inner City sharpened Columbia's distinctive identity.

A main motive of Columbia's policy of open admissions was to provide greater college and employment opportunities in the occupations of the college's interest for African Americans, as they suffered the most acute social and economic exclusion and educational neglect. While it was evident that America's Latinos suffered similarly, their resistance was less organized and vocal.

At issue were elemental democratic entitlements to economic, political, legal, and educational justice. Ironically, despite its philosophical commitments, Columbia's education was focused on occupations which were among the most severe practitioners of racial and gender exclusion. Before the mid-1970s, only a miniscule number of minority men and few women were employed in television, radio, motion pictures, journalism, and advertising or in any arts occupations, except a minimal number of African-American music performers and a few disc jockeys at segregated radio "race stations."

Apart from the fact that the percentage of minorities enrolled in American colleges and universities was much smaller than the number of whites, even after World War II, discrimination by the communication and media industries and the arts professions made education for these occupations an unrealistic choice for young African Americans, Latinos, and women. As a consequence, not only did they have little reason to attend Columbia, but also a pool of minority and women teachers with professional experience in Columbia's main subjects was virtually nonexistent. To my best recollection, African Americans constituted less than 5 percent of Columbia's student population in the late 1940s, less than 10 percent in the 1950s, roughly 15 percent in the mid-to-late 1960s, and 22 percent in 1973. Correspondingly, Columbia's Latino population was negligible until the early 1970s: in 1973 only 4 percent of total enrollment.

Columbia's open admissions policy was undoubtedly a crucial factor in encouraging the enrollment of African-American students in the late 1960s, and subsequently, of Latino students. That in one of those years Columbia's freshman class included five valedictorians of African-American high schools validates the perception that racial exclusion was a common collegiate practice, or at least, that most college institutions made little or no effort to recruit African-American and Latino students. For a number of years, Columbia was often the only local college institution represented at "college days" at African-American high schools.

Among other factors that influenced the growth of Columbia's African-American student population were new life expectations generated by the sound and fury of contemporary youth culture, and civil rights, antiwar, and campus mobilizations. Columbia had also enlarged its academic purview to include arts disciplines which were less discriminatory and where individual recognition was less dependent on industry-wide employment patterns. Of influence, too, was Columbia's reputation as a good college and its identification with contemporary themes. At the same time, the college's liberal arts extensions gave unprecedented opportunity to assemble a faculty that included numbers of accomplished minority and women artists, scholars, and writers whose credentials were earned apart from usual settings. Their visibility was reassuring to African-American and women students, though Latino students and faculty members lagged behind.

The most critical factor, however, in the growth of the number of African-American students at Columbia and later Latinos at virtually all Illinois higher education institutions was Illinois's enlightened entitlement program of state scholarship grants, which literally made a college education affordable. Indeed, the societal effect of state-sponsored student aid and national Pell grant subsidies and student loans can be likened to the vast effect of post-World War II GI Bills on America's course. Columbia had, and continues to have, a significant role in the politics of state and federal student-aid legislation.

By the mid-1960s, civil rights issues crowded the nation's agenda. While the Civil Rights Act in 1964 and Voting Rights Act of 1965 confronted southern patterns of segregation and racial exclusion, such legislation did little to contest endemic racism in northern cities. Where SNCC's militant student crusade in the summer of 1964 and Martin Luther King's SCLC demonstrations had focused national attention on southern African-American issues, the battle scene quickly spread to include the exploding resentments of northern African Americans. Harlem in 1964 and Watts in 1965 gave fuel to violent rioting in Detroit, Newark, and scores of big cities in 1967. The assassination of Martin Luther King in April of 1968 generated a firestorm in America's inner cities. Chicago's West Side burned for days, to the consternation of the city's politicians and moguls who had historically ignored and contributed to the ghettoized state of Chicago's African-American communities. These dramatic events dominated the mainstream media with vivid images of African-Americans being savaged by hostile whites, scenes that alarmed and repulsed many whites and infuriated many African Americans. The phrase "Black Power" was spoken by African-American youth everywhere, and the brief vestiges of "black and white together" were swept away by the African-American movement's reaction to the evidence of intransigent racism. In 1967 the *Kerner Report*
emphasized that America was in grave danger of becoming two nations, one black and one white, unless all the nation's agencies united in quickly remedying the suppressed state of America's African-American citizens. Chicago was then the most segregated city in America—two cities in fact, and largely remains so, except that economic class is now a factor in the equation.

In the 1960s, African-American issues had significant presence at Columbia. This was a consequence of the growing number of African-American students and faculty, many of whom were veterans of contemporary civil rights struggles, as were a number of white members of the college's community, including myself. In fact, a number of Columbia's white students and faculty marched with Dr. Martin Luther King into the Marquette Park hellspot in 1967.

As an institution Columbia directly participated only in legislative and related issues that affected the higher education community. The theatrical national events taking place at the moment were largely peripheral to the college's immediate life, whatever the impact of such issues on some of the college's individuals. The year 1968, however, was a year of unimaginable national turmoil.

Opposition to the war in Vietnam reached a climax. Gene McCarthy and Robert Kennedy were in the presidential run. President Johnson would not seek reelection. Martin Luther King was assassinated, and two months later, Robert Kennedy. A cacophony of events prefaced the Democratic National Convention in Chicago in 1968, which resulted in political theater and official panic. The Yippies came and brought an insensate, volatile coupling of antiwar passions and radical life styles. Also at the convention were thousands of local young people, serious peace partisans, and mindless joy riders, all scattered in Lincoln Park. While people milled about there was lots of pot, folk singing, guerilla theater, feckless poetry, cheap wine, indifferent sex, and dirty words. The police came in helmets and riot gear to clear the park. In a moment, a raucous nuisance became a hostile mob. A battalion of cops flailed about with nightsticks, breaking heads and bones, pushing captives into paddy wagons, and chasing scattered invaders all over the neighborhood. If the police succeeded at anything, it was the instant radicalization of legions of young people.

The greatest numbers of Columbia's students and faculty lived on Chicago's Near North Side, mostly about Lincoln Park. At the time it was Chicago's Greenwich Village: a lively place of off-Broadway theaters, music, art galleries, bookstores, bars, ethnic restaurants, and tolerant lifestyles. Whether willy-nilly or deliberately, lots of Columbia folk were part of the convention's first night of hostilities. Right at the center of it all at the Lincoln/Clark/Wells triangle were two small theaters. By odd coincidence, Bill Russo and his musical company were performing his recently composed rock cantata *The Civil War*, and right next door was Paul Sills's Story Theater. Russo's cast put a big sign outside his theater's front door that said, "CIVIL WAR TONIGHT—OUTSIDE UNTIL 10:30 P.M.—INSIDE AT 11:00"

Lincoln Park was only the first act. Quite literally, the whole world watched the next night's event. During that day thousands of young people, both veterans of Lincoln Park and new crowds, demonstrated in Grant Park across the street from the Stevens Hotel (now the Hilton Hotel), which served as the Democratic Party's

Convention headquarters. The park was rife with rumors of a mass march that evening on the International Amphitheater, the convention's site. The threat issued by antiwar and Yippie leaders was undoubtedly real, though its actuality was questionable. The mobilization was utterly disorganized, and virtually the entire Chicago police force was mobilized to cordon off the hotel and the street routes to the convention. The crowd skirmished with police all day. Early in the evening, the police just completely lost it and attacked the crowd. It was, as the Walker Commission accurately reported, "a police riot." It raged for hours, and scenes of unimaginable police brutality were televised to horrified national and world audiences. The convention was tumultuous, and the expected nomination of Hubert Humphrey as the Democratic Party's presidential candidate was virtually ignored. The events in Lincoln Park may have radicalized a few thousand young people, but it was nothing compared to the scale of combative sentiment generated by television's witness. Ridiculously, the catastrophe was compounded by subsequent federal charges that leaders of the antiwar and Yippie movements were engaged in a criminal conspiracy to disrupt Chicago's Democratic Convention.

Many Columbia students, faculty, and staff had strong civil rights sentiments and many were tuned into national antiwar and campus movements. While activists were only a small minority of Columbia's community, exhibits of advocacy were familiar, though not seriously disruptive. While the 1968 graduation ceremony was briefly interrupted by an antiwar demonstration (the class valedictorian wore a rice hat), the occasion became a magically moving and inspirational gathering, which David

Halberstam, the commencement's speaker, observed "mirrored contemporary America." Understandably, the tensions of the times had expression at Columbia, though probably less so than at many other institutions, perhaps partly because students and faculty believed that Columbia was not part of the status quo.

Viewed against the national tumult of 1968, a report on the college's state during that year may seem insignificant, but it was nonetheless a significant year in Columbia's life. At midyear, February 1968 enrollment was 5 percent greater than in fall 1967, the first time that student numbers had increased in the spring term. When the 1967–68 year ended, we had a deficit of $40,000 on revenues of $491,000 including $40,000 in donated funds, and expenses of $531,000, a sadly familiar state typically subscribed by summer bank loans. What undoubtedly was more significant than the deficit was the record of Columbia's remarkable growth during the four years after its new beginning in 1964. In that brief period, we had grown three and four times to every measure, and immeasurably more in every dimension of educational quality and vitality. Only our continually difficult finances resisted comparable remedy. We remained almost exclusively dependent on student revenues, a condition that prevails today.

In 1968, the Grenzebach firm tried mightily to organize a board effort to quickly raise $100,000 as a modest preliminary to a larger fund campaign, but this project was discouragingly unsuccessful. While board members were individually generous and loyal advocates of Columbia's cause, they were reluctant fund-raisers. I have no satisfactory explanation for that failure, except that perhaps I had failed to inspire a zealous commitment to fund-raising by the board's membership. And I have no explanation for that either. It was clearly too expensive to continue Grenzebach's engagement without far greater returns. However, we continued our association with the Taft organization, which in a short time had interested a number of major foundations in Columbia. Among these, representatives of Ford, Rockefeller, Carnegie, and Whitney foundations and the National Endowment for the Arts visited the college in the spring of 1968. All were enthusiastic, though our recentness, unconventional identity, and lack of accreditation tempered their compliment, apart from the fact that grant proposals moved slowly through the apparatus of major foundations. My quick response from the New World Foundation was certainly atypical. At the same time, the National Film Institute seriously considered, though ultimately rejected, our proposal to establish a Midwest Film Center at Columbia, though our Film Department succeeded in finding funds for a series of films for federal antipoverty agencies.

What was more important to the college's life was a need to reassess its state and course in relation to the plan embraced in the summer of 1964. Quite obviously, the 1964 plan had been an omniscient guide to the college's quick success. Back then, we had certainly never imagined that only four years later our frail waif of an institution would have five hundred students, a faculty of seventy including twelve full-time members, a library, nearly all of a Lake Shore Drive building, a number of new study concentrations in the arts and communications, and a 1968 budget exceeding half a million dollars, among a host of other advances. Unquestionably, to say the plan had been realized was an understatement. But in the interim the state of the nation had changed, as had the college. We were not yet viewed as an authentic college institution. We had not realized accreditation or distinctive public identity, and we had little more than rudimentary financial security. While we had responded to the mood of the 1960s, Columbia was still an educational experiment without a confident sense of permanence and without secure ability to sustain a genuinely distinctive contemporary college institution. We needed to go back to the drawing board.

I launched the notion of reassessment in a speech to an assembly of the college's faculty, staff, and board at the Chicago Arts Club in February 1968. On that occasion, I attempted a summary of what Columbia's community had achieved in the brief span of four years. I reviewed the state of the college's finances, which, however precarious, had not fatally impaired our success. I saluted the hard-tested loyalty of the college's trustees. But my main compliment was reserved for the college's faculty:

For you, individually and in the aggregate, no modest words apply. Our college is not made of bricks nor are we much the stuff of tradition. We are without the visibility of privilege. But we are vital, original, excellent, and contemporary. We march to the young drummer. Whatever excellence, whatever spirit, whatever we are or mean to be is made of you who provide a quality of teaching and professional and human engagement unsurpassed on the American campus.

I do not mean any of this to suggest that we are without problem or need. I am too painfully aware of these faults. But I genuinely believe that we are on to a new way, a better way, in higher education, and that we have cause to anticipate confidently that a new, more expert, and secure institution will grow from the healthy roots we are putting down.

We have come a great way in a short time. I cannot answer why simply. I do not believe it has very much to do with an expanding college population, or that being a small college, we are attractive to students alienated by a large-college environment. Instead, our special interests in the arts and media of communication, the growth of their occupational opportunities, and the fact of the faculty's immediate professionalism are most prominent in the statements of our students.

Our students are kinds of fall-outs, not quite fitting ordinary molds. They are mostly creative young people who are hesitant about a life course, which threatens to loosen their handhold on the lunch pail. And yet they have come somehow to recognize in Columbia a place of liberation where they may find a way to becoming new men and women.

I think we are succeeding because we are not like others. We have no fixed walls mortared up with old times. We are a more timely, relevant idea in which our validity comes of a responsiveness to human mission and the contemporary social dynamic.

Mindless arts cannot survive to serve men well. For these are quickly taken by those who profit in the fashions of the moments. There is a profound need now for a conscious contemporary philosophy of art and man, if we are not all of us to be left in greater darkness than before. That challenge, I put to you.

I concluded my remarks with an abstract idea that I intended in some form to be the main theme of a conference of college principals, which I would convene in the fall to reassess Columbia's course: "We need to design better ways to use the city as an active learning resource and inspiration of individual creativity—not simply, as now, to coexist with an urban environment. And as we take lesson from the city, so must we return genuine value and support."

In my zeal I may have incautiously hyped the failings of contemporary higher education in a comparative effort to distinguish Columbia's unique identity and innovative practice. In actuality, we sought only to be an influential maverick within the fraternity of higher education. Most certainly, we wanted collegiate respectability and the badge of accreditation.

I suppose I learned from my father's publicity stunts that the surest way to public recognition is an attack on sacred cows, and that even healthy animals have vulnerable flanks. But more than a bit of that would have been a tilt with windmills, though it is usefully known that nothing better mobilizes the troops than a demonized enemy. With that, we were carefully gentle.

Correspondingly, while I avoided public characterization of Columbia as an "experimental institution," which may have some connotation as "amateur," "fumbling," or "impermanent," in reality "experimental" was an accurate description. Indeed, compared to the educational mainstream, the college's very existence was an experiment in survival, even apart from our experiment with new student audiences, academic structures, teaching methods, and emphasis on part-time faculty who were working professionals.

Columbia's post-1964 path was a minefield of contradictions. We needed to preserve a familiar college identity, satisfy the strictures of accreditation, and at least sustain the inattentive neutrality of the educational community and its army of agencies and officials, all the while using an unavoidably combative rhetoric to advertise our contrasting unorthodoxy. Observing the delicacy of that equation was a constant travail. Of lesser importance was a serious need to shed public identity as a broadcasting school and simultaneously advertise radio and television which were still the college's most popular career concentrations. Surprisingly, the handicap of this narrow identity persisted even until the late 1970s, though the sharp contradictions of the college's pariah state largely disappeared after it was granted accreditation.

But also in the years after, much of Columbia's "radicalism" was subsumed by the mainstream of higher education, which embraced student diversity and minority opportunity, more permissive academic structures, close engagement of colleges and universities with their communities, and credentialing of part-time faculty who are professionals in the work of their subjects. Inspired more by fiscal than philosophical motives, higher education has neatly set aside its traditional resistance to curricula meant as occupational preparation. Today, virtually every higher institution's biggest enrollment is in business subjects, and few could do without enrollment generated by a vast array of once unfamiliar occupational specialties that are essential to the American economy. It is indeed ironic that serious study in scholarly disciplines, the traditional purpose of higher education, has been diminished by the popularity of education for business and other contemporary vocations. Perhaps even, in time, the historic identification of many colleges as liberal arts institutions may become a misnomer.

As an aside, the undeniable vocationalism of higher education today is a bit startling when I remember that only thirty years ago, Columbia was disqualified for its job-training propensities and "uncollegiate" faculty of working professionals. I suppose that knowing that many of Columbia's once embattled ideas have become common in American higher education should be satisfying enough without expecting credit for our early pioneering. But fame and fortune are illusive, as wistfully said.

I doubt if any colleges or universities in the late 1960s and early 1970s were as alive as Columbia with intense discussion of social and educational philosophies in relation to institutional mission, and with experiment in the forms and methods of education. This ferment had given vitality to the plan adopted in 1964, and it was my plan to again use an assessment of the realizations of that plan as the basis for charting Columbia's future course. With this purpose, I convened a three-day conference in October 1968. Its participants included Dean Wilkes, the board's new chair; Dwight Follett; faculty members Russo, Bouras, Schultz, and Jon Wagner; to counsel our discussion, Dr. Abbott Kaplan, the president of the State University of New York at Purchase, which was the "arts institution" of the New York University system; Dr. William Birenbaum, president of Staten Island Community College, one of the nation's most prominent progressive educators and later, president of Antioch College; and myself. We "retreated" to a suburban lodge, talked virtually day and night, and filled more than six hundred pages with notes of our discussion.

I reviewed the college's unprecedented progress during the five-year span 1964-69, during which time Columbia had successfully implemented, indeed exceeded, all our 1964 projections. Columbia had grown in that time from 200 students to more than 600 and we had tripled the college's space. The faculty had grown from fewer than twenty-five to more than one hundred, including twelve full-time members. We'd built a library of more than 10,000 volumes, created and furnished many new study concentrations in the arts and liberal arts, and provided sophisticated facilities in all communication arts concentrations. We had given new dimension to the college's urban character and occupational emphasis, sustained our pledges of low tuition and open admissions, and improved in all measures of institutional quality. We now even had a noticeable administrative staff. Though the college's current-year budget at more than $600,000 was nearly six times greater than in 1964, the college still suffered seemingly intractable financial problems, and fund-raising impediments discouragingly persisted. While comparatively Columbia enjoyed a vastly more popular image and reputation as an inventive college, the public audience remained very small and the educational community remained largely indifferent, if not hostile.

Undoubtedly, advertisement of Columbia's distinctive qualities and our charged contemporary rhetoric had convincing effects on our immediate membership. But it was probably unrealistic to expect in such short time the sympathetic interest of the larger community, and particularly, the ready approval of accrediting agencies. Such acceptances, however, remained as the college's goals. Columbia's ultimate prosperity would depend on greater student numbers and increased tuition revenues, which could only be realized if the college enjoyed far greater public presence, and that in turn depended on accreditation.

The conference's first day was spent on educational philosophies. If one would characterize the mind and mood of the conferees, it was that the college should seek ways to foster a participatory learning community that encouraged individual creativity, gave education a social reference, and caused students to take greater responsibility for their own education. The realization of such purposes involved a choice of routes. We could tinker with conventional college forms or boldly initiate a new educational pattern. We chose the more qualitative alternative, being carefully conscious, however, that Columbia's distinctiveness should not represent a radical departure from the common perception of a college institution nor subject students to uncomfortable and unproven experiments. Obviously, a genuinely participatory community requires voluntary engagement.

The conferees agreed that the projections of the 1964 plan had been achieved, and that Columbia had demonstrated the viability of a college that retained a comprehensive liberal arts education for students focused on a comparatively limited number of academic and occupational specialties. In usual college and university settings, general-education subjects are prerequisites to major field and career elections. While such study is unquestionably valuable, it is often remote from students' ultimate concentrations. The audience for general education is composed of the widest variety of students, and all, unavoidably, are expected to uniformly perform the subject's reading, memory, expository, and test-taking requirements, irrespective of a great span of individual differences in learning mechanisms, inclinations of interest, and creative impulses. In this respect, Columbia's liberal education had the advantage of a student body of similar interests, at least compared to the diverse, general-education students at most collegiate institutions. This allowed Columbia an

unusual opportunity to give students a natural motive for learning by encouraging them to express a subject's content in ways that involved their occupational focus. Write a play, short story, or poem; do a film, TV show, illustrations, or musical composition based on the subject of study. Such assignments are more likely to create an incentive for learning than tests and term papers. Moreover, Columbia had not followed the conservatory model of arts institutions which usually concentrate almost exclusively on instruction in their particular arts subject, either offering only minimal general-educational opportunity or directing students to general-education courses at other institutions. Ordinarily, serving a particular arts discipline, conservatories are unlikely to offer instruction in other arts and expect their students to be similarly focused. Alternatively, Columbia's project recognized the commonalties of artistic expression in terms of sensibility, creative impulse, and expectation of public audience—and the benefit of educating reciprocity between artistic disciplines and the enlightenments of liberal education.

The majority of Columbia students in 1969, however, did not have career expectations in the fine arts, and unlike arts conservatories, its students were not selected on the basis of esoteric possessions. Cultural biases aside, there is nothing inherently superior about "fine artists" versus artists engaged in more commercial arts expressions, nor in the dimensions of their talent or vigor of their training. Columbia students were then as now primarily interested in working successfully at professions represented by their college studies. Given the uncertainties and impermanence of employment, the relation between interdisciplinary study and employable versatility was universally understood by Columbia students, though actual instruction in these "alien subjects" met with some resistance. Knowing that advancement in one's profession might depend on knowledge of other arts or communication specialties did not easily lead to participation in studies that promised only deferred benefits.

The conference was first concerned with a restatement of the college's purposes. There were a variety of proposals that I ultimately shaped into a mission statement that remains with only small alterations today.

Significantly, the conference gave the titles "public arts" and "public information" to the college's main educational interests and characterized liberal education as "life arts." The conferees' view, "that those who choose the occupations of public arts and public information will communicate and interpret the issues and events and author the culture of their times," has remained in Columbia catalogs and publications.

At the conferees' recommendation, the existing distribution of liberal arts subjects was replaced by a requirement of forty-eight hours selected by the student, except English I/II and Speech remained mandatory; twelve hours in "basic studies" chosen from subjects shown above and including General Advertising, Radio Broadcasting I, Dance I, Theater, Music, and "The Black Experience." The requirement of a senior project was eliminated. The remaining seventy hours in a major field and elective study permitted students an opportunity to determine their principal concentration(s) and the extent of such specialization, observing study prerequisites and skill sequences required for particular subjects.

By removing a number of subject and credit-hour requirements, students presumably would take a greater range of subjects and enjoy greater control over their education. These contentions prevailed for a number of years, though their actual effect on students' course elections are difficult to measure. While students generally endorsed the benefit of freer subject choice, enrollment patterns over time did not reflect a substantial change in students' interdisciplinary inclinations, individual creativity, or embrace of personal educational responsibility.

A lessening of curricular restriction was only one element of the conferees' counsel. More central was their belief that Columbia's emphasis on the public arts and media of communication should foster socially responsive and independently thoughtful graduates and implement a recognition that the mass media and the arts needed far greater social vision and humane expression—all OK as the spiritual stuff of college advertisements, but too abstract to perform as a practical guide. Undoubtedly, we had practiced what we preached, and by word and deed had recast Columbia's identity. Learning environments can be changed. Subject content and academic structures can be altered. Unusually enlightened faculty can be engaged. But while such measures may influence an education, finding radical departures from traditional collegiate practice that will significantly better students' learning and the quality of their lives is an uncertain and often discouraging quest.

More immediately valuable was the conferees' proposal that Columbia make the city the college's campus and give public arts studies a more deliberately public character—a greater sense of audience and reciprocating social immediacy. This was to be achieved by relocating the college's theater, music, and dance departments, either together or separately, to Chicago communities, and similarly giving greater community expression to other subjects not bound to the college's central place. Moreover, the college's ability to create such satellites was enhanced by the fact that Columbia was small and without fixed educational practices and great investments in immovable facilities, in contrast to the unavoidable inflexibility of most big-city institutions. We observed that many of these had become corporate islands walled off from their communities, preserved by police and schemes of urban renewal. Instead, Columbia, without such restraints, was free to develop comparatively inexpensive satellites in neighborhood settings and to use these extensions for learning and community exchange. We did not intend to cast students in social experiments nor to use the satellites' communities for radical academic schemes. Obviously, the plan would have no merit if applied indiscriminately. It was only appropriate to subjects and departments that could be naturally extended to the public, such as performing arts, and surely not to subjects that require fixed facilities or where learning was individual and contemplative. Certainly, the satellite idea did not mean to replace the college's main location with scattered mini-colleges.

While we had previously mused about satellite projects, we had drawn no practical plans, and even with the impetus of the conferees' enthusiasm, many hazards lay in realization's path. Implementing the proposal would be difficult. The conferees observed that a strong sense of community, a "family presence," was evident among the college's members. They believed that this unusual fraternity was fueled by participation in Columbia's struggle for survival and identity, its democratic diversity and inclusiveness, and its representation of contemporary social and educational themes. It was evident that the college had the makings of a more participatory community. The conferees were uncertain how this could be put to good use and sustained. How to translate the energy of a strong sense of community into improved qualities of education and a greater learning commitment by students were unresolved questions. We felt certain that the community's feeling of participation in the college's life should be formally recognized. The conferees believed that official recognition would be signaled by reconstituting Columbia's board of trustees to enfranchise the now unrepresented constituencies, particularly students and part-time faculty. Such counsel was prompted by a belief that a more inclusive governing structure was appropriate to Columbia, and not inspired by popular agitation for participatory democracy. After three days of intense discussion, the conference adjourned. What remained were a host of decisions and ultimately difficult implementations.

In the months following the fall 1968 conference, the event's proposals were discussed carefully by board members, the faculty (both full- and part-time), and an encouraging number of students. Columbia's new mission statement and designation of the college's education as "public arts" and "public information" were popularly endorsed. Predictably, the proposal to establish satellite locations for performing arts and other subjects generated the most debate. It was generally believed that music, theater, and dance students would benefit greatly from community associations and audiences. But it was also argued that an immediate neighborhood presence would separate the performing arts from media and liberal arts studies and limit their interaction, remove many students from the services of a central college facility, and reduce the college's sense of common community. Moreover, a system of scattered satellites would be difficult and expensive to furnish and operate, and would entail expensive and inconvenient student travel. There was a strong feeling, too, that as the largest number of Columbia students had spent their lives in an urban setting, there was little, if anything, to be gained by putting their college education in noisy city settings.

In retrospect, many of these contentions were valid, or would be proven so over time. There is little evidence that neighborhood settings per se improved educational quality or performing arts students' mastery of artistic fundamentals, or that the socialization of the college's other disciplines or liberal arts subjects benefited by location in city communities. In fact, the performing arts centers—theater, music, and dance—in isolation did develop a life of their own, which consumed students' time and interest and largely erased any interdisciplinary study or liberal arts opportunity. In a sense, these outposts became focused conservatories with radical lifestyles. Despite all of this, students at these centers enjoyed extraordinary experiences, the benefit of artistic camaraderie, and unprecedented audiences of young people and community folk who mainly had never experienced serious theater, music, or dance.

Twenty-five years later, it's difficult to convey the contagious vitality of Columbia's music, theater, and dance centers and their lively and enlisting role in their communities. The centers' performances were packed with unfamiliar audiences. Russo's Free Theater, over a nearly five-year span, had a yearly audience of more than 25,000 for its musical productions. Just one play, Turgenev's *Month in the Country*, had an audience of 4,000 over a twenty-performance run at the college's Wells Street Theater. And Shirley Mordine's dance company, performing in a converted makeshift space in an old hotel at Belmont and Sheffield, was the authentic wellspring of Chicago's burgeoning modern dance movement.

Columbia's Theater, Music, and Dance Centers were located in the Near North Side and Lakeview districts, and these contiguous communities were the central sites of the city's artistic, cultural, radical, and new lifestyle activity, and included great numbers of young people in the 1960s and 1970s. The district was uniquely fertile ground for Columbia's projects, and the college enjoyed great visibility and reciprocal vitality in the community's life—so much so, that when in 1973 the college's accreditation examiners went out in the community to query public perception of Columbia, they reported that, "Every kid on the streets knew about Columbia," and all said, "Columbia's a good place," a remarkable response when it's remembered that many young people then regarded college institutions suspiciously. Such sentiments were a major cause of the college's extraordinary enrollment growth. We wrongly anticipated, however, that enrollment numbers would leap in the performing arts, and certainly in music. In actuality, while the arts and particularly music were prominent agencies of youth expression, such enthusiasms did not generate corresponding career aspirations. It was Columbia's reputation as a good college and its breadth of arts and media concentrations that made it unusually attractive to large numbers of young people.

Apart from matters of educational philosophy, the satellite project had practical motives. The college's quick growth and the prospects of this continuing made getting more space an immediate priority. We simply did not have enough room on Lake Shore Drive to improve anything, and we needed classrooms, instructional facilities, educational support services, and faculty and administrative offices. Photography and graphic arts suffered from primitive facilities, and despite the popularity of their subjects, we had nowhere to put an increased enrollment. We already occupied most of the Lake Shore Drive building, and it would take nearly two years before we could get space in the adjoining 469 Ohio building to provide sufficient facilities for these departments. And nowhere was there enough space to house a mature theater arts program, or any space at all for music and dance concentrations.

Some of the rhetoric of the satellite plan may have been idealistic "pie in the sky." But stripped of its unrealistic expectations and reshaped more practically, the satellite plan was an extraordinarily successful and economical scheme.

1968–1969: The Magic Year

In 1964, a new Columbia had risen from rubble. In 1968, the College's leap forward had a far more dependable launch site. September 1968 enrollment was up to six hundred students. The year's budget expected revenues and expenses in a $650,000 range, more than five times greater than in 1964. Faculty quality and numbers grew correspondingly. Among the new members were Milan Herzog, the Encyclopedia Britannica's vice president and authority on communication media, and its distinguished science editor, Louis Vacek; Howard Ziff, city editor of the *Chicago Daily News*; WBBM-TV director Phil Ruskin; featured journalists Earl Moses, Harry Golden, Larry Weintraub, and Lloyd Green of the *Chicago Sun-Times*; Lois Patrick, advertising manager of Carson Pirie Scott and Company; Aubrey Davis, vice president, Intergraphics, Inc.; Martin Cohen, president, Martin Cohen, Inc.; James Coufal, copy supervisor, Leo Burnett Advertising, Inc.; Bernard Lewis, President, Miracle White Company; Mary Agnes Schroeder, president, Mas-co Marketing; distinguished photographer James Newberry; Donald Newgren, director of design, Museum of Science and Industry; Father Richard Morrisroe, a hero of the civil rights movement; and Al Logan, director of human relations, Chicago Board of Education. Our faculty was particularly graced by an assembly of major African-American poets and writers, including Gwendolyn Brooks; Hoyt Fuller, editor of *The Negro Digest*; distinguished poets Haki Madhubuti and Caroline Rogers; and acclaimed novelist Ronald Fair.

Notably that year Shirley Mordine joined Columbia's faculty. Her recruitment began with Carole Russell, a prominent benefactor of Chicago arts. She had been a student and influential supporter of Martha Graham, the indisputable icon of modern dance, and Carole was rightly regarded as the doyenne of Chicago's dance community. She took me to lunch at Riccardo's (where else?) and told me excitedly about a young woman who was an extraordinarily gifted and original dancer and choreographer. "The perfect person to head a dance program at Columbia College," she said. At that moment, I had not even remotely considered beginning a dance department. But Carole argued that Columbia's arts vitality and progressive ideals could not ignore the legitimate role of dance in the arts spectrum. I readily admit that I knew almost nothing about dance, classical or modern. Indeed, my father had warned me of the "dangers of Russian ballet and mayonnaise," which I spread, I suppose, to include modern dance as well. But Carole's passionate advocacy made me feel that I was a philistine. I paid penance by agreeing to interview Shirley and promising that Columbia would have Shirley and a dance department if she was as convincing as Carole.

Shirley was a knockout, and so was the idea. I realized that the addition of a dance concentration gave the College a full complement of major arts disciplines and the opportunity of relationship between them. I don't recall what Shirley did at Columbia during the spring of 1969 except busy herself with organizing the College's dance instruction and recruiting a resident company of professional dancers, who would be paid only as part-time teachers. I did my best to learn about modern dance, which I learned to love. The dance project would be formally introduced in fall of 1969, though many uncertainties prevailed about public arts locations. Shirley had remarkable organizational skills and uncommon zeal, and I think it is fair to say that she was by example and organizing talent the authentic parent of Chicago's contemporary dance community. Most certainly the college has benefited greatly from Shirley's now nearly thirty-year presence.

Two people came to Columbia's leadership in 1968 and who would both have great influence on the college's life. In the fall of 1968, William Cobbs had resigned as the board's chairman. Dwight Follett was elected to succeed Cobbs as board chairman and he would serve in that capacity for ten years.

Follett can best be described in superlatives. Then in his sixties, he was a prominent American publisher of school and college textbooks, and the firm he headed, Follett Publishing company, was the nation's largest operator of college bookstores. He was a prominent Chicago businessman and a widely respected civic leader. Dwight was tall, slender, ruddy, and graying. A Lincolnesque figure, he had compelling dignity and grace, steely integrity, and immense charm. Utterly sensible, contagiously enthusiastic, plainspoken, and genuinely modest, he was the most gentle of men, and in every sense, a leader. He was a passionate democrat, in large sense Jeffersonian who abhorred social and economic injustice and had great compassion for individuals. He was an intense foe of racism and was the first American publisher of texts and children's books to picture African-American and white children together, and to publish books in which African-Americans were central characters.

Dwight was a thoughtful man who rejected dogma, was open to new ideas—even radical ones, and listened carefully to young people. An over age volunteer in the early days of World War II, he served as airfield commander in the U.S. Marines' Guadalcanal campaign. He had mixed feelings about the Vietnam War and understood the sentiments of the antiwar movement. A serious educator, he believed in bold experiment, and during his tenure as the board's chairman, Follett was an unfailing advocate of Columbia's mission. He was a wise counselor. I think it is accurate to say that whatever human beings are supposed to be, Dwight came closest.

And then there was Bert Gall, who has been a part of Columbia for more than thirty years. He began as a student in 1965, and in 1968 he was "the class valedictorian in a rice hat." For all my remaining years at Columbia, Bert was my close associate. At first, presumably hired to do this and that, he occupied himself as the students' tribune, advisor to Dean Wilkes and myself on student affairs, and the college's liaison to neighborhood organizations and campus activism. He was, and is, a versatile and able man. A fine organizer, he became an authoritative manager. He had endless energy, a careful eye for detail, and a firm commitment to Columbia's mission. He learned to be an excellent speaker and writer. A frail, ascetic-looking young man with a pale countenance and long blond hair, he looked then like Jesus Christ, not the tough "consigliere" he certainly became.

Columbia's enrollment had grown more than 300 percent in four years, and though we had more than tripled the college's space in the same time, what we had was utterly insufficient to an institution whose present scale had been unimaginable at the time of its skeletal beginnings in 1964. Gone now were my feckless musings about space, place, and permanence being only minimally relevant to educational quality. I suppose when the College was barely alive, I could cling to the myth that education can happen with a teacher at one end of a board and a student at the other. But suddenly we needed proper facilities for students and the variety of educational specialties we now incorporated.

As the Lake Shore Drive and Ohio Street buildings had other tenants, we could not expect to occupy large contiguous spaces in either building, though occasionally small, scattered spaces became available. And there was no possibility of creating performance spaces there for theater, music, and dance, and no expectation of attracting audiences to our peculiarly isolated location. We had no alternative to getting other locations, at least for performing arts, and only neighborhood locations would allow an economical opportunity to implement our ideas of college and community correspondence.

After some months of scouring the Near North Side, we discovered a cheap performing arts site on Grant Street near Lincoln Avenue. We thought at first to use the building principally as a theater and dance center and a graphic arts satellite. While Russo's Music Center performances were at scattered sites, we ultimately expected to include his project as part of an omnibus public arts center. The building we contemplated would amply accommodate classrooms and practice exercises, but a single rehearsal and performing space would have to serve Theater, Dance, and eventually Music. After remodeling, it would be an excellent small theater, but it would be difficult to schedule its use. The sharing of the television studio by the Theater Department was bad enough, and now to contemplate sharing a perform-

ance space between Theater Arts and the newly constituted Music and Dance Departments seemed impractical.

But that conflict was magically relieved by Bill Russo's discovery of a vacant building at the corner of Sheffield and School Streets that had formerly housed a Swedish Athletic Club. We bought it for $40,000 with a minimal down payment and a mortgage of only $400 monthly. It was a three-story building with plenty of space for classrooms and other uses, and its first floor, which the club had used for dances and socials, was an ideal place for musical performances and could easily accommodate audiences of 250 with bleacher seating. Bill named it "The Free Theater"—and that it was. The Free Theater never charged admission but the hat was passed (quite literally, a hat), and at over hundreds of performances, enough money was put in to the hat to largely pay for the building's expenses.

Now less troubled, we labored on with the public arts center project. We carefully budgeted its costs at $200,000 the first year, which included $75,000 in remodeling expenses and $25,000 in initial equipment and furnishings, and $100,000 in the subsequent years, assuming enrollment and activity remained constant. We reasoned that after the first year the expenses of the public arts center should be considered ordinary costs of the college's operations, given a reasonable expectation of enrollment growth with or without the public arts center. It was even possible, we thought, that next year we would have a surplus of tuition revenue that would help subscribe the initial costs of the center. Fortunately, we were rescued from such tortured calculations in July 1969 by the building's sale to another bidder.

I don't remember how it happened, but suddenly we had an opportunity to rent the old Esseness film studio on Wells and Eugenie. Back in the days of silent films, it was a famous movie production studio; after, a furniture warehouse of some sort; and lately, just an empty old building. It had a huge performance space without intruding pillars, and with its balcony could have comfortably seated an audience of more than five hundred. It was full of spaces for classrooms, scene storage, and dressing rooms, and it had plenty of bathrooms and, remarkably, a heating and cooling system in good order. Best of all, the building could be rented for $20,000 a year. We grabbed it.

Shirley Mordine's dance company shared space with the Theater Department at Wells Street during the fall of 1969, and then we rented the ground floor of an old hotel at Belmont and Sheffield as an independent dance center. I believe it cost $300 a month. Somehow all this good fortune erased the idea of an omnibus place of the public arts. In one stroke, Columbia's Theater and Music Departments had ample facilities, Dance had its own place, and all had opportunities to join the vitality of community settings.

In 1969 Chicago had no "off-Broadway" theater district and only minimal opportunity for theatrical or musical production of any sort apart from downtown theaters. Stage works, musical theater, and dance were rarely performed in community settings, except Bob Sickinger's Hull House Theater on North Broadway, Jim Shiflett's Body Politic in a converted bowling alley on Lincoln Avenue, Paul Sills's movable feast of Story Theater, "Second City," Val Ward's "Lumumba Theater" on the South Side, and the Old Town School of Folk Music. Modern dance was still a New York possession, and contemporary musical theater still awaited Russo's invention. In this barren scene, Columbia's three theaters and new audiences won quick visibility; and it was this sudden prominence that secured the college's arts dimension. With this, the college's narrow tag as a radio-television school largely disappeared, though it would take some time to be gone entirely.

A meeting of Columbia's board of trustees in February 1969 considered the proposals of the fall 1968 conference on the college's future course. It had taken some time to transcribe and circulate the 600-plus pages of the conference's discussion. As the faculty had done, the board endorsed the college's new mission statement and the proposal to identify the college's educational concentrations under public arts and public information titles. The proposal to create a satellite public arts center occasioned greater discussion. While board members agreed with the desirability of the project, all were concerned with its affordability. Since at that moment no specific building or location was in mind and there was no way of knowing what actual costs might be, speculations weren't practical. The members agreed, however, that a search for an appropriate facility should be undertaken, but the guide of economy should be observed carefully, particularly in regard to rental, remodeling, and operational costs. Additionally, the satellite's use should be restricted to the performing arts and other subjects only minimally considered. At subsequent board meetings in the spring of 1969, the board authorized the purchase of the Free Theater, and when the Grant Street project was abandoned, the rental of the Wells Street building and later the rental of the Dance Center space.

The February meeting's greatest attentions were given to the conference's proposal that board membership be opened to include representatives of the full- and part-time faculty and students. The proposition occasioned mixed feelings. In theory, the idea that Columbia's unusual sense of fraternity would be strengthened by inclusion of its principal constituencies in the board's governing functions was well accepted. But contemplating the actuality of such practice caused hesitation. There were concerns that serious conflicts of interest were inherent in board service by representatives of the college's constituencies, as these individuals would be answerable to particular constituencies and expected to advocate their special interests, as opposed to the all college concerns of a board independent of such influences. Moreover, confidentiality concerns would inhibit board deliberations. There was also some feeling that the college was being caught up by the current campus clamor for participatory democracy in governing colleges and universities, and that by embracing this advocacy Columbia would open the door to institutional control by irresponsible factions. It was argued that students, and to some extent part-time faculty, have only temporary campus presence and, correspondingly, would have little, if any, sense of responsibility for an institution's continuing life.

These not-unreasonable concerns were countered by arguments that board inclusion of several students and part-time faculty by no stretch meant that such constituencies would even remotely be positioned to seize institutional control, nor did the proposition threaten administration and faculty control over the educational process. The fact that students and part-time faculty would be a safe board minority did not imply that their proposed inclusion was a symbolic gesture that co-opted their voice in the college's affairs. After arguments that raged for hours, Dwight Follett, whose customary wisdom had the ring of authority, observed that democracy is always controversial and experimental by its nature. He believed there was nothing in the proposition to include students and part-time faculty on the board that threatened the college's course or traditional governance. It might be that confidentiality would be less than perfect, but there was no reason to think it would be recklessly violated. Moreover, he said, the inclusion of representatives of these constituencies could bring valuable ideas that otherwise would be lost to the board. This opportunity to codify Columbia's unique sense of fraternity should not be lost. If the plan didn't work well, it could be revoked, though he opined that such a decision might encounter some resistance. Follett concluded that, on balance, it was well worth a try. With Follett's remarks, contentions subsided and finally the board voted, with several contrary expressions, its intention to amend the college's bylaws to enfranchise part-time faculty and students.

While I supported the proposal to reconstitute the board's membership (indeed, I had developed the plan's specifics), I admit to having had some reservations about the confidentiality of board discussion and the possibility that student and faculty representation would provoke unmanageable decisions. In actuality, however, the students and faculty elected to the board acted responsibly. In fact, they all were constructive board members, and while they were genuinely representative of their constituencies, such representation, did not transcend their loyalty to the college's life and prosperity. Ultimately, we discarded the experiment, not because it was disruptive but because faculty and student constituencies, after first enthusiasms, became largely indifferent to board representation, and few participated in the process. Although Columbia's experience with elected faculty and student representatives was positive, I came to believe that their membership represented an inherent conflict of interest and blurred sensible separations of institutional responsibility. Correspondingly, I have a firm belief now in the value of an independent board. Certainly, all agencies of an institution's functions must be attentively informed by each others' intelligence, and easy lines of communication between them must be carefully maintained. Surely faculty individuals may serve valuably as board members or in any non-academic capacity if such service is not performed as a representative of a faculty constituency.

In the board's reconstitution, the service terms of board members were re-begun to correspond to the newly amended bylaws. Dwight Follett was reelected as a board member and chairman, and I, as a board member *ex officio*. Public members included Frank Anglin, Frank Fried, Seymour Gale, Don Nathanson, Don Mann, Alfred Perlman, Erwin Salk, Devorah Sherman, and new members David Logan and Alan Saks. The full-time faculty elected Harry Bouras and Gene DeKovic and the part-time faculty elected Al Peters and Albert Weisman. Later that spring, students elected Penelope Child and John Moore to serve two-year student terms. Moore has for many years been the college's associate dean of students. One hundred seventy students voted in the election, an encouraging number. Faculty participation in the election was more muted.

The reelection of Erwin Salk then represented his tenth year on the college's board, and at his retirement in 1986, his generous and dedicated board service spanned twenty-six years. Salk headed a prominent mortgage banking firm. He was and is in every sense a progressive citizen. A University of Chicago graduate in economics and lieutenant colonel on General MacArthur's staff, he served with the imposing title of "Wages and Hours Director for the Japanese Nation" in the first years of America's postwar occupation, and later, in Paris, as a senior official of UNESCO. For many years, Salk was chairman of the board's building and real estate committee with a critical role in the college's expansion. Salk's book *Missing Pages in United States History* was a popular compendium of long-ignored events in the history of African-American, Latino, and Native-American people and labor and progressive movements, and it provided the text of a Columbia course which he taught for many years. Particularly valuable was Salk introducing me in 1984 to Dr. Samuel Floyd, which led to Floyd's Columbia appointment and the organization of the college's renowned Center for Black Music Research.

The college's agenda was crowded with implementations of the 1968 Conference's curricular and governance proposals, finding performing arts locations, designing a fund-raising campaign, preparations for submitting a new application for accreditation in fall 1969, and generally, dealing with the college's many uncertainties. Full-time tuition for the 1969–70 college year was raised to $600 per semester with corresponding increases in part-time tuition. The plague of cash shortages continued, though Follett relieved some anxieties with his guiding view that the

College's deficits were not unreasonable or alarming and that borrowing money was a typical business practice, which in Columbia's instance, was satisfied by the personal guarantees supplied by trustees.

Sixty-eight students graduated in June 1969. A summer enrollment of two hundred students was expected, and fall 1969 applications indicated an enrollment increase exceeding 10 percent. Follett and Perlman urged a search for an experienced chief financial/business officer and a concerted effort to hire necessary administrative and clerical staff. Construction of new facilities for the Photography and Graphic Arts Departments was expected to be complete before the beginning of the new college year.

The 1968–69 year ended with a deficit of only $14,000 on revenues of $659,000, including $25,000 in general and Music Center contributions, a miscellany of activities incomes, and $673,000 in total expenses. An encouraging record.

1969–1970: Theater and the Chicago Seven

Seven hundred thirty-four students enrolled in the fall of 1969, an 18 percent increase over the last year. There were now sixteen full-time faculty members and, as usual, a number of outstandingly credentialed new part-time faculty members.

Among the full-time faculty was Staughton Lynd, who had a one-year, somewhat unsettling appointment. Lynd had an illustrious academic name, stemming from the renowned scholarship of his father and mother, who among their many important studies had coauthored a seminal work in American sociology. Staughton, who had earned a scholarly reputation of his own, was also one of the most controversial and activist figures in the campus ferment of the late 1960s. As a Roosevelt University professor, Lynd had been ousted for his radical advocacies, and particularly for his role in demonstrations by the university's students. Such activism aside, he was an inspiring teacher and popular with students. I hired him because of these qualities and because his engagement would publicize Columbia's academic stature and distinctive contemporaneity. While Lynd had been banished from Roosevelt as a prickly pariah, Columbia had no comparable state of campus unrest. I found Lynd to be a most gentle and thoughtful man with passionate convictions about injustice, economic inequity, racism, world peace, and issues of participatory democracy. Surely, he was not some wild-eyed agitator to send Columbia folk up the wall or against it. I have a faint memory that Lynd left Columbia to go to law school. I do know that he has had a distinguished career as a people's advocate.

While we had some added space at Lake Shore Drive and far more sophisticated photography and graphic arts facilities, there was still not enough space despite the Theater Department's relocation to Wells Street. Russo's expanded music project and a new dance concentration were, in effect, new departments, and their separate lives did nothing to relieve the college's acute space problems.

The relocation of the Theater Department to Wells Street was particularly difficult, partly because the transition had to be accomplished quickly, but far more importantly because the occasion coincided with the retirements of Lucille Strauss and her close associate, Al Peters. Unquestionably, they had been the Theater Department for more than twelve years. I had only the summer of 1969 to find their replacements. After a number of failed efforts, Paul Sills, Nick Rudall, and Frank Galati among them, Russo introduced me to Arnold Weinstein, who had a national reputation and recent notoriety for his stormy resignation as chair of the Theater Writing Department of Yale University's School of Drama. This followed a widely publicized controversy with Robert Brustein, the school's dean, which led also to the resignation of other faculty, such as Gordon Rogoff, with leading rank in the American theater. The Yale Drama School was then the premier place of theater education and closely associated with the New York and world stage. A celebrated playwright, Arnold was certainly a far bigger name than I had ever expected to recruit to Columbia's faculty, but at that moment, he was available.

Cast somewhere, I think, between early anarchism and the moods of the 1960s, Arnold was extraordinarily talented and knowledgeable, deeply humane, and generous. An intense friend, he could be sweetly gentle and mercurial in a moment. His engagement promised an exciting, if not unmanageable, time. But it seemed well worth a try.

Four weeks before opening, a new theater independent of the customary college setting was being built in a building barely adaptable to its purpose. Sixty-five unfamiliar students and only several part-time faculty resulted in a tower of problems and imponderables. With carpenters hammering, plumbers plumbing, and electricians wiring, it was an administrative nightmare. Arnold was undaunted, a happy state in part secured by Bert Gall, an instinctive organizer, whose construction skills were honed the first weeks on Wells Street. And nothing would have been possible without the tireless labors of Jake Caref. Arnold spent hours on the telephone spinning a web to catch the prominent theater folk he sought for his faculty. He got Gordon Rogoff as the department's cochair. He was joined by veteran actor Morton Lichter, Don Sanders, an extraordinary young director, and his wife, Vanessa James, who would become one of America's foremost stage designers. Hiring arrangements were vague, but all worked endless hours for miserly amounts, as did a procession of impressive theater names, who served in residence for varying lengths of time. While Arnold was a mad manager, he was an inspiring leader and teacher. Within a few weeks, students and faculty had the camaraderie of members of a kibbutz. All students had full instructional schedules and everyone was assigned to theater-support jobs with scenery, props, and costumes, and all had some janitorial duties as well. Students and faculty were enrolled in an encompassing way of life, which ignored time, personal commitments, and other studies. It was a cockamamie, disjointed scheme, but it produced a remarkable quality of education and of student enthusiasm. Arnold had no immediate plan for conventional play production, opting instead for intense scene rehearsals and improvisational theater exercises. Arnold's first term coincided with the courtroom spectacle of the Chicago Seven, who purportedly led the disruption of the 1968 Democratic Convention. Arnold created a living-theater format to replicate and interpret the daily proceedings. It was political theater made of the ultimate political theater then happening in a federal courtroom.

On many evenings, a number of the defendants and their lawyers came to add authenticity to the play-making: Abbie Hoffman, Jerry Rubin, Rennie Davis, Tom Hayden, and William Kunstler came with some frequency. Abbie, I remember, never came in the front door, choosing instead a goofy entrance through a second-story window, which required shinning up a light pole and crossing a roof or two. After a month or so, the living-theater experiment was abandoned to a theater piece, which Arnold composed of students' personal experiences and street observations. It was startlingly good theater, and the talent of the students was astonishing. In the spring of 1970, Arnold took what was to have been a brief leave to direct Lotte Lenya's off-Broadway production of Ovid's classic *Metamorphoses*. He didn't return for some weeks. In the meantime, Gordon Rogoff and Don Sanders managed the department and brought order to its chaotic life. At the end of the term, I had no alternative but to fire Arnold. It was a painful duty. I had great affection and respect for him despite his unmanageable and unpredictable presence. Even the occasion of his firing had a bit of theater about it. I had observed my father's instruction that if one anticipated a difficult firing, do it in a crowded restaurant where an alien audience would discourage a loud and uncomfortable response, and so I went to such a place to give Arnold the bitter news. I failed to reckon with Arnold's relish in an audience. I think he even stood up on a chair to deliver a virtuosity of profanities and harangues that identified me as a tinsel radical, class enemy, and anti-intellectual. I was stunned. The audience snickered. The curtain eventually went down, and we had a friendly lunch.

In retrospect, perhaps Arnold's brief tenure would have been more successful if I had had better opportunity to monitor and counsel his project. But at the time, I was preoccupied with the unrelenting demands of the college's application for accreditation. Arnold was unquestionably a brilliant faculty find, as his continuing career as a playwright, director, opera librettist, and lecturer attests. Regrettably, our twain didn't meet, but I still have every respect and affection for him.

Lucille Strauss and Al Peters had created a theater collective with similar vitality, despite severe limitations of space and student time. And they had gathered a gifted, selfless faculty who doubled as the professional core of a performing ensemble whose many memorable productions equaled the best levels of professional theater. I think that if Lucille and Al had had the opportunity of Wells Street, the whole project might have been more disciplined, though physically it would have been impossibly demanding for them.

Bill Russo also created a close fraternity among the Free Theater's students and faculty that was, if anything, more complicated by his inclusion of community members and professional musicians in the Free Theater's performing company. Russo came closest to the college's idea of a marriage with the community, and his model informed the Wells Street project and later Shirley Mordine's community-based Dance Center. Surely, Russo's introduction of new forms of musical theater and the immense popularity of its performances among young people validated whatever unorthodoxies he employed.

Theater by its nature is a collective enterprise which readily lends itself to close association of its members. Learning and performance are inseparably related, and the fraternity that develops in theater productions, or more so in repertory companies, inspires and fuels the learning and ability of its individuals. Obviously, this phenomenon has a lesson for all educational ventures. While group learning is commonly practiced at all levels of education, it might be more successful if its practitioners had the opportunity of a theater collective, or at least had been informed of it in their teacher training. Of course, Columbia then had the advantage of being a small place of interrelated studies, shared life, and an osmosis of educational methods. In time, perhaps some of these virtues were lost to the inflexibilities of greater size.

In the early fall of 1969, the college's board prepared to launch an ambitious fund-raising campaign. Its goal of $150,000 intended relief of the college's endemic cash shortages and provision of a modest working capital reserve. The plan called for a concentrated four-month campaign, which would require the most vigorous commitment by individual trustees. As president, I would have a principal role, and Alan Saks would head the board's effort. The Taft organization was engaged to man-age the campaign, and they had prepared a detailed plan and assignment of board individuals to specific campaign tasks. Foundations, businesses, and affluent individuals were gift targets, and names of prospects in these categories who were known personally by board members were carefully identified. The campaign's summary appeal was a beautifully packaged thirty-page book titled *Columbia College—A Contemporary Vision*, which I wrote and the Taft agency designed. All the campaign's lists, and materials, and special events were ready. After some months of preparation, the campaign was scheduled to begin in January and extend through April 1970. But with all that, the effort fell far short of expectations. We raised only about $75,000—half of the goal—and, of course, much less when the campaign's expenses of nearly $30,000 were charged. This was little more than the amount ordinarily received in a year's contributions.

Our campaign's failings, I suppose, were predictable. It was clear that without a full-time, experienced, in-house director of development we couldn't *ad hoc* our way to fund-raising success. It was also evident that no individual, however talented, could overcome Columbia's encompassing fund-raising disabilities. We still had no giving constituency, and our public visibility remained too slight and too recent to expect charitable generosity. We were largely unknown to foundations and funding sources. Despite the board's intense loyalty and competent counsel, it did not have individuals with usable affluent associations or the peculiar zeal to dig for donations, and our alumni were no factor at all. While alumni are usually a big source of private college support, they are much less so among big-city commuter institutions without religious affiliations, and particularly, as in Columbia's instance, when they serve students without privileged origin who are unlikely to earn enough in their careers to make significant contributions to their alma mater. Moreover, it's hard to spend years as a commuter student without the endearments of campus life and not have mixed feelings about one's college. Realistically, it would be many years before Columbia alumni could be expected to give significant financial support.

The discouraging results of our 1969 fund-raising campaign convinced me and other board colleagues that Columbia could not depend on contributed funds nor afford expensive campaigns. Also, we could not afford to support an in-house fund-raising apparatus or development officer until some future time when the college had far greater public recognition and a more supportive constituency. The best alternative was to make the college a profitable enterprise. More exactly, to fund Columbia almost entirely from student revenues, which, of course, had been and would remain the familiar financial pattern of the college's life.

Overriding all of 1969's urgencies was the college's application to the North Central Association for accredited status. The first step was to determine whether the association would even accept Columbia's application. Our previous efforts at accreditation had been summarily rejected. In retrospect, this wasn't unreasonable, as in fact Columbia fell far short of the accrediting agency's expectations, and Columbia's alternative educational practices were unfashionable. What impelled our reapplication in 1969 were the college's comparative stability, dramatic enrollment growth, reversal of many disqualifying faults, and Columbia's vitality. More compelling was our continuing certainty that accreditation was the indispensable signal of collegiate identity and the singular route to a more prosperous life. Perhaps we found motive, too, in the fact that "the times they were a changing," which might portend a changed view of Columbia's unorthodoxies by the accrediting agency.

After some months of difficult negotiations, I finally got North Central's hesitant agreement to accept Columbia's application for correspondent status, which was the preliminary institutional qualification for later seeking full accreditation. Being allowed the opportunity of making an application carried no assurance that North Central would approve the application and order the institution's examination. While we were over the first hurdle, there were many obstacles ahead. The application required a searching institutional self-study and a comprehensive narrative of the institution's history, philosophy, and expectations. If this extensive document was accepted, an on-site inspection of the institution would be conducted. This was usually a three-day visit by a team of examiners, whose recommendation would be submitted to the agency's Commission on Accreditation for final decision.

The self-study was a prodigious task, and we didn't have nearly enough hands to perform it. It required a vast compilation of detailed statistics of the college's state, measures of its performance, and defensible chart of its future course and improvement—all this within the context of a convincing narrative. In compiling this information, we had to assemble and interpret reliable statistics from years of indifferent records and disorganized bits and pieces of the college's life. We had to gather detailed resumes of every faculty member's educational and professional credentials, full- and part-time faculty alike. Perfect order was expected of current and recent student files, grade records, and transcripts of prior education. Our still-skeletal staff and all sorts of volunteers worked endless hours, nights, weekends, and holidays, from midspring to early fall, gathering data and perfecting our records. And then there was the bloody narrative to write and the application itself, which would incorporate all the data collected. These were particularly difficult. All our unorthodoxies required justification. Minuses had to be made into pluses. Our precarious finances had to be shown as evidence of confident progress, our spare college space, and performing arts satellites interpreted as ingenious implementations, and the absence of full-time faculty numbers shown as an emphasis on professionalism. In the first days of October, I locked myself away at writing the self-study narrative, interpreting data and putting the application in final shape for submission by October 15. Somehow, it got done. Then came the nervous waiting for North Central to decide whether we qualified for examination. The answer arrived in December, a Christmas present of sorts.

We passed! An on-site examination would be conducted by a team of examiners in late March. It was one thing to gather data, another matter entirely to have it in presentable form. All sorts of college things needed order and polish. And all the college's people had to be prepared for the agency's inquiry. Students, faculty, and staff needed orientation, the board needed careful preparation, and representative alumni had to be chosen for interview. Copies of the college's narrative were widely circulated. It was important, we thought, that everyone share a common perception of Columbia, and we needed to exploit the college's close sense of community.

The central themes were:

• *Columbia's main concentrations are in educating for creative occupation in the fields of public information and the public arts.*

• *Explicitly, our institutional concern is with the forms of social communication and the human potential of those artistic forces that shape the contemporary world: hence, the conscious interrelation of form and social substance within the Columbia program.*

• *Columbia gives a full, imaginative college education. It gives its students an opportunity to discover personal truth, to be involved in the life about them, and to acquire skills and use these to social benefit and personal and economic fulfillment. It is meant as an educational process whose first task is the enlistment of the student's purpose and his/her creative and social impulse as the instruments of their liberation: in short, to free students to engage their full powers.*

• *In 1964, we had fewer than two hundred students; a part-time faculty of twenty-five;*

no library; small facilities, very few resources; and an annual operating budget of less than $125,000. Today, we have more than seven hundred students; a distinguished faculty of sixteen full-time members and fifty-five part-time instructors; an established library of more than 30,000 volumes (fully contemporary, relevant acquisitions); expert facilities and working laboratories in all areas of professional study, including new performing-arts facilities in Chicago neighborhoods. The current year's budget is $857,000.

• *We have no endowment, public subsidy, or church relation, and we are not the love object of any affluent audience. Our impressive growth is the consequence of Columbia's genuinely contemporary meaning and social, personal, and career relevancy.*

• *The college is identified by its faculty whose members are serious scholars and professionals engaged with the contemporary substance of the subjects they teach. The result is a "classroom" with the real world in it. It is our experience that this faculty's teaching carries passion and authenticity.*

• *While the college makes scholarly demand of its faculty, it holds significant concern for its human relation: the rapport between student and teacher. We believe that this human connection is the source of inspiration. The genuinely good teacher has special gifts of more subtle human quality than an academic credential. Columbia seeks the gifted human being for a teacher in persons having genuine accomplishment in their art or occupation.*

• *Columbia wants an experience for students that leads them to find out who they are and what they can do. Columbia understandably has a student population with creative ability or inclination in the arts and media and motivation towards pertinent career goals or a medium of self-expression. The college makes no search for young people whose statistics seem special guarantee of college or career success.*

• *As a consequence, Columbia enrollment has not required finite screening, as there appears to be operative a form of natural selection in part explained by the evident attraction of the artistic, creative, and social focus of the institution.*

• *It is important, we believe, that we serve an unusual student population often lacking the credentials of cultural advantage, in spite of their possession of talent and career inclinations having significant potential for the entire society. We believe that our presence in this regard is important to the educational community and society and provides a largely unduplicated educational opportunity.*

No one about the college had ever gone through an accrediting examination, and though North Central provided ample instructions, we didn't know quite what to expect. Then suddenly, the appointed March day was at hand. We were assigned a team of three members headed by Dr. Erland Carlson, the president of Westminister College, a small denominational institution in Pennsylvania; the others, a dean and a faculty member, had similar small college origins. I think my colleagues and I were immediately hit with the perception that our team was utterly alien to Columbia's distinctly urban character, progressive spirit, and artistic life.

Dr. Carlson's team was courteous, friendly, and collegial. They did not seem to regard themselves as policemen of college purity. All had carefully read our self-study, and they assigned themselves to inspections of various Columbia functions and verifications of our data. They met with the board of trustees, students, faculty, staff and alumni, and inspected the college's facilities, including the performance satellites. Dr. Carlson met with me at some length. They had reasonable curiosities, though we had the feeling that team members were simply perplexed by Columbia's unusual character. To say the least, the ferment of the 1960s had escaped them. The only college event they attended was an evening performance of a rock music cantata at the Free Theater. I don't think they noticed that the cantata was based on a classical Greek theme. They seemed uncomfortable in a packed audience of young street folk, and a bit undone when a pretty young woman belted out a song and shook her décolletage at their front-row seats. The examination included an exit interview when the examiners announced their recommendation, which unsurprisingly was negative. We lost! Their reasons were virtually the same as given in our previous disqualifications. Our atypical college space was inadequate, our full-time faculty too small, our financial resources too little, and generally, our collegiate identity unproven. I don't remember whether Dr. Carlson offered any consoling or encouraging words. I probably wouldn't have heard them anyway. Gloom descended, and morale plummeted.

There was only a bit of consolation left in the fact that we had one more shot when the Accrediting Commission met to consider the recommendation of the examining team. That would be at the end of June 1970, and I planned to make the speech of my life at that occasion, though reversal of a team's recommendation would be unprecedented. In the meantime, we all stumbled along with the college's ordinary operations. Most of the college's folk never thought we'd make it anyway, and a few had even opposed the idea of accreditation at the beginning, so disappointments were muted. I was desolate and angry.

I wrote about six drafts of the remarks I expected to make at the commission's meeting; I also didn't know anyone on the commission whose support I could seek in advance. The more I contemplated the occasion, the more forbidding it became. I pictured them as stern members of a French Revolutionary Court and me transported in a tumbrel to the guillotine. The fateful day arrived. commission members smiled at me, and we exchanged pleasantries. Then I gave my lecture, which lacked neither poetry nor passion. They responded cheerily, a few even thoughtfully. Then Bill Wilkes and I went to a bare hallway to wait for the commission's decision. I hadn't known that there had been some recent debate within the commission about a need for new accrediting policies that encourage alternative forms of collegiate education and that while such advocates were a small minority, they were not without influence. After several hours, Bill Wilkes and I were summoned back to the meeting. More smiles. The chairman told us that the commission has discarded Dr. Carlson's and his team's recommendation and had decided instead to grant Columbia Correspondent Accredited Status. I was stunned and unfamiliarly speechless. Near fainting with joy, Bill Wilkes led me dumbly back to the college. Jane met me at the college door. We clung to one another. We had done it together! This time, the whole college rejoiced. We partied all night. It had taken fifteen years to get sight of the Grail.

I found out later that Morris Keaton, Antioch's president (who had aided me years before); Joe Elmore, dean of Earlham College; Laurence Barrett, provost of Kalamazoo College and Conrad Hilkenberry, an Iowa State University dean, had carried Columbia's banner in the commission's session. To the best of my memory, Columbia was the first "alternative" or experimental college to break accrediting barriers, and our advocates had chosen Columbia as the exemplar of their mission. While we suffered no immediately noticeable casualties in our March skirmish with the accrediting team, our failure would have had many troubling implications, which fortunately were avoided with the commission's June decision.

In the spring of 1970, the antiwar movement renewed on the American campus and suddenly exploded in response to the killing of four students by the Ohio National Guard at Kent State University, whose officials were held complicit in the National Guard's presence on the University's campus. The event horrified the nation and mobilized students' antiwar sentiments and their challenge to authority at many major colleges and universities. Riotous conditions prevailed widely. There was a call for a national student strike, and students walked out at many institutions across the country. Columbia was not spared the intense ferment. Albeit a minority, a significant number of Columbia students and some faculty and staff closely tied to the antiwar movement and the Kent State event organized quickly and skillfully around the strike issue. There was some threat of confrontation, more as guerrilla theater than a serious attempt to identify Columbia as a repressive institution. A number of student dissidents took over a basement storage room as a print shop to supply leaflets and posters to student strike committees at other colleges and universities in the Chicago region. All of this happened in a matter of a few days.

I quickly convened a meeting of faculty and leading staff to consider the college's response. The discussion was heated. Some argued passionately for a show of solidarity with student protesters, and some contended with equal vehemence that student dissidence should be strongly resisted. The majority sentiment, however, was that confrontation should be carefully avoided, as a show of resistance would only fuel the situation's theatrics. Ultimately, with few exceptions, it was agreed that response to the student strike, then expected to begin a few days later, should be to shut the college down and remove any likelihood of violence, damage, or confrontation between strikers and other students. All believed that Columbia's share of the crisis would peter out quickly, and a few days could be added at the end of the spring term to make up for lost classes. The alternative was to actively contend with the passions and theatrics of a comparatively small number of student dissidents, which could well lead to extended disruption and risked ugly confrontations and even a police presence. The idea of having to call police to the campus was abhorrent to everyone. Dwight Follett and representative board members agreed with the strategy. All students and faculty were notified that the college would be closed "beginning on Monday" and that everyone would be notified when classes were to resume. Without resistance, the strikers' enthusiasms waned quickly, and the college was back on track the following week, though it took a great effort to get everyone back to school. Many other colleges and universities remained in disarray, and many

called police to their campuses. A few institutions still clung to the notion that their police stance was resistance to anti-intellectual tyranny. It smacked of fascism to me.

While at the time of Kent State I was repulsed by the killing and wounding of students and had sympathy with the student protests that followed, I believed unequivocally that a strike and other demonstrations by Columbia students that cast the college as the enemy were entirely unwarranted and undeserved and served only as dangerous and disruptive exercises in the name of national student solidarity. But I harbored a private notion that Columbia's students and faculty might sense, however vaguely, that the college's inclusion in the national campus disorder was evidence that Columbia was a real college like all others, and that reinforcement of a sense of our legitimacy was important, particularly coming closely on the heels of our initial failure at accreditation. Of course, my speculations could not be validated, though they may, in some part, explain the surprisingly good morale of students and faculty when the college reconvened after the strike despite the abrupt disruption of study at nearly the end of the spring semester.

Despite the accreditation victory and continuing enrollment gains, 1969–70 was a difficult financial year. We lost $75,000 on the books, and our cash shortage was even more acute, in part owing to a recession in the national economy, a corresponding slowdown in tuition collections, and the end of draft deferments. The book loss was magnified by the start-up expenses of new performing-arts facilities and inclusion for the first time of scholarship costs, which in 1970–71 totaled $30,000. As Columbia had no independent scholarship funds, such amounts reduced tuition revenues. I had a private notion that Columbia had to provide scholarship aid and that those who could pay tuition had some responsibility for helping those who couldn't pay. I'm quite sure I didn't announce such "volunteerism," however.

Presumably a temporary measure, the board authorized an increase in the college's line of bank credit to $150,000, to be secured by larger personal guarantees by board members. While these guarantees financed the college's deficits, the practice also had the effect of severely limiting the personal contributions of individual board members, who were potentially on the hook for amounts ranging from $5,000 to $20,000; many of the board's public members remained at such risk for a number of years. Obviously, such great generosity and renewing loyalty was critical to the college's life. No board member ever had to pay any part of the guarantees they bravely made.

As we were constantly pressed for greater space and facilities to service greater and greater numbers of students whose revenues were necessary to fund the college's improvements, we were caught up in an unrelenting equation. If enrollment was capped, there wouldn't be enough money to do what had to be done in the absence of independent earnings from a large endowment, or a tuition increase of such magnitude as to price us out of the student market, even apart from the fact that much larger tuition would limit the college's accessibility to low income and minority students. As early as 1970, the whole issue was painfully evident and unsolvable. Indeed, we never entirely escaped the treadmill. Any increase in the college's expenses then could only be funded by the revenues of increased enrollment. Today, I suspect, it would take the earnings on an endowment of $200 million to be able to cap or lower enrollment and still maintain institutional quality without a dramatic increase in tuition rates, with the same consequences we feared in the early 1970s.

After Arnold Weinstein's departure in the summer of 1970, Don Sanders became the Theater Department's Chair, assisted by Gordon Rogoff and Vanessa James. They reassembled a faculty of experienced theater people which had greater stability than known in Arnold's year. Sanders was an inspiring and original theater director, and an exceptional teacher. While he, like Arnold, required a significant theater commitment by students and faculty, his plan incorporated diverse study expectations. In effect, he created a questionably successful mini-college for theater students approximating a conservatory model.

Both Bill Russo and Don Sanders organized student companies to perform in England during the summer of 1970. Their theater and music theater companies each included fifteen student performers and technical support staffs. The project was sparely financed in bits and pieces. Participating students were registered for ten credit hours at regular summer tuition rates, and the total amount went to the tours, as did all performance receipts. Additionally, the two departments independently got contributions from various sources and put gate receipts from spring performances in Chicago to the tours' fund. The college paid the project's faculty and some of their travel costs, and students paid whatever they could of their personal expenses. Russo and Sanders arranged busy schedules for their ensembles who performed separately and only occasionally on the same bill at British universities, festivals, and city locations. It was a boldly unprecedented project that required a professional level of performance by American college students in unfamiliar foreign settings involving difficult logistics and the burdens of transporting props, costumes, scenery, instruments, and sound systems. The student companies performed brilliantly to enthusiastic reviews. They left Chicago as unusually talented students and came back at summer's end as quite seasoned professionals, and Columbia enjoyed extraordinary publicity both in Europe and in America. Retaining almost all of the students who had toured in England, both Theater and Music Theater productions in 1971 and 1972 had impressive professional quality as verified in the summer of 1971 by the Theater Department's selection as the resident acting company at Harvard University's Loeb Theater, and by the great success of the Music Department's student cast in a New York off-Broadway run of Russo's *Aesop's Fables*.

The only cloud on Columbia's performing-arts horizon was a rumor that our Wells Street landlord intended to construct a high-rise apartment building on our theater space, a contingency allowed in the fine print of our lease. It quickly became a reality in February 1971, when we got a notice to vacate at the end of the spring 1971 semester, though the landlord did reimburse us for some of our remodeling expenses and costs of our brief occupancy. The cloud became thunder. We had only a few months in the spring of 1971 to find a new theater location. But again, we had good fortune. We got an old church at the corner of Kenmore and Wellington Streets, just a few blocks from the Free Theater. It was readily convertible to the needs of the Theater Department and particularly, it had a large performance space where church services had been held.

In the fall of 1970, the board had given immediate priority to a comprehensive reordering of accounting practices, an obviously critical function that had been imprudently neglected in the course of the college's renewal. For much of that time, we had only part-time bookkeeping, which barely furnished essential financial information, and only recently had hired a full-time bookkeeper, Millie Slavin, who was overwhelmed by a plethora of basic bookkeeping tasks. Millie had only the assistance of a part-time clerk who doubled as the operator of a primitive keypunch apparatus, and an antiquated bookkeeping machine little better than a typewriter with a wide carriage. Were it not for our auditor's prior reconstruction of our accounting records, it would not have been possible to even prepare annual financial statements. With everything else, and despite my questionable accounting skills, I was the college's financial manager, and given our precarious financial state, the job often consumed my attention. Even that wouldn't have been enough without the indispensable counsel of Seymour Gale and the board.

We advertised for an experienced individual who would become the college's vice president and chief financial officer. Of course, our choice was limited by the small salary we offered. Among the applicants, however, was Joe Ross, who had profitably sold his business and after several years of retirement wanted a socially useful occupation. He was closely interviewed by Gale and Follett and later by me. All of us were enthusiastic and all enjoyed excellent rapport with Ross. He was a courtly, friendly, and competent man. He had wide intellectual interests, sophisticated managerial experience, and high energy. Within a few months, he appeared to have organized us out of chaos. His deep concern for the college's welfare was quickly evident, as was his respect for me. His regular financial reports on the college's financial state were, in a word, encouraging. We seemed suddenly to be doing very much better. I wouldn't discover the explanation for several months. Joe was killing us with kindness. He simply stopped paying trade bills. I discovered piles of them in his desk drawers one day when I went looking for the college's seal. When I confronted him, he said he didn't want to worry me with distractions while I had many more important things to do. I panicked. Joe's incomprehensible news sent me "off the wall." My tantrum was interrupted by a phone call. When I returned to battle, Joe said he was resigning, immediately. He offered profuse apologies. I was a bit too stunned even to say goodbye. He was the nicest man, flawed only by excessive sentimentality.

1970–1971: A Critical Decade Begins

September enrollment in the 1970–71 college year was 814, a 13 percent increase over 1970 and consistent with annual gains in a 10 percent range enjoyed in earlier years. A bit surprisingly, the recent award of preliminary accredited status appeared to have little influence on student numbers, though without it, we might have suffered some of the enrollment loss being experienced by many small colleges. The new faculty again included a number of prominent individuals. Among them: photographer and physicist David Avison, who was an important contributor to photographic technology; featured journalists Ron Dorfman and Louis Koch; Barry Burlison, a gifted graphic artist; economist and social critic Martin Sklar; premier photographer Archie Lieberman; poet and social scientist Joel Lipman; historian Robin Lester, one of the first to use American sports as a subject of historical reference; and educator Louis Silverstein, an exceptional teacher who returned in 1970 as a full-time member of the faculty and administrative aide.

At the time of our grant of correspondent status, the North Central Association "expected institutions to seek full accreditation within a five-year period." But shortly after Columbia's award, "Correspondent" was changed to "Candidate for Accreditation" and institutions could choose to apply for full accreditation after only three years. We bravely chose that opportunity.

North Central advised us to engage an Association consultant to guide us in our preparations for seeking accreditation. They suggested Joe Elmore. It was a wonderful choice. As noted above, the dean of Earlham College, Joe Elmore, had been instrumental in the accrediting commission's decision to grant correspondent status to Columbia, which reversed the negative recommendation of our team of examiners. He spent at least one day a month with us during the nearly three-year span which preceded our final examination. In his earliest counsel, he urged us to implement a better fund-raising effort and lessen our virtually exclusive dependence on tuition revenues. In this context, he strongly advised the engagement of a development director and creation of a productive fund-raising apparatus. It took us nearly a year to implement this counsel, which would add substantially to the college's costs without immediately compensating returns.

In the spring of 1971, Herb Hoffman replaced Joe Ross as the college's chief financial officer. Herb promptly plunged into the swamp of the college's still disordered accounting and to the unpleasant task of placating creditors, particularly those unpaid during Ross's brief tenure.

At Al Weisman's recommendation, we hired Connie Zonka as director of public relations. Connie was an experienced publicist who had excellent press relations and great familiarity with Chicago's arts community. She was extraordinarily competent and was widely respected. Connie most loyally served Columbia for nearly twenty years, and at her direction, the college enjoyed excellent publicity that contributed indispensably to Columbia's growth and prosperity. Connie reversed the college's anonymity. Her first shot was to get a two-page cover feature about Columbia's virtues in *Panorama*, the *Chicago Daily News*'s weekly magazine on arts and entertainment. It was our first significant local publicity. In the same season, after a year of selling, I persuaded George Bonham, the editor of *Change* magazine, then the most influential national educational journal, to do a major piece about Columbia. Bonham recruited the highly respected writer and psychologist Thomas Cottle to write the article. He spent two intense weeks at Columbia gathering material. He did a seven-page article "Education for Survival: Columbia College of Chicago," which represented Columbia's spirit and intent well. The article put Columbia on the national education map.

In the course of the year, board membership was increased to twenty-six and its committee structure refined, including assignment of individual members to closely observe and represent the college's departments and principal administrative staff functions in board deliberations. In effect, every department was to have a board advocate. Seven new members joined the board: prominent attorney John Menk; Robert Rothschild, the publisher of *The American Encyclopedia*; Jack Behrend, whose company was the City's leading source of television and motion picture equipment; Deanna Bezark, whose son was a Columbia graduate; and two new student members, Dan Liss and Carole Coleman. Perlman and Anglin resigned because of pressing personal business, and though both remained good friends of the college, it was a big loss. Without Perlman, there wouldn't have been a Columbia College. The board voted a tuition increase to $750 per semester for full-time students in the 1971–72 year. The college's bank credit line was raised to $175,000.

Despite the fact that 1970–71 was virtually a break-even year, tuition collection remained slow and our dismal cash-poor condition persisted. In fact, we had a bit of money only because Devorah Sherman led an emergency board effort to raise $25,000 near the year's end. If anything was noteworthy about the college's finances, it was that for the first time revenue and expense figures exceeded a million dollars, an astonishing eight times greater than the first year of Columbia's new beginning in 1964. board discussion renewed about the treadmill effect of constantly having to furnish indispensable enrollment increases with new space and facilities. Particularly troubling was a report that a relaxation of subject-area requirements had resulted in an inordinate registration in courses that required expensive technology. And there was some speculation whether the policy of open admissions contributed imprudently to unmanageable growth. Neither issue was resolved.

1971–1972

The route of Columbia's success since 1964 was helter-skelter. The frenetic character of the college was increasingly unmanageable and exhausting. By the 1971–72 year, it was clear that we needed a pause to refresh and consolidate.

Nine hundred twenty-seven students were enrolled in the fall of 1971, only 5 percent more than the last year. It was a time of national recession. College draft deferments were minimal. Virtually no colleges had enrollment gains and most recorded losses. For the first time, there was a cutback in the number of Illinois state scholarship grants, which resulted in Columbia's loss of more than one hundred students who could not enroll without state aid; and federal student support was capped at the prior year's levels. At the same time, however, both Congress and, more liberally, the Illinois state legislature, appropriated money for aid to private colleges, which in 1972 resulted in grants to Columbia of more than $60,000, a state program that continues, far more generously, today. With recent preliminary accredited status, Columbia became eligible for membership in the Federation of Independent Illinois Colleges and Universities, which gave credibility to my energetic effort to lobby the Illinois legislature for institutional support and student aid, and I had a leading role in such campaigns for the rest of my presidency.

Herb Hoffman brought some order to Columbia's chaotic accounting system, but he too, quickly became disenchanted with the unrelenting duty of placating creditors who continued to complain about the college's tardiness in paying trade bills. Herb began the job on Joe Ross's down note, and it just didn't get better. He resigned in the summer of 1972, despite my entreaty that such failings were only temporary blips on a screen of noble struggles. Hoffman was succeeded by Ron Kowalski who, as the college's lead auditor for the Gale-Takahashi firm, was thoroughly familiar with Columbia's finances. After stumbling about for years, we finally had an experienced and dependable chief financial officer who was not overcome by the college's perilous financial state. In four of the preceding five years the college had lost money, the fund balance deficit had risen from $7,000 to $150,000, and cash shortages remained a constant distraction.

Television was Columbia's bread-and-butter department. The television studio was the college's most expensive installation, and its facilities had a despairingly short life because of rough handling by inexperienced students. Also, without backup gear, equipment could never be taken out of service for proper maintenance and, because of rapid technological change, equipment quickly became obsolete. Though we had installed new TV gear only a few years before, virtually everything needed replacement in 1972. That year, nearly $100,000 was invested in TV facilities, an expense made a bit less painful by comparatively comfortable lease arrangements. But it was still a big money shot. Library funding continued to be difficult, even with the help of a federal library grant of $5,000. The new space in the Lake Shore Drive building brought expensive remodeling costs. And we had the large expense of perfecting the college and preparing for the accreditation event anticipated in 1973.

With Jim Biery newly appointed as the college's director of development, the Board projected a modest fund campaign, partly inspired by Joe Elmore's counsel that we would have to exhibit some fund-raising competence to satisfy accreditation examiners, though the myriad things that had to be done for the accreditation visit suggested that a fund campaign could get only small priority. Though the accreditation die was cast, concern remained that full accreditation might restrict Columbia's unique character. Such purism had little influence. John Menk resigned from the board, as his election to president of the Chicago Bar Association would leave no time for the college's affairs. Richard Miller, who headed one of Chicago's major accounting firms, and John Naisbitt, who had been an assistant secretary of education in the Johnson administration and who would later become one of America's most popular futurists, joined the board.

Lou Silverstein was appointed as Columbia's dean and as coordinator of the self-study project, which would serve as the college's application for accreditation, though both assignments were designed uncertainly. We had twenty-four full-time faculty in 1971–72; and again, a noteworthy complement of new part-time faculty, including: Ruth Adams, editor of the *Bulletin of Atomic Scientists*; novelist Harry Mark Petrakis, who had been absent from the college's ranks for several years; Arnold Crane, a leading collector and historian of world photography; leading photographer Charles Traub; actor and theater director James O'Reilly; *Chicago Sun-Times* feature editor Robert Zonka; Helen Casper, director of retail advertising, Sears Roebuck Inc.; Jack Hagman, director of the Chicago Printmakers Workshop; Donald Miller, associate manager of WGN Radio and Television; and Jack Whitehead, a celebrated cinematographer.

At the 1971–72 year's end, it was evident that our cautious management had paid off. With total revenues of $1,352,000, which included $37,000 in contributions, and expenses of $1,299,000, we netted $53,000, reducing the fund-balance deficit correspondingly. While the college's "profitable" year could not have been accomplished without $64,000 in state and federal grants, this benefit was not a lucky windfall. Instead, it was Columbia's part in a national recognition that American higher education was a fraternal enterprise of public and independent institutions, and that the prosperity of the private sector served paramount public interest.

We expected to submit a formal application for full accreditation and our self-study document in May of 1973. If these were accepted by the North Central Association's Commission on Accreditation, the college's inspection would be scheduled in November of the 1973 year. A staggering amount of work had to be done in a short time to prepare the college for its examination. Of greatest urgency were the prodigious data-gathering tasks and the writing of a self-study document, which required a far more comprehensive statement and exhibit of institutional strength than had been required earlier as qualification for candidate status.

1972–1973

At the same time, apart from accreditation frenzies, the college's ordinary life went on. One thousand fifty-seven students were enrolled in the fall of 1972, a 14 percent gain over the year before. Tuition was now at $800 per semester for full-time students, still the lowest among the state's private colleges. The full-time faculty had grown to twenty-eight members, and familiarly, many outstanding individuals had been newly recruited to part-time faculty ranks. Among these were Thomas Alderman, executive producer at WBBM-TV; noted photographer Harold Allen; Ivy Beard, associate director of the Chicago Opera; community organizer Heather Booth; *Chicago Sun-Times* columnist Ouida Lindsay; Clarence McIntosh, executive producer, WTTW-TV; Richard Petrash, operating manager of WGN-TV; muralist Mark Rogovin; and Karel Jirak, formerly the director of Czechoslovakian Radio.

The uncertainties of Weinstein's brief tenure as chair of Theater had literally thrust the department's leadership onto Sanders, and to a lesser extent on Rogoff. Sanders, particularly, had labored without any time off through the 1969–70 and 1970–71 college years, and the student company's summer tour in England and at Harvard's Loeb Theater. James O'Reilly, a prominent Chicago actor and director and part-time member of the Theater Department faculty, became the department's acting chairman. It was a very difficult assignment, given the relocation project and faculty uncertainties, not the least of which was that Rogoff and his colleague, Morton Lichter, were not scheduled to return until the spring 1972 semester.

Despite all the handicaps, the student acting company had what *Variety* would have said was a "socko" spring 1972 season. Through their close fraternity, the result of two performing seasons at Wells Street and summers in England and at Harvard, these exceptionally talented students had become a fully professional ensemble. The highlight of the 1972 season was the long run of an original play, *Hotel*, developed by Don Sanders from perceptions gathered by theater students in the course of an assignment to study the life of a neighborhood, single-residence, "welfare hotel" with the unlikely name Hotel Diplomat. The students went about their inquiries with the zeal of seasoned investigative reporters, compiling a melange of human interest stories and evidence of exploitation (some of it criminal) of residents. The hotel was a potpourri of miseries. It would have been an appropriate setting for Gorky's *Lower Depths*.

A few weeks before *Hotel*'s opening, we began to hear all sorts of hostile rumblings and threats from the hotel's managers, and from dope dealers, pimps, shadowy policemen, and other unseemly folks who regarded the Diplomat as their business location. To say the least, the play's subject and its publicity threatened a variety of private interests. The sentiment was, "If you do that play, you'll be damn sorry you did!" It was a scary time. We did concede one thing: The name of the play, previously (and injudiciously) *Hotel Diplomat*, was changed to *Hotel*. We hired security guards and exercised some downtown connections to get police protection. The play went on uneventfully. Also, after a few official flurries, the students' exposé of the Diplomat's sleaze predictably dwindled to nothing. But *Hotel* was first-rate theater. Henry Threadgill composed the play's musical score, and his ensemble performed during its two-month run, which played to packed houses and was followed by an extraordinary production of Brecht's *Seven Deadly Sins*.

O'Reilly resigned his questionably defined role as the department's acting chair at the end of the spring 1972 semester; Sanders, Vanessa James, Gordon Rogoff, and Morton Lichter had returned, but all intended that as their last Columbia term. The Sanders, together with the principals of the student acting company, went to New York, where they founded an off-Broadway repertory theater. Rogoff became the chairman of Brooklyn College's Theater Department and senior drama critic for the *Village Voice*, and Lichter resumed a successful acting career.

I was left to scout about for a new Theater Department chairman, and by some hook or crook, enlisted Ronnie Davis, who enjoyed great national recognition as the founder and director of the famed San Francisco Mime Troupe. Davis was persuaded by Columbia's growing reputation in the national theater community, earned by association with Weinstein, Rogoff, and the Sanders. Theater students were intensely occupied during spring 1973 with Davis's unique production of *Fanchen*, an unusual play about a Chinese village. It was as much a lesson in modern Chinese history as it was a theater piece, and a remarkable project that involved a number of faculty across the college's disciplines. Ronnie Davis's Columbia engagement, however, suffered the same troubles and uncertainties that had punctuated Weinstein's tenure. These stemmed primarily from the impossibility of balancing an outside professional life with the necessary priorities of being the Theater Department's on-site chairman. Davis's tenure lasted only until midspring of 1974.

There was an unexpected change, too, at the beginning of the 1972–73 year, when Robert Edmonds asked to be relieved as chair of the college's Film Department and reassigned to the humanities faculty. He said he would enjoy such teaching far more than continuing as an administrator. While this wonderfully cultured man was qualified to teach humanities subjects, which he did until his death in 1988, he seemed an irreplaceable chair. In the brief span of six years he had literally built the college's Film Department, which quickly achieved an impressive reputation. He had assembled a faculty of fine filmmakers, among them the British documentarian Michael Rabiger, today chair of the Film Department. Edmonds was an inspiring presence. An unexcelled caster of puns, he was closely associated with the most prominent film directors and a respected colleague of the world's leading documentary filmmakers. Such film icons as Joris Ivans and Cavalcante served teaching residencies in the Film Department. But above all, Edmonds was a uniquely gifted teacher and counselor to students, rare qualities that generated exceptional student filmmaking.

Edmonds's successor as chair of the Film Department was Tony Loeb, who I hired after carefully whittling down an applicant list of more than forty highly credentialed candidates. Loeb had an outstanding professional record, a great catholicity of film experience, and an immediate understanding of what Columbia was about. As told, my recruitment was conducted in restaurant settings. In Tony's instance, it was a four-hour lunch at the Oak Room of New York's Plaza Hotel. Such a dining choice, I thought, would imply that Columbia was a big-time school. It was

the beginning of Tony's impressive and immeasurably valuable nineteen-year Columbia career.

In the fall of 1972, the Columbia College Dance Center had a new, permanent home on North Sheridan Road. Marvin Sugarman, whose daughter was a member of the Mordine Dance Company, had given the college an unimagined luxury, and Chicago its first place devoted exclusively to contemporary dance. It had an 8,000-foot unimpeded performance area with ample audience space and plenty of room on two floors for rehearsals, support services, classrooms, and offices. Jake Caref, who had almost single-handedly built virtually all of the college's facilities, constructed an immense, intricately laid dance floor and audience bleachers, and he supervised the installation of a comprehensive stage-lighting grid. It was a beautiful dance theater. Bert Gall, then officially the director of instructional services, managed the whole project. As Sugarman had also funded the Dance Center's remodeling and its equipment, the whole undertaking did not tax the college's perennially strained finances.

Apart from preparations for accreditation and submission of the college's self-study in May of 1973, the board's attention was focused on the insufficiency of the college's primary space both in terms of the scale of current operations and anticipated enrollment growth. They agreed that there was no alternative to acquiring a building, which had to be in a $500,000 to $600,000 price range, have at least 100,000 square feet of space, in a downtown or close-by location, and not exceed $1 million in remodeling costs. The real estate committee had a hard task and serious time constraints. Erwin Salk, the committee's chairman, and his board colleagues searched tirelessly for a new home. An exhausting quest, it ultimately took four years and involved great financial ingenuity. In November of 1972 they found a good possibility at 636 South Clark Street. It was an old warehouse and nondescript office building. It could be suitably remodeled, though the costs of that could only be approximated. The building was carefully inspected and the board agreed on a first offer of $200,000. It was refused, and subsequently we offered an acceptable $425,000 with a 10 percent earnest money deposit of $42,500 to be applied to the purchase price. Closing was set for November 1, 1973. We scratched up the earnest money from college funds, but board members pledged to raise the amount or increase their bank guarantees to replace the money taken from the current operating account. Where to get the rest of the purchase price and costs of remodeling was a big mystery. We first sought the help of a tax-exempt bond issue sponsored by the Illinois Higher Educational Facilities Commission, but they said we were ineligible because we could not show a substantial investment in the property apart from the amount that the bond issue would subscribe. Moreover, we had no endowment or other college funds to use as security.

This rejection gave urgency to the board's plan for a major capital gifts campaign. Jim Biery and the board spent endless hours planning the project. David Halberstam, honored in 1968, filmed a glowing testimonial to the college. All sorts of prominent folk joined in testaments to Columbia's critical contribution to American education and society. But dependable support by big foundations and big contributors remained scarce and the large gifts and grants that had to be in hand before the campaign's public launching were discouragingly absent. Although getting a new home for the college was plenty enough motive for a big fund campaign, why we believed then that we could actually raise big amounts escapes me entirely, particularly when we'd repeatedly been so unsuccessful on previous occasions. Hope, if not good sense, springs eternal, I suppose.

Our campaign was briefly encouraged when we raised nearly $25,000 at a benefit performance by China's Shenyang Dancers at the Opera House, an occasion arranged by board member Frank Fried, who was the promoter of the troupe's American tour. As this occasion was the first thaw in Chinese-American relations, a host of American dignitaries, State Department representatives, and prominent politicians greeted the dancers and Chinese officials on their arrival at the airport. I remember that we formed a long welcoming line and were instructed by a protocol officer to bow and shake hands with each of the one hundred or so Chinese visitors. Shaking hands and bowing simultaneously was hard enough, but repeating the posture quickly as each person passed resulted in a frantic bobbing up and down by the American greeters. The Chinese just broke up laughing. This scene was topped shortly after with a different response, at a formal luncheon sponsored by the State Department and state and city officials. This group was served what looked like forty-eight-ounce steaks, a surely unfamiliar repast for the Chinese, who hadn't the slightest idea how to cut and eat a big steak, not to mention that a big slab of meat was utterly alien and even repugnant to the Chinese diet. Our visitors literally blanched at the prospect. So much for the sensitivity of American protocol advisors.

In retrospect, I think that we were naively buoyed by the enthusiasm of our quick success, spurred by a need to give our accrediting examiners evidence that the college was not exclusively dependent on tuition revenues and that we would soon have sufficient space. But the illusion that we somehow could raise big money persisted for many months past the evidence that we couldn't. Once again we ignored convincing indications that major foundations, with few exceptions, were not inclined to give large general institutional support or fund expensive building projects, and large individual gifts were not given to small, unfamiliar, nondenominational institutions, whatever their virtues. Certainly, Columbia's populist identity discouraged support from affluent patrons. Nonetheless, we had no alternative to a continuing search for a building, though we quickly came to realize that we would have to find an affordable deal that did not depend on large contributed funds and foundation grants. By August of 1973, the Clark Street proposition had fallen apart. We had engaged Dubin and Dubin, a respected architectural firm, to draw a preliminary remodeling plan and estimate construction costs. They projected costs in the $2 million range, nearly double our original estimate, which had been based more on our resources than on construction cost realities. While the college's capital gifts campaign was not scheduled to begin formally until December, there was little indication that large advance gifts would be secured, with the consequence that it was most unlikely that the college would have the use of early campaign receipts to fund Clark Street's purchase and initial remodeling commitments.

In the meantime, I had discovered the possibility of getting space in the Rehabilitation Institute at Ohio and McClurg, just a block away from our Lake Shore location. The building was available because the Rehabilitation Institute was moving to a new building in the Northwestern University Medical complex. It was an exceptional building in fine condition, requiring far less remodeling than the Clark Street property, and it included a 23,000-square-foot parking lot. The building would cost $2 million, remodeling another $1 million. In short, we could get a vastly superior building for approximately the same cost as Clark Street. After careful inspection and dependable architectural and financial counsel, the board's real estate Committee concluded that the building and adjacent property was a great opportunity. They thought, too, that it would be far easier to raise money and to obtain commercial financing for an undeniably attractive building. The board authorized a vigorous pursuit, and at the same time voted to abandon the Clark Street enterprise. We tried to recover our earnest money deposit and ultimately got half of it back. The money spent on architects was just gone, though the Dubin folk were generous in their charges. Negotiations for the Rehabilitation Institute property extended for more than eighteen months until, regrettably, the property was taken off the market. Given the uncertainties, we renewed our Lake Shore Drive lease with added space until 1976, with options to terminate earlier.

We initiated a number of new programs during the 1972–73 year. These included a unique educational program, conducted cooperatively with Malcolm X College, the *Chicago Sun-Times*, and the *Chicago Daily News*, to provide study and internship opportunities to minority students interested in journalism careers. It was not meant exclusively as a minority project. This program, organized by Henry DeZutter, a Columbia faculty member, was quartered in space provided by the Field newspapers. Twenty-eight students had the opportunity to associate with a major news organization and the benefit of expert tutors, several Pulitzer prizewinners among these. A number of stories written by the program's students appeared in Field and other newspapers.

A new poetry center was sited in the theater building, which closely connect-ed students to the vitality of the city's artistic and literary community and to an audi-ence responsive to their expression. We initiated an unusual program, "The Artist as Organizer," which sought to train artists of all disciplines to develop new audiences and to be less dependent on conventional funding agencies. The college also spon-sored a mural workshop directed by creative muralist and faculty member, Mark Rogovin, which gave Columbia students an opportunity to study mural techniques and to work with artists engaged in a great variety of community mural projects.

At a March 1973 board meeting, Ron Kowalski, the college's chief financial officer, reported that there was every indication that Columbia would enjoy its "best financial year ever," a notice that replaced familiar gloom.

The year 1972–73 was one of issues and events, but nothing transcended prepa-rations for the college's accreditation visit. Everyone was marshaled to the task. It became apparent that Lou Silverstein could not lead the self-study and simultane-ously manage the dean's office. I chose a faculty member, Timothy Drescher, as a co-

dean to write the self-study, though Bert Gall and Lou Silverstein would continue to have critical roles in the whole accreditation process.

I had written the entire self-study required in our earlier examination for can-didate status, but I thought this time I would be too busy to devote myself exclu-sively to the weeks of writing the self-study document. The data gathering and con-struction were on schedule. Indeed, it was nearly done by March 1, and Drescher had begun the writing job. But, at midmonth, he told me he just couldn't do it, nor could he be persuaded to continue. I couldn't sensibly expect that Silverstein could replace Drescher at this late date. The only solution to our crisis was for me to write the self-study and by then, there was less than four weeks left to get the job done. With Bert and Lou supplying information and counsel, I shut myself away from everything else and wrote a draft of the document in two weeks of twenty-hour days, and spent another week on its revision. It got to the printer May 1, which just beat a May 12 deadline for submission. It was a terribly tough job, which at every stage required convincing justification for the college's unorthodox practices and imaginative interpretations of its data.

Somehow, it all came together impressively. Indeed, later, our document was cir-culated by the accrediting agency as a model self-study. This was not primarily because of its literary merit but because Columbia had made a candid effort to study itself in a contemporary social and philosophical context and to examine the effect of its education and distinctive college environment on its students. Such official endorsement of our self-study is a bit difficult to fathom, as I can't imagine that conventional institutions would find Columbia's description and philosophies instructive.

Forty-six members of Columbia's community had significant roles in the self-study, not counting a host of data gatherers and clerical assistants. All instructional and administrative departments, single-member functions, the board of trustees, and even the building staff were engaged in study of their purviews. Everything about Columbia past, present, and future, from its mission to the cleanliness of its corridors, was carefully studied. Literally hundreds of students and alumni, both graduates and dropouts, were personally interviewed, as were more than one hundred employers of students and graduates. We depended little on questionnaires. There were countless meetings. Nothing about Columbia escaped serious inquiry. It was a mammoth task with revelations that went far beyond the requirements of accreditation. And many of the study's insights would serve to guide the college for years.

Today, twenty-five years later, our assertions may seem only rhetorical idealism. While, undoubtedly, our implementations had mixed results, I submit with certainty that our unorthodoxy performed uniquely well then as the conscious guide of an inventive and effective educative process, which was invested with a sense of purpose and definition not common to American higher education.

The 1972–73 year ended on a good note. It had been, as Kowalski predicted, the college's best financial year. When everything had been sorted out, the year's revenues, including state and federal grants and contributions, exceeded expenses by $209,000, an amount which scrubbed the college's perennial deficit and became a $109,000 plus figure. We weren't out of the woods, but for the first time, we could see the clearing beyond.

1973–1974: Accreditation at Last

We enrolled nearly 1,100 students in fall 1973, a 5 percent gain, cheering when compared with falling college enrollments nationally. We had twenty-eight full-time faculty members. For the record: (Photography) Lynn Sloan, Brian Katz, Charles Traub, James Newberry; (Television) Thaine Lyman; (Radio) Al Parker; (Film) Anthony Loeb, Chap Freeman, Michael Rabiger; (Mass Communication) Gene DeKovic; (Graphic Arts) Barry Burlison; (Dance) Shirley Mordine, Susan Kimmelman; (Music) William Russo, Joe Riser; (Theater) Ron Davis, Vanessa James, Fritzie Sahlins; (Poetry/Literature) Paul Carroll, Joel Lipman; (Social Sciences) Betsy Edelson; (Humanities) Harry Bouras, Robert Edmonds; (English/Writing) John Schultz, Betty Shiflett, Lynn McNulty, Paul Pekin, and Dan Michalski. We had a number of new part-time faculty, including film critic Roger Ebert; Lynn Hammond, director of the Chicago Weaving Workshop; Tai Chi Chuan master Herbert Lui; theologian Father Richard Sullivan; John Wabaunsee, director, Native American Legal Fund; Quentin Young, Director of Medicine, Cook County Hospital; columnist Ruth Ratney; Bruce Jacobson, potter and director, "The Clay People." Also we had a sufficient administrative staff and a satisfying complement of instructional specialists, librarians, and student-service personnel. We had the look and feel of a real college.

In my fall 1973 board report, I noted that Columbia's Photography and Film departments had achieved prominent national rank; that the Art/Graphics Department had expanded its curriculum to include a new emphasis in craft arts;

that the English Writing department had won significant national recognition, as verified by the news that the *Journal of the National Council of Teachers of English* would devote its entire November 1973 issue to Columbia's Story Workshop, by a new grant to the department to fund training of junior college teachers, and by the fourth-year renewal of its project to train Chicago public school teachers in using Story Workshop methods; that the unusually successful urban journalism program had begun its second year; that Radio and Television continued to enjoy the highest reputation and now new facilities, expanded curriculum, and impressive enrollment gains; and that the college's community-based Music, Theater, and Dance Departments had much increased popularity and strengthened community relations. With Columbia's sponsorship, the college's African-American student organization had conducted a three-day conference in the summer of 1973 at the Hilton Hotel, which attracted a national audience of more than five-hundred delegates to plan a national campaign to increase minority employment in journalism and the media industries. Moreover, the board authorized design of health and medical insurance and pension plans for Columbia's employees, and employment security and due process agreements for full-time faculty, all to be formally considered at subsequent board meetings.

The college's paramount concern in fall 1973 was on the accreditation visit scheduled for November 26, 27, and 28. We had a swirling Rubicon to cross, and in the meantime, a welter of last-minute preparations. We rehearsed everyone. Students were alerted to the importance of the occasion. The whole college community was prepped and ready. On the Sunday evening before the visit, I met with the examining team's chairman, Dr. Laurence Barrett, chairman of the Great Lakes Colleges Association and provost of Kalamazoo College. He was friendly, encouraging, and most complimentary about our self-study. Monday morning, he said the team would meet with whomever I selected to plan the visit. He disarmed my worst fears, though my jangled suspicions were unrelieved.

On Monday morning, Lou Silverstein and Bert Gall, our best faculty spokespersons, and I were introduced to the examining team. In addition to Barrett, the team included Dr. Florence Brown, chair of the Division of Social Science, Meremec Community College; Dr. Melvin Davidson, chair of Performing Arts, Stephens College; Dr. George Langeler, dean of students, Oberlin University; Dr. Arlene Metha, professor of the College of Education, Arizona State University; and Dr. James Rose, professor of drama, Antioch College. In retrospect, I can't imagine a team of more sensitive, thoughtful, progressive educators. Together we scheduled interviews and inspections encompassing every aspect of the college's life and operation, including meetings with faculty, administrators, students, alumni, and the board. The team's inquiry was indeed thorough. The college and its satellites were spotless. Everything was perfectly accessible. We had even scheduled performances at the Music, Theater, and Dance Centers and recruited full and enthusiastic audiences for their occasions. We assembled groups of alumni, all of whom had impressive professional credentials. I suppose it could be said that we put on a great show.

The examination was a collective love-in that, as legend has it, was the most perfect example of the best intentions of the whole idea of accreditation. The team's open counsel was in every sense genuinely fraternal. We shared ideas about education with them. Quite astonishingly, the team members said they had found much about Columbia that they would try to incorporate in their own institutions. It all couldn't have been better.

On Wednesday afternoon we had the team's verdict. They announced that they would recommend that Columbia be granted full unconditional accreditation for five years, the maximum allowed newly accredited institutions. We'd made it! Twenty-five years later, I admit I get choked up writing about that time. Needless to say, we partied with great enthusiasm when the team had gone. We were damn good at doing that! But first, I called Joe Elmore. We never could have done without his wise counsel. And as for the team's remarkable chairman, Larry Barrett, I have not words enough to properly acknowledge his insightful intelligence and progressive spirit. He was a true educator in every sense of its meaning. Excerpts from the accreditation report are in the appendix.

While we celebrated the examining team's endorsement, their recommendation was not formal notice of the college's accreditation, as official designation could only be granted by the North Central Association's Accreditation Commission, which would act in the late spring of 1974. While a mishap was unlikely, some uncertainties remained. Columbia's accreditation would represent a radical departure from the agency's traditional standards, a change which would be likely to influence the views of other regional accrediting organizations. Undoubtedly, North Central's Commission would carefully consider its response, though we estimated that a commission which had boldly reversed our earlier denial would not be likely to abandon its evident sentiment in denying our eligibility now. In the meantime, however, Columbia could not advertise fully accredited status, though happily in June 1974, the award did become official. Lou Silverstein and I were invited to the commission's session after what appeared to have been a unanimous endorsement, which occasioned most hearty congratulations, even including that of our once nemesis, Dr. Carlson. I thanked the commission's members for their grant and in turn congratulated them for their break with accreditation traditions. When Lou and I got back to the college, the lobby was decorated with bright bunting, and all of the college's staff and numbers of faculty were crowded into my office and its corridor.

After the examining team's elevating visit in November 1973, the college settled down to some sort of "normalcy," though we stayed high on the examiner's report, which undeniably was a ringing endorsement of Columbia's experiment and a validation of the college's unorthodox practice. Our accomplishment was unprecedented, particularly so because it had been done in less than ten years without sacrifice of the principles which made Columbia a genuinely unique and distinguished college. In short, the grant of accreditation justified what Columbia was about and gave worth to our perseverance through hard, troubling times.

In the immediate months after, the board, persuaded by the college's first profitable year and by our expected accreditation, endorsed a pension plan for all full-time employees and an employment security agreement for full-time faculty. Both measures reflected the board's confidence in Columbia's permanence, though such expectation was fueled more by fragile promise than dependable certainty. Although its benefits were small, the pension plan adopted in 1974 was the beginning of what ultimately would be a generous retirement program.

What a year it was! Accreditation was transformative, the major event in Columbia's history: surely so in the ten-year span since the college's renewal in 1964. The immediate effect of accreditation was uncertain. In all likelihood it would be known only over time. But the fact that Columbia was now a fully accredited college would give us greater public legitimacy and greater respect by the educational community and related agencies. Until the fall 1974 enrollment was counted, we would not know if accreditation would influence student numbers. We had only the briefest time to advertise our new status.

In financial terms, 1973–74 had been modestly profitable despite some unusual expenses. While it was apparent at year's end that the college's fund-raising would be little more successful than previous failed attempts, the fiction continued with dwindling attention for some months. The death of the project was barely noticed, except that Jim Biery resigned, though he was without fault in the failure. The college's experiment with student board membership also died unnoticed. The students were as little interested in its death as they had been in its life. So perished, we thought, another of the illusions of the 1960s.

Within a year, however, the subject of student board representation was back, a revival prompted by immediate student concerns, including tuition, class fees, state and federal student aid subsidies, some complaints about the shabby state of the Theater-Music satellite, and the "secrecy" of the college's financial statements. None of this had the ideological trappings of earlier agitations for campus democracy. To mix a metaphor, this was the voice of Columbia's grass roots. Within a few weeks in the spring of 1975, the dissidents organized a student senate, formed several committees of concerned students, and enlisted the *Columbia Chronicle* staff. (It may be remembered that this was the time of Watergate, when journalism students everywhere wanted to be investigative reporters like Woodward and Bernstein.)

A special board meeting was convened to meet with the students, who were armed with a questionnaire completed by more than four hundred students. It was all quite polite. We had delayed announcement of 1975–76 tuition rates because of many uncertainties about the levels of expected student aid. The board agreed to publish rates within forty-five days and to examine class fees and, wherever possible, to reduce them. We acknowledged the shabby condition of the Theater-Music Center. We explained that a decision about its renovation depended on a resolution of the college's general building plans, which remained uncertain; but in the meantime, every practical repair would be done promptly.

Perlman and Follett, speaking for the board, emphasized that the decision to end student board representation had been made reluctantly because of lack of student interest, and that the provision would be reinstated in response to renewed student demand, and that financial statements would be made more accessible. I observed that the subject of state and federal student aid was a political issue that could not be decided on Columbia's campus, though the college, and I particularly, had a leading role in attempts to influence Congress and the Illinois legislature to significantly increase student aid funding. At the meeting, I proposed that the students organize a letter and petition campaign directed at their state legislators and congressional representatives urging support for increased student aid funds. Later, Bert Gall, Hubert Davis, and a number of students organized a Columbia campaign that gathered individual messages from more than six hundred students, and these were delivered to Illinois legislators in Springfield by a delegation of twenty students. Indeed, such lobbying, organized by then Dean of Students Hubert Davis, became a familiar Columbia "rite of spring" for many years after, leading by example to demonstrations in Springfield by students from many Illinois colleges and universities. Regrettably, except for student aid passions, activism among Columbia students rose suddenly and fell almost as quickly, though student board participation continued for several more years before succumbing again to universal indifference.

1974–1975: Enrollment Grows

If we had any doubt about whether accreditation would influence enrollment, the answer was quickly evident in fall 1974 student numbers. More than 1,400 enrolled: 900 full-time and 500 part-time, a 30 percent gain over the year before. We had some sense of this increase at the beginning of the summer of 1974 and had added space in the 469 Ohio annex, which allowed consolidation of graphics, craft arts, and photography, and taken more space in the Lake Shore Drive building. The additions required extensive remodeling and instructional facilities, and we had only limited time to complete the work. Bert Gall managed the impossible project with his usual acuity, and Jake Caref contributed his indefatigable labors. Lou Silverstein had the equally trying task of organizing teachers and classes to serve a 30 percent increase in student numbers. Somehow, everything was readied for September's opening sessions. We had not run out of miracles. The college's enrollment was quite remarkable in view of a national recession and continuing enrollment losses by most colleges.

Columbia's tuition had risen to $870 per semester ($1,740 per college year) for full-time students and $75 per credit hour for part-time students, still the lowest among Illinois private institutions. A new intensive midyear three-week session between the fall and spring semesters was offered to give students the opportunity to pursue individual projects and to earn credit hours, which, with summer enrollment, could shorten their college time to three years. Midyear intensives were abandoned after several years. Three weeks gave too little time to concentrate on a project, and the notion of graduating more quickly didn't fit the irregular pattern of Columbia's enrollment.

In September 1974, the Barry Street site of the Theater Department was closed. Building maintenance costs had become excessive and uncertainties in the department's leadership lowered enrollment projections. A less than ideal solution was to combine the Theater and Music Departments in the Music Center building. Competitions for space and authority were troubling consequences. More significantly, the whole idea of neighborhood performing-arts satellites was tattered. They had become mini-conservatories whose independent lives and singular concentrations were increasingly separated from the benefits of a college environment—its subject diversity and sense of shared community. While both departments had created remarkably successful theaters, it was questionable whether what had become a nearly exclusive focus on public performance left room for instruction and classroom practice. Such concern was more prominent in relation to the Music Department, where performances of the Free Theater Company were the main occupation, with little distinguishing Columbia students and community members, except that Columbia students had independent classroom instruction, paid regular tuition, and earned college credits, and community folk paid only a small fee for their membership in the performing company. Predictably, the satellites were increasingly expensive. Fritzie Sahlins became acting chair of the Theater Department's reduced circumstances. Charles Traub replaced Jim Newberry as the chair of the Photography Department. He was an exceptional choice. With his leadership, the department won impressive national reputation. Barry Burlison was formally appointed as chair of the Graphic Arts Department, which included a new craft arts emphasis.

Jack Wolfsohn, who was an experienced fund-raising executive and my oldest friend, became the college's development officer, a role he would perform outstandingly for fifteen years. While there was little expectation of major gifts and grants, and the large ambitions of a capital campaign were discarded, Jack quickly designed a number of more realistic initiatives that increased annual giving and secured the interest of major foundations and government agencies.

At the board's November 1974 meeting, Dwight Follett resigned as chairman, though he would remain a board member for many more years. His service to Columbia was incalculable. Dwight was succeeded as chairman by Alfred Perlman, who had returned to the board.

Though we had failed to get either the Clark Street or Rehabilitation Institute properties, the college's need for a new home remained. If anything, it was made even more urgent by the city's building department, which contended that the 540/469 buildings did not satisfy school codes. While such belated determination was inexplicable in view of the department's consistent approval during our ten-year occupancy, they nonetheless pressed their claim. The real estate committee continued to hunt. We inspected and rejected a number of prospective sites. The chase was full of disqualifications. "It wasn't the right building." "It was too expensive." "It would cost too much to remodel." "The financing was too difficult." After months of search, we came across a possibility, the Theological Seminary at the corner of Oak and Dearborn Streets. It was a splendid location, and a big enough, remodelable space likely to be in our price range. The seminary had moved to the University of

Chicago campus, so the building was vacant. However, after some weeks of deliberation, the seminary's board couldn't decide on a price and terms. We had to give up. Then a casual conversation between Perlman and Joseph Shapiro suggested that a building at Michigan and Harrison, which Shapiro and his partners owned, might be available. By coincidence, the owners were good friends of many of our board members. A meeting was quickly arranged. The owners were anxious to sell, and all had a sympathetic regard for Columbia.

It was a bigger building than any of us had ever imagined as Columbia's home. It had 200,000 square feet, sixteen floors, a marbled lobby and six elevators. Bert Gall and I went to look at it. In my head it was the Empire State Building; that this might be Columbia's home was beyond my belief. I suppose my mind was still fixed on ten years before when all of Columbia was 7,000 square feet in an old warehouse building. A 200,000-square-foot space meant we'd never need another inch. Later, Dwight Follett would share my astonishment. Our real estate committee, however, never blinked. They only sharpened their flinty eyes. They were ready for negotiations. That effort would wait for several months while Bert Gall gathered data about the costs of remodeling and code compliance. He consulted closely with architects and engineers and scores of experts: plumbing, electrical, carpentry, painting, and heating, air-conditioning, and ventilation contractors. He assembled a big volume of plans and cost figures. What's startling is that no one on our board of big-dealers even remotely questioned whether Bert was the right person to manage this critical inquiry, despite the fact that he really didn't know much of anything then about a big construction job. But he sure was the right guy; he may have begun the project as a novice but he ended it as an authority. The building was about 40 percent occupied and we planned initially to remodel 60,000 feet to serve 2,000 to 2,400 students, if such numbers were reached in 1977–78 and 1978–79. But the city required that the whole structure had to satisfy school building codes, whether or not we occupied all the space. That was an expensive discovery.

Bert's preliminary figures estimated our initial remodeling costs at $1 million, if some construction could be deferred until the following year. He calculated that it would cost $240,000 a year to operate the building and service existing tenants, who would provide approximately the same amount in rental income. Remodeling costs did not include payments to architects and structural engineers, and there was no way of estimating future building operating expenses if tenants would be replaced by the college. Somehow the numbers seemed affordable. Our negotiators, Steve Neumer and Sam Baskin, in close consultation with other committee members, finally struck a deal at the end of August 1975.

The price was $1,325,000 requiring a down payment of $150,000. The owners would issue a mortgage in the amount of $1,175,000, requiring the payment of $200,000 in $50,000 installments between September 1976 and June 1977. The remaining $975,000 balance was payable in monthly installment based on a thirty-year schedule at 7–10 percent interest rates, with a balloon payment of the balance due on October 15, 1985. If the outstanding principal was paid before 1980, the owners would refund $100,000 to the college. Additionally, the college would be obligated to pay $20,000 annually for a 115-year term to the holders of the building's ground lease. Real estate taxes would have to be paid until the college occupied the entire building. Figures on this would depend on negotiations with tax authorities.

Getting a building of such size and price with a prominent Michigan Avenue location was a great deal. Nonetheless, it was awfully big bucks to pikers like us. Kowalski prepared all sorts of financial projections which contended that the venture could be afforded if we could subscribe initial remodeling costs and the down payment by squeezing college revenues, securing a line of bank credit, getting significant capital gifts and foundation grants. Erwin Salk banged away at the Continental Illinois Bank until they agreed to provide a $600,000 line of credit. Jack Wolfsohn believed that he and I could get a few significant capital gifts and foundation grants for our specific project. On September 4, 1975, the board unanimously endorsed the purchase of the 600 South Michigan building. The minutes of that occasion included my editorial comment, "Hooray!"

Spurred by anticipation of accreditation and a prosperous year, the board's endorsement of a rudimentary pension plan and the extension of health and medical benefits to all employees were expressions of confidence in the college's maturity. The faculty's new concern with employment security was a similar expression. Such a quick leap of faith was mind boggling when only a few years before survival was Columbia's preoccupying issue.

As politics is a fact of life even in small tribal societies, it is not surprising that Columbia's little faculty had political strains and interest in due process protections against arbitrary discharge. It was inevitable, I think, that the faculty sought to bridle the power of deans and department chairs and establish forums and rules to resolve hiring and retention conflicts. The full-time faculty, deans, and I worked fraternally at the design of a fair and practical code to govern academic employment. We produced a brief document without lawyers or expert consultants. While it was not a tenure arrangement per se, it had such effect. It was superior in many ways to the formal tenure systems embraced then by most college institutions, and certainly it was more liberal in its avoidance of the typical seven-year probation period, when promotion to tenured status was decided. With little alteration, except the added opportunity of appeal to a committee of the board, this simple code was satisfyingly effective during all the years of my tenure. To my memory, its provisions were exercised on only three occasions, when separations were not amicable. Faculty employment disputes ordinarily were negotiated reasonably without having formally to invoke policy statutes. In more than twenty years, there were only two instances involving litigation. Few, if any, colleges can claim such an uncontentious record, particularly in today's litigious times. Columbia's 1974 due process document focused on the engagement and separation of Chairpersons and faculty and established a committee to monitor the employment process identified as the Elected Representative Committee of Chairpersons (ERCC).

After several years, it took some urging and reminding to get the chairs to elect their ERCC members, which probably reflected the infrequency of the committee's convocation. The first instance in which the policy was exercised had a regrettable consequence. Jim Newberry, the brilliant chairman of the Photography Department, sought to dismiss one of his faculty members, who took his appeal to the ERCC, where Jim's intransigent stance gave the committee no alternative to deciding in favor of the appellant. The decision provoked Newberry's resignation. It was a big loss.

While getting a Columbia building would have been enough event for the year, it wasn't the year's only business. In 1975 Columbia entered the computer age. After a year of discussion, a decision was made to computerize the college's operations, though it would take some years before everything was swept up by the tides of the new technology. With the counsel of a board committee and a bevy of experts, Kowalski chose a comprehensive system supplied by the Wang Corporation, then a major player in the world of computers. We leased the system at a cost of $40,000 a year. Suddenly, it seemed, everyone's desk was cluttered with read-outs, screens, and mouses, and typewriters disappeared. Within a few years I couldn't find a pencil sharpener. Some quickly became skilled, while others muddled far behind. Glitches were common. Everyone talked in tongues. We were quickly awash in a sea of information. It's hard to believe today that a world once existed without computers. I held out to the end of my Columbia days, learning to suppress my Luddite impulses. Indeed, people came to my office just to see my old Underwood typewriter and primitive adding machine. (I've since graduated to an old Olivetti.)

In 1975, the college began long-term disability and life insurance benefits for all full-time faculty and staff. The lease for Columbia's space in the Lake Shore Drive and annex buildings was renewed to 1978, with a six-month cancellation clause, which anticipated we'd move before the lease term's end.

All the elements of prosperity were in favorable alignment in the 1974–75 year, most importantly the added revenues of a 30 percent enrollment gain and some generous federal and State benefits and foundation grants. Important, too, was a doubling of contributions to scholarship and building funds compared to the prior year, a record largely attributable to the energies of Jack Wolfsohn, who at the time had been the college's development officer for less than a year. At the year's end, revenues exceeded expenses by $275,000, a mighty amount which later enabled the college to buy a new building and show our bankers a prosperous balance sheet.

Also that year, the college originated a unique project in Chicago's Uptown community. It came about in an unusual way. I had been seeking foundation support for a folk art and "lost trade arts" program I hoped to initiate as a division of the college's arts studies. In the course of my inquiries, I had talked on several occasions with Alan Jabaar, who led a division of the National Endowment for the Arts. He was a musical ethnologist, an accomplished country violin player, and an authority on Southern music. He suggested that I talk with Howard Klein, who was then the chief program officer of the Rockefeller Foundation's music department. Later, in a conversation with Klein, we somehow got on the subject of the migration of Southern culture to Northern cities. By way of example, I described the Uptown community which included large numbers of white migrants from Appalachia, who lived as aliens and outcasts in conditions of great poverty. I observed that they had been stripped of all the distinctive and familiar cultural ties that had given them expression and a sense of community. Indeed, there was no agency in Uptown, nor anywhere in Chicago, to give these migrants reason and opportunity to come together, even to learn to cope with the vicissitudes of life in a big city. The idea of a Southern Regional Cultural Center in Uptown was born at this discussion. Klein invited me to submit a proposal, which I did (within days). My proposal, written with Bert Gall's close counsel, incorporated many things I had learned in long association with the Highlander Folk School in Tennessee. Bert knew a lot about Uptown and its Appalachian community, and he had all sorts of valuable connections and contacts there. (I learned never to be surprised by the useful stuff in Bert's head.) Klein was enthusiastic. We got an initial Rockefeller Foundation grant of $40,000, and they continued to support the project for four years.

We rented a big storefront on Montrose Avenue, minimally remodeled it, and hired Doug Youngblood to head the center. Doug was a young man of about thirty with sinewy build, weathered face, and the look of a club fighter. An Uptown street guy who had come out of the Appalachian back country, he had some 1960s politics, was a talented organizer, a leader by nature, and a very sensitive, untutored poet. His mother was Peggy Terry, a legendary organizer and leader of the poor and exploited.

Doug, with Bert's guidance, filled the center with all sorts of activities: quilting and sewing sessions, clog dancing and bluegrass music, storytelling, singing groups, wood carving, and other indigenous Appalachian crafts, and a great variety of musi-cal and social gatherings. There were special programs for children, seniors, and women, and assemblies for men. The center quickly became a singular meeting place for Uptown's Appalachians and a way in which they could connect with their cultural heritage and escape from loneliness and separation. In time, all this led to a number of critical human services: legal aid, access to welfare agencies, employment services, fostering understanding and respect for Appalachian children in the public schools, instructing families how to adapt to unfamiliar social expectations, and conducting classes to prepare neighborhood people to take GED tests. The center's work was aided significantly by Judy McLaughlin, who joined the project during its first year. She was a very bright and original young sociologist from West Virginia with intimate knowledge of Appalachia. She was particularly responsible for the center's social services and many of its arts programs. Among these was an impressive mural project that sent teams of young painters into the community. After two years, Doug Youngblood left the center, and Judy became its director. The neighborhood, however, was rapidly changing. Appalachians dispersed to other locations, and the center's distinctive cultural themes and audience were disappearing. In the last year of the center's life it functioned mainly as a social service agency, and its program was merged with "Alternatives," an organization that has become, with Judy's leadership, one of Chicago's most important social agencies devoted to the welfare of children and young people. (Judy later became Bert Gall's wife. All in the family, as it were.)

In retrospect, the most impressive accomplishment of the Southern Regional Cultural Center was its unique demonstration of the power of the arts when they are used to implement human welfare and constructive social change. Perhaps there is even a valuable lesson in the center's example of combining art and culture with social service. Why not a neighborhood sports center or educational place that includes social service? I wish that Columbia's project had been a more contagious model.

I don't know whether any other college enjoyed Columbia's quick success. I think few, if any, did it as well on their own without external subsidy or the support of special constituencies. Columbia had unusually enlisting qualities and the benefit of timely accreditation, but the paramount element of the college's success was the zeal and competence of its dedicated faculty, staff, and board. The intense loyalty and fraternity that existed among them was not simply the accidental outcome of Columbia's democratic and missionary spirit. As fundamental as that spirit was, the college's sense of family was deliberately cultivated. Not finding any comfort in hierarchy, I consciously tried to minimize "upstairs–downstairs" distinctions based on job ranks. All of the college's jobs and the people who did them were important, and all deserved respect and a sense of human equality. This was not an abstract maxim—it had to actually happen, and that it did was mostly Jane's doing.

The creation of a sense of family was not some sentimentality, but in fact, a recognition of the genuinely important role played by each of the college's employees. If Columbia was to fulfill its educational purpose and provide a humane learning environment, such achievement depended on the dedication and quality of service that students received from those appointed to serve them. If each of these people were imbued with the sense that as members of a special fraternity they were servants of a common purpose, they might find greater motive for putting the best of themselves to their college occupation. And if that persuasion wasn't enough, we insisted, students paid the college's freight, and they were entitled to the most conscientious, courteous, and patient attentions. Whatever the source, the quality of Columbia's student service was outstanding.

Many of the college's members then regarded their employment as more than a job. They wanted to participate in Columbia's mission. There were countless examples of unselfish loyalty and voluntary work that went far beyond ordinary expectation. Jake Caref was a shining example of such dedication.

Jake is an exemplary Columbia loyalist. I hired him in 1965 for his mastery of a range of building trades and his exceptional carpentry skills. The college always had something to build or repair. He worked tirelessly for pitiful pay, though he could have worked for union scales anywhere else. When Columbia had no money at all, Jake somehow found a way to personally finance many of the college's early constructions. It took us years to repay him. As a stateless Pole and a Jew he had suffered every inhumanity, yet he emerged from the War's degradations as a most kind and generous human being with his faith in man's goodness somehow preserved. Jake is genuinely wise, literate in six languages, and a consummate reader. He has a rare intelligence and perception of reality, and a deep appreciation for the arts and respect for education, though he had no formal training in either. As a young man he was a notable gymnast and he remains immensely strong. He is an incomparable carpenter (no intricate cabinetry is beyond him) and he has an enormous knowedge and sense of interior architecture. Jake performed many miracles of ingenious construction. But more, he is an unparalleled friend. Jake Caref retired in 1990, and at eighty now he is still Columbia's great partisan.

Many others helped to make Columbia what it is. Irv Meyer, an expert at many crafts and surely the nicest and most helpful man, has served Columbia for twenty-five years. Larry Dunn, once a Columbia student and a talented artist, became the manager of the technical staff of the college's many buildings. Richard Wood, who runs the 600 South Michigan building's freight elevator and does everything else to make the college's life comfortable. Mark Gonzales, officially the college's "runner," scurries about the city on Columbia's errands. Jim Grady, the 600 South Michigan building's engineer, came with the building, as did so many more who were my splendid colleagues. When I retired, fourteen of them joined in a big photograph with a caption that said, "With great pleasure, we helped you to build the college; and on your retirement we find ourselves with great sorrow." What could be more beautiful than that? Surely, the Columbia family had no members more important than them.

As reported, Columbia's Board of Trustees was an important agency in the college's life, particularly in the acquisition of the 600 building. It couldn't have happened without their counsel and zeal. A little band of "friends of the family" only a few years before, the board had become an unusually generous and intensely engaged assembly of individuals with credentials of public service. For the record, the board membership in 1975–76 included:

Samuel Baskin, attorney, Baskin, Server, Miner and Berke; Deanna Bezark; Harry Bouras, artist; Gus Cherry, Vice President, Metropolitan Structures; Patrick Crowley, attorney, Crowley, Barrett and Karaba; Patricia Crowley, President, Space Inc.; Roger Davis, President, Goodwill Industries; Dwight Follett, Chairman, Follett Publishing Company; Jacob Fox, attorney, Altheimer and Gray; Franklin Fried, President, Triangle Productions; Sydney Gordon; Myron Hokin, President, Century Steel Corporation; Casimir Jaskowiak, President, Bowers Printing Inks; Milton Klein, (ret.) Chairman, Klein's Sports Stores; H. Ernest Lafontant, attorney, Lafontant and Lafontant; Stanton Leggett, President, Stanton Leggett Associates; Richard Miller, managing partner, Wolf and Company; John Naisbitt, President, Urban Research Corporation; Steven Neumer, attorney, Katten, Muchin and Zavis; Donald Nathanson, President, North Advertising Agency; Alfred Perlman, Vice President, Arthur Rubloff and Company; Richard Rosenzweig, Vice President, Playboy Enterprises; Robert Rothschild, President, Lexicon Publishers; Erwin Salk, President, Salk, Ward and Salk; Warner Saunders, anchorperson, Channel 5, NBC Chicago; Alan Saks, President Saxon Paint Stores, Inc.; Hope Samuels; Devorah Sherman; David Solomon, M.D., psychiatrist; Walter Topel, President, Walter Topel Productions; Albert Weisman, Vice President, Public Affairs, University of Chicago; William Wilkow, managing partner, M and G Wilkow Real Estate; Mirron Alexandroff, President, Columbia College; and faculty members Barry Burlison, Jack Hagman, Lynn Koons, and Thaine Lyman.

While all of Columbia's board members were noteworthy civic, business, and professional leaders, the college was particularly privileged to have Patrick and Patricia Crowley among its governors. The Crowley's had world prominence for their leadership of humanitarian causes and their advocacy of peace, justice, and interfaith harmony. They had true nobility.

While many Columbia board members deserve more than fleeting mention, three deserve particular attention: Stanton Leggett, John Naisbitt, and Milton Davis. All gave the college valuable counsel, and all made noteworthy contributions to Chicago and to the nation's welfare. Stanton Leggett was a prominent expert on public education and the common schools. He was uniquely insightful, imaginative, intensely practical, and ahead of his time. Among many respected roles, Leggett was the principal consultant to Dr. Joseph Hannon, the superintendent of the Chicago Public Schools in the mid-1970s, when the city's schools were extremely disorganized by the issues of desegregation, school busing, and political manipulation. Legget was an early advocate of magnet schools and voluntary school choice, and though he was only partially successful, if his plan had been adopted more universally then, it could have significantly eased the turmoil of the desegregation effort and the school busing controversy. But he did give Columbia an influential voice and respected presence in the councils of Chicago's schools at a time when the college had only faint public recognition. John Naisbett was a former undersecretary of education, chief executive of a national news reference bureau, and later had an illustrious career as a best-selling author of books on America in a future world shaped by technology. Naisbitt gave Columbia important help in navigating the swirls of government agencies and national foundations. Milton Davis has served the College as a board member for more than twenty years. As chairman of Chicago's South Shore Bank and co-chair of Chicago United, Davis is nationally recognized as "the principal leader of efforts to enlist the resources of America's banking institutions in serving their communities." Davis is a champion of human cause. His contributions to Columbia are legion, and his board service has been invaluable.

1975–1976: A New Home

We had 1,677 students in September 1975, a 19 percent gain over the previous year, thirty five full-time faculty, and a number of new part-time faculty. These included journalist Barbara Reynolds; radio broadcasters Art Hellyer and Buddy Black; dancers Jan Erkert and Nana Shineflug; recording artist Eddie Baker; sociologist Howard Becker; Ron Freund, director, Clergy and Laity Concerned; dance therapist Jane Ganet; and a number of Columbia graduates who enjoyed distinguished careers: photographers Ozier Muhammad, Brent Jones, and Vandell Cobb; radio and TV personality Bob Sirott; TV directors Howard Shapiro, Ron Weiner, and writer, Larry Heinemann.

Charles Traub, the chairman of the Photography Department, and his colleagues organized a photography gallery which occupied a small space in the 469 Ohio building. In addition to a schedule of exhibits of the work of local and national photographers and Columbia faculty, they hoped to gather a permanent collection of outstanding photography. At the time, a collection of significant scale seemed a bit ambitious, but from little acorns big oaks grow. A faculty member, Howard Kaplan, took on the job as gallery director, and Traub transformed into a confident entrepreneur. Within a few years, the Photography Department became a prominent American center of photographic education. The minigallery became today's Museum of Contemporary Photography, and the value of its collection grew to exceed $1 million. After a brief life in a makeshift location, the North Bank at McClurg Court offered 2,000 feet at no rental cost for a comparatively spacious

gallery and provided an interest-free loan of $12,000 for remodeling expenses—indeed, manna from heaven. The gallery prospered there until in 1979 it moved to a more elaborate space on the ground floor of the 600 South Michigan building, and later achieved museum status.

For several years, we had sought foundation support for a number of comparatively large-scale programs. These included development of a curriculum that more closely related arts studies and liberal education; a project to publish and exhibit graduates' work and give alumni the opportunity of a continuing intellectual and artistic community; compilation of a catalog of folk and craft arts represented in the Chicago region to create associations between artisans and a teaching resource for the college; and development of a humanities and history curriculum based on national and regional cultures.

Perseverance was rewarded. The Lilly Endowment in Indianapolis agreed to fund these projects with a grant of $100,000, and subject to their evaluation of our first year's progress, to extend support with an additional $250,000. It was a big leap ahead from the times when large program grants to Columbia were unknown.

But the 1975–76 year had troubles, too. As nearly 70 percent of the college's full-time students received Illinois state scholarship awards and/or federal Pell grants, and the college enjoyed significant benefit from state and federal grants to private colleges, student and college aid politics were always a critical concern. That year such concerns became matters of alarm. Inexplicably, federal and state agencies announced increases in individual grant amounts but failed to appropriate corresponding funds to provide for increased numbers of applicants. The consequence of this bungle was that Columbia's spring enrollment declined 5 percent. One hundred twenty-one full-time students were lost, with some offset by a greater number of part-time students. More than one hundred newly expected students were denied any aid; all state-aided students had their spring awards reduced by 12 percent; and state aid for summer enrollment was withdrawn entirely. To make matters worse, state and federal aid to independent college institutions was reduced by 50 percent. The cost of lost tuition was $125,000 and a similar amount was lost in college aid. More woe, the governor vetoed a bond issue to support college renovation, whose benefit to Columbia would have been $220,000. These were hard blows, particularly at a moment when the college badly needed every dollar to finance the new building. While student aid levels were restored the following year, what was lost stayed lost.

In February 1976, at the initiation of Tony Loeb, with the support of the American Issues Forum, the Film Department sponsored an extraordinarily successful public meeting on "Blacklisting in the Entertainment Industry." It featured Ring Lardner, Jr., representatives of the Hollywood Ten, and other prominent victims and observers of blacklisting and McCarthyism. More than seven hundred attended, at least a like number were turned away, and many were informed by extensive television, radio, and press coverage organized by Connie Zonka. Her public relations department also received more than twelve hundred requests for copies of the meeting's discussion, including many from schools, colleges, and influential citizens. As in the instance of the college's 1968 conference on "The Arts and the Inner City," the blacklisting event performed a widely complimented public service which spurred national discussion of an important issue and renewed understanding of America's civil liberties.

The year's main preoccupation was, of course, preparing the college's new home. We had bravely anticipated that the building's remodeling would be done in time to move by September 1976, but it was soon evident that our expectations couldn't be realized. There was just too much work to be done. In fact, it would be a big stretch to get in by the beginning of the 1977 spring semester, and even then, it was likely that some college functions would be left at Lake Shore until later that summer. That's what actually happened. The big move came just before the spring 1977 term began, and the Film and Photography Departments didn't move until August. In the interim, we organized a regular bus service that transported students and faculty between the Lake Shore and Michigan Avenue locations. It was all terribly impractical, but it didn't last long.

In retrospect, all of the effort of getting the 600 South Michigan building seems minor in comparison to the agonies of remodeling and financing. To make everything more difficult, a quarter of the building was occupied by tenants who had leases with various ending dates, some even extending for two years. Working around them and simultaneously being a good landlord was a hard trial.

The first big pitfall was that after four months we determined that our architectural arrangement with Luizzo Associates was unworkable, and they were replaced by Patrick Shaw Associates, Chicago architects who had greater familiarity with school building codes and better relations with the various code agencies. Drawing architectural plans and sifting through engineering and building code data was difficult. To remodel a big old building is to confront a catalog of rude discoveries that require expensive and time-consuming remedies. Tear down a wall, and rotting studs, rusty plumbing, and frayed wiring may be revealed. Most unanticipated and terribly expensive were a new roof, new cars and cabling for the elevators, and lots of tuck pointing, plumbing, and electrical work. Understandably, city school-building codes were far more strict than those for office buildings. A fire alarm system independent of the building's electrical system had to be installed and special fire walls constructed. And as much of the college's education depended on technical facilities, extensive equipment installations, and specialized uses of space, Bert Gall and the architects could only proceed in close consultation with department chairs, faculty, and technical staff, which made for slow and tedious architectural work. Early on, it was clear that we'd have at least $500,000 in unexpected costs above budgeted amounts, even without considering the second and third stages of our remodeling plan.

Money wasn't the stuff of dreams anymore; this was real life, and we couldn't turn back. City building inspectors were pressing us to get out of the Lake Shore Drive building. Somehow we just had to put the big bucks together. What could ultimately be provided from college funds was questionable. The $600,000 bank line of credit would be quickly spent in ongoing construction costs. All the subcontractors had prompt pay-out schedules. Jack Wolfsohn organized a campaign for funds. It was a spirited chase that mostly had to be done in little more than a year, and much of the campaign depended on Jack's and my personal solicitations. board members gave nearly $200,000, including Myron Hokin's gift of $50,000 (the largest). Other individuals gave another $200,000; again, Kenneth Montgomery was the biggest donor. Corporations and foundations supplied $400,000. Jack got a $150,000 challenge grant from the Kresge Foundation, which required that we reach a $1,200,000 goal by August 1977. Somehow we scratched up that amount just in time. We still needed a lot more and had to divert college funds to cover urgent building and moving expenses; to buy and install new instructional equipment; to pay the interest on our line of bank credit; and, after September 1978, to begin repaying the principal amount.

It was all pretty amazing. We had never really raised any significant amount of money before. Columbia's abortive fund campaigns of the past had usually cost nearly as much as the amounts realized, and all had involved many planning sessions, consultants, feasibility studies, and elaborate materials. The building fund campaign had few if any of these accoutrements. Jack and I talked a lot with each other and a small number of board members. We didn't have any consultants, but Jack was knowledgeable and experienced. We prepared a number of convincing proposals and went after only a short list of foundations and a limited number of prospective major donors. We had a minimum of campaign literature: only an eight-page appeal and a few circulars. I had a lot of lunches, and Jack and I traveled to foundations.

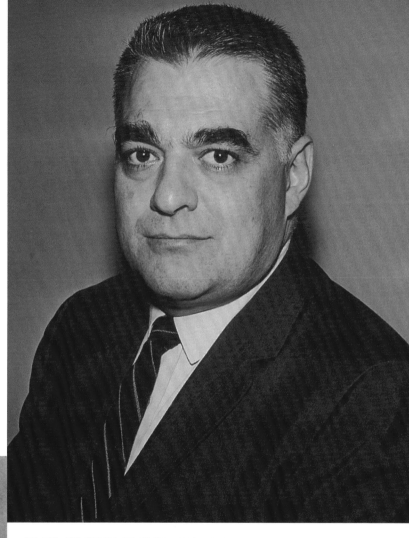

TOP LEFT: DON SANDERS AND VANESSA JAMES; BOTTOM LEFT: THAINE LYMAN; MIDDLE: JAKE CAREF; RIGHT: THE 1950s MA.

LEFT: THE 1960s MA; RIGHT: BRIAN KATZ. FACING PAGE: TOP LEFT: MA WITH EDGAR (YIP) HAR[...] BOTTOM LEFT: 1960s COLUMBIA REGISTRATION; TOP MIDDLE: GORDON ROGOFF; TOP RIGHT: AC ([...] GALL; BOTTOM RIGHT: JOHN FISCHETTI CARICATURE OF MA.

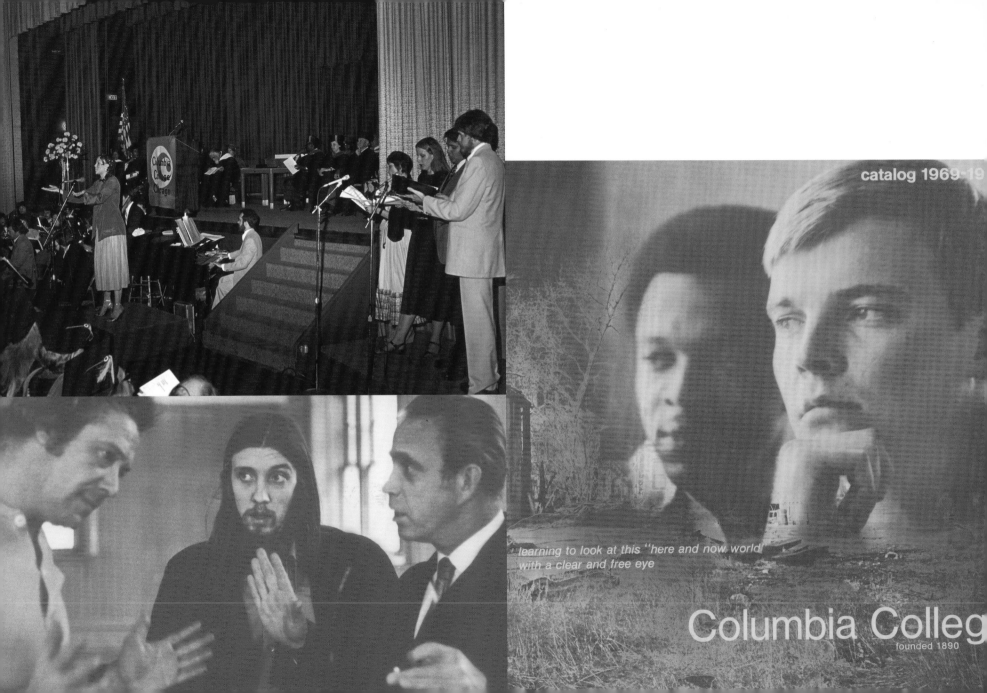

catalog 1969-19

learning to look at this "here and now world" with a clear and free eye

Columbia Colleg

founded 1890

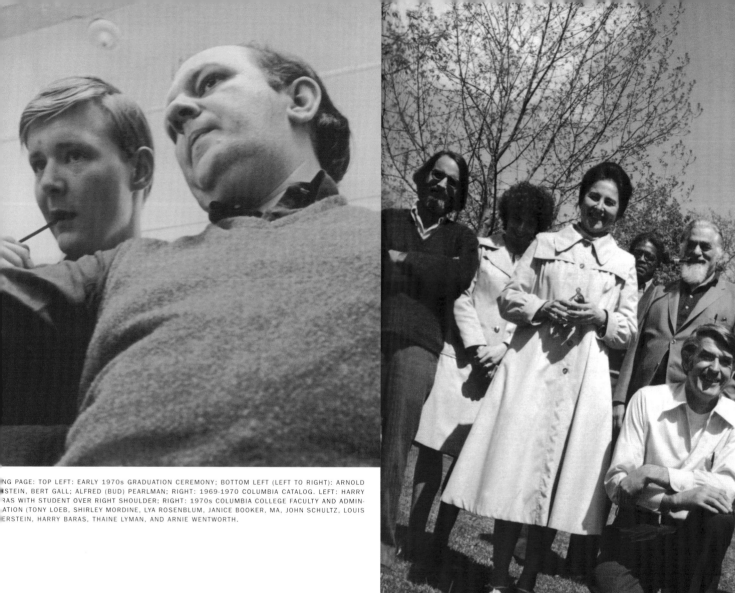

FACING PAGE: TOP LEFT: EARLY 1970s GRADUATION CEREMONY; BOTTOM LEFT (LEFT TO RIGHT): ARNOLD [EPST]EIN, BERT GALL; ALFRED (BUD) PEARLMAN; RIGHT: 1969-1970 COLUMBIA CATALOG. LEFT: HARRY [BA]RAS WITH STUDENT OVER RIGHT SHOULDER; RIGHT: 1970s COLUMBIA COLLEGE FACULTY AND ADMIN[ISTR]ATION (TONY LOEB, SHIRLEY MORDINE, LYA ROSENBLUM, JANICE BOOKER, MA, JOHN SCHULTZ, LOUIS [SIBE]RSTEIN, HARRY BARAS, THAINE LYMAN, AND ARNIE WENTWORTH.

TOP: MIDDLE 1970s COLUMBIA FACULTY AND ADMINISTRATION, BOTTOM: MICHAEL RABIGER. FA▨
PAGE: TOP LEFT: PAULA EPSTEIN, TOP MIDDLE LEFT: EUGENE (GENE) DEKOVIC; TOP MIDDLE R▨
CATHERINE SLADE; BOTTOM: JOHN TARINI, JANE ALEXANDROFF, AND SUZANNE COHAN-LANGE; RIGHT:▨
SOUTH MICHIGAN.

LEFT: NEWTON MINOW, MA, AND THAINE LYMAN (SEATED FOREGROUND); TOP MIDDLE: FRED FINE; B
MIDDLE: JANICE BOOKER; TOP RIGHT: IRV MEYER; BOTTOM RIGHT: JOHN WAGNER. FACING PAG
LEFT: RANDY ALBERS; TOP MIDDLE: BETTY SHIFLETT; BOTTOM LEFT: AL WEISMAN AND DANCERS;
BERT GALL.

LEFT: RICHARD LOECHER, KAREN FISCHETTI AND JAMES MARGULIES; RIGHT: JOHN FISCHETTI. FACING PAGE: TOP LEFT TO RIGHT: CAROL LOVERDE, PAUL HOOVER, AND HERMANN CONAWAY; BOTTOM LEFT: HUBERT DAVIS AND SANTA CLAUS; MIDDLE RIGHT: LYNN SLOAN; FAR RIGHT: SHEILA BALDWIN; BOTTOM RIGHT (LEFT TO RIGHT): CHUCK ZIELER, BOB KECK, AND CHRIS BURRITT.

LEFT: HOLLIS SIGLER; TOP (LEFT TO RIGHT): SYDNEY SMITH GORDON, JOHN OLINO AND MARY JOH[...]
MIDDLE (LEFT TO RIGHT): STEVEN RUSSELL-THOMAS AND PETER THOMPSON; BOTTOM: DANIEL HOW[...]

The college's general story and record of quick achievement was most persuasive. We continued to get lots of publicity, and we had a wealth of activities to publicize. Board members participated in the campaign with great energy. Jack was the real hero of the fund campaign, and Bert Gall was the author of the whole building project. In that mighty task, Trustee Gus Cherry gave invaluable help.

Excluding funds restricted to the building project, 1975–76 showed revenues of $355,000 over the year's expenses, though this momentary gain and more was quickly gobbled up by building expenses. The year would, of course, have been much better if we hadn't lost $250,000 in the shortfall of state and federal funding, but then again, we weren't sunk by this big hit, which would have fatally swamped us only a few years before. That was most encouraging.

At the year's end, August 1976, there were two significant changes in Columbia's leadership. The college's Chief Financial Officer Ronald Kowalski and Academic Dean Louis Silverstein resigned. Kowalski had served the college well for five very difficult years. He had reordered Columbia's financial systems, computerized its methods, and provided the information vital to our building's purchase and to projections of the college's financial course. Perhaps his greatest accomplishment was that he had been a master juggler of Columbia's finances, which kept us a few steps in front of the sheriff, as it were. Kowalski was replaced by John Scheibel. A very experienced business manager and accountant, Scheibel was a sweet, intensely loyal, and very literate man who was committed to Columbia's mission and the welfare of the college's community. He would have a leading role in Columbia's life for more than twelve years.

At the close of the year, Lou Silverstein became the chair of the Life Arts and Liberal Education Department. He had served well as the college's principal education officer during the critical years when accreditation was won. As an immediate response to Silverstein's resignation we made a concerted effort to find an experienced educator of leading national reputation to serve as academic dean. We expected it would be difficult, particularly as we sought a person who had a distinguished record as a creative college educator in tune with Columbia's distinctive character and mission. We advertised nationally in education journals and asked a variety of foundations and knowledgeable individuals, a process that led to a number of applications and subsequent interviews. Among respondents was Dr. Merv Cadwallader who had been suggested by George Bonham, the editor of *Change Magazine*. Cadwallader was an ideal candidate. He was a distinguished scholar with wide interest in the arts and a principal founder of Evergreen State College in Olympia, Washington, perhaps America's most innovative public college. After several interviews and a number of convincing recommendations, my nomination of Cadwallader was endorsed enthusiastically by department chairs and faculty representatives. Cadwallader accepted and was expected to take the dean's office in September. He was delighted with the house that Bert Gall found for him in Oak Park. But at the last minute, he decided not to come. His reason was that his wife of several years, who had spent the first years of marriage on Evergreen's pastoral campus, just couldn't take to the idea of life in a big city. Cadwalader was regretful, and we were even more so. Later, Dr. Cadwallader would serve for many years as president of Union Graduate University, a unique institution that pioneered external degree programs, and more recently as President of Northern Arizona University. Apparently, the Cadwalladers were happier in bucolic settings. Columbia hardly had that.

We had, however, a worthy alternative in the appointment of Lya Rosenblum as the college's academic dean. A Ph.D. in political science, she had served as assistant dean during the preceding year, and with that beginning Lya had a leading Columbia role. It has been a remarkable tenure. Lya is an attractive, liberal woman and an articulate and imaginative educator with great energy. She is a skillful negotiator and arbiter of controversy, essential attributes of a successful academic dean who, in Columbia's instance, was responsible for the college's entire educational purview and its not easily managed faculty.

Apart from such preoccupations, Lya was the main organizer of Columbia's graduate school and a principal participant in the self-study process. She was and continues to be the cause of a succession of major U.S. Office of Education grants for many millions of dollars, which funded a great variety of valuable Columbia projects, most of which would probably never have happened without government support. She also secured the Getz family's $750,000 gift, which funded reconstruction of the college's Eleventh Street Theater, now identified by the name of the donor. And she's secured millions more to support undergraduate and graduate programs she initiated in teacher education. Lya is an exceptional public representative of the college to important civic constituencies, government and educational agencies, and foundations. After serving for many years as the college's vice president for academic affairs, she was vice president and dean of Columbia's graduate school until her retirement in 2000.

The final months of construction were hectic. There was great difficulty in installing television and radio studio equipment and computer gear. Moving was a jumble. It took a small army of movers three nights to complete that. We had only one large freight elevator and a small passenger elevator at 540, so getting everything out and on trucks was very slow work, and much had to be carried laboriously down narrow flights of stairs. The movers weren't in the best mood. Somehow, it all got done and, within a week, we were ready for students and the spring registration. Bert Gall, of course, managed the move out and in with customary efficiency. Not a surprising feat for someone who'd managed Hannibal's storied crossing of the Alps centuries before! As usual, we'd underestimated the costs of moving and the last-minute cleanup of construction debris. It was a crazy time.

In the following months, classroom instruction and administrative functions had to contend with noisy construction, the traffic of remaining tenants, and the inconvenient distance between the college's two locations. While classroom activities were only temporarily disordered, administrative and clerical functions were acutely disrupted. For many months, much of the college's business was done out of packing boxes, some of which only turned up after weeks of searching. And some boxes just stayed lost.

While a few of the building's tenants did not leave until 1979, most leases expired earlier. This was not a problem, as we had not planned, nor could we have afforded, to entirely complete the building's reconstruction until after 1980. In the meantime, tenant income did cover a significant part of the operating costs. The Kodak Company occupied the building's prime ground floor space and mezzanine, which they used to display their products. Their lease ran four more years, but they wanted a quicker termination, and we promptly accepted an offer of $70,000 in settlement of their lease obligation. A bit of debate ensued about how we would use the "Kodak space." It was argued by some that it was an ideal setting for the college's admissions office and various student recruitment attractions. My doubtfully popular choice, endorsed only by the Photography Department faculty, was to use the Kodak space for the photography gallery and exhibits of folk and craft arts, a view persuasively supported by Bill Wilkow among his board colleagues. And that was that! The Kodak pay-out was spent in making a beautiful gallery, now the Museum of Contemporary Photography. Earlier, I had prevailed similarly in assigning two floors of the 600 South Michigan building to the college's then comparatively small Art Department. It was my rather singular estimate that the Art Department's concentrations of graphic, commercial, and craft arts would have great popularity, in part because we would have little competition from other local colleges and because of Columbia's unique opportunity for allied studies in photography, film, theater, and advertising. Indeed, within a few years, the Art Department had the college's largest enrollment.

While Columbia hadn't yet moved to Michigan Avenue, our new building was pictured and described in all of the college literature and advertisements. The first dividend of the college's new home was realized in fall 1976. Two thousand fifty students enrolled: 1,250 full-time, 800 part-time, a full-time equivalent of more than 1,600. These numbers represented a 20 percent gain over the year before. We had projected only a cautious 7 percent increase in view of continuing economic uncertainties and doubts about the sufficiency of state and federal student aid. Coupled with a 4 percent tuition rate increase, 1976 enrollment figures renewed confidence that we would be able to finance the immediate requirements of our building commitments, though it would still take ingenuity and daring to put the project on a firm financial footing. Most pressing was Bert Gall's estimate that at least $600,000 more would be necessary to fund construction of the eighth, ninth, and eleventh floors, which would house the Film and Photography Departments in the summer of 1977. It was quickly evident that the costs of the whole remodeling project would be about $2 million, nearly double our earlier optimistic projections. Moreover, we would soon have to begin repayment of our bank loans (now $700,000), make large monthly payments on our mortgage obligations, and operate the building without benefit of tenant incomes, which would entirely disappear within two years. And suddenly we had the added costs of servicing a 20 percent greater enrollment. There was much woe in the hard-come-easy-go equation.

To relieve acute financial strains from the remodeling project, the board decided to seek an additional loan of $500,000 from the Continental Illinois Bank. It was a pretty iffy prospect; but after some weeks of negotiation the bank agreed to consolidate this amount with our previous $700,000 credit line. All told, it came to

$1,200,000, with the requirement that the college make semiannual payments of $150,000 beginning in February 1978. At an interest rate of 1.75 percent over the prime rate, it was a very favorable agreement. The college's board was unbelievably brave. A number of board members worked hard to get contributions of furnishings and materials needed to prepare the building for occupancy. Noteworthy among such efforts were gifts of carpeting for all the building's space arranged by Devorah Sherman, and Alan Saks's contribution of library and other shelving. Such gifts relieved the college of many thousands of dollars of expense. The board's intense commitment to Columbia was an extraordinary act of faith. What a wonderful bunch they were. There was something remarkable, too, in the support of Continental Bank officers Roy Davis and Bill Marcou, more accustomed, I'm sure, to a flinty-eyed view of poor suppliants like us.

In the 1976–77 year Columbia had forty full-time faculty members and a part-time complement of 120, all respected academics and professionals recruited to the faculty and monitored with as much care as were full-time appointments. The academic pattern initiated in the early 1970s still largely prevailed. Graduation required 124 credit hours of study, including forty-eight semester hours of liberal education, eight semester hours of English, and sixty-eight credits in elective subjects guided only by necessary course sequences and skill and knowledge prerequisites.

In 1977, a comprehensive sound-engineering program was initiated by the Radio department, though its subjects covered audio functions in radio, television, film, theater, and music. The project had immediate popularity, in music particular-ly, stemming from the prominence of the recording industry in American youth culture and the increasing employment of computer-generated techniques in musical reproduction. Initially, sound-engineering students could choose a two-year associate degree concentration or incorporate such study in a bachelor's degree program. Though the associate degree opportunity had brief duration, and Film-Video reincorporated sound studies within its department, the sound-engineering program continues to prosper with sophisticated, state-of-the-art facilities.

Also in 1977, while descriptions and advertisements of Radio and Television linked them together under the title Broadcast Communications, the departments retained independent lives and separate Chairs. Given the increasing relation between film and video techniques, the Film department reflected this in a new title, Film-Video Department, though the department's new video emphasis did not intrude significantly on the Television Department's purview. That year, too, Columbia initiated cooperative study arrangements with the School of the Art Institute, the DuSable Museum of African-American History, the Adler Planetarium, and the Midwest Academy for Community Organizing. Also, through a cooperative arrangement with the Associated Colleges of the Midwest, Columbia students could enroll at other institutions in their special programs in urban teaching, urban studies, work assignments in urban areas, and language and cultural studies in Latin American countries.

That year, Al Weisman, Columbia Trustee, faculty member, and singularly influential Chicago publicitor, died suddenly. His death occasioned an impressive memorial luncheon which enlisted the membership and audience of Chicago's communication industries and launched the Weisman Scholarship Fund and an annual Weisman Memorial event, both of which continue. These yearly memorials and associated seminars for Columbia students and the public feature the leaders of the communication professions. The Weisman luncheons regularly attract audiences of 700 or more, and the Weisman Scholarship Fund, with assets now of about $1 million, continues to provide scholarships to Columbia's students. The initial Weisman tribute had David Halberstam as its principal speaker, with an audience of more than one thousand. The success of the Weisman memorial event is properly credited to Connie Zonka; Al's son, Tony Weisman, who became a member of Columbia's board; the Weisman family; leaders of the communications fraternity; Irv Kupcinet; Howard Mendelsohn; Sherman Wolf; Jon Anderson; and many others who were Al's loyal friends.

Also that year, the Lilly Endowment, while complimentary about the college's achievement in the first year of their grant, abruptly changed their priorities. Their second year contribution became $50,000 instead of the $250,000 expected. As the college was committed to at least a three-year project, its continuation would now depend largely on college funds. New faculty and support personnel had been hired, and many programs begun. These couldn't be abandoned, but they required an expensive shift in already strained college resources.

More disquieting was an unavoidable recognition that time had run out for the Theater-Music satellite. City inspectors insisted that the building more closely conform to school building codes, which would require expensive and impractical renovation, but at best only temporarily rescue a facility whose purpose was no longer viable.

The college's performing arts satellites had a brilliant seven-year run, which significantly influenced the city's artistic life and contributed mightily to Columbia's success. By 1977, Columbia had become a settled institution, and inevitably, no longer a youthful educational and social experiment. While we sought to preserve the college's inventive spirit, this could no longer be expressed in old slogans and tattered settings. It was hard to abandon the Theater-Music Center and the Free Theater. They represented Columbia's earlier soul, but ending it was imperative. Discouragingly, the Theater-Music Department and suitable performing spaces could not be put in the 600 South Michigan building. But, again, we were lucky. We were able to lease the Eleventh Street Theater building at a yearly cost of $36,000 (not including operational costs) for a three-year term, with an option to buy the building at the end of the lease. We could get by with minimum remodeling expense; but most attractively, though needing extensive repair, the building included a proscenium theater with main floor and balcony seating for an audience of six hundred. Oddly, the Eleventh Street Theater was the site of Columbia's theater performances in the 1930s and early 1940s. What goes around comes around, I suppose.

Bert Gall, finishing construction and moving the Film and Photo Departments to the 600 South Michigan building, had the added task of supervising the Theater-Music Department's move to Eleventh Street and preparing its space for its occupancy. The big miracle was that it all happened on schedule, though Bert then seemed to weigh about seventy-one pounds and hadn't slept for eight weeks.

He didn't come to work on Labor Day, but he was there to help manage registration when it began on Tuesday morning.

Combining the Theater and Music Departments at the Sheffield Avenue location had never been a satisfactory arrangement. Whatever inherent difficulties may have existed in associating different disciplines, undoubtedly crowding them together in a small facility served neither department's needs. It was a shotgun marriage that only satisfied the college's need for an economical solution to the loss of the Theater Department location; though that event reflected the absence of strong Theater Department leadership and the consequent diminution of the department's program and enrollment after Don Sanders's departure and Ronnie Davis's brief tenure. While continuing the association of the theater and music disciplines in the Eleventh Street building, its far greater space allowed both disciplines to effect instructional separations without acute space restrictions, though competition continued for main-stage performance time.

In 1977, however, the renewal of the Theater Department by new leadership was a paramount concern. We conducted an extensive search over many months for a Theater-Music Department chair whose purview would include a close fraternity with Russo's less structured music project, which in effect was an independent college department. We sought a prominent member of the American theater community, with a record of important professional accomplishment, comprehensive experience in theater education, and strong musical interests: in short, an inspiring, creative, mature leader who could restore the deserved respect the department had

enjoyed locally and nationally as an important place of theater education. We advertised widely and received many applications. I interviewed a number of outstanding candidates.

Finally, after several meetings, I was certain that in Paul Carter Harrison I had found the right person. Paul Harrison was a distinguished African-American playwright and director with an international reputation, extensive theater education experience, and great musical interest. He was a very sophisticated, contemporary, and talented man. He agreed with Columbia's mission. There are exceptions, but artists generally are a bit goofy. Paul did not seem given to temperamental excesses. He would begin in September 1977, just in time to manage the department's first semester at Eleventh Street. It would be a big test of his patience.

Simultaneous to all this juggling, we were suddenly notified of Marvin Sugarman's intent to sell the Dance Center building on Sheridan Road. Sugarman's extraordinary generosity to the Dance Center and its program had exhausted his charitable resources. The value of the building exceeded $170,000, an amount we simply couldn't pay. It seemed the end of the Dance Department's rope, but we weren't done with miracles. As a final generosity to the department and, in effect, to Chicago's dance community, Sugarman agreed to sell the building to Columbia for $95,000, a big but remotely affordable sum. The good folk at Continental Bank loaned us another $50,000, God knows why, and we scratched up $45,000 to complete the purchase. I said earlier that the college's board was brave and Continental Bank officials uncustomarily sympathetic. If anything, my observation was an understatement.

At the 1976–77 year's end, the college had qualified for Kresge's challenge grant of $150,000. It was a profitable year if mortgage, construction, and loan obligations were excluded. Whatever was left over was quickly used up in greater expenses budgeted for the new year's operation.

Albeit a paper figure which avoided longer-term obligations, it was evident that Columbia enjoyed a reasonable state of financial health, particularly so in view of the many new and unanticipated expenses that had been incurred in the 1976–77 year. In a personal sense, I was beginning to be more comfortable with big money numbers that would have been unthinkable only a few years before, though living without daily anxiety was yet too unfamiliar to be easily enjoyed.

1977–1978: New Board Leadership

In November 1977, the board leadership changed. Not unexpectedly, Bud Perlman resigned as chairman. In succeeding Dwight Follett, Perlman had emphasized that he would serve only a short time. He was replaced as chair by Devorah Sherman, who had an outstanding record of civic service in causes concerned with the welfare of children and young people. She had been vice chair and for several years one of the board's most active and generous members. While she met every challenge with gracious competence, her term was abbreviated by illness within a year. Steve Neumer, who then headed the executive committee and had served with great distinction in getting the 600 South Michigan building and in other college affairs, was elected in October 1978 to serve temporarily as chair until the board's official annual meeting a month later. I had anticipated that Neumer would be elected to a full term as chairman. The board's nominating committee, however, nominated Charles Bane for the office. Though perfectly commendable, it was a surprising choice.

Charles Bane had every civic credential. He was a prominent and respected lawyer and senior partner of a major law firm, Isham, Lincoln and Beale, which had President Lincoln's son as a founder and now included former Governor Richard Ogilvie as a partner. Bane had headed a variety of blue-ribbon commissions, had been president of the United Charities of Chicago, was the founder of the United Way, and a past president of the Chicago Council on Foreign Relations. The son of a coal miner, he was a Harvard Law School graduate, a Rhodes Scholar, and chairman of the Rhodes Scholars' Selection Committee. Bane was a dedicated civil rights advocate and had been appointed by President Carter as chairman of the Lawyers Commission for Civil Rights under Law. Bane's son had been a Columbia student, which had led to Charles's enlistment as a Columbia board member in 1976 and to his becoming a vigorous partisan of Columbia and its mission. The nominating committee believed that as board chairman, Bane would give the college an important public dimension and access to an affluent and powerful constituency whose notice and support we had never attracted. It was a persuasive nomination, hard to ignore. Of such stuff the dreams of glory are made. Bane was elected as the board's chair for a term until 1981. His representation did give the college an unassailably respectable identity. Regrettably, it didn't lead to big money, though he was otherwise a most excellent and attentive chairman.

At the meeting of Bane's election, Don Nathanson and Richard Miller resigned as board members as both were moving to California. Newly elected to the board were Joel Henning, a lawyer and legal journalist; Dori Wilson, one of the city's foremost publicists; Dr. Jorge Prieto, Chief of Medicine at Cook County Hospital and a leading advocate of Mexican-American and minority interests; and Milton Davis, the inventive and celebrated officer of the South Shore National Bank.

In the spring of 1978, the board appointed a committee charged with the design of an expanded pension plan for the college's faculty and staff and expected their report at an early date. Tuition was increased to $2,300 a year for full-time students in 1978–79 and was also increased for part-time students, though the tuition increase was voted hesitantly in view of the college's traditional commitment to low tuition rates. In the discussion of this, it was observed that the revenue take from a 5 percent increase in tuition could be replaced by $250,000 in funds generated by dependable gifts or endowment incomes. Such a prospect, however, seemed remote then.

Looming over everything was the realization that our reaccreditation examination was scheduled for the spring of 1979 and a new self-study would be due in the fall of 1978. What was hard to believe was that nearly five years had passed since Columbia's first accreditation. If anything, our reexamination would be more demanding, as the award this time would be for ten years and the college would need to present itself as a far more mature institution than was expected in 1973. We had a mountain of work to do and, again, only a short time to do it.

In describing the self-study project at a March 1978 board meeting, I emphasized that even if this scrutiny was not required at the moment, a searching inquiry and self-assessment would have been necessary. Columbia had become a much different place than it was just a few years before. I stated, "While the college has many serious matters of education and student service to attend to, many of our problems are not unique to Columbia. American education remains in serious crisis, higher education no less so than the common schools. There is growing debate about who shall be educated, how, and for what, and what federal and state resources will be directed to the sectors of education. Moreover, there is continuing uncertainty about how to better impart the constituents of intelligence, cultural literacy, and humane citizenship to a youth population manipulated by the mass media and contemporary culture."

I believe now that my report of national debate on such subjects was unfounded, and surely so in implying the possibility of resolution or influential consensus. At best, even now, educators only nibble at the main issues of education as they swirl about in hostile political currents and peripheral controversies.

I believe, however, that such disabilities are not the result of an absence of enlightened educators or creative ideas, but stem instead from educators' distaste for controversy, resignation to the contention that nothing can be done, and from the absence of a significant popular movement whose agenda includes serious educational reform as a cardinal element of a national commitment to greater social and economic democracy. At present, the sheer size, entrenchment, and adhesion of American education makes it, and even individual institutions, largely resistant to comprehensive change. This largely precludes higher education's timely incorporation of new study and career concentrations that reflect vast technological changes and new directions of the national and world economies. I observe, too, with the whimsy of hindsight, that while Columbia tried mightily to preserve its earlier zeal and vitality, over time this effort was blunted by our singularity, by an absence of sufficient financial resources to sustain and renew the college's experiment, and, with great growth, by the loss of easily manageable size.

At the end of the 1970s, Columbia had begun to exhibit a sense of institutionality with corresponding expectations of permanence and personal security. And inevitably, as faculty, staff, and board numbers were multiplied by new individuals who had not shared the college's earlier ferment, the creative energies and aspirations of those times became less and less instructive.

Minute gradations of change are, of course, imperceptible. Nothing signaled that Columbia's earlier vitalities and guides were exhausted. Indeed, many tracings of these prevailed in different forms and strengths.

In the late 1970s, Columbia was a shaky success, surely neither mature nor secure. Such prizes still had to be won. That a raggedy, irregular educational experiment had become a real college disguised the fact that Columbia then was only fifteen years old. I recognize an inclination of memory to regard that time as Columbia's golden years of great deeds and inventions, but such sentimentality ignores the acute anxiety, uncertainty, and missteps of those times. Nonetheless, those fifteen years were special and unrepeatable times of discovery, sense of community, and less guarded effort to create a new kind of college place. In 1978 and 1979, while critical financial matters, construction problems, and relocation of college functions remained the most prominent subjects of board discussion and my own occupations, increasing time was spent on pension and employee benefit plans, computer improvements, and response to faculty rumblings about governance, presidential succession, turf controversies, and other issues that are part of institutional territory.

In 1964, it would have been impossible to imagine that I might alone reinvent an urban, private college focused on communications media and arts specialties. Surely I did not envision a college of Columbia's present scale. Viewed accurately, Columbia then was a worn-out name attached to an obscure bit of an enterprise: penniless and without subsidy or sponsor. I don't know what I had in mind for

Columbia then. My surviving memory is that I was preoccupied with the vicissitudes of survival and some inexact notions of greater prosperity.

While my effort was informed by my perceptions of American society and the state of its education, I only vaguely perceived how these views might be harnessed to Columbia's life. Undoubtedly, Columbia's separation from PFTC and relocation on Lake Shore Drive resulted in immediate enrollment gains, but such results were more accidental than planned. Indeed, it would take several years and the counsel of colleagues to form even a primitive plan for the college's promotion. The earliest elements of this were advertisements of Columbia's distinctive qualities and contemporary vitality. Columbia's identity did not incorporate a comprehensive arts program until several years later. Our greatest possessions initially were an educational focus on communications media, lively liberal arts opportunities, a learn-by-doing emphasis, and a faculty of experts who taught what they did professionally. Successful student recruitment and public recognition of our collegiate identity would depend on a persuasive exhibit of Columbia's educational excellence, inventive instruction, faculty commitment, professional environment, and contemporaneity.

In most instances then, collegiate advertising and publicity efforts were only minimal interests, a neglect which reflected the comforts of established identities, familiar audiences, a sense of rank in the collegiate hierarchy, and a largely noncompetitive environment. While customary institutional postures and practices were shaken up by the influx of nontraditional students in the years after the war in Vietnam, and more rudely by campus disorders in the 1960s and early 1970s, except for an elevated regard for public relations as a defensive agency, there was little reorder of collegiate advertising and promotional priorities. That was only to come on a large scale in the mid-1970s after competition for college-age students intensified and the educational expectations of a radically changed economy created a large student market among adults seeking college credentials and contemporary skills. Until that happened, student recruitment followed conventional patterns. college and university catalogs were mostly recitations of course offerings, faculty listings, and informational essentials, often in stilted academic language and without graphic distinction. Other student recruitment materials were similarly routine.

In contrast, everything Columbia issued was meant deliberately to convey the college's distinctive quality and contemporary spirit. This was a time when I wrote all Columbia's publications: catalogs, course descriptions, self-studies, grant proposals, even form letters sent to prospective students. I viewed nothing as routine communication. As conventional advertising was unaffordable, and as we were only beginning to enjoy media attention, Columbia's virtues were extolled mostly person to person. The exception was the college's annual catalog. It was our greatest promotional expense, the main instrument of student recruitment, and the vehicle of Columbia's message within the college and externally. Columbia's catalogs and recruitment publications had bold colors, creative graphics, and enameled paper stock, enlisting course titles, many popular media names among the faculty, and pithy expositions of the college's unique and timely qualities.

In retrospect, I think that Columbia's aggressive entry in the local collegiate market and our bold promotional style may have been the keys to our success, at least as much as the substance of what we were selling. I observe this to contend that Columbia's success, if that is a fair assessment, was more impelled by gritty entrepreneurship than by philosophical imperatives or unique intellectual insights. And certainly I was not inspired by a sudden epiphany to make a college. As the mountain climber said when asked why he climbed the mountain, "Because it's there."

Ordinarily, organizers, promoters, impresarios, and the like enjoy only fleeting recognition. More durable respect is rightly reserved for those whose work is real stuff. Mine wasn't. I was only an entrepreneur there at the beginning of Columbia's renewal as others may be at critical moments later. Obviously, without me, there wouldn't have been a Columbia College. But inevitably, time devalues even founders, inventive ones no less so. In that sense, institutions are impersonal places, despite the critical role of particular individuals. (Said a bit wistfully, of course.) But, hey! The span of Harrison Street between Michigan and Wabash is named "Mike Alexandroff Way," though I challenge you to try to direct a cab driver to Michigan and Alexandroff.

During my tenure, I viewed everything about Columbia as having a promotional dimension. In early years, our first need was to break the binds of anonymity and to gain public respect as a legitimate and distinctive college institution. As noted, we had few resources then to devote to such priorities. In our orphaned state, we had only a little flock of partisans: a couple of managers, a minimal staff, a few board members, a small number of part-time faculty, several hundred students, and scattered alumni to carry Columbia's message to a largely indifferent public. We had no alternative to enlisting everyone in Columbia's crusade.

It was promptly evident that our membership's strong sense of fraternity and family represented a great strength. Talking up Columbia was a deliberate instruction. Indeed, every volunteer was furnished with a brief script of the college's virtues tailored to the "ambassador's" familiar milieu. Faculty were urged to tell about Columbia on their jobs and in their professional associations. Similarly, board members were asked to advertise their Columbia service, and staff, to talk up Columbia wherever they went. We organized student visits to their former high schools and to college counselors, and encouraged students to help us recruit new students among their families and friends. We gave tuition premiums to students who got others. I think the most effective thing we did to get student support was to create deliberately a gracious, cooperative, and genuinely friendly college environment. Students weren't herded about and treated indifferently. If a student wanted just to talk to someone or had some problem, all official doors were open—mine, too. The college was scrupulously clean. Class sizes were small. Instructors came on time. Student services were not forbidding. It wasn't accidental that even as late as 1974, the greatest number of students had independent connections to other Columbia students or that, as our 1974 accrediting team discovered, Columbia had a reputation as a "good place."

The college got great public visibility from its theater, music, and dance satellites whose performances and community presence introduced Columbia to thousands of young people and audiences of all sorts. These performing-arts colonies were major generators of Columbia's rapid enrollment growth, an effect distributed among all the college's studies.

While radio and television had long been Columbia's most prominent identity, the college's emergence as a more substantial and comprehensive institution gave rise to greater notice and respect by local and network stations and to greater interest by those who contemplated careers in the broadcasting industries. By 1970, nearly every Chicago station had numbers of faculty who taught at Columbia and employed many of the college's alumni. Within a few years, Columbia had a near monopoly of part-time and entry-level jobs in Chicago television and radio stations. This benefit gave a rare foot-in-the-door opportunity to great numbers of Columbia students, who later graduated to the broadcast industry's professional ranks. Television and radio faculty, prompted by Thaine Lyman and Al Parker and their faculty, were literally an employment agency for the college's broadcasting students.

The quickly evident success of John Schultz's Story Workshop method of teaching writing and English led promptly to replications in Chicago's public schools and in colleges in other states. Story Workshop was a hot topic at the national conventions of English teachers, in educational journals, and in the local press. Similarly, Columbia's adoption of the Lessac method of teaching speech enjoyed valuable publicity. It was important that Columbia gain recognition and respect for its innovative pedagogy apart from its media and arts specialties. Such reputation gave Columbia convincing collegiate dimension.

The Photography Department's rapid ascent as a respected national center of photographic education won a wealth of publicity; and the department's organization of the college's photography museum and sponsorship of an annual public lecture series featuring the stars of world photography contributed valuably to Columbia's reputation. Charles Traub, the department's chair, was an exceptional leader and instinctive entrepreneur.

Tony Loeb led the college's Film Department to quick prominence, too. The department's sponsorship of film festivals, annual juried screenings of student films entered in Academy Award competitions, and yearly events showing outstanding short films and documentaries at Chicago film theaters all attracted large audiences and provided forums for exchange between Midwest filmmakers. Tony was also instrumental in founding the State of Illinois and Chicago Film offices to encourage feature film production in the city and state. Funding of Film Department projects by the National Film Institute and other major film agencies added to the department's cachet and correspondingly to Columbia's reputation. The department's symposium on blacklisting in the film and entertainment industries was a national event.

Bill Russo was a fount of recognition and publicity. Harry Bouras had a ubiquitous presence in the cultural and artistic life of Chicago. For many years, he was the city's most visible arts figure, and he was consistently identified with Columbia. His and Russo's close associations with the college were taken as testaments to the virtues of Columbia's instruction in the arts and humanities and as confirmations of the college's intellectual quality. Such respects were not small matters for Columbia. Most recently regarded by the public and educational community as a broadcasting school, Columbia's collegiate pretensions were viewed suspiciously at best.

Shirley Mordine was the harbinger of Chicago's burgeoning modern dance movement. Her great publicity stemmed from her extraordinary creativity as a dancer and choreographer and from the fact that the Columbia College Dance Center was then the city's only performing venue devoted exclusively to contemporary dance. The Dance Center gave a unique opportunity to legions of local, national, and foreign dancers and dance companies. The center's dance programs were the most publicized Columbia activities.

I spent a long time in publicitors' kindergarten and in a similar grade as a fund raiser. I was, as told, a habitué of Mike Fish's restaurant. Among Fish's customers was an elderly fellow, I believe named Red Morey, who was reputed to have been a notable gambler. He always dined alone, and I had only a nodding awareness of him. But one evening, he came over to my table to tell me that he wintered in California with his good friend, Jake Factor (more commonly known as Jake "The Barber" Factor, a notorious name from the 1930s). Red said that Mike Fish had told him a bit about me and Columbia, and that when he saw Jake, who was a generous fellow, he would ask him to make a gift to Columbia. I hopefully assembled a kit of Columbia materials to furnish Red's appeal. I didn't see him again until the spring when he told me with tearful regret that Jake had said, "I'd do anything for you, Red, but this year I'm only giving to Jewish hospitals." If nothing else, it's always good to know your competition.

My early and sustaining vision of a contemporary urban college was of an institution that combined an excellent quality of instruction and student support with an extension of its services to the general community. Typically, college and university extension programs offer instruction to adult learners, whose study interests are not usual components of curricula, or to extend college opportunity to off-campus and irregular students. My interpretation of "extension" did not emphasize instruction. Instead, I sought to organize activity centers that had independent public lives, and projects and events related to the college's specialties.

Columbia could not find a model in major comprehensive universities, whose research concentrations, particularly in science, and focus on graduate studies were designed to serve the common welfare and the diverse expectations of the national and world economy. Columbia had far more modest ambitions, and whatever extensions we contemplated would obviously be limited by the college's specialized educational purview and minimal resources. I was influenced, however, by the impulse and energy of the extension project performed by Southern Illinois University and its later maligned President Delight Morris, who pioneered a remarkable program that served the people of southern Illinois in the 1950s and 1960s. I found lesson, too, in UCLA's imaginative extension program during the same period.

It was clear to me that nothing we might do to perfect our educational quality could more quickly relieve Columbia's anonymity and generate greater public notice and constituency than giving the college a visible and valuable presence in

Chicago's cultural affairs. In short, we needed to find ways to give public expression to Columbia's mission.

If I had any doubt about this perception, it was quickly cured by the experience of the college's performing-arts satellites, whose artistic and community vitality gave the public a sense that Columbia was a far more substantial college institution than it actually was. What was born as an educational experiment was unintentionally a public relations coup.

The 1968 conference, "The Arts and the Inner City," marked Columbia as an important center of contemporary ideas, and the myriad public activities generated by Columbia's faculty and the blizzard of enthusiastic rhetoric issued by the college and its small band of advocates created an institution of mythic proportion. As reported by our accreditation examiners in 1974, "Every kid on the street knew about Columbia College." It seemed that whatever the issue or event, someone identifying themselves with Columbia had noticeable presence. As said, everything Columbia did had a promotional implication.

In Columbia's earlier times and currently, the college's "extensions" and an array of projects and events have been a prominent part of its institutional interests and public identity. I doubt if there is a college or arts institution anywhere that remotely rivals Columbia's assortment of public expressions and arts agencies. Indeed, I am perplexed by the absence of recognition that Columbia is and has for years been Chicago's major arts organization, especially when the comprehensiveness of Columbia's arts engagements are properly valued. Apart from the fact that Columbia is the largest educator and employer of the city's arts professionals, I submit that no agency or venue for the arts has comparably generated such a variety and scale of significant arts activities.

For example, in 1978 alone, Dr. Amy Horton, Columbia's extension director, and other Columbia folk, organized an array of general public and community-focused conferences, workshops, and lecture series. These included:

Arts and Community Life, a three-day conference of African-American, Latino, Native American, and other community arts organizations.

Alinsky in Retrospect, a series which featured labor, social work, political, and church leaders.

The Literature and Politics of Irish Nationalism, a series involving prominent playwrights, novelists, musicians, and scholars.

Workshop for Elder Craftsmen, held in a south-suburban African-American community.

Street Vision: Photography and the City, a community course in photojournalism for nonprofessionals.

Mexican Folk Arts Workshop, a course for Latino young people in the Pilsen community.

Needlework Crafts, a workshop for older women in Uptown.

Art and Architecture, a series done in cooperation with the AIA.

New Life in Five Older Communities, a one-year series done with the Metropolitan Housing and Planning Council and social scientists, educators, and community leaders.

Community Education for Media Access, a continuing program for African-Americans, Latinos, women, and older adults.

An *Intergenerational Arts Program* sponsored in a number of communities.

A *Cultural Resource Project on Native Americans in Chicago,* developed with the Tribal Council of the American Indian Center.

An *Arts in Prison Program* done in cooperation with minority arts organizations and prisoner support groups.

A three-day *National Mural Conference,* organized by Mark Rogovin, who painted the beautiful mural that decorates the entire west end of the 600 building's lobby, brought together prominent muralists and advocates of public art and sculpture in outdoor neighborhood settings.

At the same time, the inventive work of Columbia's Southern Cultural Center in Uptown continued, as did work on Susann Craig's compilation of a Directory of Ethnic Arts and Artisans. Thaine Lyman, chair of Columbia's Television Department, quite singularly generated great public resistance within Congress and among many civic organizations to the Frey Bill, which would have allowed commercial broadcasters to virtually ignore federal regulations governing the industry's public service responsibilities. Additionally, Columbia was prominent in a two-year project concerned with the rehabilitation of Chicago's South Shore district, which included representatives of the main agencies of the community's life and commerce and enjoyed great citizen participation. Funded by Title I, a cooperative state and federal program, the South Shore project became a national model of community redevelopment.

In 1978, the college's coordinator of veterans affairs, Ron DeYoung, made an important contribution to the nation's welfare. DeYoung, in the course of his job, together with a small cadre of Vietnam veterans, discovered information that led to initiation of what became a national and world alarm about the dangers of Agent Orange, the dioxins widely used by the army as defoliants in Vietnam and by forest management agencies in the United States. Their efforts prompted a national movement which enlisted great numbers of Vietnam veterans, medical professionals, environmentalists, scientists, politicians, media principals, and ordinary citizens and the major veterans' and countless national organizations, in advocating compassionate remedy for veterans who had been disabled by the effects of Agent Orange. Worthy of special note was the help of CBS's Bill Kurtis, who initially publicized the plight of veterans exposed to dangerous chemicals during the Vietnam War.

The record shown refers only to ad hoc "extensions" in 1978 and excludes many of the college's public projects conducted by arts, media, and liberal education departments. A similar catalog of ad hoc projects could be compiled for any other year. In ensuing years, many permanent and influential public agencies of Columbia's interest were established.

Columbia has always been a uniquely lively and activist place. Faculty, students, alumni, and staff participate prominently in the artistic life of the city and in all manner of human services. Columbia's emphasis on a community mission gave unusual vitality to its education, but it also gave the college remarkable visibility and public presence. Arguably, in the last twenty-five years Columbia has enjoyed more media publicity than other Chicago educational institutions, many of far greater size and prestige. Perhaps Columbia had a greater wealth of valuable happenings.

In my earliest attempts to get Columbia greater public visibility and respected distinction and to instill greater institutional pride, I speculated that Columbia needed to be associated in the public mind with notable people. I learned this from my father's publicity stunt of giving an honorary degree to Jimmy Durante, and when he honored more appropriate individuals twenty years later in Los Angeles.

As recorded, Gwendolyn Brooks was the first recipient of Columbia's honorary doctorate in 1964. That event, begun with the idea that commencement could be used to give the college greater public visibility and respect, was the precursor of what has become Columbia's annual celebration of "Artists in Human Service."

The Columbia College Chicago commencements each year honor outstanding individuals in the arts, public information, education, literature and the humanities, science, and politics, who have engaged their great talents in important human service, and whose life work and example embodies the college's ideals and spirit. Some of these have leading prominence, some ennobled by courageous labor in unpopular causes would not be awarded usual recognitions, and some are only at the beginning time of their great promise. . . . Columbia College Chicago has conferred these recognitions for itself and to represent this city whose healthy traditions and aspirations are honored by these honors – this whole city which is the college's campus and the vital spring of its learning.

For my entire tenure, I chose, with some counsel, nearly all the recipients of Columbia's commencement honors and wrote all the citations that heralded their awards. It was my pleasure to put Columbia in the company of human nobility. Commencement occasions were Columbia's largest public events, and we enjoyed exceptional publicity from the media exposure of our distinguished honorees, who over the years graciously put themselves to the college's service.

Among those Columbia has honored:

Gwendolyn Brooks, Poet

Curtis D. MacDougall, Distinguished Teacher

John Brademas, Leader of Congress

Frederick Douglas O'Neal, President, Actors Equity

Eugene Rabinowitch, Editor, Bulletin of Atomic Scientists

Langston Hughes, Poet

Norman Corwin, Writer, Poet, Playwright

Kenneth F. Montgomery, Attorney

Dwight W. Follett, Publisher

Ralph Nader, Citizen

Louis J. "Studs" Terkel, Writer

Edward Kennedy "Duke" Ellington, Composer

David Halberstam, Reporter and Pulitzer Prizewinner

Charles Wilbert White, Artist

Sr. Ann Ida Gannon, B.V.M., President, Mundelein College

William M. Birenbaum, President, Antioch University

Fannie Lou Hamer, Chairman, Mississippi Freedom Democratic Party

Frank Reynolds, Broadcast Journalist

R. Buckminster Fuller, Architect

Aaron Siskind, Photographer, Teacher

Joseph Papp, Director, New York Public Theater and Shakespeare Festival

Kay Boyle, Writer

Newton N. Minow, Public Servant, Attorney

William "Bill" Russell, Sports Commentator, Coach, Athlete

Neil Sheehan, Pulitzer Prizewinning Reporter, *The New York Times*

Chester "Howlin' Wolf" Burnett, Musician

Pauline Kael, Motion Picture Critic

Quentin D. Young, National Chairman, Medical Comm. for Human Rights

Myles F. Horton, Director, Highlander Folk School

Rosa Parks, Montgomery, Alabama

Bob Fosse, Film, Theater, and Television Director

Harrison E. Salisbury, Associate Editor, *The New York Times*

Charlemae Rollins, Acclaimed Librarian

Ruth Page, Dancer

James Farrell, Writer

Ivan Albright, Artist

Seymour Hersh, Pulitzer Prizewinning Reporter, *The New York Times*

Alexander L. C. Wilder, Composer

Arthur Mitchell, Director, Dance Theater of Harlem

Ed Bullins, Playwright

Jonathan Kozol, Educator, Social Critic

Katherine Kuh, Art Critic, Curator, Writer

Roman Vishniac, Biologist and Microphotographer

John Hammond, "Columbus" of American Music

Daniel Schorr, Broadcast Journalist

Gordon Parks, Sr., Photographer, Filmmaker, Writer

Maria Martinez, Potter

Oriana Fallaci, Journalist and Novelist

Carlos Chavez, Composer-Conductor

Addie Wyatt, Labor Humanist

Abby Mann, Television-Film Writer

Henry Aaron, Hero

Edgar Y. "Yip" Harburg, Lyricist

Many remained good and helpful friends of Columbia, and many remained my friends, too. A number of our honorees returned to Columbia as speakers and resident scholars. Most memorably: David Halberstam, who was the featured speaker at many college events; Neil Sheehan and his wife, Susan, also a distinguished journalist, who served a two-week residency; and Tom Wicker, Harry Edwards, and Oriana Fallaci, whose residencies were signal occasions. The Fallaci residency was particularly extraordinary. Among its exhausting schedule of events was a public lecture (more like a mass meeting) by this remarkable woman, who spoke about graffiti authored by political prisoners on the walls of their cells, which she had recorded all over the world. Her lecture was a staggering piece of theater.

At the 1967 commencement, which honored Norman Corwin, the greatest of all radio dramatists, the centerpiece of the program was the closing prayer from Corwin's poetic drama *On a Note of Triumph* broadcast to a world audience in May 1945, to celebrate the victorious end of World War II in Europe. The "prayer" and its facing illustration, created by Gerry Gall, were included in every commencement program during my tenure.

Columbia's commencements were carefully staged and designed to show the college at its best. Bill Russo's music was dependably spectacular. The occasion usually began with a brilliantly sung medley of "America the Beautiful" and "Lift Every Voice." I have a poignant memory of standing on the stage next to Henry Aaron when the orchestra and singers began "Lift Every Voice." He asked me how we happened to do that music, and I replied that it was what Columbia was all about. He held my hand while the song was played.

At another memorable occasion, the faculty gave me a baseball autographed by all of the White Sox players and a private dinner with Willie Mays, which Jack Brickhouse had arranged. I had a mixed mind about meeting my hero. Viewing stars from afar avoids the risk of discovering that one's hero's feet have turned to clay. To lessen the shock and to overcome some trepidation, I invited sports columnist and later Pulitzer prizewinner Tom Fitzpatrick to join me at dinner with Mays. It turned out to be a wonderful time, except for a stream of insistent autograph seekers. Mays was charming, perfectly friendly, and genuinely bright. Fitz told me later that he had interviewed Mays many times and he had never revealed so much of himself as he did at our dinner.

I tried many times to honor Doris Lessing, Robertson Davies, Pete Seeger, Nadine Gordimer, Saul Alinsky, and Bill Veeck among others, but our commencement dates never fit their schedules. As most of the members of Columbia's graduating classes until the 1980s were the first of their family to get a college degree, commencements had an unusually festive and celebratory mood. The house was always packed, even for occasions at the Prudential Building Auditorium in the 1960s when we had fewer than one hundred graduates (only twenty-five in 1964). In the mid-1970s, we moved the commencements to the Auditorium Theater, which seated 3,000 people. By 1988, there were nearly 1,000 graduates, both undergraduate and graduate students, requiring an even larger arena. So Columbia's commencements moved to the Amphitheater on the University of Illinois Chicago campus, which could seat an audience of 7,000. Despite an unwieldy number of graduates, we continued to announce every graduate's name and each walked across the stage to get his or her diploma. It was a slow go, made even slower by irrepressible family cheering.

After-graduation parties are part of our commencement traditions. It's hard to imagine now that our earliest parties included all of the faculty, staff, board members, honorees, and introducers, students who worked the graduation, and even some of the graduates and their families. Somehow, the 250 or so of us fit into a downstairs room of the Blackhawk Restaurant at Randolph and Wabash. When the numbers got too big, there were two parties: one which Jane and I hosted for commencement principals, friends of the college and board and media folk at Deni's Den, and years later, at Andy's, a premiere jazz club; the other, a separate faculty gathering at the University of Illinois Faculty Club, though comings and goings between the parties was a usual part of our late-night festivities, which often ended in after-hour locations and next-day breakfasts.

1978–1979

Our new Michigan Avenue identity contributed to the college's enrollment growth. We had projected 2,800 as the number of students who could be comfortably housed in the 600 building without the reconstruction of the last space vacated by tenants. We hadn't expected to reach 2,800 students until 1980, which would have given us time to settle some obligations and to gather the funds for the final remodeling project. It was unimaginable, even weeks before, that the college would almost immediately be pressed for greater space, particularly when our judgment was that the 600 building was as big a place as Columbia would ever need. The board's immediate response was a futile gesture to limit the college's enrollment in 1978–79 to 2,750 students, a measure that ignored the fact that Columbia's prosperity depended on continuing enrollment growth.

We had planned to move the Film and Photography Departments and everything else that remained at 540 at the end of the summer of 1977. This schedule, however, could not be kept because of construction delays and greater than anticipated costs, so part of the Film Department and other functions could not be moved to 600 until the end of the 1977 fall semester. The enrollment gain allowed us to budget $110,000 to complete the remodeling of the twelfth floor, but we lost the luxury of time when the city's building department insisted that the college vacate all of 540 by the first of the 1978 year at the latest. Everything did get done and moved during the Christmas break.

We had sold the Theater-Music building to a Japanese fraternal organization for the astonishing price of $60,000, $25,000 more than we'd paid originally. Suddenly, we had an unexpected $60,000, and we promptly used it to pay off the Continental Bank loan, which we'd just taken to finance the purchase of the Dance Center property. What a delightful windfall.

In January 1978, the newly constructed Photography, Craft, and Folk Arts Gallery opened with speeches and a ceremony. With more than 1,000 people attending the gallery's first exhibit, it was a big event.

That year was the beginning, too, of a new study concentration in Arts and Entertainment Management and of a Labor Education Division. An educational emphasis on the business and management functions of the arts and entertainment industries was a logical expansion of Columbia's arts and communications interests. The project began in conversations I had with Fred Fine, who had been the vice president of Triangle Productions, then the largest national booking agency of popular music concerts. Most recently, Fine had been the vice president of the Madison Square Garden Corporation, whose president, Frank Fried, was a longtime Columbia board member and had previously headed Triangle.

Fred Fine was (and still is, at age eighty-eight) a remarkable man. He loves the theater. Indeed, as a prominent member of the Jefferson Committee, whose coveted annual awards celebrate "the best in all categories of professional theater," Fred attends virtually everything performed in the Chicago region, an exhausting self-assignment that has prevailed for more than thirty years. He is a national authority on popular music and arts policy, and a respected friend of the arts and artists of every discipline. A genuinely wise man, he has a lively and insightful intelligence about politics, history, and literature, and has an abiding commitment to human welfare. He was responsible for organizing the Illinois Arts Alliance and other arts advocacies. If one had to define the ideal qualifications for the head of a college department of arts and entertainment management, a description of Fred Fine would be perfect. I cannot imagine a more decent, kind, compassionate, productive and loving man or a better and more loyal friend. At a time when very few colleges and universities had much interest in arts and entertainment management, Fred Fine's Columbia project anticipated what has become a popular college concentration and career.

Fred Fine and I together planned a program in concert management and other careers in the popular music industry. Ultimately, it would embrace the business functions of all of the college's arts specialties. Fred's first course offering was "Pop Concert Management." If everyone who wanted the class had been registered, it would have had more than 500 students. Whatever else, it was surely a testament to the immense popularity of music in contemporary youth culture. By the fall of 1978, the Arts and Entertainment Management program offered business courses in a number of the college's concentrations, even "How to Manage a Photography Store." Predictably, some of Fred's efforts occasioned turf wars with other departments who insisted that their purview included anything related to their department title. It wasn't the first time, nor would it be the last, when an innovative project was compromised by college politics.

The Labor Education Division was planned as an extension program which could reach an atypical college audience. The project intended initial focus on trade union subjects: union organizing, training shop stewards, and labor negotiations. We were encouraged in this effort by a number of trade union leaders who wanted to educate workers in trade unionism, and to extend college opportunities to their memberships. At the urging of these union officials, I hired Paul Johnson, an experienced union organizer, a Ph.D. candidate in Latin American history, a member of the University of New Mexico's faculty, and former director of the Boston Labor School. Johnson was an ideal choice as the labor program's director, and would have been similarly ideal for a great range of Columbia positions. Expert in labor education and American history, he was intensely interested in literature, jazz music, and the theater, and is an enthusiastic sports fan. An exceptional organizer, Paul was kind and fair-minded, honorable and committed to human service. He is a strong-looking, quiet, and confident man, who quickly inspired trust and affection. Impatient with pretense, he was entirely comfortable with lofty and lowly alike—and all with him. These descriptions apply equally today.

Columbia's labor education program got off to a rousing start. Paul had organized a one-day conference on "The Media Image of Labor," which had as its principal participants Lloyd McBride, president of the United Steel Workers of America; William Wimpisinger, president of the International Association of Machinists (IAM), Robert Johnston, regional director of the United Auto Workers (UAW); James Hoge, publisher of the *Chicago Sun-Times*; Phil Boyer, manager of ABC-TV Chicago; Joe Flaherty, a novelist and notable writer on labor issues; and

TV news anchor Bill Kurtis. Studs Terkel was the moderator. The audience was filled with labor and media people, members of university faculties, and representatives of business and industry. The local and national media gave great publicity to the event and to Columbia's sponsorship. It was a confident beginning.

But while the program had labor's encouragement and despite Paul's diligent efforts, organizing classes from the membership of participating unions reflected the growing indifference, even among unionized workers, to trade union causes, a phenomenon that presaged the diminution of trade union sentiment, locally and nationally. After two years, the labor education program was abandoned. Paul left Columbia then to become the manager of the Rosemont Horizon, which became a major sports and popular entertainment venue. After five years at that, Paul served as the personnel manager of a prominent company before returning to Columbia in 1989 as the college's director of human resources, a critical position he holds today.

September 1978 began a year of decisions: the big one, the tests of reaccreditation in March 1979; and a number of other resolutions which confirmed that Columbia had become a real college and was a pretty big business to boot.

At the same time in 1978, two new offices were created. Bert Gall was appointed as dean of administration; and Hubert Davis as dean of the Office of Institutional Research, though Davis retained some supervisory role in the college's library and continued to counsel the student aid programs. Valjean Jones, an experienced administrator of student affairs, replaced Hubert as the dean of students.

Valjean left in 1981 to manage a department at the University of South Carolina, and she was replaced as dean of students by Ed Navakas, who had been Columbia's director of admissions. But Navakas, too, left after a brief time. And so began the remarkable tenure of Hermann Conaway as dean of students, a term that lasted until 1992 when he died suddenly. Hermann was a wonderful man, critical leader, and wise counsel of Columbia's life. We thought of him as indispensable. What an awful loss.

Hubert Davis was a valuable and versatile Columbia mainstay. He originated the college's library, introduced Columbia to the opportunities of state and federal student aid, and was authoritative in the uses and languages of computers when they were alien garble to nearly everyone else. Hubert left Columbia several years later to become an Episcopal priest, a response to an earlier calling. He died in 1988.

Two thousand eight hundred fifty-three students enrolled that fall, a 14 percent gain over the year before. A significant part of that increase resulted from the quick growth of the Arts and Entertainment Management Department, whose enrollment became 4 percent of the college's total, and greater numbers enrolled in art, graphics, and craft subjects, which validated the controversial decision to devote two floors of the 600 South Michigan building to the Art Department. When Charles Traub resigned as chair of the Photography Department to become the head of a major New York gallery, he was succeeded by John Mulvaney, who had been a member of the Photography faculty in 1975 and 1976 before leaving to become chair of the Art Department of Illinois Wesleyan University.

When Mulvaney returned in 1978, it was as chair of a combined Art and Photography Department, a role he performed with great distinction for twenty-one years until his retirement in June 1999. During John's exceptional tenure, Columbia's Art and Photography Department achieved national rank and became the college's largest in credit-hour enrollment. Mulvaney influenced the development of Columbia's prestigious Museum of Contemporary Photography, and the department's very successful concentration in Fashion Design and Merchandising. He led his department's comprehensive incorporation of the sophisticated computer technology that has revolutionized contemporary graphic arts and photography. In Mulvaney's first year, Art and Photography got a ready-to-wear department and career emphasis in interior design. Columbia gave a home to ninety students and several talented faculty of a failed school in that specialty, which nonetheless enjoyed a respected reputation. One of these faculty transfers, Anthony Patano, remained at Columbia for twenty years until his recent retirement as head of the department's interior design program, which prospered under Mulvaney's inventive guidance.

A gifted leader and unusually skillful manager, Mulvaney was a dogged negotiator and consummate politician, a man to be reckoned with. He had a ruddy look and Irish charm. Academia's gain was City Hall's loss. John was an excellent photographer and compelling teacher, a New York City blue-collar guy who drove a truck to support his intense determination to become an educated man. Mulvaney was a compelling and thoughtful advocate and principled adversary, who unquestionably had an influential role in Columbia's life.

In 1978, Columbia made an arrangement with Roosevelt University to share libraries. As Roosevelt University had a mature collegiate library with more than 300,000 books and a great array of library services, Columbia paid an annual fee to Roosevelt of $10,000, which was a small price to pay for the great opportunity the arrangement gave to Columbia students. The deal also compensated for our library deficiencies when Columbia was measured for reaccreditation.

In September 1978, the full-time faculty numbered fifty. Only eight of the faculty had served more than ten years, and in 1998, five of those and thirty-one from the 1978 list were still active members of Columbia's faculty. Also by 1978, a host of new administrative, student service, and technical staff people had joined the college, many in capacities unimagined only a few years earlier. Including part-time faculty, more than 330 people worked at Columbia in 1978, exclusive of student workers.

At its December 1978 meeting, after months of study, the board adopted a new defined-benefit pension plan for the college's full-time employees. The pension plan previously in place projected limited benefits and required employee contributions of 2 percent of an individual's annual salary, matched by a like contribution by the college; though employees had additional opportunity to make tax-sheltered contributions to individual retirement accounts. While ultimate pension benefits of the earlier plan were comparatively small, these did represent an effort to share the college's prosperity with faculty and staff, whose extraordinary loyalty had made Columbia's success possible. Undoubtedly, the new retirement plan, fully paid by the college and adopted in 1978, stretched the boundaries of affordability. Some board members believed that providing such a scale of uncertainly funded retirement benefits was premature and even imprudent, in view of Columbia's still precarious finances and the newness of its minimal prosperity. Notwithstanding such arguments, the board finally supported my contention that Columbia had come of age enough to have confidence in its continuity and in its ability to subscribe the costs of a commitment to the long-range security of its employees. I doubt if such a decision could have been won without John Scheibel's tireless and imaginative effort to document the retirement plan's affordability and to design a plan with unusual benefits.

I continue to be amazed at the audacity that led to the adoption of Columbia's pension and benefit plan when I remember that only a few years before, the best any of us could hope for was that we would have a job the next year, and during the 1960s, that we'd even get paid next month. In the late 1970s, Columbia began (and continues) to provide a most generous employee benefit package including, in addition to retirement benefits, very liberal medical coverage, disability insurance, and life insurance (equal to two and three times an individual's salary).

I was a firm believer, too, in giving sabbatical leaves to faculty, particularly to those, in Columbia's instance, who worked so assiduously at teaching and at counseling students and monitoring part-time faculty. Many of Columbia's full-time faculty had credit loads of sixteen hours and more, and all had occupation with their department's administration and community extensions—all this usually at the expense of their own artistic, professional, and scholarly work. Obviously, chairs and full-time faculty had great need for a periodic opportunity to renew themselves and to pursue independent projects.

After the pension decision and feeling I was on a bit of a roll, I again summoned Scheibel's statistics, which helped me to persuade the board to adopt a sabbatical leave policy that had been drafted by faculty and chairperson representatives. Initially, some board members questioned the sabbatical plan, grumbling that "other folk work hard and they don't get sabbaticals." But opposition quickly waned. Albeit then a minimal policy, it was a big step over what had been an utter void.

Over time there were some modifications to the sabbatical leave policy, and one significant change in the grant of full pay for leave time. As recipients usually tacked on a summer absence to their sabbaticals, in practical effect, the leave extended over a nine to ten month period. I never used my sabbatical opportunities, as neither I nor the board had any idea how the college could function without me for an extended time. By the time it probably could have, I was already in sight of retirement. But, let no one doubt, there were occasions when the crown of indispensability weighed heavily.

I have no memory whatsoever about what prompted the board's adoption of procedures to choose a successor president. It probably had something to do with faculty discussion about the college's governance, a subject of only occasional interest. While I had no intention in 1978 to leave the president's office, I suppose, as in contemplating a sabbatical, I had expressed some notion of the pleasures of leisure. Whatever, fixing the presidential succession was a sensible and prudent course. It was a comparatively simple procedure that, with minimal alteration, remained in force until its first exercise when my successor was chosen in 1992.

The board agreed to fully computerize its administrative operations. John Scheibel had submitted a brief, supported by expert consultants, that urged the purchase or lease of a sophisticated compatible computer system to replace piece-meal acquisitions and by now obsolete instruments and systems we'd assembled in the past. Scheibel's report recommended that the college lease a system manufactured by the Digital Equipment Corporation which would use POISE software adapted to our needs, and both companies would train the college's personnel in the system's use. Scheibel and his consultants had selected Digital hardware and POISE software after bids by a number of companies had been evaluated. If purchased outright, the hardware and software components would cost $125,000 (many, many times that in today's dollars); but a lease with a five-year term, at roughly $35,000 a year, would be a far more affordable choice that would relieve the college of a big cash payment. The board concurred with Scheibel's proposals to acquire and lease the computer system described. The introduction of the new system was, of course, chaotic, but in time reasonable comfort was restored and far greater efficiency enjoyed.

When Columbia first contemplated a building purchase in 1974 and 1975, we had inquired about using a bond issue supported by the Illinois Higher Educational Facilities Authority to finance the acquisition. At that time, the authority decided that Columbia's current and projected resources didn't qualify for bond-issue eligibility. Surprisingly, only three years later, the college was judged to have sufficient financial strength and promise to qualify for the authority's support. It was surely a convincing validation of Columbia's quick success. Scheibel, Ira Kipnis, the college's legal counsel, the board's finance committee, and I, and authority representatives labored for months at negotiating the terms of a bond issue. What was finally agreed to was an issue of revenue bonds in the amount of $2,600,000 to refinance the purchase, remodeling, and major maintenance costs of 600 South Michigan, these bonds to be secured by a first mortgage on the property and the college's commitment to repayment. The Continental Illinois Bank committed to the purchase of the bonds for a fifteen-year term at an interest rate of 7.5 percent.

Annual payments during the fifteen-year term would be approximately $300,000, and as bond issue proceeds would be used to retire the college's building mortgage and bank loan indebtedness, the bond issue resulted in a reduction of $200,000 to $300,000 in annual operating expenses and relieved the college of the burden of having to make a $900,000 balloon payment on the mortgage in 1985. Wow! What a grand benefit the bond issue was. Apart from large savings of interest payments, bond issue proceeds allowed the college to pay off the 600 building's mortgage within five years, which earned a $100,000 rebate recorded in the purchase document. In effect Columbia had bought the building for $1,225,000.

There was encouraging news, too, in Wolfsohn's report on fund-raising in the 1978–79 year. New gifts and grants were secured from the Woods Charitable Fund, Inland Steel-Ryerson Foundation, People's Gas, R. R. Donnelley and Sons, International Minerals and Chemicals, the Joyce Foundation, Interlake Steel Corporation, the *Chicago Sun-Times,* Oscar Mayer, Sears Roebuck, Santa Fe Railroads, Motorola, Shell Corporation, Carson Pirie Scott and Co., Esmark Inc.,

and the UOP Foundation. Also, we received government grants of more than $150,000 from the National Endowment for the Arts and Humanities, the U.S. Office of Education, the Illinois Arts Council, Chicago Office of Manpower, and the Illinois Humanities Council.

While some of these grants had the assistance of faculty members and several board individuals, the main work was done by Jack Wolfsohn, and a grant writer, Victor Margolin, with some proposal writing and visitation by me, though Jack was the spur of it all. This, in addition to managing all the activity of capital and annual giving campaigns.

With the evidence of a profitable 1977–78 year, similar results were forecast for the current 1978–79 year. Anticipation for the following years, however, was uncertain. Double-digit inflation was an immediate prospect, and it was certain that the number of college-age students would fall 20 percent by 1985. To what extent these factors would influence Illinois state and federal student aid subsidies was entirely unknown. Moreover, the costs of the college's operation in a highly inflationary environment could not be dependably estimated. Albeit with great hesitation, the board voted in spring 1979 to increase Columbia's tuition in September to $1,250 per term for full-time students and to $87 per credit hour for part-time enrollments. Entirely abandoning any fixed enrollment ceiling, the board voted also to reorder the 600 building's space allocations and to finish the building's remodeling to minimally accommodate an enrollment of 3,600 students. And that seemed an awfully big stretch.

While the board was encouraged by the results of the Minter Report, a comparative study of all Illinois independent nonpublic colleges and universities sponsored by the Illinois Board of Higher Education, enthusiasm was tempered by Columbia's ratio of debt to net worth. The Minter Report, however, confirmed Columbia's dramatic improvement over a four-year period, 1974–78. In almost all respects, Columbia had far surpassed the results of the greatest majority of Illinois private institutions. Columbia's full-time-equivalent numbers increased by 133 percent, while group four colleges (four-year undergraduate) had increased 13 percent, and all Illinois institutions, taken together, by only 2 percent. In total revenue generated, Columbia's increased by 119 percent, compared to a 36 percent average increase by all other Illinois institutions. Columbia's total educational and general expenses increased by 95 percent, whereas the average increase for all institutions was 23 percent. Even more striking, Columbia's unrestricted fund balance increased by 494 percent compared to a 1 percent average for all institutions. In 1977, Columbia College ranked fifth of fifty-three independent Illinois institutions in terms of percent of net revenues to total revenues. Columbia's appearance of profitability was, however, misleading when compared with the financial state of other institutions. Unlike most colleges and universities, Columbia had no significant endowments or reserve funds, and whatever net revenues it produced were promptly reinvested in the college's improvement. For most Illinois colleges, educational and general expenses are funded at about 70 percent from tuition and fees and 30 percent from other incomes. In Columbia's instance, the ratio is 95 percent from tuition and 5 percent from other resources. Our success, too, has acutely contradictory elements. While some of Columbia's investment in capital assets was financed by new revenues, the largest part was funded by long-term debt commitments. Though this was incurred most prudently and its retirement well within the college's expected financial resources, debt had a heavy claim on whatever prosperity the college enjoyed. In the meantime, we were buoyed by the Minter Report that Columbia's enrollment had grown by 269 percent in the four years studied. Regrettably, tuition had increased in the same period by more than 70 percent, though Columbia's tuition remained substantially lower than any other Illinois institution.

In 1978–79, Columbia's board newly included Louise Benton, president of Encyclopedia Britannica Films; architect Norman DeHaan; and distinguished attorney Albert Jenner. Columbia's agenda in 1978 and 1979 was crowded with a range of critical issues, but the primary concern was reaccreditation, which required submission of a comprehensive self-study in November 1978 and on-site inspection in March 1979. While the tasks of preparation for the college's examination were no less consuming than five years before, at least this time we had some experience with the accreditation process and could better organize for its expected trials. Most importantly, in 1979 Columbia sought reaccreditation as an already accredited college, which was far different from seeking accreditation without prior credentials. Of equal benefit was that in 1978 the college had sufficient staff and resources to prepare a mature and comprehensively documented self-study, which was impossible in 1973.

The self-study, spanning a year and a half, was again a massive task of information gathering and interpretation. It was headed by the college's dean, Lya Rosenblum, with the close assistance of Doris Salisbury, who was appointed to supervise assembling the data. Sixty-two members of the faculty and administration participated. With detailed and individualized guidelines, every academic and administrative department and function conducted its own self-study, including instructional technicians, and maintenance and custodial staff. All were asked to evaluate the quality of their services and their relation to students' welfare and benefit. The research firm Daniel Coffey and Associates was hired to question 3,000 students and alumni, both graduates and nongraduates. Ultimately, 1,760 individuals responded with detailed information about themselves and their Columbia experience. A market research agency, Goldring and Co., conducted twenty-five extended focus group sessions with students and alumni. Faculty members interviewed more than fifty employers of students and alumni, to ask them to evaluate the on-the-job competence of students educated by Columbia. Terry Sullivan, Columbia's registrar, did an in-depth study of every member of the college's 1978 graduating class. Dr. Laurence Barrett, who had been the Chairman of Columbia's 1974 accreditation team, and Dr. Joseph Elmore, whose counsel had been invaluable in our first accreditation adventure, advised the 1978 self-study. And I, as intended, wrote the self-study document, though this time I had far more dependable and orderly information to use in my exposition.

The self-study had two main themes. One was an assessment of Columbia's educational, vocational, cultural, and civic effect on its students; in essence, how well the college served them. The second was how well Columbia managed its growth and change.

We began our answer with a brief summary of Columbia's state in the autumn of 1978:

This is the document of a young college whose cardinal characteristics are unusual, at least so when occurring in close constellation. Columbia is a big-city, downtown, independent, open-admission, and comparatively specialized liberal arts college, whose students reflect the social, economic, racial, cultural and educational complexities of contemporary urban America. Columbia has a strong sense of social, educational and artistic mission and the ingenuity to perform its purposes successfully. As evidenced by a comparison of numbers, Columbia's life has been shaped by great growth during the five years since last official review.

	1973–1974	1978–1979
Total enrollment	1,014	2,853
FTE of total	861	2,286
Total faculty	117	264
Faculty full-time	23	52
Main educational plant	40,000 sq. ft. (rented)	200,000 sq. ft. (owned)
Theater-Music Center	12,000 sq. ft. (owned)	
Theater-Music Center		26,000 (rented sq. ft.)★
Dance Center	15,000 (rented sq. ft.)	15,000 (owned sq. ft.)
Library	22,000 (vols.)	35,000 (vols.)
Library Shared with		
	Roosevelt University	300,000 (vols.)
Annual operating budget	$1,462,000	$5,331,000
Fund balance	$109,000	$2,200,000★★

★present Eleventh Street building with option to purchase
★★fund balance excludes building and physical assets

Other current statistics shown in the 1978 self-study:

AGE OF STUDENTS

44%   18–21 years

25%   22–25

14%   26–29

14%   over 30

3%   unreported

FAMILY INCOME

32%   less than $6,000 annually

20% $7,000–$10,000

14% $11,000– $13,000

34%   over $14,000

RACIAL COMPOSITION

54%   white

37%   African-American

3%   Latino

1%   Asian

.05%   Native American

4%   unreported

Of full-time students, 50 percent are first-time college students. Fifty percent attended other colleges before Columbia. Fifty percent of all full-time students graduated from inner-city Chicago high schools.

Given Columbia's commitment to open admissions, students' prior academic records and tests of college aptitude mainly are useful as evidence of delimiting educational handicaps and shaping student guidance. As a matter of record, in 1978, of all full-time students, 51 percent ranked in the upper half of their high school graduating classes; and half of these, roughly 25 percent of Columbia's total numbers, ranked in the upper quartile. Of the 49 percent who ranked in the lowest half of their high school graduating classes, 20 percent, or 10 percent of all students, ranked in the lowest quartile.

While Columbia did not have official subject "majors," in effect, student choice is revealed in departmental enrollments as a percentage of total college enrollment.

12%   Film

15%   Photography

28%   Radio/Television

6%   Theater/Music

2%   Dance

4%   English/Writing

5%   Art

5%   Advertising/Journalism

4%   Arts and Entertainment Management

19%   Unreported and scattered Liberal Arts

In general, retention of students to graduation is a thorny problem; and for Columbia, even more prickly. In Columbia's self-study I submitted that expecting graduation within four years for first-time freshman students was unrealistic and unreasonable and that retention is subject to a variety of interpretations. And worse, that judging institutional quality on the basis of such measures has minimal, if any, validity. I would argue similarly today that extension of the measure to six years is not much better, particularly as the graduation rates of transfer students are not incorporated in an institution's retention statistics; nor are students tracked from one college to another to determine graduation rates or other evidence of individual or institutional success. Student characteristics differ widely from campus to campus, and often even within single institutions. In fact, there is no universal student, and present efforts at standardization only pretend that individual characterizations can be commonly factored, a contention that ignores the individuality of students and institutions. I submit, too, that the present clamor for uniformity and standardized test score performance is influenced by political opportunism and the abdication of enlightened educators.

In 1978, without today's sophisticated computers, tracking students' enrollment and calculating retention rates was, at best, a difficult and uncertain task. Students often dropped out and returned in subsequent terms and many attended full-time one semester and part-time another. Sorted out, 23 percent of Columbia's first-time freshmen and 37 percent of sophomore and junior-year transfers who entered in 1974 graduated by 1978. These percentages would have been greater if six-year spans had been used as they are today. Given the large number of Columbia students who were questionably qualified for college and negatively influenced by a variety of social and economic deprivations, this retention-to-graduation record was good. What was most encouraging was the great number of individuals who ordinarily would not have had college opportunity, who became successful college students.

While my colleagues and I were acutely distressed by the evidence that many Columbia students dropped out, first-year students particularly, and we were often occupied with a search for remedy, it was unrealistic to believe that Columbia's retention rates would ever be competitive with conventional expectations. With open enrollment it is inevitable that many students, despite efforts at remediation, will become discouraged and quickly opt out. In contrast, a good number stay to master the rigors of college study. It remains elusive whether success is a matter of perseverance, an unpredictable reflection of individual differences, or the result of a combination of these and other factors.

To characterize all questionably qualified students as high risk begs the question: High risk to whom and to what? Is it that the admission of high-risk students would jeopardize the scholarly standards of institutions of higher education if some of their resources and energy were diverted from the education of "the best and the brightest"? Might institutions that have individuals capable of mapping the most distant galaxies of the universe be incapable of academic remediation? Or is "high risk" just shorthand for saying that individuals who just won't make it will find no benefit in and even be injured by exposure to more failure? The biggest risk, it seems to me, is that arbitrary designation of students as high-risk puts all those initially unqualified students in the same swamp, even though many could pull themselves out of the muck. And I am troubled by the fact that the wounds of most of those identified as high risk were not self-inflicted, and that injury was done to them by the neglected quality of their lives and by indifferent education. Unmistakably, Columbia failed many of them, too, and I have never become reconciled to that.

Understandably, with open admissions, Columbia's greatest student loss occurred among first-term and first-year students, many of whom were quickly discouraged by their failure at classroom assignments and grade reports and were unresponsive to offers of help. Usually, these students just disappeared. An inability or lack of motive to satisfy even minimal classroom expectations may have influenced their abdication. Academic insufficiency was seldom the reason. Often, a sense that they wouldn't make it was copped out with expressions of disinterest and not caring. Many failed as a result of the whole complex of influences that poverty's culture exacts on individuals. Obviously, not all of Columbia's students were poor, but many were. Not having enough money, even with student aid, to satisfy the ordinary costs of living was the most frequent reason for dropping out given by individuals interviewed for the self-study. It should be noted, also, that the late 1970s and early 1980s were times of national recession and wild inflation. Correspondingly, part-time jobs for students were scarce, and acutely so for minorities.

Although it was comparatively easy to get into Columbia, once in, Columbia was a difficult college even though its tests were not confined to expressions of academic skills, which is usually the case in freshman and sophomore years. In a learning-by-doing environment, Columbia emphasized students' learning the crafts of their subjects and exhibiting their creative energies. That Columbia was a tough go was a discouraging discovery for many students who had unrealistic notions of careers in the college's specialties and had not imagined that the route to them was difficult, competitive, and required serious commitment. Such revelations caused many to abbreviate their Columbia studies.

Self-study interviews disclosed that many students' initial career interests and choice of Columbia lacked certainty, and they simply decided to transfer to colleges that offered choices among a greater number of majors. Certainly, changing majors is not atypical nor is it unusual that exposure to unfamiliar subjects influences students to make new career and college decisions. As Columbia's focus on the arts and communications media left little room for career and study alternatives, its curricular peculiarity led numbers of students to leave Columbia for more comprehensive college institutions.

Every self-study response confirmed again that students came to Columbia because of their educational and career interests in one or several of the college's artistic or media specialties, and because at Columbia students had the opportunity of hands-on education and a faculty of professionals. They believed that Columbia was a friendly place and liked its mix of ages, races, social, economic, and cultural backgrounds. Those entering as transfer students were more comfortable than freshmen with an absence of strict course requirements. There was some indication that giving freedom in course choices may be of little benefit to those who are not prepared for the opportunity. Similarly, there was some expression of a preference for more structured course requirements, though neither emphasis had high priority among students. While Columbia had, in effect, offered itself as a college alternative for those disenchanted with conventional institutions, our inquiry did not show this to be an influential factor in students' choice of Columbia, nor was Columbia seen as an opportunity for success after prior college failure.

A large majority of students and alumni endorsed open admissions. There was some dissent among those with highest college ability and among some "lower-ability" students. Inexplicably, only 20 percent said that open admissions had figured in their decision to come to Columbia, despite the contradictory fact that a larger percentage of students wouldn't have been admitted if admissions had been more restrictive. I can only speculate that self-identity as an open admissions beneficiary may be threatening to an individual's self-image, in the same way that affirmative action is believed to demean its recipients. In a related sense, high-ability students may not want to be identified as attending a college with low admissions standards. Ninety percent of students surveyed recognized that a great variation in student abilities is unavoidable in open admissions, and 80 percent believed that Columbia satisfied the needs of students with widely different talents. This was reassuring, however inaccurate. The study of 1978 graduates confirmed that Columbia students had little interest in organized campus activities: even less so than Columbia students in 1948. On the other hand, 50 percent said that Columbia had prompted their participation in the city's cultural life and social affairs. As these activities are, in effect, the urban equivalents of student life, this verifies Columbia's contention that the city is the college's campus.

However comfortable relations between African-American and white students seemed, the self-study revealed some class and racial distinctions in attitudes to government-sponsored student aid. Students of least privilege, disproportionately African-American students, rightly viewed these subsidies as just and necessary, though not enough to survive on or to catch up with more privileged white students. In a few instances, a combination of state and federal student aid was regarded as "profitable" by students who had questionable college intentions. Some white students regarded this occasional corruption in the same way that "welfare queens" are used to discredit the grievously inadequate systems of welfare. Similar strains were present on America's campuses many years before when veterans with GI Bill benefits were aided and non-veterans were not, though such controversy then was without racial tensions. In an unjust society, any form of publicized welfare demeans its recipients, and the assumption anywhere in the educative process that a student is disadvantaged (eligible poverty implies a whole complex of disabilities) has some self-fulfilling qualities about it.

One of the self-study's principal interests was an attempt to measure Columbia's effect on students during their enrollment and in their lives after college. With this purpose, our inquiry centered on what students learn to do; their happiness, self-regard, and self-realization; their social attitudes; their intellectual development; and the occupational consequence of their education.

Together, all these have to do with students' and graduates' "quality of life." Individuals are, of course, neither reliably objective nor accurate reporters, even of themselves. Nor are those who make and ask questions and record answers entirely dependable. Presumably, a college would want to show that it makes students better than they were. Thus, evidence of change in the individual attributable to enrollment was sought. We suspected that even when it seemed evident that Columbia was the source of such changes, these may really have resulted from nonschool influences. The student is actually at a college for only a brief time. This is particularly true of a big-city commuter college like Columbia.

As only a few Columbia students had the opportunity of prior instruction in arts and media subjects or the rudiments of the college's career disciplines, nearly all began study at Columbia with minimal preparation. Thus, the evidence is unusually compelling that to individual and collective measure, Columbia's students learned the crafts of arts and media disciplines quickly and well and produced an abundant exhibit of mature talents and creative expressions. This was true of every department of the college's instruction.

The self-study detailed countless examples of student professionalism. Among these: collections of student writing in the editions of *Hair Trigger*, which has consistently won national awards as the best of collegiate prose; the many prominent awards won by film students whose professional creative quality was verified by such critics as Pauline Kael; the remarkable employment record of scores of Columbia students at commercial television and radio stations; frequent exhibits in major galleries of the work of photography students; and impressive media reviews of the performances of theater, music, and dance students.

Columbia observed that college is not simply a preparation for the next school grade or the employment market. college is an important time of life in itself and should be a happy and satisfying time of self-discovery when students can find out and enjoy what they learn to do well. Columbia's contribution to students' self-regard and self-realization was confirmed by the self-study's report of hundreds of students, parents, and recent graduates. Many said that at Columbia they got themselves together, found themselves, got confidence, straightened out, and felt they could amount to something. Such feelings did not come from test scores or grades, but from the fact that at Columbia they had become artistically and professionally competent and knowledgeable and confident in their choice of careers. Self-confidence is, of course, an essential part of an individual's self-esteem. At Columbia, many students discovered that they must do well for themselves if they are to merit their colleagues' approval, engage their teachers' respected professionalism, and in many instances, to satisfy an audience. In succeeding at these, there is self-respect.

When we began our inquiry, we anticipated that Columbia would be shown to have a liberalizing effect on students' social ideas and civic participation, but such expectations were not evidenced by student response. It was clear that students in 1978 were a sea change away from the ferment of the early 1970s.

Only some very tentative generalizations emerged from our inquiry. General social attitudes were worked in personal situations, seldom as politics. Students were sensitive to injustices, had little sense of class and race distinctions, and were very tolerant of eccentricity. It was not evident that the social attitudes of students were substantially changed by their Columbia experience. Of recent graduates: 17 percent participated in community activities; 12 percent attended church regularly; 14 percent worked in local volunteer agencies; and 10 percent in political campaigns. There was evidence that African-American and white students usually enjoyed a comfortable, if not entirely trusting, relationship within the college, a hopeful sign given the polarity of these groups elsewhere. African-American students were more involved than whites with social issues and events, and for them, racism was an inescapable constant. The social attitudes of the majority of Columbia students were formed much more out of college than in it. The most usual student and alumni response was that Columbia had not impressed a particular view on them. But many interviewed offered a quick contradiction in statements of concern about such issues as racism and the environment.

We had great difficulty in measuring Columbia's effect on students' intellectual development and the evidence of it in the lives of graduates. It's confusing now whether we meant "intellectual" to be an amalgam of cognitive skills or as a synonym for lively, scholarly, culturally responsive intelligence. We should have stuck to cognition or dropped the inquiry entirely. It would have been better to simply declare we had won the war and send the troops home. To have tried for anything more was an exercise in futility. It's enough that a fair measure of cognitive skills is had or inferred in the tests and term papers of customary undergraduate education.

But as Columbia made limited use of such examinations and was more largely dependent on faculty estimates of the quality and creativity of students' work and performance, it had even less objective evidence of students' intellectual development. And evidence of graduates' intellect was, at best, only subjective and anecdotal. Most Columbia students and graduates testified that Columbia gave them an excellent opportunity to be as well educated as they wanted to be. Most felt that Columbia had helped them to read, write, and speak better. And a surprising number said that Columbia had influenced them to attend theater, dance, and music performances—even symphony concerts—and to enjoy art galleries and museums. Eighty percent reported that they regularly read books, fiction and nonfiction. Sixty-three percent read three or more magazines monthly and 52 percent regularly read daily newspapers. When it's remembered that many of these students began at Columbia with only ordinary literacy and with little cultural appetite, their report is impressive, even if it's a bit hyped.

According to their own report, 25 percent of Columbia's students learned to write far more successfully than they had ever imagined and nearly twice as many believed their writing was much improved. Some students, of course, never learn to write well. But many of these learn to do other things well, some remarkably so. Columbia furnished both writers and nonwriters with college opportunity, and both flourished. Most Columbia subjects require extensive reading. While some "doing" subjects do not emphasize reading assignments, serious reading is often important to expert performance. Apart from immediate utility, the college tried to give students a personal reason for reading. Reading may begin as a requirement, but lifetime literacy does not often have such origins. Students learn to read for themselves, and at Columbia, they often had the opportunity of exceptional literature courses and inspiring teachers.

The one subject of the self-study that enjoyed universal agreement was Columbia's occupational effect on students. The idea that a college education should have an occupational consequence was a fundamental tenet of Columbia's mission. When the college set sail in 1964, the issue was unsettled. Then, many educators and the agencies they influenced still held to the archaic notion that liberal arts education and an occupational emphasis were antithetical collegiate values. In fact, a leading reason for disqualifying Columbia's early efforts at accreditation had been the college's vocationalism. Within ten years that prejudice largely disappeared.

In 1978, nearly 300 students had internships and part-time jobs at radio and television stations, newspapers, advertising agencies, film and photography studios, graphics and printing companies, and art galleries and museums. Nearly 50 percent of alumni who had graduated in the five years past, and many who had not completed study, were successfully working in jobs directly related to their Columbia studies. This figure did not include alumni who freelanced at various arts and media specialties nor those not regularly employed as artists, writers, and performers, though most of these reported satisfaction with their career progress. Only 15 percent reported that they had not found work in jobs related to their Columbia studies and had taken other employment. Eight percent were unemployed at the time of inquiry.

The down note in these statistics was that only 36 percent of minority graduates, mainly African-Americans, had found employment in jobs related to their Columbia studies. This figure was encouraging only to the extent that a few years before, minority hiring in the media and entertainment industries was pitifully minimal. Economic success as an aspirant artist, musician, performer, writer, or filmmaker was a long-term pursuit. Despite this, a number of African-American photography students enjoyed remarkable success; noteworthy, Vandell Cobb, who became *Ebony* magazine's chief photographer; Ozier Muhammad, a Pulitzer prizewinner for newspaper photography; and Brent Jones, who has had a very successful career as a fine-arts photographer. Another finding of the self-study was that an unusually high number of graduates had successfully developed their own businesses.

The whole college was mobilized in the interest of the self-study. We had spent more than a year and a half on it. Obviously, our greatest motivation was to secure a ten-year accreditation grant from our North Central examiners. But if successful at that, the self-study's greatest value would be its revelation of Columbia's future course. In the fifteenth year of the college's renewal, a ten-year accreditation grant would signal a qualitative change in the college's life and the focus of its management. In the first years, we had been preoccupied with survival. When this was in sight, our main emphasis was on getting accredited and gaining public respectability, and finally on securing these credentials. Again, assuming a ten-year reaccreditation, we would be relieved of the consuming occupations of serving what had been Columbia's leading priority since 1968. For the first time, the college would have the opportunity to consolidate its strengths without the uncertainty of questionable status, and be able to focus on new directions and responses to influential changes in the nation's state and educational environment.

The self-study—the student responses particularly—had made it evident that Columbia's contemporaneity and embrace of themes of the 1960s and early 1970s had limited currency in 1978 and would certainly have little influence in the 1980s. While the ferment of the '60s and its youth energies had temporarily disrupted the national tranquility and signaled important changes in American life, the 1960s were not really a revolutionary time, but, its agitations did lead, albeit belatedly, to the end of the Vietnam war, to the rise of the women's movement and greater gender equality, and to an end of the statutory denial of civil and human rights for America's minorities and their greater enjoyment of social, economic, and educational opportunity and their political enfranchisement. Though the slogans of the 1960s discontent may have lost their bite and immediacy, the ideas they represented reshaped America. And though no longer suited to Columbia's specific advertisements, many earlier themes are incorporated into Columbia's mission and spirit.

Columbia was never a loosely experimental institution. In departing from conventional models, the college was an experiment in survival as a competent collegiate alternative interested in new methods and arrangements of instruction and in commitments to community service. It was these we sought to preserve after 1978 when Columbia had confirmed its permanence.

Despite the critical importance of reaccreditation, the examining occasion had a peculiar anticlimactic quality or, more simply, perhaps, we were just exhausted.

While we were confident that our self-study was convincing and comprehensive, and that our preparations for examination had been so thorough as to make failure unlikely, anxieties nonetheless prevailed. In fact, we couldn't have been more readied and organized. We had carefully arranged the examining team's meetings with students, alumni, board, faculty, librarians, and administrators. Briefs of the self-study had been widely distributed, and extensive discussion sessions held with all agencies of the college. A series of letters had been sent to all students explaining the examination process and expressing the importance of accreditation to all of Columbia's students. We scheduled an array of departmental events and exhibitions to demonstrate the college's instructional excellence, creative vitality, state-of-the-art facilities, and the professionalism of its students. Despite ongoing construction, everything was clean and polished.

In our maiden voyages to accreditation in 1970 and 1974, the college had been most helpfully and sympathetically counseled by Dr. Patsy Thrash, who headed the North Central Association's consultant-evaluator staff. She had chosen Dr. Elmore as our special guide and consultant and Dr. Barrett and the six other remarkably spirited and insightful members of our 1974 team. In 1979, the team of examiners was more typically constituted. Apparently, Dr. Thrash believed Columbia was less of an anomaly in need of unusual regard in 1979. The team, all higher-education heavyweights, was headed by Dr. Ilmer Jagow, president of Ohio's Hiram College and included Dr. Reatha King, president of Metropolitan State University in St. Paul, Minnesota; Dr. Robert Ray, dean of Continuing Education at Iowa State University;

Dr. Kala Mays Stroup, vice president for academic affairs and professor of speech, Emporia State University in Kansas; and Dr. Van Deren Coke, director of the art museum of the University of New Mexico. The team examiners were conscientious, thorough, and not receptive to glib explanations. All were experienced evaluators and serious educators, competent in their disciplines and unfailingly courteous, cooperative, and businesslike. If they lacked anything, it was only the enthusiasm and intensity of our 1974 team. But then again, such vitalities might have been reflections of the times. The occasion was stressful, but comparatively uneventful. At least it was without troubling surprises. The college's self-study and supporting documents had such a wealth of verifiable data and candid interpretation that challenge was minimal and infrequent. Moreover, the evidence of Columbia's great progress since its last inspection left little room for damaging criticism. Accreditation teams are not on site to make value judgments, but only to determine if an institution is an orderly enterprise with sufficient faculty, facilities, and resources to accomplish and perpetuate its educational purposes. At the requisite exit interview, after three grueling days, our examining team recorded their recommendation that Columbia be reaccredited for a ten-year term to 1989. While formal award would await the June meeting of the North Central Association's Accreditation Commission, the deed was done.

Columbia had been yoked to the issue of accreditation for ten years. Then, quite suddenly that chafing harness was gone. Relieving? Oh yeah! But only briefly. There were still lots of big rocks to carry up the hill.

1979–1980

The fall 1979 term began with 3,309 students, a 12 percent gain over 1978 which included a 14 percent increase in full-time equivalents. Columbia now had the largest enrollment among four-year independent colleges (excluding the major universities) in Illinois. Implausibly, college space was again at serious issue, and it would be acutely so if enrollment projections for the next two years were accurate. In the past five years, the college's enrollment had tripled, a phenomenon that often occasioned notions of enrollment caps and other interventions, none of which altered the inescapable reality that without large enrollment growth, Columbia could not generate enough revenue to support itself. While regular increases in tuition were unavoidable, the amounts realized only barely met the ravages of inflation and were small compared to the income from enrollment gains. The only alternative was a quick development of endowment and gift revenues, and there was no immediate prospect of that. With repetition of such logic, the board reached a reluctant consensus. The growth-revenue treadmill was Columbia's vehicle of necessity. I wouldn't have predicted it then, but twenty years later my successors are still driving that old car.

In 1979, policy doubts aside, it was impossible to avoid cheering at such evidence of success as the growth of the college's Art Department. In the fall of 1976, all art subjects enrolled 700 credit hours. Just three years later, the Art Department's enrollment exceeded 5,000 hours.

At its fall 1979 meetings, the board approved development of a graduate program, tentatively scheduled to begin in the spring of 1981. A determination of which

Columbia disciplines would most appropriately offer graduate study and have best enrollment expectations was yet to be made. The board also authorized a combination of advertising and journalism in a single departmental concentration. Subdepartments of these specialties had prospered, despite not having any full-time faculty or independent departmental life. With a formal departmental identity and serious support, we believed enrollment would grow. If it did, it might even become practical to reconstitute separate advertising and journalism departments.

As continuing at Eleventh Street was a questionable prospect, the board renewed discussion of combining the Theater-Music and Dance Departments in a single performing-arts facility, which would provide greater opportunity for instructional exchange among related performance disciplines and productions that joined the resources and talents of the departments. There was some possibility that the college could acquire a building well suited to such purposes at Adams and Sangamon Streets, though this required careful architectural and cost study. The board committed $5,000 for a six-month option on the property, which would give Bert Gall time to estimate remodeling and building operating costs and allow Jack Wolfsohn time to investigate federal, foundation, and major gift sources.

At the board's February 1980 meeting, Jack Wolfsohn reported a gift of $250,000 from the Elizabeth Ferguson Trust, secured by Seymour Gale through his association with Sam Pfeffer, the trust's administrator. The gift funded construction of the lecture and recital theater that occupies the west end of the 600 building's ground floor. The board voted to name the theater for Elizabeth Ferguson. Later,

Sam Pfeffer became a member of Columbia's board, a generous service that continues today. Wolfsohn reported, too, receipt of government grants of $153,000 and individual gifts of $25,000 and $8,000 from the Friends of Columbia College. Additionally, the Kresge Foundation had made another $100,000 grant, to be matched by new contributions before June 30 of the current year.

The board authorized an expenditure of $60,000 to create a comprehensive college library on the building's entire third floor and to fund construction of additional art classrooms on the eleventh floor. Gall also asked the board to approve the lease of 3,800 feet in the 624 South Michigan building at an annual rental of $24,000 for the enlarged development and public relations functions. The board responded to Gall's plea that there was not any room left in the 600 building.

Columbia's arrangement to share Roosevelt University's library was renewed for a two-year term at an annual cost of $10,000. After that time, Gall said, Columbia's library would be fully able to provide comprehensive library services to all of the college's students. That would be no small accomplishment. It's simply astonishing that a college library, able to serve the diverse interests of the 4,000 students anticipated in 1982, was created from nothing in the late 1960s. It couldn't have happened without the dedication and ingenuity of Hubert Davis, Bert Gall, and, immodestly, the little band of us who faithfully reserved money from the college's meager piggy bank to invest in the library's development.

That year, the board voted to fund the past-service obligations of the pension plan in five yearly installments of $85,000 rather than hold to the twenty-five-year schedule set when the plan was adopted. This decision represented a long-term saving of $600,000 and would give the college's employees an immediate sense of security.

No Columbia year was easy. It was just that some years were harder. We always seemed caught up in a maelstrom of changes and anticipations. In that sense, 1979–80 was an ordinary year, or perhaps it only seemed so in the absence of familiar accreditation anxieties. Apart from events and issues described earlier, Dr. Donald Canar, who had been president of Chicago's YMCA Community College, came out of a brief retirement to share my busy effort to lobby the U.S. Congress and the Illinois Legislature for student aid appropriations and other college benefits, and representations to federal and state educational agencies and the organizations of higher education. Another great dividend in having Canar was that a few years later I was able to hire his former secretary, Patricia DeWitt, to serve me in that capacity. To call Ms. DeWitt a secretary grossly underestimates her remarkable talents and the great pleasure that I and many others enjoyed in her company. She retired with me in 1992, but five years later, I got her back to type the first draft of this manuscript.

The board had its usual ins and outs. That year, Enid Long, an alumna of the college; Aaron Cushman, who headed a major public relations firm; Ben Gould, one of Chicago's most prominent attorneys; and David Ruttenberg, a notable real estate developer, joined Columbia's trustees. The board allocated $25,000 for developing feature films, a potentially profitable idea of Tony Loeb, the Film Department's chair, and Mel Pearl, a law colleague of Steve Neumer and a very successful developer of feature film properties. We bumbled around with this venture for a year or so, ultimately abandoning it after exploring its risks.

Peter Thompson joined the faculty. A talented photographer, filmmaker, and anthropologist, Thompson had inventive curiosity about learning and teaching, which I had only known once before, in John Walker, a faculty member in the late 1960s who had strongly influenced Columbia's educational methods.

The board voted a 10 percent salary increase for the college's faculty and staff. Revenue for 1979–80, including gifts and grants was $1,090,000 greater than expenses, though virtually all of the surplus was promptly committed to a variety of college improvements, new full-time faculty, student services, library personnel, and to the initial funding of the graduate program.

Obviously, student recruitment was Columbia's constant priority, indeed, our life blood. In the 1960s and early 1970s, I was the manager of the recruitment effort, aided by a succession of exceptional registrars, who interviewed prospects, answered telephone inquiries, and handled the great paper flow. After 1964, without exception, Columbia's enrollment increased every year, a record compiled despite demographic negatives, national recessions, the handicaps of the college's anonymous and spare state, and sharp competition from other institutions. After Columbia's accreditation in 1974 and greater prosperity, what had been a skeletal recruitment effort, however ingenious, was far better staffed and more sophisticated. Earlier recruitment had been mainly confined to newspaper advertisements, when affordable, and a great variety of mailings, scripted responses to telephone inquiries, and personal interiews.

Most student recruitment was Columbia's word-of-mouth advertisement by students, alumni, and faculty, and later, publicity on a remarkable scale. Until the college was fully accredited, Columbia was viewed suspiciously by high-school college counselors, and though we were not barred from soliciting students, Chicago high schools were not cooperative, except at inner-city schools, which were not usual targets of college recruiters. For some years, Hubert Davis and whatever faculty he could enlist covered high-school college days. Hubert was Columbia's main link to Chicago's schools.

By 1978, the all-purpose registrar's office had disappeared and was replaced by an admissions director and professional staff. Margaret Lyman (Thaine's wife), who had managed a very successful recruitment agency for a Catholic women's college, came to Columbia to give the college an active presence in Chicago-region high schools. Margaret Lyman remained for ten outstanding years, and she organized and trained a staff of outside representatives, among them the talented Judy Dyke, who still carries on Margaret's exemplary tradition. By the mid-1980s, though only 7 percent of all high-school seniors in the six-county Chicago region recorded career interests in Columbia's arts and media specialties, to the best of our calculation, ultimately 45 percent of that 7 percent would enroll at Columbia. That statistic, I submit, is convincing validation of Columbia's career emphasis, focus on arts and media studies, and reputation for excellence in the subjects of the college's concentrations.

With 3,828 students enrolled in fall 1980, 15 percent more than 1979, the effect of the damnable equation "more students equals more space," was again a high priority concern with no immediate solution. While Bert Gall continued to juggle the 600 building space, his ingenuity was unraveling. If similar growth was realized next year, a hard problem would become acute.

In the meantime, a decision had to be made about exercising the college's option to purchase the Eleventh Street Theater-Music property. Though the building was structurally sound, it was shabby, and expensive remodeling of a rented facility was an uneconomical prospect. To complicate the situation, board member Gus Cherry wanted to buy the building for an unrelated purpose if we did not exercise our purchase option. After some months of indecision and in the absence of a practical and affordable alternative site for the Theater-Music Department, the board decided to buy the Eleventh Street property if reasonable financing terms could be arranged. Bud Salk headed the negotiations, which established a price of $525,000 for the 90,000-square-foot building, requiring an immediate down payment of $50,000 and an additional payment of $100,000 in advance of a June 1, 1980, closing date, and a conventional mortgage of $375,000.

Eleventh Street's owner was the Board of Jewish Education, which occupied the building's third floor, but expected to move within the year to Spertus College. The Theater-Music Department, however, did not occupy all the remaining space, some of which has in poor repair. The big rub was that when Columbia was the building's owner and sole occupant, we would have to spend $300,000 immediately to bring the whole building into compliance with school building and safety codes, and it was likely that another $2 million would be needed to remodel the entire building to suit the college's occupancy and to fully restore the Eleventh Street Theater. The acquisition was a formidable project that would badly strain Columbia's financial resources, even anticipating continued prosperity. But once again we plunged ahead and scratched up the money needed for building-code compliance and a start at remodeling. The plan to acquire another theater-music-dance site was abandoned. The board pledged to give and get at least $100,000 during the current year to help with Eleventh Street's costs, and Jack Wolfsohn recharged his efforts to get foundation and grant support. Somehow, again, we muddled through, with the timely generosity of a loyal old friend, Kenneth Montgomery, who made a gift of $150,000, and a $50,000 gift by trustee Myron Hokin. Board members Hope Samuels and David Solomon led a board effort to increase the membership of the Friends of Columbia College from its present 200 to 500 members, not so much because of the $50 membership fees, but as a way to create a greater pool of potential larger contributors. Regrettably, such potential was never realized on any significant scale.

Familiarly, there was again a serious shortfall in Illinois State Scholarship funding, resulting in a retroactive cutoff in awards back to August 31, 1980, eliminating benefits for more than 150 Columbia students already enrolled in the fall 1980 term and jeopardizing student aid awards for all new students expected to enroll for spring 1981. An effective lobbying effort by the Federation of Illinois Independent Colleges and Universities got some scholarship funds and eligibility restored. But Columbia took a $250,000 hit in fall term drop-outs, spring no-shows, and unpaid tuition accounts.

That year, Paul Carter Harrison resigned as chair of the Theater-Music department to become the college's dramatist in residence, which relieved him of the consuming responsibilities of chairing a department. Harrison was replaced as chair by Sheldon Patinkin, founder of the National Jewish Theater, who was and remains a seminal figure in Chicago and in the American theater. A founding member of the legendary Compass Players and Second City, a distinguished director including a Broadway run of Leonard Bernstein's *Candide* and a host of other plays, Patinkin was chosen as Theater-Music's chair in competition with a number of theater luminaries, and he still serves as the department's leader.

Sheldon Patinkin is an enlightened educator with an abiding commitment to the theater arts and to his department's students and faculty, and he enjoys the respect and affection of theater professionals everywhere. During his Columbia tenure, Sheldon has presided over one of the largest theater arts programs in the country. His department offers a full range of theater subjects: playwriting, acting, directing, producing, scenic design, stagecrafts, technical theater, speech, stage movement, and dramatic literature.

While Sheldon's purview has also included music studies, the Music Department has been, in effect, a virtually independent department headed by Bill Russo, though both concentrations enjoy close relations. The Theater Department's enrollment customarily exceeds 400, and Music numbers more than 150 students.

In 1999, with the college's acquisition of the Sherwood Music School's building, next door at Eleventh Street and Michigan Avenue, the Music Department now has a separate identity and life.

The Theater Department for many years has produced a full season of classical and contemporary plays and musical-theater productions for public audiences at the college's Getz Theater. These main-stage productions have student casts sometimes supplemented by Equity actors, student production crews, and directors and scenic designers chosen from the faculty or from professional ranks seconded by advanced students. Also, there are a number of studio productions that feature students in all performance and production roles.

Unlike conservatories, theater schools, and most university theater departments, where students are chosen selectively, Columbia's theater students represent a wide range of abilities, few having had theater experience or training. It is hard to explain why a large number of the college's students have chosen to be theater majors or to aspire to careers in the theater, or for that matter for careers in the arts. My only explanation is that individuals (and there are lots of them) with artistic natures seek expression in their careers, often despite the absence of prior opportunity or immediate evidence of talent. Nonetheless, it is important that such individuals be given an opportunity to realize themselves, and that, after all, is an elementary part of Columbia's mission.

An encouraging number of Columbia theater students become working members of Chicago theaters, and others work in education or community theater settings in Chicago and elsewhere. A few make it in Hollywood or New York. Some organize their own theater companies. Sheldon and his faculty's prominent association with local and national theater communities and the respect that the department enjoys lead to many opportunities for the college's theater students. But, realistically, only very few really make it in the theater. Indeed, it is discouraging that so many talented and well-trained young people fail to find opportunities in the theater, as is the case in all fine-arts disciplines. And it is shameful that this richest of nations has failed to support a nationally funded system of regional theaters and music, dance, and art venues even to the extent of many European countries. Certainly, many educated in theater arts work in nonprofessional and community theater settings, many engage their theater talents in film, radio, television, and related occupations, and for others, theater training has a strong personality and self-confidence effect, which has great life and occupational value. But I doubt that such benefits satisfyingly compensate for the absence of the real thing.

The board grew to thirty-six members with the addition of Barry Crown, a scion of one of Chicago's first families and a manufacturer of recreational equipment; Lowell Sachnoff, a notable attorney and zealous civil libertarian; and Ron Williams, president of Northeastern Illinois University and a distinguished leader of American higher education. Regrettably, the board lost the valuable services of Steven Neumer and Patti Crowley.

Columbia's Michigan Avenue neighbor, Spertus College of Judaica, offered an opportunity to purchase their building and the lot between the colleges. At a price of $5,500,000, it was a fine piece of property, though where we would have gotten that kind of money taxes the imagination. Negotiations went on for several months, but ultimately, the Spertus board withdrew the offer and Columbia got its sanity back.

April 15 is memorable as the day when taxes are due. In my instance, April 15, 1981, was unusually memorable because it was the day I had a heart attack. I think taxes and the fact that my day was spent on Columbia's budget were only coincidental events. Jane carted me off to the hospital to endure the reassurances of family and friends and the indignities of medical repair. Columbia folk rallied sweetly around me, and Bert Gall, John Scheibel, and Charles Bane ably manned the bridge in my absence, which lasted more or less until the end of May. I was back in time to preside at commencement when Columbia honored that most exemplary man, George McGovern; renowned scientist Franklin Long; sociologist and civil rights leader Dr. Harry Edwards; Michael Cacoyannis, the celebrated motion picture director of *Zorba the Greek*, *Iphigenia*, and other fine films; and feminist writer Marilyn French. That made the 1981 spring season more genuinely memorable than my brief encounter with mortality. At the year's end, though many college issues remained unresolved, Columbia enjoyed a very good year at the "box office." Otherwise, pains and pleasures evened out.

More than anything that happened that year, the death of John Fischetti in November 1980 is my most vivid memory. Fischetti was the *Chicago Sun-Times's* nationally syndicated, Pulitzer prizewinning political cartoonist. He was a world treasure and dear friend. He had immense talent and consummate humanity. His art was a profound editorial on the human state in a hostile world: Goyaesque creations made uniquely accessible by his humor. He also invented the four-hour lunch.

When I first contemplated the abyss of John's departure, I thought to design a way to commemorate him. I consulted with John's indomitable wife, Karen, and we together planned an annual memorial occasion. The response to our project was magical. Without any solicitation, the college's perennial godfather, Ken Montgomery, called to tell me that if Columbia would create a vehicle, he would contribute $150,000 to such purpose; and soon after, John's good friend Lee Freeman, and Columbia's peerless Trustee Bill Wilkow, each volunteered $25,000; and beginning in the fall of 1981, both also entirely funded the first three annual Fischetti Dinner, which attracted audiences of more than 500 people and featured such nationally prominent speakers as Jimmy Breslin, Seymour Hersh, and David Halberstam. The Fischetti Endowment, enlarged by the proceeds of these annual events and stock market growth, has provided scholarships to more than 270 Columbia journalism students. The fund's present value exceeds $1 million.

1981–1982

Enrollment increased by 4 percent in fall l981 to 3,986. But half of this increase included 98 graduate students, who represented sixty full-time equivalents. At the same time, fall 1981 enrollment improved the numbers of full-time students to 67 percent of enrollment totals. While 1981 was one of the few occasions in which yearly gains were comparatively flat, tuition revenues reflecting a greater percentage of full-time students were roughly the same as budget forecasts based on more than 4,200 students. Several factors explained the brief leveling-off of Columbia's annual enrollment increase. That year and for several years after, national college enrollment began to reflect demographic predictions. Correspondingly, many Illinois colleges and universities lost enrollment in the early 1980s. In Columbia's instance, however, the most important cause of a relative drop-off in enrollment was the reduction of $40 million in Illinois appropriations for state scholarships, which led to a rationing of student aid and cost Columbia nearly 200 anticipated students.

Despite a mild disappointment in total student numbers, graduate school enrollment results were most encouraging, particularly as graduate students did not depend on state and federal student aid benefits. The graduate school's initial subject concentrations were Interdisciplinary Arts, Photography, and Film-Video. Arts, Entertainment, and Media Management, and Creative Writing and Teaching of English were added in 1982; and Dance Therapy and Journalism in 1984.

The graduate program in Interdisciplinary Arts predated Columbia's graduate school. It had been a joint project of Loyola University and the Great Lakes College

Association, which served a number of regional colleges. When we joined this venture, Columbia became the site of the program, and when our graduate school was accredited, Columbia replaced Loyola as the degree-granting institution. The program was developed by the uniquely creative Suzanne Cohan, still the chair of Columbia's graduate department of Interdisciplinary Arts Education, which integrates study of arts and media expression with principal focus on education. A simply wonderful person, Suzanne's enthusiasm and energy are boundless. She is an exemplary educator and colleague. Though in student numbers, the Interdisciplinary Arts Program is comparatively small, its graduates have an outstanding record of successful employment. This is similarly true of Jane Ganet-Sigel's graduate program in Dance Therapy, an unusual specialty which reflects the increasing importance of the arts as a method of psychotherapy.

Though 1981–82 is best described as a year of consolidation, the pace of events was no less hectic. Again, the college was engaged in preparations for the 1984 accreditation of the graduate program, the inspection of which unavoidably involved some elements of the college's general operations and of undergraduate departments newly offering graduate studies.

That year, the board voted an expenditure of $150,000 to replace the college's antiquated phone system. By the time the new system's complications were sorted out comfortably, Columbia's growth would require an entirely new telephone system. The board also authorized $250,000 for the 600 building's remodeling, particularly to create science laboratories and a computer-learning center on the eleventh floor; and a $250,000 reserve for Eleventh Street constructions, which proved far short of estimates.

The quick growth of the Science Department was a convincing exhibit of Columbia's educational maturity and surely a testament to the extraordinary talent, energy, and imagination of the department's chair, Dr. Zafra Lerman. She, as Harry Bouras had earlier, gave Columbia impressive public recognition and stature in American higher education and in the scientific community.

The college's bookstore, now a booming operation, was moved to the ground floor of the 623 South Wabash building. After years of starts and stops, Columbia finally got a radio station, WCRX (87.3 on the dial). The University of Illinois at Chicago decided to transfer their broadcasting license to Columbia in return for a broadcast opportunity for their students, though this was only minimally used. WCRX gave Columbia regular access to a large radio audience, and a professional on-the-air opportunity to our radio students. While radio audience measures do not ordinarily include noncommercial stations, within a few years, Columbia's station was shown to have the largest audience of Chicago's alternative radio stations. The college's only expense was $25,000 for a transmitter, new studio equipment, modest remodeling of the Radio Department's space, and a nominal fee to the University of Illinois for the transmitter's location.

At its May 1982 meeting, the board elected Jay Fox as chairman to succeed Charles Bane, who planned to move to Florida. While Bane had not developed an affluent constituency, he was a very constructive and dependable board chair who brought order to the management of the college's affairs. Bane was a pleasure to work with, and his courtly manner had a settling influence on the college's customary turmoil. Jay Fox was an excellent choice as Bane's successor. He had served outstandingly for several years in a number of board assignments and enjoyed close association with a number of board members, Dwight Follett particularly. That was an impeccable credential. The board again voted an 8–10 percent increase in faculty and staff salaries for the 1982–83 college year and an 8 percent increase in tuition charges. The board also established a fund reserving $50,000 a year for five years in anticipation of a $253,000 balloon note due in 1988 on the Eleventh Street mortgage. There was some discussion of the city Landmark Commission's interest in designating the 600 South Michigan building as a civic landmark, a questionably desirable identification. Ultimately the Commission abandoned such intents. The board instructed that all college funds not necessary to current operations, then roughly $500,000, be deposited in an interest-earning short-term asset management account at the Continental Illinois Bank, and whenever any subsequent accumulations reached $1 million, such sums would be designated as an endowment fund. While the year ended on a very profitable note, Columbia's wealth was illusory, in that bond issue, mortgage, and other debt obligations were correspondingly much greater, and reserve funds, however identified, equaled only several months of college expenses. Hardly a generous cushion, though light years better than the fragile security of earlier times.

The year ended on another big up-note with my prideful announcement that Daryl Feldmeir, one of America's most distinguished journalists and newspaper editors, would join Columbia's faculty in the fall 1982 as chair of a newly established Journalism Department, with expectation of a graduate program in 1984.

1982–1983: Coming of Age

By comparison with the 1960s and 1970s, by 1983 Columbia had come of age. While not yet a genuinely mature institution, the college's most prominent disabilities had been overcome. In the nineteen years since 1964, enrollment had grown twenty times to more than 4,000 students. What at first was rented space was more than fifty times greater in owned buildings. Columbia's educational program, including a graduate school, was greater in every dimension. Faculty numbers, three hundred in 1983, including sixty full-time members, had grown twelve times in the span of a few years. A modern college library had grown from nothing in 1967. In 1964, only Jane, Wolf Dochtermann, a part-time bookkeeper, and I constituted the college's administration. In 1983, administrators, student services, educational, and library staff numbered more than 160. An in-house board of five had grown to thirty-six prominent, independent members. Columbia had become a fully accredited institution; a scratched-up yearly expenditure of less than $100,000 had become a $10 million budget; and college funds had grown from less than zero to nearly $3 million in reserves and endowment. Indeed, everything about Columbia had grown in similar multiples.

It was inevitable that by 1983, I was president of an entirely different institution than I had headed even a few years before. Though a subtle transformation, in 1983 and in the years that followed, my occupations were increasingly those of a typical college president whose job description is not dissimilar to that of a CEO of a comparatively big business. I was pretty well done with having my hands in the educational stuff. It was a dispiriting discovery. Or perhaps, it was just hard to accept a role in which I was no longer the mogul of Columbia's life. The college had simply become too big and complex to be managed and inspired by one person, an uncontestable fact reflected in a dispersal of authority and inevitably in a maze of virtually independent duchies. This was particularly the case among educational departments, whose turf was zealously defended. No longer could I hoist the regimental standard and expect the troops to fall in neatly behind. In retrospective, it was fortunate that a rush of policy and management issues and fund-raising, public relations, and political functions left me no time to notice a loss of personal authority and initiative. Moreover, I could not have had a more talented and compatible coterie of lieutenants.

Despite discouraging forecasts of national collegiate enrollment and our own hesitant projections, Columbia's September 1982 enrollment was 4,250, a 9 percent gain. Total credit hours increased 15 percent to more than 50,000 in the year's first semester. Full-time-equivalent numbers grew by 14 percent. Obviously, these were record numbers in all respects. As anticipated, space issues had reached acute proportions.

Prominent among the year's issues and events were a number of important board decisions. At the board's December 1982 meeting, a $1,800,000 construction plan was authorized. This included such costly jobs as replacing windows and making extensive elevator repairs in the 600 building. Half of the year's construction expense, $900,000, would be paid with college funds, and $900,000 would be subscribed by a three-year, Continental Illinois Bank loan.

Most unprecedented was the board's decision to formally establish a Columbia College endowment fund with an initial deposit of $1 million. At a subsequent meeting, after reviewing a number of proposals, the board chose the Harris firm to manage the college's endowment investments.

Prior to 1983, Columbia, as most colleges, universities, and not-for-profit organizations, was not included in the Social Security system. But after January 1, 1983, Congress mandated the inclusion of all not-for-profit entities in the Social Security system and the payment of FICA taxes by these institutions and their employees. Compliance with this required significant changes in Columbia's Pension Plan, as this had not anticipated Social Security benefits or the expense to the college and its individuals of contributions to the Social Security system. Correspondingly, what was in effect a new retirement plan provided an annual retirement income equal to 80 percent of the average of the five highest years of an employee's earnings, including pension plan benefits and Social Security expectations. Together with the benefits of individual personal retirement accounts, this could easily result in an annual income exceeding the highest paid year of the individual's Columbia compensation. The new retirement plan also liberalized the terms of eligibility to require a minimum fifteen years of service to qualify for maximum retirement benefits at age sixty-five. In making this generous provision, we speculated that it could help Columbia's recruitment of talented faculty and experienced administrative specialists, who would not otherwise consider a midlife career change. Fortunately, it did. As before, the college's pension plan did not require any employee contribution, and as the greatest number of Columbia employees elect individual, tax-deferred retirement accounts, virtually all Columbia employees could now anticipate satisfying retirement incomes.

Bert Gall proposed that the board consider purchasing the land immediately to the west of the college's Eleventh Street property, then a parking lot, to construct a new 96,000-square-foot multi-purpose college building. This would include a new dance center and an opportunity to consolidate the college's performing arts departments at a unified site. While the cost of the whole project would approximate $10 million, not including land costs, it would be possible to construct interior spaces in affordable stages over several years to respond to the college's needs and growth. The board's real estate and finance committees spent nearly a year exploring the project, which ultimately floundered on an inability to come to any agreement on the price of the parking lot, though ultimately we bought a parcel of it, which is now a sculpture garden.

Tracing back to the 1950s, even the 1940s, neither advertising nor journalism were formally designated as departments or study concentrations. While both were usually included in the college's advertisements and in catalog listings of subject specialties, and their curricula reflected gradations of instruction, enrollment was comparatively small. It was a peculiar neglect not remedied by incorporation in an omnibus Advertising/Journalism Department several years later. The issue was revisited in 1982 when a decision was made to reconstitute separate departments. This choice was largely prompted by the nearly simultaneous opportunity to get Daryl Feldmeir and John Tarini to head newly created subject entities.

Tarini had never entertained the notion of joining Columbia's faculty before Lya Rosenblum sought his interest, and similarly, Daryle Feldmeir had no thought of Columbia when I began my effort to engage him.

John Tarini fits no mold. He is a piece of theater. An athletic man with a great flowing mustache, he looks like an Italian grandee. Bright, entertaining, literate, and articulate with an easy fluency in French and Italian (and English, of course), John is a very talented, caring, and liberal man, and an intense and loving friend. There was and is great pleasure in his company.

A Ph.D. in psychology and a University of Chicago faculty member, Tarini was among early scholars in the field of motivational research, which led him to a twenty-five-year career as executive vice president of Edward Weiss and Company, a major advertising agency, as its director of Analytical Services, which included marketing and research, and to national prominence in the advertising industry. While Tarini had contemplated early retirement, he was dissuaded by Columbia's offer of an opportunity to create a department of advertising and marketing, which he did admirably. Within three years, the department's enrollment grew to 5 percent of the college's total credit hours. Tarini's wide association with Chicago's advertising and marketing agencies gave him unusual opportunity to recruit full-time faculty who were central to the department's instruction, and a cadre of part-time subject specialists with outstanding credentials. A great benefit of his ready familiarity with the city's advertising and marketing agencies was a wealth of job opportunities for graduates and a similar opportunity for internships, which gave students a monitored opportunity to get on-the-job experience and a head start in the employment market. By 1984, seventy-five students had internships and the number multiplied in succeeding years. In 1989 the Advertising Department was renamed the Marketing Communications Department. John continued as the department's chair until his retirement in 1997. He was a talented, inventive educator.

In having Feldmeir, a nationally respected newspaper editor and journalist, who had retired as the managing editor of the *Chicago Daily News*, then one of America's premier newspapers, I envisioned a major Journalism Department that would attract distinguished faculty and a significant number of students, and boost the college's reputation. Feldmeir was an extraordinarily talented journalist and a princely man. In his first Columbia year he satisfied every promise. He recruited an exceptional faculty, which included Nicholas Shuman, Eric Lund, and Lester Brownlee. Shuman had served as foreign editor of the *Chicago Daily News*, when that section of the paper was universally celebrated for its reporting of foreign affairs, and later was financial editor and a senior editorial writer of the *Chicago Sun-Times*, when the two Field newspapers were merged. Eric Lund had been the city editor of the *Sun-Times,* and Brownlee had had a very successful newspaper career and as a television news reporter. From a small, scattered enrollment, the new Journalism Department quickly gathered more than one hundred undergraduate majors. In anticipation of a graduate journalism program in the spring of 1984, Daryl and his colleagues organized a demanding graduate program designed for a selective number of the best-qualified graduate students, and created a fully professional newsroom for graduate and experienced undergraduate students. Fifteen very talented students were accepted for the first graduate class.

Then suddenly, in the fall of 1984, Feldmeir became gravely ill, and after a terrible lingering time, he died in early 1985. It was an irreplaceable loss. His cruelly abbreviated Columbia tenure had lasted only a bit more than two years.

Just before Daryl's illness, I had introduced him to Nat Lerman, who had recently retired as the associate publisher of *Playboy* magazine and president of *Playboy*'s publishing division. It was my intention that Lerman would join the Columbia faculty part-time to organize a magazine and periodical publishing emphasis within the department. I had known Nat for many years, going back to the 1960s when he taught creative writing courses at Columbia, succeeding, as I remember, the legendary Jack Conroy. Daryl was enthusiastic about getting Lerman. But just after Nat started, Daryl became ill, and it was soon evident that he would never be able to return to Columbia. Though a painful necessity, the Journalism Department would need a new chair.

I consulted with a number of Columbia colleagues and leading Chicago journalists, all of whom said I already had an outstanding candidate in Nat Lerman. After scrambling about for several months and interviewing prospects, some with very commendable credentials, I, too, concluded that none were remotely as well qualified as Lerman for the chair's job. Though his experience was mainly with magazines and not with newspapers, Lerman was a seasoned executive, with a sterling reputation as one of America's most respected magazine publishers. Moreover, he had every respect for the traditions and skills of the news media and good knowledge of radio and television news operations. He had chosen early retirement with some notion of greater leisure and the opportunity to write, so I was a bit surprised when he responded to my entreaties. To build an important Journalism Department from Feldmeir's brief beginnings was no leisurely task. Lerman took over a ship that was badly adrift and questionably seaworthy. This was, after all, ten years after Watergate, and the glamour of investigative reporting had worn thin among young people, and correspondingly, student election of careers in journalism was only minimally popular. But the department prospered with Lerman's leadership, particularly because of the addition of a magazine and periodical emphasis in the journalism curriculum, though education in news media retained its customary prominence.

The Journalism Department developed a vigorous program of undergraduate and graduate studies, which continued to attract students. The department's enrollment grew quickly to nearly 4 percent of the college's credit-hour totals. In cooperation with the television and radio departments, the Journalism Department developed an emphasis on broadcast news. Internships and graduate job opportunities increased significantly, and so did the department's reputation in educational and professional communities.

The Journalism Department published an annual directory and review of Chicago arts and entertainment and publishing media, which had surprising newsstand sales and won a number of national awards for Best of Student Publications. This was (and still is) an entirely professional publication: really a "slick bit," whose considerable costs were largely subsidized by a variety of publications, printers, paper suppliers, and magazine distributors, whose contributions Lerman regularly secured, though the magazine's editorial content, art direction, and production was a student project counseled by the department's faculty.

Apart from his managerial skills, professional competence, and very valuable association with magazine and periodical publishing and with a great array of writers and editors, Lerman was an inspiring teacher who was esteemed and fondly regarded by his colleagues and his students. Nat served a fourteen-year Columbia term, retiring in 1998. He captained a good ship.

By February 1983, we had a year's experience at what was a novel experiment in financing employee health and medical benefits by combining self-insurance with "stop-loss" coverage. Scheibel reported that despite an unusually high claim year, the college had saved $85,000 in comparison with what would have been the costs of a group policy with fewer benefits issued by Blue Cross or a similar carrier. This method of financing employee health and medical insurance is still used by the college.

We had engaged Charles Feldstein and Company, premier fund-raising consultants, to evaluate the state and direction of Columbia's fund-raising efforts. Feldstein recognized that Columbia was severely handicapped by the absence of an affluent constituency and had only limited alumni numbers. They observed, however, that we could significantly increase results by even a small increase in professional staff, which at that moment only included Jack Wolfsohn, Victor Margolin, a secretary, and a part-time student clerk. When I look back at it, it's simply remarkable how much Jack and his little band got done. We hired Sonya Gutman, who had been the associate director of the University of Chicago's development office, to head a major gift and corporate support focus. Though a very experienced fund-raising professional, Sonya encountered the same obstacles that had confounded large scale fund-raising in times past. Despite Columbia's greater visibility, public respect, and enrollment growth, the college still had a scattered and uncommitted constituency, a small alumni pool that was not affluent, little access to major donors and corporations, and a board who, with few exceptions, were reluctant and inconstant fund-raisers.

I have tried many times, with little certainty, to fathom my failure and that of expert staff and consultants to inspire the board to zealous fund-raising engagement in even very well conceived and organized campaigns. It seems reasonable to attribute fund-raising failures until the late 1970s to the fact that Columbia was then too small, unimportant, and invisible to raise any significant amounts of money, and to understand that board members would be discouraged by meeting nearly universal resistance.

But, perplexingly, efforts to inspire and enlist the board in serious fund-raising continued into the 1980s, when many earlier barriers had been overcome. However futile its pursuit, fund-raising efforts in the 1960s and 1970s did not lack a sense of urgency, but board individuals in the 1980s were not similarly spurred. In fact, it may well be that Columbia's evident prosperity in the 1980s, achieved without hyped fund campaigns and board mobilizations, had the effect of suppressing any sense of urgency about fund-raising within the board. Great personal generosity was, however, common among board members.

Undoubtedly, the 1982–83 year was the best in Columbia's brief history. The graduate school had grown to 150 students, and its accreditation in 1984 was expected confidently. The year's revenues from all sources would exceed expenses by $2 million, though nearly half of this had already been spent on the year's construction projects. An enrollment of 4,600 students—a 10 percent increase—was forecast for the next college year.

At a spring 1983 meeting, the board increased tuition to an annual full-time rate of $3,550; part-time tuition per semester hour to $125; and to $147 per semester hour for graduate students. Faculty and staff salaries for the 1983–84 college year were increased 10 percent for all individuals earning less than $23,000 and 7 percent for those earning more than that figure. The variation reflected the fact that lowest paid workers paid a disproportionately greater amount of their earnings in FICA deposits, and the board wanted to lessen that disparity.

Only a few years before, it would have been hard to imagine the omnipresence of computers in the college's life. But that moment was surely at hand, both in terms of ordinary operations and educational programs. Accordingly, we hired a computer expert, Dr. Edgar Eddins, to manage the college's computer usage. I barely knew then that such persons as Eddins even existed. The computer revolution had sure started without me.

My generation was pretty well fixed with the notion that one retired at sixty-five or earlier, if possible, to allow a few years of leisurely dotage. When I actually got to sixty in 1983 with the expectation of retiring in 1986, my whole scheme began to collapse. Happily, the board extended my contract to August 31, 1991, with the option that I or the college could terminate after 1989 with a year's prior notice.

The year 1983 was one of great sorrow, too. Thaine Lyman died unexpectedly. I really don't think that anyone was more important to Columbia's life than this wonderful hard rock of a man. He had come to Columbia thirty-three years before when television was an infant industry. Surely, there was no expectation then that television would become Columbia's most identifying subject and for years the greatest source of student revenue. Whatever Columbia was and whatever we became, Thaine Lyman's loyalty, perseverance, inventive talent, and compelling humanity were indispensable to Columbia's life and success. I am gratified to have the opportunity of this narrative to salute Thaine again.

That year, Columbia lost another exemplary human being: Bill Wilkow. He had served the college with singular distinction and generosity for more than ten years as a trustee and dedicated friend. He was an extraordinarily sweet man and a wise counselor.

1983–1984: Graduate School Accreditation

In fall 1983, 4,628 undergraduate and 172 graduate students enrolled, and we had to turn away another 200 because we'd run out of class space. As enrollment was the elemental stuff of Columbia's health, capping the college's size, even temporarily, was like dumping mother's milk down the drain. Nonetheless, there was plenty of cause to rejoice. Enrollment was up 13 percent. At the year's beginning, Columbia had 533 full- and part-time faculty, more than 150 student-service professionals, instructional technicians, and eight librarians. The college was really a big place.

When we expected in 1979 that we had ten years of relief from the trials of accreditation, we obviously hadn't contemplated that we'd be back in the hunt only five years later, seeking accreditation of a graduate division. At least now, the preparations would be easier and the college's strengths more confidently exhibited. When the graduate program began in 1981, two North Central Association representatives had conducted an on-site examination of the plans and prospects of Columbia's graduate project. And they, together with Lya Rosenblum and her colleagues, had identified a number of concerns that would be principal subjects of the formal accreditation inspection now expected in spring of 1984. While Columbia's graduate division was still comparatively new, great progress had been made in the program's brief life. Initial concerns had mainly to do with selection and counseling of graduate students and measures of their academic performance, organization of curricula, faculty recruitment, graduate library provision, and degree requirements. We had every confidence that these concerns had been amply satisfied.

We had filled a critical need in getting Dr. Dennis Peacock as the graduate division's director. Peacock had been the assistant provost for Institutional Research and Academic Planning and a member of the linguistics faculty of the Illinois Institute of Technology. He was a very able and versatile administrator and a most talented assembler of data required for the graduate program's self-study. Submitted in November 1983, the self-study document written by Lya Rosenblum with Peacock's assistance was a convincing preface to the on-site examination of the college's graduate division in April 1984. Our examiners were experienced graduate school administrators, and though not expert in Columbia's subject specialties, they had valuable counsel to offer about the process and management of graduate education. While we didn't seriously doubt the examiners' favorable recommendation, inevitably some anxieties persisted until official notice in June 1984 of the accreditation of Columbia's graduate program. The few "whoopees" that followed were quickly sobered by the thought that the accreditation cycle would start again in less than five years.

The imperative need for more space was hardly an unfamiliar problem. Where, at what cost, and how we would pay for it were, as usual, the questions. Building at Eleventh Street was prohibitively expensive, and finding an appropriate older building reasonably close by was a doubtful prospect. Then, once again, our provident star. The old Studebaker Building at 623 South Wabash quite suddenly came on the market. The building had 160,000 square feet, and it could be remodeled at reasonable cost. It was sparsely occupied by short-term tenants, including the college's bookstore. Best of all, the building was virtually across the alley from the 600 South Michigan building. The owner agreed to sell the property for $2,400,000, a bargain. We expected that buying and renovating the 623 South Wabash building would solve the college's space needs for years ahead. That forecast would prove as faulty as our belief five years before that the 600 South Michigan building would give the college ample space forever.

Of the $2.4 million purchase price, $700,000 would be paid by college funds and $1,700,000 subscribed by a new Higher Education Facilities bond issue, though the bond amount would be $5,530,000 to include $1,800,000 in the initial 623 South Wabash building remodeling costs; $200,000 for reconstruction of 600 South Michigan building space vacated by the shift of facilities to 623; $900,000 to repay Continental Illinois Bank loans used for 1983 construction projects; $800,000 to create a required debt-service reserve, which would be recovered in the final (eleventh) year of the bond term; and other bond issue expenses, including the cost of bond insurance, which gave Columbia's bonds a "triple A" rating and the lowest interest rate. Standard and Poor's highest rated bonds!

Bert Gall was confident that 70,000 feet of 623's space could be readied for college use by September 1984 within the budget constraints. The rest of the building could be remodeled in stages as necessary and affordable.

The remodeling of 623 South Wabash was another example of Bert Gall's extraordinary talent for managing construction projects. His impeccable planning incorporated his great personal knowledge of Columbia's subjects, instructional technologies, and the counsel of faculty and department heads. He was the project manager, general contractor, and close monitor of every construction detail. Bert's buildings had remarkable utility, many beautiful qualities, and consistently cost much less than comparable construction. He cut his teeth on the college's comparatively modest construction projects in the early 1970s, and that experience and his first work at 600 South Michigan were the foundation of what would become our successful construction pattern. The critical element of this was Bert's recruitment of Michael Arenson, an unusually talented young architect, who over time has designed all of Columbia's building projects. Around Michael, Bert organized a team of the best of Chicago's major contractors: carpentry, electrical, HVAC, and plumbing, who have worked together now for nearly twenty years, though each of these familiar "subs" still must compete with the lowest bids of other contractors.

We expected great difficulty in finding a new chair for the Television Department. On an interim basis, Al Parker added Television to his Radio Department purview. In the meantime, an intense but ultimately unsuccessful search for Lyman's replacement was conducted locally and nationally. Among those whose counsel I sought was an old friend, Edward Morris, who then managed a Chicago TV station, Channel 44, which broadcast White Sox baseball and other popular local programs. Previously, Ed had spent nearly thirty years as WTTW's program manager and director of station development, and as a leading executive of the Corporation for Public Broadcasting. Also, as an officer of the National Television Academy, he knew many of the leading people in the television industry and was an unusual source of candidates. In my conversations with Ed, I realized that he would be the ideal candidate, though at first neither of us had entertained the possibility. After many weeks of my persuasion and Ed's soul-searching, we had a meeting of minds. Ed was it—the TV Department's new chair. An exemplary choice, he remained in the job for nearly fifteen years until 1999, and remains a faculty member and senior consultant.

There was an unexpected vacancy in the leadership of the Arts and Entertainment Management department. Fred Fine, the department's founder and chair, was nominated by Mayor Harold Washington as Chicago's Commissioner of Cultural Affairs. Reminiscent of the times of Senator Joe McCarthy, Fine's confirmation hearings by the Chicago City Council were similarly acrimonious. Fine publicly admitted to having been a member of the American Communist Party until 1955, when he ended this association. While never denying his earlier political advocacy, he had subsequently compiled a thirty-year record of exemplary contribution to the national and local arts community, to higher education, to the entertainment industry, and to American democracy.

Fine's confirmation hearings by the City Council had a ludicrous quality. Opposition was mostly confined to Alderman Pucinski, a few befuddled Council colleagues, and a little band of archaic protesters. Mayor Washington spoke eloquently in support of Fine's nomination. Leading members of Chicago's arts community, including the heads of the city's major arts organizations, prominent representatives of business, labor, higher education, clergy and citizen agencies joined in

Fine's acclaim. The City Council voted overwhelmingly to confirm Fine's appointment. Apart from that critical endorsement, the impassioned testimony of a cross-section of Chicago's life and variety of opinion represented a powerful reaffirmation of democratic ideals and respect for the arts. If that sounds a bit high blown, I submit that virtually no one left the Council hearings that day without a sense of exultation and national pride. The only loser in the whole affair was Columbia. We were left to find a new department chair to replace the irreplaceable Fred Fine.

In his eight years at Columbia, Fine had invented a department which added an important dimension to the college's arts and media studies, developed a very successful graduate program, and had served very valuably as Columbia's ambassador to Chicago's arts community. There's an old vaudeville instruction that says, "Never go on after kids or animal acts." Similarly, Fred Fine would be a tough act to follow.

Few universities, and no arts schools, then offered a specialty in arts and entertainment management. Only a few people had the requisite experience and qualifications in the field. Our search for Fred's successor finally narrowed to one candidate, Carol Yamamoto, who had the experience, vision, and familiarity with education to perform the chair's job. A UCLA MBA, she had been the manager of the Lyric Opera Theater and development director of the Seattle Opera Company. While no one could have been expected to duplicate Fred's verve and ubiquity, Carol was knowledgeable and communicative about arts administration and entertainment management, and most expert in their business practices. She served as the department's head until 1991, when she resigned as chair but remained as a member of the faculty, and has since become a leading national consultant to arts organizations, foundations, and government arts agencies. Carol was succeeded by Dennis Rich, a University of Wisconsin Ph.D. and a very experienced arts manager. He remains the department's chair today. He has extended its purview and educational quality, which now includes instruction in sophisticated business functions at both undergraduate and graduate levels.

But the Fred Fine story isn't done. After Harold Washington's tumultuous first term ended in 1987, Fred resigned as the Commissioner of Cultural Affairs, saying he was too old for the job's demands. What he really needed, I think, was just a pause. With Mayor Washington's encouragement, Fred had begun a vast civic enterprise, which gave unprecedented prominence to the city's cultural and artistic life. It was an awesome challenge. To amply catalog his accomplishments would take a book in itself. Unquestionably, Fred had become the universally respected dean of the Chicago arts community and the champion of democratic access to its benefits. With such ornaments, Fred returned to Columbia as the Director of Public Affairs. He became our advocate to myriad city, state, and national arts activities, many of which he initiated. He created bridges between Columbia and a great range of arts programs and gave public presence to a number of the college's arts projects. His indefatigable energy was as before, and continued for twelve more years, until June 1999, when he decided again to quit, which in view of his precarious health might not be unwise. But on the other hand, he's only eighty-eight and I suspect will come to his senses—and be back.

Whatever the year's events, none would be more significant than the beginnings of the Center for Black Music Research and Dr. Samuel Floyd's tenure as its founder and director. With these, Columbia would became a leading place of distinguished musical scholarship. Sam is a tall, handsome man with an athlete's build and great presence. Articulate and persuasive, he is gentle and modest. He is an extraordinary musical scholar and exceptional writer, who has an international reputation for his books and articles on music subjects. He has great energy and dedication. Sam is visionary and original, and his value to the college is inestimable. At great personal and scholarly sacrifice, he served several years as undergraduate academic dean and in a present emergency is Columbia's chief academic officer.

In the Columbia library, what had been the Lurie Collection on Fine Arts, a gathering of texts and references on arts subjects funded by a $100,000 grant from the Robert Lurie Foundation, became the Lurie Library of Fine and Applied Arts with a new $100,000 grant from the Lurie Foundation and a $50,000 gift from Lenora Wexler. Remodeling and capital projects during the year also included construction of two sophisticated science laboratories, a $35,000 expense for increasing the broadcast power of the college's radio station, and $50,000 to acquire and equip a TV truck, which duplicated the mobile units of major TV stations, except that Columbia's truck included greater video recording capacity than mobile units that can feed directly to their stations.

At its spring 1984 meeting, the board authorized a 7.5 percent increase in tuition rates and a general salary increase of 7 percent, both reflecting high rates of inflation within the national economy. Alton Harris, a prominent attorney, and Kenneth Riskind, president of the Northwestern Steel Company, were elected to the board.

Again, the year ended profitably, despite more than a million dollars in capital expenses. Endowment and reserve funds exceeded $3.5 million. Though this was a miniscule accumulation relative to Columbia's present and anticipated size, it did represent a very big step above the college's acutely precarious state only a few years before. Notwithstanding my uncertainties about retirement, I agreed to an extension of my tenure to August 31, 1991, though in 1984, the 1991 date seemed a century away.

1984–1985: Gifts and an Anniversary

Despite enrollment anticipations of 5,200 students in fall 1984, only 4,900 enrolled, less than a 3 percent gain over the past year. While full-time numbers increased by 5 percent, there was no increase in part-time students. Total tuition revenues were greater, however, because of an increase in full-time equivalents and in part-time credit hours. Nonetheless, even Columbia's small enrollment gain compared very favorably to that of other public and independent Illinois institutions, a majority of which reported enrollment losses. While 1984 marked the twentieth consecutive year of Columbia enrollment increases, why 1984 numbers were not greater is difficult to explain. It may have been that the college's forecasting had become less accurate or that we had underestimated the effect of a reduction in the size of the college-age population, cheaper public college tuition, and the growing intensity of college marketing campaigns. It was also quite possible that our large tuition increase in fall 1984 was influential. There was nothing alarming about the college's smaller enrollment gain, but the 1984 figures signaled a need to improve recruiting. In the course of the year, the whole recruitment and admissions system was computerized. This allowed new methods of direct mail advertising and easier telephone follow-up of prospects. We also hired and trained additional field representatives and admission staff and developed new recruitment literature. The student aid effort, critical to student recruitment, was also improved.

The 1984–85 budget included a reserve for student-aid losses as a consequence of a staggering variety of complex new state and federal student-aid regulations. In response to this administrative nightmare, five new staff positions were created in the college's student-aid and records offices, and the computer system was comprehensively reordered to reflect the maze of new regulations.

While the whole collegiate community was equally troubled, it was possible that Columbia had previously unimagined retroactive liabilities. Though state and federal levels of student aid had not been curtailed, there was ample evidence that such was the deliberate intent of restrictive new student-aid regulations, which were more palatable politically than reducing student-aid appropriations. It ultimately turned out that Columbia suffered only minor penalties, though excessive administrative costs were permanent.

On a more encouraging note, my State of the College report to the board at its January 1985 meeting reminded members that almost to the day, it was the twenty-first anniversary of Columbia's move to Lake Shore Drive and the beginning of the college's renewal. On that bitter cold night in January 1964, if I had been more sensibly realistic, I would have run away; though that would have been an ungrateful response to Bud Perlman's generosity. I offered a familiar litany of the trials of Columbia's earlier life to mark a magical coincidence of January events in 1964 and twenty-one years later as a preface to an announcement of gifts to the college of more than $1 million: $750,000 from Emma Getz; and $291,000 from Trustee Myron Hokin. With the help of board member Enid Long, I had tried unsuccessfully to interest Oscar and Emma Getz in making a major gift. It finally happened because of the personal and persuasive effort of Lya Rosenblum. The Getz gift was certainly then the largest gift Columbia had ever received from an individual donor. The money was used to remodel entirely the college's Eleventh Street Theater, which was named in perpetuity the Getz Theater. Myron Hokin's generosity was used to create the Hokin Student Center, which occupies the ground floor of the 623 South Wabash Avenue building.

The January 1985 meeting was an appropriate time to recognize Columbia's influential role in civic affairs and in the arts, media, and education. Consider that:

• *Columbia had leading identity in a major program that joined the city's higher education community, city officials, and business and industry leaders in promoting Chicago's economic development. This was part of a national project of the Association of Urban Universities (which I then chaired) to more closely involve urban higher education institutions in the life of their cities.*

• *The Chicago Metropolitan Higher Education Council (CMHEC), which I also chaired, included the Chicago region's colleges and universities and the Chicago community college system in an active coalition with Chicago's public and parochial schools to improve the quality of common school education and to create greater harmony among its racial divisions.*

• *Columbia was the organizer of the Grant Park Cultural and Educational Community (GPCEC), which closely associated the central city's colleges and universities with the major arts and museum institutions in identifying and promoting the Grant Park district as a common cultural and educational campus, and in developing mutuality and cooperative programs.*

Also prominently visible then: Columbia's Museum of Contemporary Photography and the national reputation of the college's Photography Department; the impressive celebration of the tenth anniversary of the Columbia College Dance Center; the Theater Department's important contribution to the vitality of Chicago theater; Bill Russo's many musical events and celebrated rank in American music; Harry Bouras's leading role in the cultural community; the growth and reputation of the college's graphic arts concentrations; the college's prizewinning literary journals and frequent recognitions in local and national press reviews of Columbia as an important source of contemporary fiction and poetry; the college's radio station, which broadcast to a large part of the Chicago region; the stellar reputation of Columbia's education in television; the widely attended film festivals sponsored by the Film/Video Department and the prizewinning films produced by its students and faculty; an influential state-wide arts advocacy movement by Fred Fine as chair of the college's Arts and Entertainment Management program and now as the city's Commissioner of Arts and Cultural Affairs; the South Shore Neighborhood Revitalization project sponsored by Columbia; local and national publicity of the Southeast Chicago Historical Project; the college's Southern Regional Cultural Center in Uptown; early sponsorship of the Children's Museum, the Peace Museum, and mural and ethnic arts projects; the Center for Black Music Research; and Columbia's prominent role in the political issues of higher education in Illinois and nationally. These were among many other examples of Columbia's cultural and educational vitality.

The year went by with the usual travails. The greatest part of the Wabash building's construction was completed without unexpected dislocations. The Illinois Board of Higher Education asked the legislature for a big increase in the state's student-aid appropriations, though as action on this was deferred until the fall 1984 session, any significant increase in student awards had little, if any, effect on fall 1985 enrollment. Congressional debate over the amount and number of Pell Grant awards continued without resolution. A campaign within the college to get students and their families and friends to send messages to their Congressional representatives in support of increased student aid gathered more than 10,000 messages. These were broken down by Congressional districts and a delegation of Columbia students went to Washington to deliver these appeals and to lobby Congress. Columbia was instrumental in enlisting a number of Illinois independent colleges and universities in a similar effort, which ultimately influenced an increase in student-aid funding, though it was smaller than the amounts sought by the 1985 campaign. Columbia's effort did, however, establish a pattern and campus apparatus which was exercised with great effect by some Illinois institutions in student-aid campaigns in subsequent years.

1985–1986: Growth and Growing Pains

Tuition was increased by 6.5 percent for the 1985–86 college year to $4,064 for full-time students, to $138 per credit hour for part-time enrollment, and to $172 per credit hour for graduate students. The board authorized a general 5 percent salary increase for all faculty and staff and allowed upward gradations in individual instances.

Board meetings continued to emphasize the need for greater board participation in fund-raising and the familiar recognition that Columbia remained precariously over-dependent on tuition revenues. Jack Wolfsohn reported that some gifts and grants were jeopardized by the low record of board giving and getting. The board adopted a proposal by Chairman Jay Fox that the board subscribe to a special effort to raise $100,000 to be used for undergraduate scholarship aid as a partial offset to the nearly $750,000 from the college's funds then being spent for scholarship aid.

Wolfsohn also reported that with the Getz and Hokin gifts, if a number of ifs could be satisfied, it was quite possible that the year's gifts and pledges might exceed $2 million, and even much more if Columbia were to be awarded a federal endowment grant, which we did not qualify for the previous year. Wolfsohn said the U.S. Office of Education, which calculates endowment grant eligibility, employs a questionable formula that creates a barrier to Columbia's inclusion, though he hoped that this handicap might be overcome this year. Again, as described the year before, if Columbia became eligible, it would be at a late date, which would give only several months to raise the matching amount required of recipients. As in all likelihood Columbia would only ask for an initial grant of $300,000, reserving the opportuni-ty to ask for $500,000 the next year, it would still be very difficult to raise the $300,000 match. This had to be in demonstrably new money, which ruled out the use of college funds or preexisting sources.

In the ensuing months, we repeatedly tried unsuccessfully to persuade U.S. Office of Education monitors that they had incorrectly interpreted their own regulations. Unsurprisingly, to expect government officials to confess error was an utterly alien concept.

We had come to the end. Jack and I agreed that the only possibility of rescue lay in the faint hope that we could persuade the intervention of a higher government power. I asked for the help of Dominic DiFrisco, a prominent public relations executive who had in the past helped me organize support for student-aid legislation in Congress and in the Illinois legislature. He thought that it might be valuable to enlist the interest of a leading Republican in the Congress (this was, after all, during the Reagan administration), though Congressional Republicans were not ordinarily strong advocates of higher-education benefits. DiFrisco believed that the best bet was to try to get to Congressman Robert Michel, the Minority Leader of Congress, who certainly was the most influential Illinois Republican in Congress. And as Michel was a good friend of Jack Brickhouse, both coming from Peoria, Brickhouse might be helpful in getting us an appointment with Michel.

It seemed a long shot, but with nothing else going, it was worth a try. While I knew Jack Brickhouse, I was hardly a good enough friend to ask a big favor, though he had arranged my dinner with Willie Mays a few years before. Dominic talked to

Brickhouse, who said he'd be most happy to help us with Michel; indeed, he'd even go with us to Washington. Jack quickly arranged a meeting and soon, Brickhouse, DiFrisco, Wolfsohn, and I were off to the capitol.

Michel was masterfully courteous, and he and Brickhouse exchanged stories about growing up in Peoria. Then I was on. I promptly deferred to Wolfsohn who explained our difficulty with the U.S. Office of Education in establishing Columbia's entitlement to an endowment grant because of the agency's insistence on a questionable interpretation of eligibility rules and the intent of Congress. Michel very patiently heard us out, including Wolfsohn's carefully detailed argument. Michel asked a number of probing questions, and followed these with an observation that Columbia may have been done in by an arbitrary comma. He asked his secretary to summon four or five key members of Congress and an Under Secretary of Education, including Congressman John Porter, whose constituency included 300 or so Columbia students. Within thirty minutes, all had filed into Michel's office. Without endorsing its merit, he reviewed Columbia's case, telling them only that he believed it deserved attention; and if they found our argument valid, he would expect a remedy. All said they would give their best attentions to our appeal. In a little more than an hour, Michel had cut through a jungle of bureaucratic red tape. He promised us nothing but a fair hearing, and that was all we had asked. And certainly, he asked nothing of us. That done, Michel took our little delegation to lunch in the Congressional Dining Room where, again, he and Brickhouse talked about their salad days.

Undoubtedly, prompted by affection for Jack Brickhouse, Congressman Michel had done us a great boon. Though his generosity was expressed politically, it had no political inspiration. Michel was very impressive and had great charm, and I felt that he was a decent man who used power conscionably. Did I say that about a prince of the Republican Party? I must be getting soft.

Jack Brickhouse was more easily described. I got to know him better after we had gone to Washington together. He was just the nicest man. I can't imagine anyone who served more good causes than Jack. He was a delightful raconteur, gracious and charming, innately and unpretentiously democratic. When I had dinner with Willie Mays, I asked him about the racial attitudes of prominent sports broadcasters. "None better than Jack," he said.

I wouldn't have had a reason to tell about our adventures in the Land of Oz if the story didn't have a happy ending. For nearly a month, the Office of Education was silent—nary a hint or a query. Then a brief letter arrived which said that after a recomputation of Columbia's eligibility score, we qualified for a $300,000 grant if the college raised a matching amount in new funds within the prescribed time period. The lateness of our notification left less than three months to satisfy the matching requirement. Even apart from severe time constraints, the task was unusually formidable because donors and foundations customarily prefer to support more specific projects than general endowment funds, and the few who will support the latter ordinarily require long periods of cultivation.

We quickly drafted a plan to solicit every even remotely possible prospective donor, corporate contributor, and foundation. This had to be done selectively because we had to concentrate our effort on getting comparatively large contributions. We had no time to prepare elaborate appeals. But with Jack's perseverance we put the dollars together by the end of summer 1985, barely before the deadline. Board members replaced—even exceeded—their give-and-get pledges to the $100,000 scholarship fund with contributions to the endowment match. Jack got sizable unrestricted gifts from a small number of local foundations and family trusts. Bert Gall hit up the college's suppliers. Our familiar savior, Ken Montgomery, sent a big check. And I did a lot of begging. But it was well worth the frantic effort.

While it meant $600,000 more in the college's endowment and opened the way to a million dollars more next year, (a possible $500,000 grant plus the matching $500,000), the long-range benefit would be much greater. The intention of the endowment grant program was to help developing institutions (Columbia was so classified) and historic African-American colleges create permanent endowments. Specific grant terms required that grants, institutional matches, and compounded investment income be preserved intact for a minimum of five years, when these funds would have grown significantly. It was a most enlightened idea and first-rate legislation.

Fall 1985 enrollment was 5,200, a 5.6 percent gain over last year's disappointments. Seventy percent were full-time students, and the full-time equivalent was 4,300, unusually high for an urban institution. The ratio of men to women was balanced at one-to-one. Sixty percent (3,120) of 1985–86 students were white, and 40 percent (2,080) were minorities. African-Americans were 31 percent (1,612) of enrollment totals; Latinos 7 percent (364), a 25 percent increase over fall 1984; and Asians and Native Americans 2 percent (104). Among African-Americans, women outnumbered men two-to-one. Only a few years before, that ratio was one-to-one. Our ratio may have been influenced by the intense collegiate competition for minority students and by recruitment efforts of the military services. But as this gender disparity was repeated nationally, it evidenced a significant increase in the numbers of African-American males not capitalizing on even the minimal, recently won opportunities of the American mainstream.

At the opening of the 1985–86 college year, there were eighty-six full-time faculty members, twenty-five specialists identified as artists in residence and adjunct faculty, and more than 450 part-time faculty. There were fifteen instructional departments and two graduate subdepartments, Interdisciplinary Arts and Dance Therapy, and a variety of special subject concentrations.

Until the early 1970s, only 18 percent of Columbia's students were women, with a lesser percentage on the faculty. Both counts reflected the systemic discriminatory practices of the media industries, which were the main focus of Columbia's education. As the college's educational emphases expanded to include a variety of arts disciplines, the number of women students increased, and the growth of liberal education studies increased opportunities for women faculty. But by far, the greatest influence on the numbers of women students and faculty was the women's rights movement and its continuing insistence on equality in American society. This opened up career opportunities for women in the media and arts professions and attracted women in sizable numbers to Columbia's educational specialties. While the college had consistently sought women students and faculty, such efforts were only modestly successful when women were largely excluded from Columbia's professions. By 1985, however, the number of women students equaled the number of men, and women were 21 percent of the college's faculty, though a smaller percentage of these were full-time appointments.

It would take some years before any reasonable gender equality could be achieved in the number of women chairs and faculty leaders. In 1985 and for some years after, a highly competitive employment market prevailed for women faculty in academic and media disciplines (lesser for the arts), and Columbia could only attract a small share of them. But even in the College's earlier years and over time, Columbia did assemble an outstanding representation of women faculty. To name only a few: the very distinguished photographers, Lynn Sloan and Ruth Thorne-Thomsen; the eminent director of the Museum of Contemporary Photography, Denise Miller; widely exhibited artists Phyllis Bramson and Hollis Sigler; writer Betty Shiflett; dancer Jan Erkert; Margaret Sullivan in Advertising; theater director and undergraduate Academic Dean Caroline Dodge Latta; poet Maxine Chernoff; dance therapist Jane Ganet-Sigel; Suzanne Cohan, the director of Columbia's graduate program in Interdisciplinary Arts; video artist Barbara Sykes; journalist Carolyn Hulse; filmmaker Doreen Bartoni; theater producer Mary Badger; singer Carol Loverde; weaver Lynn Hammond; actress Pauline Brailsford; scientist and educator Zafra Lerman; and a bit later, actress and stage director Catherine Slade and social anthropologist Joan Erdman.

Student aid was and remains critical to the enrollment of minorities and is similarly essential to Columbia's prosperity. While both federal and state student aid had increased in the current year, stricter regulations governing eligibility were expected to become even more limiting in 1986 and after. In this respect, Columbia had an encouraging record. I reported to the board that both federal and state student-aid agencies had recently completed a comprehensive audit of the college's current and prior student-aid programs, which closely scrutinized $15 million of complex student-aid transactions relating individual financial data to academic records and a bewildering assortment of regulations. Columbia's record was virtually perfect and officially complimented as a model of student-aid administration at a time when many colleges suffered expensive penalties. The board extended its compliments to Student Aid Director Ray Pranske and to Hermann Conaway, the college's dean of students. My report also noted an explosion in the technology of the arts and media subjects that constitute Columbia's main educational interests, and the compelling necessity of furnishing our education with contemporary instructional technology. "Yes, we have been successful; indeed, remarkably so. But success is an impermanent possession and change comes in quick time. We must be ready." I warned that great technological change in the subjects of Columbia's instruction would require large and continuing capital investment in rapidly obsolescing instructional facilities, a continuing reordering of space, faculty retraining, new faculty, and sizable maintenance expenses. The cost would be far greater than even the amounts that we had customarily financed from current funds. I estimated that within the year we could expect to spend at least $1 million, and by 1990, a $4 million investment was a reasonable anticipation.

I submitted, too, that as my tenure would end in five or six years, there was a noticeable anxiety within the college's community about what would follow my term. Moreover, concern was expressed for the continuity of the college's leadership even apart from the president's office, as Columbia's leading administration had remained unchanged for many years. In fact, the same number of people, in most instances the same individuals, who managed a comparatively simple institution, then directed a complex institution of thousands of students and faculty and a budget of many millions. In short, I observed that our system was archaic and ultimately imprudent.

In a subsequent meeting that year, the board adopted a presidential succession procedure and elected Bert Gall as the college's vice president. The board regarded both Gall and Scheibel as indispensable to the college's life and continuity.

At the beginning of the year, when the college became eligible for a $300,000 endowment grant, at Wolfsohn's prompting the board decided to apply for an additional grant of $500,000 during the current year and to immediately begin a campaign to raise the required matching amount. Wolfsohn and the board were confident that the matching requirement could be subscribed, as this time we would have nearly a whole year to gather the funds, though the amount necessary was $200,000 greater than what was raised in 1985's brief campaign. The application was submitted in April 1986 and again, with Wolfsohn's guide, the board's energy, the

generosity of individuals and local foundations, and by "hook and crook," we satisfied the matching requirement that qualified the college for the $500,000 endowment grant. In little more than a year's time, the college's endowment had grown by $1,600,000.

In 1986, Jay Fox had completed three years as the board's chairman. He had accepted the post with the understanding that he would only serve a three-year term. Fox had most ably presided during a time of many accomplishments. Among these: the accreditation of Columbia's graduate school; the acquisition of the 623 South Wabash building; qualitative improvements in the college's fund-raising; and most importantly, the college's consolidation after years of disordered growth.

In 1986 Fox was succeeded as the board's chairman by Alton Harris, who was the managing partner of a very prominent law firm, had served as legal counsel to important government and business agencies, and was closely associated with the upper echelons of Chicago's business and financial communities. A cultured individual, Harris was seriously involved in civic affairs, and had dedicated interest in education and the liberal arts. He even had been a Columbia photography student. I was influential in Harris's recruitment to the board and felt that he was exceptionally qualified to become the board's chairman. The moment came much sooner than I had expected. When several long-serving members declined the office, Harris was persuaded to accept. His chairmanship has extended to fourteen years. Harris is a compassionate man, committed to Columbia's mission and welfare. His judicious counsel is readily accessible, and while comprehensively engaged in the college's life, during my term he carefully observed his and the board's exclusion from the president's and the faculty's educational purviews. He regularly attends college events and is a munificent host and extraordinary cook who works hard at making friends for the college. The college has been richly rewarded by his extraordinary loyalty and competence and, I add, limitless patience.

At its April 1986 meeting, the board voted a 6.5 percent increase in 1986–87 tuition rates, which would still be the lowest among Illinois's independent colleges and universities, and a 5 percent general salary increase for faculty and staff, though a greater amount would be given to a number of faculty and staff who had served for many years without any merit recognition beyond general institutional salary increases. As a result, faculty salaries for the ensuing college year averaged 8.7 percent higher and part-time teaching compensation was increased by a similar amount, with a commitment to a continuing increase in part-time teaching rates.

The college continued to enjoy a run of profitable years, due in significant part to continued Illinois aid to the state's independent college institutions based on undergraduate student numbers. Columbia's great growth was reflected in the increasing amount of this award, then $600,000.

By 1985, Columbia was safely beyond its earlier life-and-death struggles to survive. But even if the stakes were now smaller, the college was not immune to trouble. It came in the form of a faculty controversy in the Writing/English Department. I would have believed its intensity alien to Columbia's sense of community and traditional harmony and collegiality. As faculty warfare is not unknown on American campuses, I suppose it goes with the territory, though my immediate colleagues and I were unprepared for its excesses. I suppose, also, that in our case it was a signal that Columbia had reached sufficient size and maturity to suffer, perhaps even expect, occasional turf warfare. The issues that divided the English faculty were complicated, and both sides could reasonably claim to have a good argument; though inevitably, these became uncivilly personal.

Story Workshop® techniques were nearly the only method of teaching writing and English used in the department. Invented by John Schultz and seconded by his close associate Betty Shiflett, the Story Workshop method was an unusually strict system of teaching informed by Schultz's published theories of how language and writing skills are learned. Though the method incorporates an emphasis on standard expository writing, grammar, reading skills, and conventional elements of English instruction, its distinguishing quality is its employment of an intricate system of classroom exercises, student participation, and a distinctive oral component, none of which are part of ordinary English instruction.

Teachers, identified as Story Workshop directors, underwent rigorous training, and their continuing participation in directors' workshops was a strict requirement. In these in-service sessions, student and faculty performance was carefully reviewed. This was in addition to classroom observations by Schultz, Shiflett, and the department's leading cadre. Obviously, the whole process required the consummate dedication of the department's faculty who, in addition to their department preoccupations, were also expected to pursue personal writing projects, which Schultz aided.

Unsurprisingly, the department's members functioned as a family, with Schultz and Shiflett as presiding figures, and in many instances, the faculty shared a social life.

Whatever view might be held of the department's exhausting expectations, there was no denying its remarkable success in teaching English and writing, subjects that have long perplexed experts, and the extraordinary quality of student writing. Nor could the evidence be ignored that Story Workshop methods had proven successful at every level of the educative process, were being adopted by increasing numbers of schools and colleges, and enjoyed prominent recognition in the associations of educators and teachers of English. It was arguable that these could not have happened without the method's precision and the dedication demanded of the department's faculty. One can only speculate that these might have been eased enough to repair the schism, though by the time the dispute erupted openly, it would probably have been too late to fashion a remedy.

In all likelihood, a rising in the ranks was inevitable. It was a long time in coming, and at first was only the grousing of a few individuals who complained that faculty expectations were unreasonable and that the system prevented any exercise of individual teaching initiatives. Unsatisfied by Schultz's response, their complaints became more strident and contagious, and a sizable faction of dissident faculty quickly developed. Predictably, a caucus of loyalists rose to the provocation. Both sides contributed to a rash of manifestos and countercharges. The dissidents contended that the Story Workshop community was more a cult than a family, and that faculty who deviated from the party line were rudely cast out like discredited angels.

They also charged that the Story Workshop method was overly rigid and dismissed alternative teaching techniques as alien pretensions, and that some students were not well served by Story Workshop's classroom experiences. The battle raged for nearly a year. Positions hardened irreparably, and both sides insisted that their opponents be expelled.

Despite Herculean efforts by Lya Rosenblum, who as academic dean was the administration's frontline soldier, and by Bert Gall and myself, all efforts at compromise failed. Not only was the English/Writing Department abusively divided, but many of the college's faculty and students chose sides as well.

It should be understood that the contestants were responsible and principled people and talented and dedicated educators, many with impressive reputation in academic and literary communities; none more so than John Schultz, who has served Columbia with singular devotion now for more than thirty years.

Finally, the controversy became too unsettling to be allowed to continue, and with the counsel of Lya, Bert, and a number of chairs, I imposed a resolution that created two departments: one, English Instruction and Literature Subjects; and the other, Creative Writing, which included fiction and nonfiction writing, and the old department's graduate programs. Poetry courses, as literature subjects, formerly part of the omnibus English/Writing Department, were transferred to the English Department. There, poetry flourished as a distinct study emphasis, headed by the distinguished American poet (and later a novelist, too) Paul Hoover, whom I vaguely remember to have been one of the dissidents. Hoover was joined by his wife, poet Maxine Chernoff, and together they developed Columbia's study emphasis in poetry writing, which has many students and a national recognition and publishes an annual anthology of contemporary American poetry. (Columbia is among a few American colleges to offer a major study emphasis in poetry.) The largest number of faculty joined the English Department, irrespective of their factional affiliations, because teaching English and literature were their specialties. In the reconstitution, the Creative Writing Department was initially assigned five full-time faculty members, including John and Betty, though this number has grown over time. While after the separation of faculty many English classes continued to use Story Workshop methods and adaptations of it, a number of classes, particularly those with new faculty, used more conventional methods. But, absent John and Betty's presence and the control they exerted, and without Story Workshop's teacher-training emphasis and continuity of instruction, even reassigned faculty loyalists could only imperfectly sustain Story Workshop methods in teaching English to Columbia's students. And with the college's continuing growth and the influx of new teachers, a diminishing number of students had the unique benefit of the method.

Relieved of responsibility for teaching undergraduate English, the new Creative Writing Department prospered. The numbers of students and faculty increased significantly, as did the quality of undergraduate and graduate student writing. The publication record of graduates and faculty was encouraging, and the department's anthologies of student writing have consistently won coveted awards.

But it was all a tragic episode in which the college turned out to be the big loser. A number of splendid faculty members, discouraged by the struggle, resigned; among them, Larry Heinemann, who only a few years later would win the National Book Award for *Paco's Story*, a novel about the Vietnam War. He had learned to be a writer as a Columbia student and as a Story Workshop director. There were other faculty casualties. The greatest injury was the ultimate loss of the Story Workshop approach as a principal method of undergraduate English instruction and a return to the more customary college English courses.

At the great separation of the two departments and after an extended search, Dr. Philip Klukoff was chosen to chair the English Department. Among his qualifications was his long service as a tenured professor at Stockton State College in New Jersey, a college with student characteristics similar to Columbia. In my view, however, Klukoff's outstanding credential was his bravery in accepting responsibility for an unimaginably chaotic situation. He was a tough, talented, and patiently judicious man, virtues which were put to immediate test. He had to minister to many wounded souls and recreate a critical agency of Columbia's education.

Potential for serious discord within a department is undoubtedly present in Columbia's system of chair appointments and in the expectations of their performance. To cop a bit of history, when I was virtually the college's only manager during the early years of Columbia's renewal, there was no academic hierarchy and no departments or chairs, excepting the de facto status of Radio and Television and their chairs Al Parker and Thaine Lyman. There was only a small number of part-time faculty then, most of whom I chose. Later, when departments and career concentrations developed, they formed at my direction around and at the initiative of particular individuals, who became chairs of their disciplines. While it was implicit then and subsequently that choice and retention of department chairs was a presidential prerogative, such power was refined in 1977 by adoption of rules for hiring and retention of department chairs and faculty. While I retained the power to initiate a department and to nominate the chair, as I did in the instances of Arts and Entertainment Management, Journalism and Advertising, and with Lya Rosenblum's guide, Interdisciplinary Arts and Dance Therapy, both presidential acts required the endorsement of the Chairpersons' Council. Ultimately, though I had the authority to nominate a chair, it became more usual that a search committee referred its nominations to me for final selection.

Chair qualifications continued to emphasize accomplishments and professional reputation in the department's subject, administrative and communication skills, personality characteristics suitable to a leadership role, high work energy, evidence of an entrepreneurial spirit, and compatibility with Columbia's mission. I had learned to add to these measures a subjective estimate of the prospect; though I recognized that a degree of egocentricity, even eccentricity, was not unusual in outstanding individuals. Indeed, I believe strongly that in higher education, energy spent on the indulgence of eccentricity may be justifiably tolerated in the instance of brilliant individuals. I'm probably attracted to dramatic personalities, and I think I'm one, too.

On my watch, Columbia's chair system was poles apart from most colleges and universities that had a hierarchy of deans who presided over departments, and whose chairs were chosen on a rotating basis from department faculties. In contrast, Columbia's academic structure was headed by the college's dean and principal educational officer, who directed the affairs of all instructional departments and a range of educational services. It was a loose federation in which departments had considerable autonomy, and their chairs enjoyed job security and my consistent support if they performed to expectations and their departments prospered. Among the measures of a department was its quality of student service, enrollment gains, public recognition, educational ingenuity, addition of talented faculty, administrative competence, and departmental harmony.

Columbia's department chairs had far greater responsibility than those at other colleges and universities; and few, if any, institutions were as dependent as Columbia on the energy, entrepreneurial spirit, and talent of its department leaders.

The corollary of such dependence, however, was that Columbia's chairs became paladins of virtually independent provinces at a great distance from the capitol city. (There is an old Russian proverb that says, "God is a long way up and the czar is a long way off.") Chairs reigned successfully to the extent that they sustained the consent of their faculty and avoided excessive exercise of arbitrary power. As college teachers are by nature an independent lot, the chairs' management style was tested continuously. It could be said fairly, I think, that at Columbia, faculty strife was minimal, except the schism in the English Department.

A new season of discontent came in 1988 in a contretemps within the Science Department. It defied reasonable explanation. It mostly had nothing to do with educational issues, at least initially, which were raised later only to embroider the rhetoric of what was essentially a clash of personalities.

Under ordinary circumstances, science studies would have been included among liberal arts subjects. If anything, science and mathematics were often alien to the aptitudes and career interests of many of Columbia's students. Correspondingly, the college's science courses had been confined to the rubric "Science Today," which offered a sketchy history of science and a survey of contemporary scientific discoveries, and to several elementary science courses which satisfied the certification requirements of teacher education.

When Dr. Zafra Lerman came to Columbia's faculty in 1976, the college's benign indifference to science education was swept away. Her distinguished reputation in the scientific community, scholarly credentials, and published research would have easily qualified her for the faculty or a prominent research position at any major university. In accompanying her husband, an important scientist who had accepted a Northwestern University appointment, she had simply arrived too late to find a local faculty opportunity. In fact, Columbia was the only Chicago institution not already in session. When Louis Silverstein, then the chair of the Liberal Arts Department, interviewed her and reviewed her credentials, he rushed to tell me that we simply had to hire her, even though we'd have to make up courses for her to teach. Lya Rosenblum and I concurred, and Zafra was in our midst.

It would take a magazine profile to describe Zafra. She grew up in Israel; served its military obligation; completed her undergraduate work at the Technion, graduate work at the Weizmann Institute, and her doctorate in physical chemistry at Cornell University. There, she was a postdoctoral fellow, a member of the university's faculty and a research associate of Dr. Frank Long and other scientific luminaries. She was widely published in leading scientific journals and lectured frequently all over the world. As the chair of the American Chemical Society's Commission on Human Rights, Dr. Lerman had world prominence for her passionate and effective advocacy of human rights issues, and she was personally responsible for assuring the safety of an impressive number of scientists from political tyranny and repression.

Zafra's original teaching methods and programs have been and still are funded by grants in the millions of dollars from the National Science Foundation and leading grant-making educational and scientific agencies. At this writing, Zafra heads a large-scale project sponsored by Chicago's public school system, which is retraining its science teachers.

She is the respected colleague of many of the world's most celebrated scientists including many Nobel prize winners, and she is herself the recipient of a host of prestigious awards. In my opinion, she was and is a very attractive and charming woman who has a bit of theater and high fashion about her. She has a mercurial temperament, an inexplicable vulnerability, and a perplexing susceptibility to unnecessary battles. And she is flat-out the best classroom teacher I've ever known (besides, perhaps, my mother).

Within three years, Zafra had created a Science Department which began at nothing. Suddenly, hundreds of Columbia students were taking science courses. She assembled and trained a credentialed faculty of full- and part-time teachers, and scouted up the funding to equip sophisticated science laboratories. She designed an accessible science curriculum for students who had no expectation of careers in science. It was quite literally meant as science for intelligent citizenship. The genius of it was that its instruction was based on the expressions of science in contemporary life and on the use of scientific principles in learning to think and reason. Students were encouraged to interpret the lessons of science in terms of their own artistic and career inclinations. A dance student choreographed scientific principles. Art, photography, and film students employed their talents similarly. Television and radio students programmed the issues of science, and journalism students wrote articles. These student illustrations of science themes were of such quality that delegations of Columbia students were invited to share their methods with students and faculty of other colleges and universities, Princeton and the Indiana Universities among these.

Then, in 1988, the Science Department imploded, literally falling in on itself. Over time, Zafra lost the consent of some of her faculty. In a sense, like the English Department before, the chair and faculty of the Science Department had a family cohesion. In both instances, the departments sailed ships of radical design in the unfriendly waters of conventional practice in their disciplines, and both departments had in common a sense of embattlement which brought their members closely together. It was not unlike Columbia's earlier feeling of being a pariah in the community of higher education. But, as in many families, when close ties are shredded by the neutrality of former enemies, the English and Science Departments became less mindful of the collegiality both had long enjoyed.

In retrospect, I speculate that Zafra believed, as did Schultz, that requiring a preoccupying intensity of faculty effort and sustained fraternity among members were indispensable elements of her department's continuing success. It may have been, too, that she believed, however abstractly, that fraternity with her faculty would shield her from their resistance to her expectations. While there may have been substance in her estimate of indispensables, any expectations of safety in fraternity tumbled like a house of cards. Indeed, as when families fall apart, all sorts of dysfunction are revealed.

I've no reliable memory of the event that set the Science Department ablaze: only that in my opinion it was a goofy occasion involving personal frictions between a faculty faction and Dr. Lerman, though these may have been fueled by an accumulation of grievances. To faint memory, however, there were no innocents. But once the fire started, it quickly sped through faculty ranks, gathering partisans as it spread. While the department's dissident faculty—full-time members, mainly—contended that they were exploited and suppressed by Zafra's arbitrary demands and expectations, charges which she hotly denied, the whole course of the controversy was punctuated by intense personal feelings, bizarre charges, and threats of lawsuits. When the argument reached a point when the faculty faction centered its demands on Dr. Lerman's ouster as the department's chair and she countered with an insistence that they be expelled from the Science Department, it was compellingly clear that no pacific resolution was possible. To worsen matters, a number of other faculty and students had become embroiled in the controversy, some, I think, viewing it as entertainment. Whatever, putting an end to the fight was urgently necessary.

Once again, as in the instance of the English Department, a resolution was imposed from above, meaning by my authority with the advice of legal counsel and the mixed endorsement of the college's deans and chairs of other departments. Although it was not an easy or satisfying conclusion, any alternatives, like expelling the combatants, impermissibly risked damage to the quality of Columbia's education and the welfare of students. What was imposed was the creation of a Science Institute, which Zafra Lerman would head, to encompass the college's graduate program in teaching science and Zafra's independent projects in science education, and a separate Science Department with new leadership, which would be responsible for the college's undergraduate science instruction. Dr. Charles Cannon was chosen as the department's chair, a position he still holds; Dr. Lerman continues to head Columbia's Science Institute, which enjoys national reputation as a leading center of innovative science education and the support of major funding agencies and school systems. Utilizing Dr. Lerman's concept of science instruction for students with no expectation of science careers, and many of her methods, which relate instruction to the artistic and media interests and inclinations of Columbia's students, the undergraduate Science Department has developed a competent life, regrettably independent of its stormy past. I wish that I could report that everyone lived happily ever after. But inexplicably, some volatile debris of the "science war of '88" still litters Columbia's landscape, even twelve years after.

1986–1987: Comparative Serenity

In my message to the board at its October 1986 meeting, I reported that the college had returned to a peaceful state. Obviously, I didn't anticipate another brush war. I've no memory now of what it was that gave me such comfort, except that I may have been buoyed by encouraging enrollment statistics. We opened the year with 5,550 students, a 6.5 percent increase over the prior year, and a full-time equivalent of 4,620, which confirmed Columbia's rank as the fifth largest of Illinois' independent colleges and universities. The percentage of African-American students, however, fell to 28 percent, a more than 25 percent loss in the last four years; and African-American women continued to outnumber men by two-to-one.

Full-time faculty members increased to 121, eleven greater than the previous year, but still forty to fifty below an appropriate number of full-time faculty. Of 121 full-time faculty members: ninety-two (76 percent) were white; twenty-two (18 percent) African-American; five (4 percent) Latino; and two (1 percent) Asian. Of these, sixty-three had doctorates; thirty-six had MAs or MFAs; seventeen had bachelor's degrees; and five had no degrees. In September 1986, the part-time faculty numbered 505 and taught 60 percent of Columbia's classes. Columbia's problem of disproportionate numbers of part-time faculty worsened in relation to increased numbers of students, and adequate orientation and supervision of part-time faculty by departments was increasingly troubling. Regrettably, qualitative improvement in the faculty ratio remained limited by financial barriers, in the short term, at least. Columbia, however, was not a rare exhibit of such disproportion, as it was patently evident that nearly all of American higher education was similarly dependent on part-time faculty and graduate teaching assistants (which Columbia did not employ).

The college's operating budget for 1986–87 topped $18 million, and after all capital expenditures, revenues were projected to exceed expenses by $500,000 and even more if heightened fund-raising efforts were successful, though fund-raising at that moment was even more uncertain than usual. Jack Wolfsohn had decided to step down as the director of development at the end of the college year, when he hoped to serve in a staff capacity for two years until his retirement. I know his job as director had been terribly difficult and stressful, because the task of persuading the fund-raising efforts of the board had fallen to him alone, and perhaps as a result, his harangue had grown thin. With regret, I accepted his decision and endorsed his wish to serve in a staff position. Jack was a talented and experienced fund-raising executive. While not among Columbia's earliest pioneers, he was surely a most loyal and committed veteran of Columbia's long march. When he joined the college's ranks, the college had no record, reason, or savvy to sensibly expect public, foundation, or government agency support. He was the paramount guide of what became a successful fund-raising and grant-getting enterprise. Jack would be very hard to replace.

Columbia's library collection had increased to 80,000 volumes. This was still only half of the American Library Association (ALA) standard for an institution of Columbia's size, though the college's library was more than ample for an institution with specialized educational focus and in many instances serving a nonbook curriculum. This was particularly true since Columbia's collection was augmented by

Roosevelt University's general library holdings and by computer access to the library resources of other institutions in Illinois and the nation. In comparison to college libraries with decades of acquisition, Columbia's library collection was contemporary. Ironically, the ALA book-count standards would soon become passé with the explosion in information technology and computer access to literally a world of study and reference sources. In this respect, with a timely, albeit costly, new technology and information systems and a staff of sophisticated librarians, Columbia quickly achieved parity with far older and better established college libraries. By 1989, even the library sharing arrangement with Roosevelt University had become unnecessary. The little bit of library planted by Hubert Davis and diligently cultivated over time had become a modern college library.

Corresponding to Columbia's great growth, the college's bookstore had become a big business, with annual revenues of $700,000. While it had only recently begun to return a small profit, this was hardly worth the amount of time spent on the bookstore's management, most of which, as did many Columbia things, fell to Bert Gall. While surveying a number of college and university bookstores in search of efficiencies, he discovered that most collegiate institutions farmed their bookstores out to national college bookstore chains, who paid royalties to the institutions they serviced. It seemed a sensible arrangement, which led us to ask for bids from the most prominent operators of campus bookstores. We narrowed the prospects to Barnes and Noble and the Follett Corporation, and ultimately selected Follett, whose bid was the most attractive. They paid $117,000 to purchase operating rights

and a reasonable share of the bookstore's profits. The Follett College Bookstores were part of the national company, which had been headed by Dwight Follett, who had given many distinguished years to Columbia as board chairman. While he had counseled the development of Columbia's bookstore, doing business with the college would have been unthinkable to him. And to me, too, until long after he had retired from the Follett Corporation and resigned as the college's board chairman

In the course of the year, we began preparations for a reaccreditation examination by the North Central Association scheduled for the spring of 1989, which included a new self-study to be submitted in December 1988. Obviously, the college had changed dramatically in the ten years since the last comprehensive examination in 1978, and even in the five years since the college's graduate program was accredited in 1983. While Columbia's mission statement and the greater part of its history could be taken from prior reports, the 1988 self-study would have to incorporate newly compiled institutional data. This was again a formidable task, despite the fact that the college had recent experience with the self-study process and the benefit of computers. We were benefited, too, in having Dennis Peacock as the college's director of Institutional Research to direct the self-study and to write much of its narrative.

When, in 1987, Dennis Peacock became the director of Institutional Research and was given responsibility for preparing the college for reaccreditation, he was replaced as the director of the Graduate School by Dr. Keith Cleveland, who had been the assistant dean for Academic Affairs. Cleveland is an exceptional scholar and teacher, who had been a member of the University of Chicago faculty, and his tenure as the director of Columbia's Graduate School continues today.

The college continued its profitable run. Looking back, I suppose there must have been some truth in my earlier observation that the college's life was comparatively serene. At least, a review of the year didn't prompt any memorable anxieties or noteworthy events, the latter excepting Jane Alexandroff's organization of Chicago Artists Abroad, which ranks high among Columbia's contributions to the Chicago arts community. A brief account of it is in the appendix.

1987–1988

The 1987–88 year began with 5,700 students—5,465 undergraduates and 235 graduate students. Two-thirds of Columbia's students attended full-time and one-third attended part-time. Sixty percent of the college's students were white, 26 percent African-American, 7 percent Latino, 4 percent Asian, 1 percent Native American, and 1 percent not identified.

Though Columbia had no officially defined major fields of study, it did to the extent that students identified themselves with particular study and career concentrations and followed the curricular expectations of departments, albeit with some individual variation. Nonetheless, it was difficult to calculate the number of departmental majors with any precision because students were unreliable reporters; many changed the emphasis of their studies in the course of their enrollment, and departmental records of student declarations were undependable.

Columbia's Liberal Education Department fits no customary collegiate pattern. English, which includes literature courses, and Science, which includes math studies, are separate departments, reflecting the college's emphasis on English skills and scientific literacy as fundamental to successful college study and life quality whatever an individual's occupation. The Liberal Education Department is an omnibus agency of liberal-arts disciplines (previously gathered under the rubric Life Arts) none of which has been formally designated as a department. In effect, these disciplines function as subdepartments, each with a faculty complement, a distinctive academic life, and student choice among a large number of subjects. Study in each discipline is required of all students.

Columbia offers no major fields of study other than in arts and media concentrations and their career specialties. Despite the fact that one of Columbia's distinctions is the exceptional quality of its liberal arts studies, students do not come to Columbia with the expectation of pursuing any of these as their major concentrations, though it would be possible for a student to get an excellent general education by concentrating on a combination of liberal arts studies without electing arts or media subjects.

The Liberal Education department, however, has the greatest student numbers among the college's departments, a large full-time faculty and the largest number of part-time teachers, which reflects the high value Columbia places on liberal education, and the fact that the college is both a liberal arts college and an institution of special educational interest. We have avoided a proliferation of departments, each with a separate administrative apparatus and supporting staff, in instances when a discipline has no major field of study. But, unquestionably, liberal education is an important part of Columbia's educational substance, verified by the fact that if the enrollment in the college's English, Science, and Liberal Education departments is viewed together, one-third of all student credit hours are taken in what is traditionally described as liberal arts studies. The department's arrangement is unorthodox and perhaps is an unwieldy system, and may even inhibit faculty initiative and student opportunity. Nonetheless, it has created a strong sense of collegiality and connection among faculty representing a variety of disciplines and a lessening of the departmental competitions which often occur in conventional liberal arts colleges.

For many years, Dr. Leslie Van Marter presided as chair of the Liberal Education Department. He retired at the end of the 1999 year. Van Marter is a respected scholar and experienced academic administrator, and he has regularly taught Columbia courses in philosophy and ethics, including a very popular course on the Holocaust. A University of Chicago Ph.D., he was a Fulbright scholar at the University of Paris and a student at Oxford University, professor of philosophy and department chair at California State College, dean of the School of Arts and Humanities at Pennsylvania State College, and dean of Lake Erie College. He has published books and articles in leading journals. He served Columbia with great distinction in a difficult job that required unusual patience and judicious temperament in managing diverse individuals and academic disciplines.

At the board's October 1987 meeting, I observed that it would be difficult to arrest the decline of Columbia's minority-student enrollment. Chicago's public high schools had been the nearly exclusive source of Columbia's minority enrollment, and the graduation rates of minority students from these schools were at discouragingly low levels. While I could only get sketchy figures, as nearly as I can calculate, in 1985, Chicago public high schools graduated 15,494 students, an astonishingly low figure when cast against an elementary/secondary school population of more than 400,000. Three thousand one hundred (20 percent) of 1985 graduates went on to attend four-year colleges. Three hundred fifty of these (11 percent) enrolled at Columbia, of whom 250 were minorities, 220 African-Americans, and 31 Latinos. Of 1985 graduates of Chicago's high schools, 9,000 were African-Americans, 1,350 of whom went to a four-year college, and of these, 220 (16 percent) attended Columbia.

Starting in the spring of 1987, a special committee of the college's deans, department chairs, and faculty and board representatives sought a comprehensive reorganization of the college's terms of faculty employment, which included an examination of the issue of professorial rankings. These deliberations extended over seven months and resulted in a series of proposals that were submitted to the committee's constituencies for discussion. Understandably, debate was intense, particularly among chairs and faculty councils, but consensus was finally reached and the board ratified the plan at its January 1988 meeting.

The membership of the old Elected Representatives of Chairpersons (ERC), which had been restricted to department chairs, was changed to include three chairs and three nonprobationary faculty members, with accompanying provisions for review and appeal. Apart from issues of faculty employment security, the new ERC would also hear grievances filed by faculty who claimed discrimination or affront by chairs or their faculty colleagues based on race, gender, religion, national origin, physical handicaps, or sexual orientation.

Those joining the faculty after September 1, 1987, would have probationary status for six years before being eligible for ERC review in the event of their dismissal by their department's chair in consultation with senior members of the department's faculty. Faculty who had served a year or more by September 1987 would achieve full faculty status after four years of continuous employment.

The performance of all chairs was subject to formal written review by the academic dean and their department's senior faculty every two years; and all full-time faculty, adjunct faculty, and long-term artists- and scholars-in-residence to annual review by their department chairs and senior faculty. All performance reviews were to be open to inspection and response by individuals reviewed. In establishing a system of performance reviews, we emphasized that its intent was fraternal, not punitive, and that the purpose was to improve the quality of chair and faculty performance. The college's deans, too, were to be subject to periodic review, though no satisfactory procedure for this was ever developed. Over time, chair and faculty reviews were practiced less formally than originally intended. Claims of discrimination were virtually unknown.

The issue of traditional professional ranks, which had rumbled about the college for a number of years, was resolved, albeit imperfectly, by designating all full-time faculty, except those in probationary status, as professors, which omitted the preliminary ranks of "assistant" and "associate" professor. Those still in probationary status continued to be identified as "instructors." Neither title was commonly used within the college, though "professor" had occasional currency. At the time, the decisions on faculty employment security and rank seemed a bold change in the college's rules. But in retrospect, I think the changes were less significant and the college's life continued to be shaped, during my tenure, by the fraternal reasonableness that had long prevailed, though undoubtedly much of Columbia's old informality was inappropriate to an institution of far greater size and complexity. At the very least, Columbia's new rules for faculty engagement avoided the arbitrary harshness of traditional tenure systems, which only offered faculty tenured appointment at the end of six or seven years or ignominious dismissal and often embroiled senior faculty and deans in bloody dispute.

Apart from difficult issues of institutional process, Columbia faced the immediate prospect of large capital expenditures which could not be financed from current revenues. These were to fund unfinished work in the 623 building, new construction to respond to the growing technological emphasis of Columbia's instruction, and to anticipated enrollment increases, new computer installations, and major deferred maintenance projects. So it was back to bond-issue financing. The board agreed to a new bond issue indebtedness of $1,650,000. But unlike previous bond issues, which were secured by the college's buildings and real estate, the new issue would be secured by endowment and reserve funds, making stability of these a compelling necessity.

The board and John Scheibel also created a five-year budget projection based on no enrollment growth and increased revenue only from tuition increases and fund-raising. This restrained budget could be promptly exercised if circumstances warranted. And even if a worst-case scenario did not happen, the board instructed that yearly budgets continue to avoid commitments that anticipated revenue growth until evidence of fall-term enrollment was recorded. While we had always carefully observed this prudence, it was valuable to be reminded that hard old times ought not be forgotten in the throes of success.

Also that year, at the board's spring 1988 meeting, I nominated Albert Gall as Columbia's executive vice president and provost, and the board unanimously concurred. This was in recognition of Bert's cardinal role in the college's management. While his myriad duties remained unchanged, at least now he was appropriately titled. And maybe he got a pay raise, too.

1988–1989: Merger Discussion

Among the year's important miscellany, an 8.9 percent increase in tuition rates was fixed for 1988–89, the largest tuition increase in the college's history. While Columbia's tuition of $2,498 per semester ($4,996 per year) for full-time students, $170 per credit hour for part-time enrollment, and $205 per credit hour for graduate study was still the lowest among Illinois independent colleges and universities, it was the first time that a combination of maximum state and federal student-aid awards did not exceed Columbia's tuition and fees and allow some small amount for students' living costs.

The board established a minimum give-or-get expectation of $3,000 for individual board members. William Hood, who had managed Columbia's earlier bond issues for the Continental Illinois Bank and who was in 1969 a member of the college's Photography faculty, was elected to the board. At year's end, the college's endowment and reserve funds reached $8 million. The $500,000 lost in the stock market's 1987 crash had been recovered. And the board's Investment Committee reported that Columbia had averaged a 17 percent return over the five-year life of the fund.

Apart from the year's happenings, a new interest jumped out of the blue. Despite Columbia's current prosperity and popularity in the student market, the college's financial security was marginal; and with nearly exclusive dependence on growing tuition revenues, the college did not have the financial strength or public confidence to survive a serious recession or a large reduction in federal and state student-aid subsidies. Nor did Columbia have any real expectation of a sufficient endowment fund, whose investment earnings could significantly relieve dependence on tuition revenues, or consistent gift receipts from a generous public or prosperous alumni. And there were no guarantees that Columbia's virtual local monopoly in arts and media education would continue if other commuter institutions chose to compete for students in Columbia's subject concentrations, or designed a replica of Columbia's comprehensive program in arts and media specialties, particularly if our competitors were public institutions with low tuition, state subsidy, and the interest of state legislators. While there was no cause at the moment to believe that such a glum scenario was imminent, the possibilities could not be prudently ignored.

I had speculated that while Columbia prospered in its focus on arts and media career specialties within a context of liberal education, it might be possible to build a comprehensive university around Columbia's successful concentrations. Indeed, a number of respected individuals, both within and outside Columbia, had urged serious consideration of such a course. But it was more likely, I suspected, that the distinctive and relatively prosperous institution we already had would be destroyed in an effort to create a comprehensive urban university of, at best, questionable quality and societal value.

I had never thought, however, of the possibility that Columbia could preserve and even strengthen the quality and focus of its education and have the opportunity of a comprehensive liberal education curriculum and mature faculty in a merger with a respected, secure, local, urban university. But, somehow, the possibility arose in a conversation I had in a snowed-in airport in Springfield with Rolf Weil, then president of Roosevelt University.

Roosevelt University was founded in 1944 and became a comprehensive university in 1947. Roosevelt's founding inspiration was a noble and largely unprecedented effort to democratize access to American higher education, whose institutions had traditionally excluded minorities, African-American students particularly, though then most private colleges and universities also restricted the enrollment of Jews and other minorities. Roosevelt's founder, Sparling, had been the president of the Central YMCA College, a modest-sized institution of small distinction, when he resigned as a protest against the institution's discriminatory admissions policies. The city's liberal community rallied around Sparling's example, and in the succeeding furor, a new college was born, pledged to admit students without regard to race, religion, or national origin.

The new college was named for President Franklin Delano Roosevelt, and Eleanor Roosevelt participated in the inaugural ceremonies and continued to support the fledgling institution. Fueled by the great wave of GI Bill veterans and by a non-discriminatory admissions policy, Roosevelt grew dramatically in immediate post-war years and recruited an outstanding faculty attracted by the opportunity of teaching at an exemplary democratic institution. Roosevelt in those early years had extraordinary vitality and humane spirit, which, as a Roosevelt alumnus, I can enthusiastically confirm. Roosevelt's road after was less encouraging.

Despite its popular beginning, Roosevelt increasingly embraced conventional collegiate respectability, though I suspect this appearance was first cultivated as a defense against reckless charges that Roosevelt was a communist institution. Whatever the motive, the university's academic structure followed a familiar pattern of deans and divisions, study was shaped by typical systems of subject requirements, and enrollment was reserved for those with usual collegiate qualifications. These measures probably reflected the fact that Roosevelt's managers, Sparling included, were not educational radicals, except in their advocacy of nondiscriminatory college admissions, which Roosevelt could justly claim to have pioneered.

Roosevelt clung to this as its principal virtue long after the issue had lost distinguishing currency; and though the general quality of its education had commendable excellence, the university failed to develop a bold public identity and student appeal based on distinctive educational initiatives and community services. I think Sparling had this in mind in 1963 when he sought to join Columbia and me to Roosevelt's community. By then, however, Roosevelt may have lost the opportunity of creating an identity as a leader of an American cultural renaissance. This could have been achieved by casting the university's umbrella over a luminous faculty of arts and culture creators who were not then, as now, sought by other institutions of higher education. Such individuals were then usually disqualified by their lack of conventional credentials. I suspect that Roosevelt's academic bureaucracies would have made such bold steps impossible; though, in my view, Roosevelt could have gathered the resources to ride the crest of popularity and respect it enjoyed from the spirit and reason of its founding. Perhaps, in 1963, I might have contributed to such purpose, though Roosevelt and I had different styles.

Collegiate respectability had imperatives, however, which were rudely tested in the 1960s and early 1970s. I believe the result of these tests was that Roosevelt missed out on the spirit of those turbulent times. The university summoned police to quell campus demonstrations and discharged dissident Staughton Lynd from the faculty, acts that Roosevelt may still regard as having preserved the sanctity and ideals of university life.

When Rolf Weil broached the possibility of a merger between Columbia and Roosevelt, Columbia was a hot college, on the rise with rapidly growing enrollment and more students than Roosevelt, particularly in the count of full-time equivalent students. Moreover, where Columbia was increasingly prosperous and enjoyed great public notice, Roosevelt's finances and publicity were much less encouraging, though its fund-raising apparatus was far superior to Columbia's. Nonetheless, Roosevelt had an important graduate business school, mature undergraduate and graduate programs in teacher education and in various science specialties, an impressive library, a respected labor-education division, and a very competent faculty in the many disciplines of a comprehensive curriculum. Unquestionably, Roosevelt was a formidable and deservedly respected institution. Educationally, Roosevelt and Columbia were a good fit.

I don't know whether Rolf and I shared the same motivations towards a merger, but after several conversations, I think I gained his enthusiasm for the idea of creating a new urban university that would draw on the strengths of both institutions. But my private interest was in a new university invested with Columbia's vitality and sense of social engagement that would retain emphasis on arts and media education. Undoubtedly, Rolf had a Roosevelt agenda in mind.

I promptly told Al Harris, our chairman, of my exchange with Weil. After consulting with several members of the board's executive committee, Harris told me to continue discussions, though it was understood that these were to be held in strict confidence. Weil told me that he had held a similar conversation with Jerome Stone, Roosevelt's chairman, who had advised him to continue merger explorations. Obviously, there were endless complications to consider, and both of us agreed to appoint two surrogates to explore the merger proposition in greater detail. I appointed Bert Gall and John Scheibel, and Rolf chose two Roosevelt officers of similar rank. They worked at the project for many months and finally created what they named New University, even casting budgets for the merged institutions, though they made no effort to address questions of educational policy or personnel, which would require the participation of other institutional representatives. What they did design was a financially viable entity, with anticipated revenues and operational costs, with some economies of scale and elimination of duplicate functions. It was an insightful and convincing document that strongly suggested a merger, the main benefit of which would not so much be cost savings as superior education.

Before any effort was made to resolve disparities in admissions requirements, tuition, faculty tenure, academic structures, governance, and other imponderables, Harris, Stone, Weil, and I met together on several occasions to sort out our attitudes to a merger and to decide whether continued exploration of the proposition was warranted.

My initial discussion with Rolf Weil was prompted by our mutual intention to retire in the next several years; subsequently we informally agreed that if a merger was ultimately fashioned it would take at least several years, during which time both of us should remain to manage it. And when board memberships were consolidated—or, however, a single board was constituted—a procedure would be adopted for choosing a new president. But, as events would later prove, our speculations were unnecessary.

What emerged in our discussions with Stone and Weil was that despite Columbia's genuine willingness to regard the merger as a marriage of equals, Stone viewed Columbia as the junior partner. He believed that as Roosevelt had been a university for more than forty years and enjoyed greater presence and respect within civic and educational communities, his university deserved seniority. That was unacceptable to Columbia, and though we met several more times, Stone's attitude remained unchanged. With that, the whole merger plan collapsed. Jerry Stone is a most honorable, generous, and reasonable man, and in his many years as Roosevelt's board chairman, he served the office with distinction and generosity. I suppose that given his intense loyalty to Roosevelt, he may have had an unrealistic view of his institution's comparative strength, though with Columbia's great spurt in recent years, perhaps he has had second thoughts.

The five-year projection in the spring of 1988 had anticipated modest enrollment increases of about 2 percent annually over a five-year term and corresponding improvements in the college's space, facilities, and personnel. Actual enrollment results in fall 1988, however, threw recent projections into a cocked hat. Six thousand fifty four students enrolled, a 6 percent gain, representing a full-time equivalent of 5,146 students, an amount not expected until 1990. Numbers would have been even greater if we had not turned away 150 students. This big leap badly stretched already strained resources and prompted a rush of efforts to preserve the quality of the college's services. Space and instructional facilities were again at great premium, and so were the full- and part-time faculty, academic counselors, department secretaries, assistant deans, and library services. While we were quickly able to recruit additional people, and had the benefit of additional space and facilities made available by recent construction, it was clear that we could not continue to crowd the college's limited space. Even with an enrollment ceiling, which the board set at 6,350 students, a number that would presumably be reached in 1989, we could not avoid the issue of substantially increasing the college's space. Undoubtedly, this would require another building.

A casualty of this recognition was a burial of prevailing notions that the college's prosperity could be sustained without dependence on increasing numbers of students and greater tuition revenues, even in the absence of sizable endowment and gift revenues. Columbia's financial managers and I had consistently rejected the idea that Columbia's enrollment growth had to be limited because the expense of new buildings and accumulated debts would be greater than the revenue returns generated. Nonetheless, we carefully observed the cautions inherent in this contention in weighing greater tuition revenues against the costs of major capital investments.

a conference for statement and discovery

the arts and the inner city

to make new men everywhere

May 13, 14, 15, 1968
Columbia College, Chicago, Illinois

TOP LEFT: LERONE BENNETT; TOP MIDDLE: PAUL SIMON AND MA; BOTTOM LEFT: MA WITH HAROLD WASHINGTON; RIGHT: THE ARTS AND THE INNER CITY CONFERENCE BROCHURE.

We made it — FULL ACCREDITAT
CONGRATULATIONS TO US

Columb

540 33

FACING PAGE: MA IN FRONT OF 540 LAKE SHORE DRIVE; TOP RIGHT: MA CELEBRATING FULL ACCREDITA-
TION IN 1974; BOTTOM RIGHT: MA AND LYA ROSENBLUM. TOP LEFT: JOHN MOORE; TOP MIDDLE: ZAFRA
LERMAN; TOP RIGHT: TONY LOEB; BOTTOM (LEFT TO RIGHT): STUDS TERKEL, MA, RAY NORSTRAND AND
JAMES HOGE (1985); TOP RIGHT: JOHN SCHULTZ; BOTTOM RIGHT: SHELDON PATINKIN

TOP LEFT: JOHN SCHEIBEL; BOTTOM LEFT: MARCEL OPHULS WITH MA; TOP AND BOTTOM RIGHT: THE 1970s MA. FACING PAGE: LEFT: JEFF MACNELLY CARICATURE OF MA; RIGHT LOUIS SILVERSTEIN WITH MARIA WEIDERMANN.

To Mike,
with many thanks — JEFF MACNELLY.

TOP LEFT: PAUL JOHNSON; TOP MIDDLE LEFT: HAROLD WASHINGTON; TOP MIDDLE RIGHT: MULVANEY; TOP RIGHT: CHARLES TRAUB; BOTTOM LEFT: MA WITH BUD SALK; BOTTOM RIGHT (LEFT TO RIGHT): DOREEN BARTONI, PAUL CARTER HARRISON, AND JOAN ERDMAN. FACING PAGE: TOP LEFT: KARKOVICE WITH MA; FAR LEFT MIDDLE: JANE ALEXANDROFF; MIDDLE LEFT: NORMAN ALEXANDROFF JANE; BOTTOM LEFT: MA AND JANE; RIGHT: THE 1980s MA.

TOP LEFT: 1992 COLUMBIA GRADUATION AT UIC PAVILLION; BOTTOM LEFT: ALTON HARRIS; RIGHT: JOHN B. DUFF.

Without having sufficient endowment or reserve funds, or the assurance that a capital campaign would successfully fund a new building, Columbia had no accessible alternative to a speculative venture that depended on the accuracy of enrollment projections and on finding an unusual opportunity in the South Loop real estate market.

The 6,350 enrollment ceiling was an arbitrary figure representing a rough estimate of the number of students and institutional functions that could fit in the college's space. The ceiling, however, had some flexibility. Finding and outfitting a new building would take time, during which efforts to improve Columbia's quality could not be suspended, and some enrollment growth would have to be supported. But at the moment, no good building prospects were in sight.

In revenue terms, it was evident that if enrollment and year-to-year rates of increase could be sustained, the college's tuition income over the next four years would increase to $5 million; and apart from unavoidable building costs, the college would be able to fund a much accelerated schedule of institutional improvements. Given 1988 enrollment numbers, which far exceeded the no-growth prudence of the college's five-year guide, and if 1988 was not taken to be an aberration, Columbia could reasonably anticipate continued popularity in the student market. This was especially true due to new career specialties within existing subject concentrations, the introduction of an undergraduate and graduate teacher-education division, a continuing education program, and a new emphasis on regional, national, and foreign student recruitment. However, whatever the success of these efforts,

even if 1989 student numbers were within the 6,350 ceiling, any growth in subsequent years would result in a pressing need for much greater college space.

Apart from enrollment statistics, bond issues, and building speculations, in the 1988–89 year the college gained a $100,000 gift to establish the Al Weisman Library of Contemporary Journalism and a $100,000 gift to the Weisman Scholarship Fund; a three-year MacArthur Foundation grant to support the Dance Center's national dance series; a commitment by the Rosenbaum family to fund the Theater/Music department's productions of new musicals; and major investments in a sophisticated central computer system to link all administrative and academic functions, incorporating new computer technology in all of Columbia's instruction, a computerized newsroom for the Journalism Department, a new study concentration in computer graphics, and the purchase of one hundred new computers for general student use. That year the college budgeted $1,240,000 for scholarship aid and work-study stipends, and while the amount was not nearly enough, it did represent a major improvement in college-sponsored student-aid funding.

Columbia added ten new full-time faculty positions, which was a good start at having forty new full-time faculty positions by 1993. Among the new adjunct faculty members were Pulitzer prizewinners John White (in news photography) and Jeffrey Lyon (in science journalism). More than one-half of Columbia's full-time faculty published, exhibited, or performed professionally in 1988. The Film/Video Department was ranked among the three leading collegiate film programs. Columbia's Science Institute won a number of new accolades, as did the graduate program in Interdisciplinary Arts. A Columbia project in computer-aided English programs received special recognition by the Fund for Post Secondary Education, and Columbia was designated as a development site for a national project in teaching English. We expected that when this effort was completed, Columbia would join MIT, Chicago State University, and ten other national institutions in becoming regional resource centers for English instruction and associated research. Regrettably, it didn't happen.

That year also saw the first issue of a new Columbia College poetry journal initiated by Paul Hoover, and *Hair Trigger*, the college's annual anthology of student writing again won top awards. A tutoring center in mathematics was established, and the English tutorial center much enlarged. A new comprehensive Science Demonstration Laboratory was constructed and equipped by a grant from the National Science Foundation. The college's library got 50 percent more space. All in all, it was a very good year.

In the summer of 1988, after an extensive national search, Dr. Dennis Lavery was chosen as Columbia's vice president for College Relations. With the assistance of Jack Wolfsohn, Connie Zonka, and an augmented staff, Lavery would head a newly created office that joined fund-raising and public relations functions.

Though the board had authorized a $2,650,000 Higher Educational Facilities bond issue, the amount was marketed as part of an omnibus $11 million bond issue that refinanced remaining obligations of the 1979 and 1984 bond issues. This refinancing arrangement would save more than $100,000 per year during the issue's twelve-year term. A more immediate benefit, however, was that the new bond issue included a debt service reserve that freed $854,000 that the college had deposited as the reserve required by prior bond issues.

Seven hundred fifty thousand dollars of this unexpected windfall was spent to purchase the land between the Eleventh Street Theater-Music building and Wabash Avenue, with the idea that a new college building might be constructed on the property or be used as the site of a dormitory, though it was again recognized that a new building would be a very expensive venture. We thought that the property might, in time, become a very profitable investment whenever the city's plan to develop the South Loop was realized.

The year's big event, of course, was that Columbia received the enthusiastic endorsement of the North Central Examiners, who reaccredited the college for a ten-year term and removed all limitations on Columbia's graduate program first accredited in 1983.

Among the examining team's exit observations, though their enthusiasms were a bit tempered in their final written report, was a strong confirmation that Columbia had excellent physical, financial, and human resources to perform its mission competently, and that Columbia's community knew, understood, and concurred in that mission. The team submitted that Columbia College was exceedingly well managed, its faculty unusually talented, enthusiastic, and original, and that clearly Columbia has enjoyed a unique and deserved success. All members of the team agreed that the college was an exciting educational place. They acknowledged that the practice of open admissions presented a mind-boggling challenge to educational ingenuity and perseverance, but that our effort to confront this challenge was a valuable source of Columbia's vitality. The team's report often included words such as "remarkable," "amazing," "inventive," and "entrepreneurial" in describing Columbia's process and achievement. They complimented the board's serious and knowledgeable sense of purpose. It was a flattering endorsement.

Columbia's annual commencement had been held at the Auditorium Theater for many years, but by 1989, it had simply grown too big for this splendid site. Now, with graduating classes of 1,000 undergraduates and graduate students and an army of families and guests, getting a far bigger arena was urgently necessary. The weather was too unpredictable to safely schedule an outdoor event. Indeed, I can't remember a Columbia commencement event that didn't have a rainstorm. Our only option was the giant fieldhouse on the University of Illinois Chicago campus. When Bert Gall and I first saw it, I, at least, was staggered by its immensity, and the logistics of managing a commencement there seemed overwhelming. But, as usual, Bert was undeterred. In June 1989, we had about 7,000 people and it all went like clockwork. Bert marshaled virtually all of the college's staff, whose captains had a careful script and communicated with one another with radios. I readily admit to a renewing thrill at seeing a sea of caps and gowns, college regalia, and the columns of graduates, faculty, trustees, and honorees, though no more so than I did at the first commencement at the University of Illinois's amphitheater.

At its late spring 1989 meeting, the board voted to increase tuition for the 1989–90 college year by 8.5 percent to a full-time tuition rate of $2,710 per semester ($5,420 a year) and to $185 per credit hour for part-time enrollment and $224 for graduate studies. The board also voted a 6 percent salary increase for faculty and staff, but insisted that pay raises begin to reflect merit and not be regarded simply as a general institutional salary increase. In this respect, Paul Johnson, who had returned to Columbia as the director of Human Resources, reported that his office was completing a classification of the college's administrative, clerical, and professional staff jobs to establish a coherent, consistent, and equitable basis for comparing Columbia's pay scales with other collegiate institutions and local business organizations. This information, he believed, might also be useful in rewarding particularly deserving individuals. Moreover, he hoped to develop a system for incorporating performance evaluations by supervisors to serve as a basis for salary judgments. For faculty and departmental chairs, performance evaluation had only recently been adopted, and it was probably too early to reflect individual performance in year-to-year salary decisions. The informal practice of rewarding particularly deserving individuals would continue until a more uniform system was developed. In the meantime, with some variations, the board's customary grant of salary increases was expected to prevail generally within the college. Johnson also submitted that Columbia's part-time teaching rates were still not competitive with other local institutions, though the college had, in the last several years, made commendable efforts to remedy this disparity, as evidenced by the board's current decision to increase part-time faculty compensations by 10 percent in the 1989–90 year, and he urged similar efforts in succeeding years. Aided by a leap in tuition revenues and by an unexpected refinancing windfall, Columbia enjoyed its most profitable year, which was a fitting context for the college's ten-year reaccreditation.

Columbia at Age Twenty-five

When the new Columbia had reached its twenty-first year, I think Jane and I were the only ones to notice that January 1989 marked the twenty-fifth year of the college's renewal. But, then again, we were the only real "ancients" left. Then and now comparisons are only curiosities. Columbia in 1989 was only barely the same institution it had been twenty-five years before.

I have some memory of a dictum that contends that qualitative change occurs as a leap from what may be imperceptible incremental changes that preceded it. Whether the contention applies universally to all states of change, it at least described what happened to the character of my job, which over time nibbled away at my self-perception until I suddenly discovered that I was barely, if at all, an educator and had imperceptibly become a corporate chief executive. While I observed this unwelcome phenomenon earlier in this narrative, my college role had changed significantly by 1989. I continued to make Columbia's principal decisions, but preoccupation with the college's business left me little opportunity to exert a creative influence on Columbia's educational substance, a role filled by a talented cadre of college individuals. Perhaps Columbia had finally become a genuinely collective enterprise.

1989–1990: The Implications of Growth

While the 1989–90 agenda was crowded with important subjects, none was even remotely as critical to the college's life as finding a resolution to the issue of enrollment growth and the educational and financial implications of it. In recent years the issue had been confronted and even presumably satisfied by, first, the 600 South Michigan building, and subsequently, the 72 East Eleventh Street and 623 South Wabash acquisitions, which allowed the college brief plateaus in the effect of the enrollment-space equation. But these had proven to be only temporary solutions, quickly followed by futile efforts to impose enrollment ceilings, flirtation with the idea that Columbia's quality could be enhanced without recourse to enlarging tuition revenues, and that a more insistent commitment to fund-raising would lessen tuition dependency. Notwithstanding voluminous inquiry, college officials, the board, and senior faculty reluctantly concluded that Columbia was already beyond the point of buying a big new building and that the college had no present educational or financial alternative to encouraging continued enrollment growth to be prudently served by greater space, facilities, and personnel whenever necessary and affordable. Whatever hesitations survived were silenced by the evidence of fall 1989 enrollment figures. Six thousand five hundred and three students registered, a 7 percent gain over 1988 and 150 more than the proposed ceiling of 6,350. Three hundred students were turned away. Seventy percent of fall 1989 students enrolled full-time.

The numbers of African-American students was the same as in 1988, but they now represented 22 percent of all students, down from 26 percent the year before.

Latino students now constituted 8 percent of Columbia's student population, up from 6 percent in 1988. Asian students doubled to 2 percent. The leap in numbers of students created many problems, of course. There was a large unanticipated increase in students requiring English and math remediation. Student life, library services, and faculty and staff office space were badly strained. Indeed, all college functions were overcrowded. The greatest problem, however, was that 1989 enrollment numbers equaled expectations for 1993, and corresponding improvements in college services were now four years behind schedule. There was much catching up to do, though the tasks were less forbidding because of unexpected revenue gains, except that adding new full-time faculty could not be done hurriedly. While improvement projects were manageable, everything, particularly enrollment anticipations in 1990, hinged on our ability promptly to find a new building.

In the late spring of 1989, John Scheibel told me that for health reasons he would retire in August. The news was an awful blow. In his fourteen-year tenure as Columbia's chief financial officer he had been indispensable to the college's success. His competency was boundless. He was a magician with figures, had extraordinary managerial ability, and a rare quality of common sense. He was a very literate writer who could make the most complicated financial garble understandable. An exceptionally skilled negotiator, he most ably represented the college in bond-issue and building-purchase transactions, and he supervised a maddening succession of computer installations. He treated everyone with grace, courtesy, and affection. He was one sweet man. He understood and sympathized with Columbia's mission, and he surely served it well. Replacing him was unimaginable. We searched hard for months among local and national candidates for the job. We finally settled on an exceptionally qualified individual, Mike DeSalle, who had served as comptroller for Vanderbilt University and Michael Reese Hospital, and he, like Scheibel, had exceptional talent and quickly earned the respect of Columbia's community. And he, too, in his now ten years of service, has become indispensable.

The year's nearly $28 million budget included $130,000 for English and math remediation, a figure expected to grow in subsequent years; $1,450,000 in scholarship and student work/aid grants; medical insurance costs of $1,530,000, rising at a rate of 15 percent a year; retirement plan contributions of $1,200,000; $1,350,000 in Social Security taxes; and revenue of $1,077,000 (based on enrollment numbers) from Illinois State Aid to Independent College Institutions.

Fourteen new full-time faculty were added in 1989–90, which brought the college's full-time faculty to 150, including adjunct faculty, and artists- and scholars-in-residence. For all Columbia folk who suffered years of maddening telephone service, a new telephone system was installed at a cost of $250,000.

The board adopted a government-mandated revision of all pension plans. Changes included the following provisions:

• *The inclusion of employees who were (or are) first hired when over the age of sixty.*

• *All employees still working past normal retirement age of sixty-five are to be continued in the plan.*

• *Effective January 1, 1989, the plan benefit formula can no longer be offset by anticipation of a participant's primary Social Security benefit.*

• *100 percent vesting must be accomplished by the end of an individual's seventh year of employment.*

The search for a new building was disappointing. One possibility did exist, but its ultimate purchase was questionable. It was an empty office building at 1006 South Michigan Avenue that had usable space of only 80,000 feet, less than half the footage we needed. The purchase price was in the two- to three-million-dollar range and would require an estimated $6 million to remodel. It was hardly a bargain. The building also had the handicap of "mill construction," which would require an unlikely waiver from the city building department of the sort denied to us fourteen years before at the college's Lake Shore Drive location. In the absence, however, of an alternative, and given our pressing need to get a building by midspring 1990 to have greater space by September, we played around with 1006 South Michigan's figures for several months in the fall of '89. At the same time, we continued to speculate about constructing a 100,000-square-foot building on the college's Eleventh Street and Wabash property, though its estimated cost of $14 million seemed prohibitively expensive. After all of our decisions about uncapped enrollment growth, only a few months later we had to reimpose a ceiling of 6,900 students (an absolute limit) in the likelihood that no building would be found in time to remodel it for occupancy in fall 1990. Even the 6,900 figure would require rented space, which hopefully could be found in the immediate neighborhood.

Columbia had been consistently and inordinately lucky in finding last-minute solutions to perplexing problems. Utterly unexpected, the 624 South Michigan building came on the market. It was a beautiful building once identified as the Blums-Vogue building when it housed that high-fashion enterprise. The building was in excellent repair, had 180,000 square feet, and was a fine example of art deco architecture. A purchase price of $8,045,000 was quickly negotiated. Its terms required a 10 percent down payment and the balance to be subscribed by an 8 percent mortgage, providing a thirty-two-year schedule with a balloon payment after fifteen years. Within a week, a mortgage commitment was secured. (I might add, it paid to have some powerhouse real estate folk on the board.) Bert Gall estimated that remodeling costs for the balance of the current year and through the 1991–92 year would be approximately $3.5 million, though some of that amount would be spent for construction in the 600 and 623 buildings. Gall also observed that the 624 building had a profitable aggregate of tenants whose removal could be scheduled to correspond to the college's space needs. In the meantime, tenant income could be sufficient to fund the building's operating costs through 1992. At the moment, the college's reserves and anticipated revenues were sufficient to afford an $800,000 down payment and mortgage costs, though these expenses were recovered by incorporation in a new bond issue secured in 1992. Moreover, the building was of such quality and location to insure a profitable sale in the unlikely event that Columbia's enrollment could not support its possession. Needless to say, the board's authorization was unanimous and enthusiastic. Gall was confident that 30,000 square feet could be constructed for the college's September 1990 enrollment, and 60,000 square feet more by September 1991. In one stroke, we had gotten the college off the "more students-more space" treadmill, at least for some years ahead.

Anything after the new-building event would seem anticlimactic. But life went on. Unremarkably, some board members served a number of terms and others served shorter spans, and as initial election to the board was to a one-year exploratory term, the greatest board turnover usually occurred among those with short service. In the 1989–90 year, the board had an unusual number of new members. Among those newly elected were Wayne Fickinger, until recently vice chairman of the board of Bozell Jacobs Kenyon Eckhart, a major advertising agency, and executive director of the Mid-America Committee, which joins the CEOs of leading Midwest corporations; Tim Wright III, who served as commissioner of economic development in the Washington administration; Averill Leviton, an active participant in Chicago's civic affairs; Emmet O'Neill, executive assistant to Senator Alan Dixon, and well known for his influential role in local and national civic and political affairs; and Dr. Thaddeus Kawalek, president emeritus of the Chicago Osteopathic Medical School and distinguished educator, who in earlier times had been Columbia's executive dean. These new members were representative of the quality of the board's membership and Columbia's coming-of-age in Chicago's civic community.

The chairman of the board's development committee, Nick Van Hevelingen, reported that the fund-raising efforts of the newly reconstituted Office of College Relations had yielded $1,316,000, exclusive of government grants, in the 1988–89 year, which, with the exception of the year of the government's endowment grant, was Columbia's best ever fund-raising year, a result that included initiatives begun earlier by Jack Wolfsohn. Similar success was anticipated in the current year. Such encouragement led me to approve Van Hevelingen's and Lavery's plan to reorder the focus of the college's public relations efforts. Only after the fact did I conclude it was a cockamamie scheme that ran against Columbia's remarkable publicity record. Most regrettable was that the plan's implementation resulted in Connie Zonka's departure. The plan, undoubtedly well meant, was to develop new local and national constituencies that would be responsive to the college's fund-raising appeals, and to farm out to a public relations firm what had been a very successful in-house publicity program. The earliest draft of the plan even entertained the notion that Columbia might in time be repositioned as a liberal arts college with a strong emphasis on the arts and communications media. Though emphatically rejected, even the mention of this should have been enough to inflame my suspicions. Nonetheless, we circulated a proposal among a number of Chicago's leading public relations agencies, and with the counsel of board member Aaron Cushman, who headed one of these agencies, the firm Porter-Novelli was chosen to represent the college's publicity interests. This presumably would free the college Relations office to concentrate on developing new constituencies and a heightened fund-raising effort. Both ventures were unsuccessful, the publicity firm expensively so, because apart from what I thought extravagant service costs, we had to provide all the story leads, an effort that proved more costly than the whole of the college's previous public relations effort. More disap-

pointing was that Columbia's publicity decreased dramatically. At the same time, gift revenues were considerably less than the year before, and new constituencies remained elusive. After nearly a year's trial, both projects were scrubbed. An in-house publicity emphasis was restored, and the college's search for new fund-raising constituencies refocused on familiar audiences. It took some years to recover from the experiment. Dennis Lavery resigned to return to university teaching, and Nick Van Hevelingen left the Pulitzer newspaper organization to replace Lavery.

I have no memory of a year when the institutions of American higher education did not raise tuition, and 1990 was no exception. Illinois colleges and universities increased their tuition in a 5 percent to 10 percent range, Columbia at the midpoint of 7.5 percent to $5,928 per year for full-time enrollment, $198 per credit hour for part-time students, and $239 per credit hour for graduate students. These figures were still substantially below those of Illinois's independent institutions. Similarly, as the national rate of inflation in the costs of college services continued in 5 percent to 6 percent range, Columbia's faculty salaries were increased by 6 percent, and staff's by 5 percent, both amounts allowing individual exceptions.

Gall reported at the board's midspring meeting that negotiations for the 624 South Michigan building were nearly complete and that construction plans were done and ready for the moment when the building was purchased. At the same meeting, chairman Harris reported that at the instruction of the executive committee he had secured my agreement to extend my tenure to August 31, 1992, a year later than anticipated; and also that a search for my successor would begin in the spring of 1991 after careful preparation. Until then, contemplation of my retirement had an abstract quality and now, with a date formally fixed, the reality was startling.

Also at the meeting it was announced that the U.S. Office of Education had made a Title III grant to Columbia of $2,500,000 over five years to fund a number of college improvements and new initiatives. The board expressed its compliments to Lya Rosenblum for her mighty efforts to secure the grant and to Jack Wolfsohn, whose Washington skills had facilitated the award. Sixty-eight hundred students were anticipated in fall 1990. And Columbia again enjoyed a prosperous year.

But whatever 1990's good fortune, the year was marked indelibly by the deaths of Harry Bouras and Robert Edmonds, both of whose extraordinary faculty service had spanned thirty years. Their scholarship gave Columbia genuine intellectual dimension and invested a generation of students with the riches of the arts and humanities.

Columbia College has a unique campus with extraordinary cultural opportunities and the vitality of downtown Chicago. For a big-city college, or a college anywhere, Columbia is ideally located, literally across the street from Grant Park, one of the most beautiful park settings in the world. It includes four of the world's great cultural and museum institutions: the Art Institute of Chicago, the Field Museum of Natural History, the Shedd Aquarium, and the Adler Planetarium. The Chicago Symphony Center and the city's central library are only two blocks away. This inspiring assembly also includes Roosevelt University and its renowned Auditorium Theater, the School of the Art Institute, the Chicago Cultural Center, DePaul University's downtown campus and its Merle Reskin Theater, and Columbia's Getz Theater. For whatever reason, a cooperative association of cultural and educational institutions who shared a common campus was never developed, probably simply because no one or no institution had taken the initiative of organizing a common forum.

It was a natural idea that only awaited a spark. This was lighted by Susan Aaron, who was then the administrative director of the college's Arts and Entertainment Management department. Susan had been active in an effort to develop support and city approval for a lakefront garden project proposed for the southwest corner of Grant Park at Michigan and Randolph Streets. She asked my counsel in getting the Grant Park institutions to endorse the project. Our discussion led to the idea of organizing an association of Grant Park's cultural and educational institutions that could address a number of common issues and develop active relationships among the district's institutions. So we gave it a shot. Reception was enthusiastic. All the institutions rallied around. In a surprisingly short time, the Grant Park Cultural and Educational Community was launched. We had hoped that Willard "Sandy" Boyd, president of the Field Museum, would take the lead, but he demurred, which left me to be the Community's chair and Susan Aaron its executive director. The organization was housed at Columbia. The Grant Park Community's membership included Columbia, Roosevelt, DePaul, the School of the Art Institute, the Field Museum, Shedd Aquarium, Adler Planetarium, the Art Institute, Chicago Symphony Orchestra, Auditorium Theater Council, the Chicago Public Library, and the Cultural Center. A comfortable dues structure based on institutional budgets was adopted and all members agreed to participate in efforts to solicit the support of prominent Chicago foundations. Other officers were chosen, and a schedule of monthly meetings fixed. The organization was off and running. A variety of issues were considered as priority concerns. These included getting better police protection for the Grant Park District, developing cooperative educational programs, attracting greater city and suburban numbers to the museums, expanding parking facilities, and the rerouting of Lake Shore Drive traffic to create a common campus for the Field Museum, the Shedd Aquarium, and the Planetarium. Undoubtedly, achievement of a museum campus and a reroute of traffic would require influential civic support to overcome the city's reluctance to spend the millions of dollars needed for construction costs.

While individually the community's institutions had immediate public identity and enjoyed good publicity, together they were a formidable and influential association. Susan and other representatives of the community were often invited to participate in the planning of major civic, cultural, and economic development projects, and regularly involved by city agencies in everything concerning the Grant Park District. Police presence, parking, and sanitary services were noticeably improved. Columbia developed a number of cooperative programs with the museums, even scheduling classes at their locations. The college enjoyed great public benefit from its leading role in the Grant Park Community and from publicity that featured the college's campus. When a new commissioner was appointed to head Chicago's Park District, I introduced him at his inaugural event, which gave Columbia great cachet

in the Park District's councils. The community's campaign to increase museum audiences was only nominally successful, in part because we lacked the funds to mount a major effort. While the community worked to win public support and city accord for the traffic reroute, it was the project's movers and shakers, Sandy Boyd, president of the Field Museum, and the presidents of Shedd and Adler and their boards, who won the support of Mayor Daley, though the museum campus would not be a reality until 1997.

But even good things come to an end. By the time of my retirement in 1992, only a few of those who had formed the Grant Park Cultural and Educational Community remained at their jobs. It would take someone else to renew the organization. DePaul's John Richardson held out for a year or so, but then he and Susan finally closed up the shop. Now seven years later, no one and no institution has tried to fill the void. Getting people to act together in their own self-interest is inexplicably difficult.

When the new college year began in September 1990, all sorts of sentiments crowded my head, prompted by the realization that in fixing the date of my retirement, my separation from Columbia had already begun. It was hard to handle that. I suppose I suffered a moment of funk before being caught up in the seasonal rush of college events.

We had a bit more than 6,800 students, about the number expected. The college was also overcrowded as expected, and the new building's construction would have little effect until midyear. But at least relief was in sight. We added ten new full-time faculty and some improvements in college services, though this effort was lessened by space limitations. Columbia's graduate program continued to prosper. In its six-year time, enrollment had grown to 300; more than 200 students had completed their graduate studies, and a great number of them enjoyed professional success. We anticipated that the number of graduate students would increase significantly with the introduction of a new program in teacher education, whose approval by the Illinois State Teacher Certification agency was expected momentarily.

At the board's instruction, Bert Gall, Mike DeSalle, and I had begun in summer 1990 to develop a new five-year college plan, which would be submitted at a three-day board retreat scheduled in November. These projections were to be presented together with a contemporary restatement of Columbia's mission and a projection of its implementation in the years to 1996, which I would prepare, both to be incorporated in a document titled "Columbia College in 1996."

Often in the past we had developed reams of detailed projections and plans to improve the college's condition and educational quality. In most instances, these had served as practical guides for much shorter periods than intended because projections did not, or could not, accurately anticipate revenues and expenses reflecting actual enrollment and tuition revenues in subsequent years. Variables included variations in the national economy and government policy, particularly as these affected federal and state student-aid grants and the college's benefit from Illinois's aid to independent colleges and universities. The greatest difficulty in predictions was Columbia's endemic uncertainty about enrollment growth in relation to the college's space. By 1991, however, we could safely estimate that the 624 building would give Columbia sufficient space to serve an increased number of students for some years ahead without having to confront the familiar imponderables of the enrollment-space equation.

In casting a new five-year plan, we created a number of alternatives that reflected a variety of conditions incorporating different enrollment projections, tuition revenues, schedules of college improvements, investments in facilities, library resources, full-time faculty, professional staff, salary expectations, curricular emphases, and the cost implications of these and other variables.

Our projections did not include unpredictable fund-raising receipts and self-liquidating program grants, though these, as in the instances of Title III and science grants, generated important educational improvements and gave us opportunity to focus college funds on other priorities. Nor did we include investment earnings, as these were usually reinvested or reserved for major capital projects, such as building construction. As these resources then only constituted 7 percent to 9 percent of

Columbia's income, we expected some comfort in committing the college to our projections, which were mainly based on tuition and related revenues.

In developing our projections, we assumed a 3 percent annual enrollment gain, year-to-year tuition increases of 6.5 percent and a renewing inflation rate of 5.5 percent. Thus cast, student numbers would be 7,100 in 1991–92; 7,461 in 1992–93; 7,655 in 1993–94; 7,915 in 1994–95; and 8,152 in 1995–96. At that rate, there would be 8,400 students in September 1996.

Using 1990–91 as a base year, our plan expected over a five-year span to add sixty-two to 108 new employees, including forty to seventy-five new full-time faculty, and to spend one to two million dollars on scholarship subsidies and two to four million on new instructional facilities and library resources. These figures were shown in a range of affordability depending on the accuracy of revenue/expense projections.

While my report at the board's retreat was meant to accompany the five-year plan submitted, I anticipated that my impending retirement would give my remarks a valedictory cast. So I used the occasion to emphasize Columbia's history and mission since the college's renewal in 1964, and to offer this exhibit as a guide to Columbia's future course. This exposition was apart from explanations of the plan's proposals for improving the college's state and educational quality. A brief excerpt:

It would be entertaining to imagine that at some magic moment in the early 1960s I had a transcendent vision of Columbia that sprang full blown, and that now again, I can call up a new vision to shape the college in the time to 1996 and beyond. Regrettably, making a vision to order is a forbidding assignment. Moreover, as visionaries are regarded skeptically as charla-

tans or nuts, I submit that there is nothing about me that suggests that I have mystical qualities, though I admit, had I imagined Columbia's present scale, my seer's medal might be more authentic. If anything is proved, it is that pie in the sky is sometimes edible.

I claim only some early inspirations that enlisted the energies and talents of many others who contributed to Columbia's prosperity and confidence in its perpetuity. Columbia is, in fact, a shared possession that enjoys the renewing vitality of students.

Such abstractions and disclaimers aside, it is true that Columbia's life has been informed by an evolution of what once were largely unproven ideas of a college institution mainly unlike those customarily known. But Columbia's idea was not a personal invention without tie to enlightened educational philosophy or practice, nor simply a new implement that begged marketing. Columbia's success had crucial assist, indeed, coincidence with the 1960s' dramatic burst of new ideas, new technologies, and new human expectations. Columbia would not have happened at another time. We might be credited with anticipating education's direction and successfully exploiting its opportunity, perhaps ingeniously so.

In casting a perception of Columbia in 1996 and after, I begin with a renewed recognition of Columbia's elemental purposes, which emphasize a collegiate focus on arts and media concentrations within a context of liberal education, and a policy of open admissions and accessible tuition. Undeniably, performed successfully, I cannot imagine a significant change in these familiar essentials.

It is Columbia's purpose, too, to perform a distinctive urban mission, which combines an unduplicated higher educational service to metropolitan Chicago and to national and foreign students, with a vital presence in the city's life and culture.

There are certain themes that I observe as implicit constituents of Columbia's strategies. We are a serious educational place and we proudly regard our identity as educators. It follows that we have obligation to perfect the quality of our education and its enlightening effect on students. Implicit in Columbia's mission is an intent to educate students who will realize themselves humanely in shaping public perception of contemporary issues and events and in authoring the culture of their times.

Such idealism has been a conscious guide to Columbia's life. Some may view this idealism impatiently, but I submit that it is an important part of Columbia's successful uniqueness and quickly won public recognition. Surely this idealism has invested the college's membership with a unifying and special spirit. Understandably, Columbia's coming-of-age has been viewed mostly as a success measured in financial terms, enrollment gains, and in exhibits of educational ingenuity. It is too seldom appreciated that Columbia's elemental quality is the vitality of its distinctive educational ideas, whose implementations are exceedingly well performed.

My perception of Columbia in 1996 emphasized that the board could only determine the dimensions and financial imperatives of efforts to improve the college's educational quality and remedy its failings; but that the shape, content, and implementations of such efforts were reserved for faculty initiative shared with administrators of the college's academic process.

Among the subjects of such dialogue, I emphasized a need to rethink the occupational outcomes of Columbia's educational specialties in light of my certainty that the work world would continue to change dramatically. New jobs, new skills, new knowledge, new expectations. Few individuals remain permanently in the same job, and most have multiple careers. Correspondingly, the college's education would need greater variety and emphasis on technological competencies, and students would need better guidance to the interdisciplinary opportunities of Columbia's instruction.

A common theme of perceptions of Columbia in 1996 and after was a cardinal intent to significantly improve the college's efforts to help academically troubled students to greater mastery of the expectations of successful college study. In this effort, the faculty has paramount role. Thus, discovery of more effective methods of teaching is a principal college concern, which, I cautioned, cannot be satisfied without the faculty's intense commitment to explore new methods of teaching and student relation. At the same time, ways must be found to give faculty larger competence in fields other than their specialties and to give them more command of contemporary technology.

While Columbia's faculty is outstanding, its individuals, like faculty everywhere, are educated primarily in their disciplines, specializations ordinarily intensified in the course of their careers. The whole activity allows little, if any, attention to pedagogy, and after becoming teachers, the character and psychology of learning and the educative process is seldom studied. Inevitably, teachers learn by doing and by observation of others. But together we must develop a far greater opportunity for our faculty to study the arts and sciences of education and to encourage incorporation of this in our faculty's teaching. Similarly given the college's unavoidable dependence on part-time faculty and the sheer numbers of them, we must promptly find ways to imbue part-time faculty with a sense of Columbia's unique purpose and spirit and better monitor their teaching competence. If this is not done attentively, we put the largest part of the college's education to the risks of indifferent teaching, an utterly self-defeating equation.

While the absence of pedagogical substance in college teaching and dependence on part-time instructors may be general phenomena of American higher education, Columbia can find no comfort in common faults. We must be an exception, because we are not and never meant to be like other college institutions. And though we cannot invest our faculty with ultimate pedagogical insights, nor can we even remotely afford vastly improved ratios of full- and part-time faculty numbers, we can significantly improve our faculty's pedagogical sensitivity and the quality of part-time teaching. After long discussion, the board endorsed the basic enrollment, income, and cost assumptions of our five-year projections and a range of institutional improvements based on realization of income projections. Retrospectively, of course, our projections seem remarkably predictive of the next five years, and the plan did provide a valuable guide to college decisions, though as in any plan, however prescient, subsequent events and new views influence interpretations.

In my amplifications of improvement proposals, I appended a wish list of speculative capital investments, which included a dormitory, a day-care facility for the children of college employees and students, a new Dance Center, and a separate building to house the college's music program. In 1995, Columbia got a modern dormitory at Polk Street and Plymouth Court that now serves 350 students, though more dormitory space is now necessary. In 1998, the Sherwood Music School build-ing at Eleventh and Michigan was purchased for what is now a separate college Music Department. And in the same year, the college bought a building at 1415 South Wabash that houses theater shops and film stages. We now have a splendid new Columbia College Dance Center at 1306 South Michigan Avenue. A day care cen-ter hasn't yet happened. Virtually everything else in the 1996 plan has been far sur-passed, except that scholarship funds still lag behind anticipations.

Apart from concentrations on preparing data for our five-year projection and on developing institutional improvement plans, the college's 1990–91 agenda was crowded with important questions. While the most paramount of these was to define and initiate the presidential search process, we had also to determine an occupancy schedule for the 624 building, whether to refinance the building's purchase and con-struction costs with a new bond issue, and the feasibility of a major fund campaign.

The 624 building was an urgent issue. As discussed in contemplating the build-ing's purchase, the Illinois Department of Public Aid leased, with a June 1992 expi-ration date, 100,000 square feet of the building's 180,000-square-foot space, and this tenancy generated $900,000 in rental income, which largely covered the costs of operating the building. The Department of Public Aid fully occupied floors two, four, five, eight, ten, eleven, twelve, and thirteen, and one-third of six; the Torco Company was on the seventh floor; and the college occupied one, three, seven, four-teen, and part of six, which was being readied for college occupancy in June 1991. It was Bert Gall's impression that Public Aid wanted to remain in the building indef-initely, at least in most of their present space, though they might be amenable to a one-to two-year extension beyond June 1992. What was at issue was how firm and dependable our enrollment projections were for 1992 and beyond. If we had confidence in these projections, we would obviously need the space as soon as possible; and moreover, the revenues from a much greater number of students would more than compensate for the loss of tenant income.

It was a difficult subject. Our new enrollment and revenue projections were being put to a hard test, even more so by a recession in the national economy, the renewing danger of high inflation, and uncertainty about the resolution of the crisis in the Middle East, which carried the threat of war and, conceivably, reimposition of the draft. It was impossible to estimate the effect of these disturbances on student-aid appropriations and other essential benefits of the collegiate community. Albeit a comparatively small concern, it was hard to risk the comfort of income from the 624 building's tenants. To the contrary, if we extended tenants' leases until 1993 and if enrollment projections were realized, the linked idea of Columbia's growth and improvement would lie in chaos. While the first stage of the building's conversion would help, it would be nothing if the course of continuing construction was interrupted or precipitously scaled back.

With such recognitions, the board decided to continue with the original plan and to negotiate a settlement of tenant leases that best suited the college's construction and occupancy schedule and enrollment expectations. This, despite potential losses in tenant income and the possible effects of national and international troubles.

The Department of Public Aid and the Torco Company were entirely out of the building by the end of 1992, though Bert Gall was unable to negotiate away the big electric Torco sign on top of the building. It still is there today. Happily, our earlier enrollment projections were accurate. Columbia continued to grow and improve and quickly needed even more space. The worst fears of 1991 were never realized, that is, if one exempts the war with Iraq.

I omit a lengthy description of what seemed Columbia's umpteenth major fund campaign and a record of countless hours spent in its preparation, reams of consultants' advice and efforts to organize the participation of board members. Over a twenty-year span, the idea had often been trotted out, given a bit of exercise and sent back to the barn, lamed by evidence that Columbia had no affluent constituency, insufficient numbers of influential partisans, and too limited alumni expectations. Buoyed by the college's evident success and anxious to relieve the extent of dependence on tuition revenues and accelerate the college's improvement, the board once again embraced the notion of a major fund campaign. And once again, the wish prevailed over more realistic assessments of Columbia's fund-raising potential. Despite the board's commitment to the campaign and its expenses, estimated in a $250,000 range, agreement to a $25 million goal over five years, the assembly of an experienced campaign staff, and what seemed careful planning, the campaign, begun in 1992, never really got off the ground. It lingered about, I think, until early 1993, after I had gone, and I have no memory if anyone even noticed that the horse had died. It was undoubtedly an error to have mounted a major fund effort during the transition to a new president, and I suspect that there were serious faults in the campaign's management. And I might have done more, though it was hard to do in a farewell role. But I believe the campaign would have failed inevitably because Columbia's prominent viability was too recent to expect great public generosity and because Columbia simply didn't have the horses to pull a big campaign wagon. It may even be that Columbia will remain a peculiar place with little, if any, likelihood of going successfully to the well of public generosity, and that in the absence of this, the college may have to continue to depend mainly on its educational and business ingenuity. Perhaps, too, there are some features in the operations of the proliferating number of profit-making colleges which might serve Columbia as better models than heavily endowed colleges and universities.

The Search for a New President

At the board's January 1991 meeting, Alton Harris, the board's chair, formally initiated the search for a new Columbia College president. He proposed a letter be sent to Columbia's community, announcing my retirement on August 31, 1992, and described the procedures that would be employed in the search for my successor. "The selection, though dauntingly difficult," he said, "invokes a process specified by a prior resolution of the Board of Trustees. The final choice of a president is a board prerogative, which requires the affirmative vote of two-thirds of the board's membership, whose choices are limited to candidates who have been screened and nominated by at least a two-thirds vote of the members of a search and nominating committee. This committee is composed of the board chair; two board members elected by the board; two administrative officers of the college, the executive vice president and vice president for Academic Affairs; two members of the full-time faculty elected by their colleagues; two department chairs elected by the Council of Chairs; and President Alexandroff."

Harris said that the board would elect its representatives at a meeting in February, and he urged faculty and chairs to promptly select their representatives in whatever way they decided was appropriate. Gall was asked to facilitate this election at the earliest possible date.

Once formed, the search committee would prepare a job description and develop search procedures. Harris expected that candidate interviews would begin by late spring 1991 and should be completed by midfall, with a choice made by January or February of 1992.

It was important, Harris said, "that everyone understand that the committee's deliberations must be held in strictest confidence and that committee members must observe an absolute prohibition on discussion of the committee's business or candidates with anyone who is not a member of the search committee. Thus, members of the committee will not report to their constituencies, nor will it be appropriate for members of these constituencies to attempt to lobby or influence committee members. It must also be understood, that as most candidates who submit themselves to the committee's inquiry are presently employed, they must have every trust in the committee's perfect discretion, which if breached could have damaging consequence for the individuals. Each committee member is expected to bring to the search process their independent judgment and commitment to Columbia's best interests and not that of any group or viewpoint."

I don't suppose that anyone reading my narrative imagines that I am a selflessly modest fellow. So, if I include here bits of Harris's references to me in his message to the college's community, it won't jar the readers' illusions.

The Columbia we know—unique and remarkable institution that it is—would not exist were it not for the vision and energy Mike has provided during the more than thirty years of his presidency. His accomplishments are legion. The approaching end of the Alexandroff era at Columbia is a time for praise, sadness, reflection, and excitement over the beginning of a new era in the college's history. We will need to shower Mike with encomiums and honors in appropriate profusion in recognition of an astonishing career and a wonderful accomplishment. We will need to take stock of the institution he has shaped, to measure how far Columbia has come and to assess the nature and strengths of this extraordinary college. And we will need to plan and prepare for Columbia's future, a future that preserves the best of what Mike has helped to build.

Sometimes, immodesty is nourishing.

Harris's message had an unexpected caveat in the board's instruction that in what remained of my tenure I should devote the greatest majority of my time to the proposed fund campaign and to the college's civic and community relations. Accordingly, I was asked to delegate responsibility for most internal matters to Bert Gall, the executive vice president. All heads of college functions were to report to him, except the vice president for College Relations and Development. Apparently, I was to be a lamer duck than I expected to be. If memory serves, after some practice at limping, I meddled as usual, though I did delegate controversy to Bert. It was too good an opportunity to pass up.

The aggregate of continuing uncertainties in spring 1991 about the national economy and the reality of war in Iraq led to the adoption of a preliminary 1991–92 budget based on an enrollment of 6,600 to 6,800 students and smaller than usual institutional expenditures, the first time in recent years when the same or a reduced number of students was contemplated for a succeeding year. Despite these limitations, the budget draft funded a number of new full-time faculty appointments, usual salary increases for faculty and staff, and set a 6.3 percent increase in tuition rates. What was known was that increases in federal and state student-aid appropriations were unlikely, though current inflation rates exceeded 5 percent and a greater number of students were expected to apply for student-aid grants. And while in the past

Columbia had consistently run against downtrends in college-age numbers, such demographic direction might influence Columbia's 1991–92 enrollment.

The board deferred action on a new bond issue to fund the 624 building's expenses until tenant negotiations were completed and fall 1991 enrollment figures were known. By March 1991, the membership of the search committee had been chosen. Al Harris would serve as the committee's chair and members included Bert Gall and Lya Rosenblum, who by office represented the college's administration; David Rubin and Lerone Bennett, who represented the board of trustees; John Schultz and John Mulvaney, the chairs; Bill Russo and Caroline Latta, the faculty; and myself. The committee met three times in April and at least three times in succeeding months through March 1992. The earliest sessions were devoted to establishing search procedures, drafting a preliminary job description, and choosing a consulting firm to assist the committee. None of the members of the committee had any experience in conducting a presidential search, and we quickly recognized that the committee needed seasoned professionals to guide its work. Harris, principally, and several other committee members interviewed nine executive search agencies recommended by other colleges and universities who had conducted similar searches. The number was narrowed to four, and the Heydrich and Struggles firm was chosen as the committee's consultants. They assigned a very competent team headed by a senior executive, Bill Bowen. Without him, the committee may have floundered badly. In May, the consulting team had a long session with the board, which solicited members' views, focused particularly on the draft of a job description, which had been refined by the consulting team, who assured board members that the search would include candidates from law, business, and government and not be limited to those with higher education credentials. Subsequently, the consultants prepared and placed advertisements in a wide range of publications and generally publicized Columbia's search for a new president. All advertisements welcomed applications from women and minorities.

During the many months of search, 120 candidates were considered. Members of the consulting team interviewed all applicants and closely examined their qualifications and references. Some number of clearly unqualified applicants were eliminated after review by the committee. Thirty survived committee and consultant scrutiny, and all were personally interviewed by committee members. Fourteen candidates were chosen for interview by the whole committee, and finally, five were asked to return for a searching interview. Committee discussion about these candidates was intense and involved information about candidates solicited from colleagues and professional sources that had not been shown as the candidate's references. While it was the Committee's intention to narrow the search to at least two nominations to be submitted for board choice, one of the five finalists was convincingly more qualified than the others. Thus, only a single individual was nominated and submitted to the board. This was John B. Duff, then Chicago's library commissioner. Duff had a Ph.D. in American History from Columbia University, was a published historian, and had served as provost of Seton Hall University, president of the University of Massachusetts at Lowell, and chancellor of the Massachusetts Board of

Higher Education. He had an impressive record in public and independent higher education and in civic and governmental affairs. The nominating committee determined that Duff had exceptional talent to give Columbia influential presence and representation in academic and public communities, a secure familiarity with the political and legislative process—and mature ability to extend Columbia's cause among foundations and fund-raising constituencies. He was an experienced manager of large-scale enterprises and had a competent sense of college finances. Duff expressed respect for the faculty's centrality in the collegiate process and devotion to student welfare. He was in full accord with Columbia's emphasis on the arts and media together with education in the liberal arts and sciences. He was enthusiastically committed to Columbia's unselective admission policies and to a strong program to help students in remedying their collegiate difficulties. The committee unanimously recommended Duff's selection as Columbia's president by the Board of Trustees. Dr. Duff was introduced to the board at its March 16, 1992, meeting. A lengthy colloquy ensued. Before the board voted on Duff's nomination, however, members insisted that the meeting's record reconfirm Bert Gall's appointment to a five-year term as the college's provost and executive vice president and that this be secured by contract. With that done, the board elected John Duff as Columbia College's president to take office on September 1, 1992.

The statutory requirement of an affirmative vote by at least two-thirds of the board's membership was exceeded. Twenty-six members voted affirmatively and three dissented or abstained. Some members observed that though they did not question the election of Dr. Duff nor the search committee's recommendation, they were disappointed at the committee's singular nomination. A choice among two or more candidates would have been preferable. Moreover, they said, there had been too little communication with the board, particularly after press leaks reported prematurely that Duff's selection had already been made. Harris responded that while greater choice would have been preferable, it would have been artificial and not honorable to recommend other candidates who did not enjoy the committee's fullest confidence simply to satisfy an appearance of choice or competitive qualifications. No one had any idea of the source of the leaks. Bennett emphasized that the committee had acted with integrity and respect for the need to preserve confidentiality. I stated unequivocally that I, and surely Harris, had in no way manipulated the committee's choice and the board's concurrence, and I repeated my conviction that John Duff was an outstanding choice and that his selection had been made with perfect fairness and objectivity. All of the board's members joined in grateful compliment to the members of the search committee for their exhausting and selfless service to the college.

When the whole presidential search was done, and I suppose even while it was happening, I mused about the sorts of individuals who had submitted themselves as candidates. Somewhere in my head was a faint notion that giants would be discovered among them: some Robert Hutchins with the populist vitality of Bill Veeck, someone articulately committed to the welfare of human society with abiding faith in the glories of education, someone who would carry Columbia to great heights and would influence the course of American education. No such giants were discovered. It was probably because the sorts I imagined simply didn't want to be college presidents or maybe that there aren't many giants out there any more. Undoubtedly, a number of candidates were very decent, talented, competent, appropriately credentialed people with requisite energy, management skills, collegial personalities, humane convictions, and political savvy. Indeed, they were quite like typical college and university presidents. No one but Duff fired my interests, however, and, I suspect, that of my committee colleagues. I didn't seek to replicate myself. My stewardship was done, and I chose it to be so. I knew it was time for somebody new. It was just that my colleagues and I thought Columbia was a very special place that deserved a very special leader. We hoped it would be John Duff.

I have limited this narrative to a time span ending with my retirement in 1992, excepting a brief show in my preface of some statistics of Columbia's dimensions in 2000 and occasional notes that an individual's college service extends to today. The impressive accomplishments of John Duff's presidential tenure (1992 to 2000) deserve an independent narrative.

My lifelong concern for Columbia's state and welfare remains undiminished. While not having had an intimate role in the college's life and decisions since my retirement, I could not become an impersonal reporter of the college's recent years. Undoubtedly, constructing this narrative has given me a far more complete understanding of Columbia than I ever had before, but such insights belong to my time and not to my successor's.

I do record, however, that on John Duff's watch, Columbia has prospered and grown mightily. Student and faculty numbers have dramatically increased. In the number of buildings and college space, Columbia is many times greater. In fact, Columbia is now identified as a major player in the remarkable renewal of Chicago's South Loop and the district's development as a center of higher education. The college's endowment has more than doubled, as has its operating budget. With the leadership of Alton Harris and the talent and dedicated service of David Rubin, William Hood, and many other members, the college's board has become a mature agency of Columbia's life. And in Provost Albert Gall, Chief Financial Officer Michael DeSalle, Human Resource Director Paul Johnson, and Dean Lya Rosenblum, the college continues to have incomparable administrative leadership. Unquestionably, Columbia now enjoys impressive public recognition, respect of the higher education community, influential civic presence, and prominence in local and national arts, media, and intellectual communities. Columbia is no longer a doubtful Johnny-come-lately.

1991–1992: The Final Year

As I have occasionally mentioned in the course of these recollections, our unique approach to departmental chairmanships has been both a source of strength and, occasionally, a locus of conflict. One final instance awaited me in my final year. the faculty of the Film/Video Department petitioned for the replacement of the chair, a man who had served in that role for over twenty years, who had hired many of the faculty and had nurtured both the department and many individual careers. Efforts at mediation proved unavailing, and I concluded that it was in the best interest of all concerned that there be a change in the chairmanship. There was no question about the continued faculty role of the individual involved, but he decided to retire as of the end of the academic year.

Bert Gall, Sam Floyd, who had become the academic dean for undergraduate studies, Lya Rosenblum, and I interviewed all the members of the Film/Video faculty and concluded that no compromise was possible. The greatest number of faculty simply refused to continue to serve under this chair. Their unity was unshakable.

While no less a crisis than the controversies in the English and Science Departments, Film/Video's troubles did not carry the baggage of excesses and contagion of passions of those earlier struggles. But there was no alternative to relieving this man of his appointment as the department's chair, which I did with great reluctance. He remained a faculty member without assignment until the end of the college year.

I observe only that by the end of my tenure, Columbia's chairs system and the expectations of a chair's performance had changed significantly as compared to the college's earlier times when chairs were chosen and renewed at the pleasure of the president. Moreover, it was evident that department chairs were not vested with the power they once commonly exercised; though even today, the college's president has final say in the choice of chairs and can cause their dismissal if the action is consistent with college protocols. While I would still argue for old measures of a chair's qualifications and performance expectations, I suspect these would be exacted only with great difficulty, because chair searches and performance expectations have become less demanding and are more subject to the comfort level of a department's faculty. If there is advantage in this, it is that at least serious friction between faculty and their chairs is less likely. And perhaps this new state of things was inevitable with the college's greater numbers of faculty and students.

To return to the here and now, the college's enrollment of more than 7,100 students in September 1991 dismissed all prior uncertainties, and the preliminary budget was recast to reflect Columbia's renewed prosperity. This was with the caveat that there was a compelling need to improve amounts realized from unrestricted gifts in the current year, particularly as such receipts had been disappointing in the previous year. David Rubin, who chaired the board's Finance Committee, cautioned that this effort could expect little or no benefit from the major fund campaign just initiated.

In my message to the board at its November 1991 meeting, I observed that as this was the final year of my tenure as Columbia's president, it was likely that the board's January 1992 meeting would be the last of my reports on the state of the college, and that neither now nor then would I attempt a summary of my more than thirty years as Columbia's president. It would serve no purpose, I thought, as I had already offered a review of Columbia's modern times and a perception of the college's future course at the board retreat a year ago.

I supposed as a product of my ruminations about Columbia's life and safety, and as I viewed my prospective successor, I had come to a certain conviction that even if our best ambitions were realized, the college will continue to depend on familiar entrepreneurial and management qualities and educational and social commitments, which have prevailed successfully during all of Columbia's modern life. In short, we've done well. And if we are to continue to prosper and have a safe foundation on which to get to a higher state, what we've done must be valued and cherished.

It is rewarding to observe that the college began my lame duck year with undiminished vitality. Indeed, Columbia enjoyed a big leap in civic engagement and public notice in just the first weeks of the new college year. Among other events, Dance Africa and Dancing in the Streets festivals had audiences in the many thousands and a wealth of media notices; Columbia's Black Music Repertory Ensemble was the centerpiece of the city's Library Inaugural ceremonies; a large-scale arts program was launched, jointly sponsored by the college and the Chicago Park District; an extensive literacy and tutorial effort was begun in the Chicago Public Schools, to be expanded to include public housing projects and Park District centers; and Columbia's Center for Science Education hosted a major public event, which featured the eminent world scientist and hero of the Chinese democratic movement and Tiananmen Square, Dr. Iang Lizhi, whose "release" from China was helped prominently by Zafra Lerman.

In the final months of my tenure, while familiarly occupied, it was without the usual intensity. I was happily distracted by a succession of fetes, farewells, and recognitions by many of the organizations served by my Columbia representations and by a bounty of luncheons and dinners with a host of Columbia colleagues. The best of my farewell occasions was Mike Alexandroff Day at White Sox Park. It was a day for Jane, too. Everyone knew we were devoted baseball fans, I for more than sixty years and Jane for forty-five. Three hundred or so Columbia folk came out to cheer. I got to throw out the first ball. My seventy-year-old arm failed me. My pitch sailed ten feet wide of the plate. With a few more throws, I would have had my old stuff back. But one was enough to know I was still unhittable. Right up there, too, was a wonderful alumni event in Los Angeles, where Jane and I were honored by more than 400 alums and their guests. Some went back to the 1940s. It was a grand evening filled with talk of old times and wistful memories. What was most rewarding was to hear about the great success so many alumni enjoyed in their careers and to know the great affection everyone felt for Columbia. I realized how dumb and shortsighted it was to have neglected so many who shared Columbia's spirit and so valued their college times. I can't leave this without acknowledging the great dedication of Ron Wise, Gerry G. Bishop, Ira Miller, and Bob Cosentino. I wish space allowed me to name many others.

I think the last important act of my stewardship was to initiate a comprehensive review of the policies and formulas that guided the college's investment of pension, endowment, reserve, and operating funds. It was a bundle of more than $30 million.

In this inquiry, Mike DeSalle and David Rubin had paramount roles, exercised with the help of the board's Finance Committee. To counsel our analysis, we engaged the Stratford Group, a financial consulting firm of highest reputation. After four months of work, it was decided that to maximize safety and earnings of the then $8 million pension fund, it should be removed from the insurance company that had managed the fund's assets and earnings since the plan's inception, and a new fund manager chosen who would allocate 60 percent of the pension fund to equities and 40 percent to fixed-income securities. Endowment and quasi endowment funds were allocated 80 percent to equities and 20 percent to fixed income securities, and operating funds allocated 25 percent to equities and 75 percent to fixed income instruments and cash. It was also decided that equity investments would be divided evenly between growth and value style investing. After a long discussion that extended over several sessions, the board endorsed the investment plan. Another month was spent in choosing fund managers, whose results would be compared at the end of one year when presumably some would be replaced and the portfolio of others enlarged.

These decisions included a reconfirmation of the board's instruction to the new managers of the college's investments. This emphasized that no Columbia funds were to be invested in the securities of companies doing business in South Africa. Similarly excluded were companies with discriminatory employment practices, those with notorious employee relations or that countenanced oppressive workplace behavior towards women and minorities, companies engaged in the sale of armaments, and companies that have a record of indifference to the environment.

Mike DeSalle became the principal manager of Columbia's investments, though the Finance Committee continued to closely monitor results. The whole effort was extraordinarily successful, though obviously, all ships rose on the stock market's rising tides. But this takes nothing away from DeSalle's acuity. I may have pointed the way, but Columbia got a lot bigger and richer after I'd gone.

At the board's April 1992 meeting, tuition for the 1992–93 year was increased by 5.9 percent, which again sustained Columbia's tuition as the lowest among Illinois private colleges and universities. Faculty salaries would be increased by 5 percent and staff compensations by 4 percent. A preliminary budget for 1992–93 expected revenues and expenses in a $41 million range and anticipated an enrollment in September 1992 of 7,450 students. (In actuality, that forecast was right on the nose and quite perfectly consistent with earlier five-year projections.)

Then suddenly it was my last day. My stuff was packed up and carted away to a little suite on the fourteenth floor of the 624 building that said President Emeritus on the door. Now there is only a number. I wanted to leave unnoticed, without ceremony or tears. No trumpets or drum rolls. Everyone honored my choice. Earlier that day, all the wonderfully loyal people who labored downstairs crowded my office to give me a treasured picture of their assembly, captioned, "We helped you to build the college and on your retirement, we find ourselves with great sorrow." They were no lesser colleagues and friends than vice presidents, deans, and faculty. Late that afternoon, Jane came for me. We hardly spoke. We just numbly left together and shut the door. Even the corridors were empty. I had a troubled feeling of repeating a scene played fifty years before when I had allowed my mother and father and myself only minimal expression when I left home for the army.

There was some talk of having a big dinner party, but I suppose my indifference discouraged its happening. I might have been more receptive if some had not viewed such an affair as a fund-raising opportunity. I did have a very gracious luncheon a few months later when Dominic DiFrisco persuaded the city to name a short stretch of Harrison Street "Mike Alexandroff Way."

For some years, I harbored a diminishing hope that the success Columbia enjoyed in its emphasis on open admission, its civic engagement, and use of a part-time faculty of working professionals might serve as a contagious example to other college institutions. It was possible, too, I thought, that Columbia might influence other colleges and universities to modify their traditional exclusion of so-called at-risk students, and that in doing this, such institutions would have cause to commit a greater part of their enormous creative potential and resources to the challenge of educating large numbers of historically neglected young people.

Columbia's example, however, found few takers. If anything we did impressed the collegiate community, it was Columbia's remarkable growth, which most assumed to have been accomplished by clever marketing and publicity. As for influencing changed admission practices and getting others to seek remedies for students initially without customary college qualifications, Columbia had little, if any, influence. Indeed, in the view of many of our brethren, the practice of open admissions cast Columbia as a dubious college institution.

Since the 1980s, American higher education has discovered on its own that students expect their college education to have an occupational consequence. Indeed, students view college as the way to a good job. colleges and universities have discovered, too, that civic service is a valuable institutional function, though few regard it as a part of students' educational experience. And most colleges have found that wide use of part-time faculty is a necessary economy; though in this, I observe that using large numbers of graduate teaching assistants as instructors of undergraduate classes is a poor substitute for hiring working professionals and already credentialed academics as part-time teachers.

Though regrettably it was not infectious, Columbia's quality of education and the competence of its faculty were of highest order. In fact, I am certain that no college offering undergraduate arts and media studies could rightly claim a quality of practical education, instructional facilities, or faculty competence superior to Columbia. The quality of Columbia's liberal education was similarly exemplary, though its subjects were not major fields of study. The difficulty of such comparisons is that, to the best of my knowledge, no other college institutions offer such an assembly of arts and media subjects in close, cross-fertilizing constellation. So the only comparison that can be made is between Columbia's arts and media concentrations and corresponding departments of other institutions; and in this respect, none of Columbia's departments would be found wanting.

Had Columbia not incorporated in its mission an intent to give college and career opportunity to a significant number of students without traditional collegiate qualifications, and had we restricted enrollment to only those most qualified, the quality of Columbia's instruction would be widely advertised and the most gifted would compete for entry. But, of course, such an elite institution wouldn't be Columbia College.

What is true of Columbia's students is that many would qualify for highly selective college institutions, many more are quite typical of students on most American campuses, and some need help to master collegiate expectations. What is also true is that Columbia students are more creative, independent, and focused than the general college population.

Columbia students have the benefit of an exceptional education and benefit from it to the extent they exercise the best of themselves. That many do is verified by their life and career successes. Most colleges can claim similar confirmations, and I mean no criticism of other colleges and universities and certainly not of the quality of education they perform in disciplines similar to Columbia's. I contend that college institutions have different purposes, but validity is held commonly. That a great diversity exists among the institutions of American higher education is the system's glory. What's disturbing is that many who praise the diversity of higher education's opportunities in the abstract are quick to censure college institutions that don't conform to conventional models.

I appropriately close this narrative of Columbia College's history with a tribute to the college's executive officers, faculty, board of trustees, administrative cadre, professional staff, and the many, many others who served the college's renewal with uncommon loyalty and talent. There is no artifice in saying that despite whatever I contributed, Columbia would not have lived or prospered without the dedication of its rare assembly of extraordinary men and women.

An inclusive listing of the members of Columbia's family would take pages and pages. Regrettably, I can list only a small number of individuals to represent the many who served Columbia with equal distinction. As in any hierarchy, Columbia's leading cadre had responsibility for the management of the college's life and contributed valuably to Columbia's success. Some had comparatively brief presence and others served for many years, some even to today. But all were champions of Columbia's welfare.

Bert Gall served at Columbia's helm as my friend and colleague for twenty years. Lya Rosenblum guided the course of Columbia's education for the last fifteen years of my tenure. Sam Floyd succeeded Lya as undergraduate academic dean. The stalwarts who went before them were Wolfram Dochtermann, Ted Kawalek, William Wilkes, and Louis Silverstein. We were all honored by the presence of the revered deans of students Hubert Davis and Hermann Conaway. And I am certain that few, if any, colleges and universities have enjoyed Columbia's unusual quality of financial management found in John Scheibel and Mike DeSalle; and similarly, Paul Johnson, who serves with rare distinction as the college's director of Human Resources.

In any college institution or common school, the faculty is the primary instrument of its educational quality. I cannot imagine a more educated, professionally accomplished, and humanely engaged faculty than Columbia's, nor a faculty more invested with a sense of educational mission and commitment to inventive teaching.

TELEVISION

Virginia Butts, Wolfram Dochtermann, Jack Jacobson, Thaine Lyman, Edward Morris, Michael Niederman, Ken Ponte, Phil Ruskin, Barbara Sykes, Harry Trigg, Barbara Yanowski

RADIO

Art Hellyer, Terri Hemmert, Al Parker, Charles Rowell, Chuck Schaden

FILM/VIDEO

Doreen Bartoni, Jack Behrend, Judd Chesler, Dan Dinello, Roger Ebert, Robert Edmonds, Chap Freeman, Fred Lasse, Anthony Loeb, Michael Rabiger, Paul Rubenstein, Gordon Weisenborn, Jack Whitehead, Barry Young

PHOTOGRAPHY

David Avison, Kerry Coppin, Arnold Crane, Jonas Dovydenas, Archie Lieberman, Lyle Mayer, John Mulvaney, James Newberry, Lynn Sloan, Stephen Marc Smith, Joseph Sterling, Robert Thall, Peter Thompson, Ruth Thorne-Thomsen, Charles Traub, John White

ART, GRAPHICS AND DESIGN

Phyllis Bramson, Barry Burlison, Susann Craig, Gene DeKovic, Marlene Lipinski, Carol Haliday-McQueen, Lynn Hammond, Ruth Migdal, Donald Newgren, Ed Paschke, Anthony Patano, Herbert Pinzke, Hollis Sigler, Leo Tannenbaum, Irving Titel, Ernest Whitworth

THEATER

Robert Borelek, Ron Davis, Paul Carter Harrison, Vanessa James, Caroline Latta, Michael Maggio, Terry McCabe, Michael Merritt, James O'Reilly, Sheldon Patinkin, Al Peters, Gordon Rogoff, Don Sanders, Paul Sills, Catherine Slade, Chuck Smith, Lucille Strauss, Arnold Weinstein

MUSIC

Eddie Baker, Orbert Davis, Carol Loverde, William Russo, Howard Sandroff, Henry Threadgill, Bobbi Wilsyn, Tony Zito,

DANCE

Jan Erkert, Susan Kimmelman, Herbert Lui (Tai Chi Chuan, Master), Shirley Mordine, Tim O'Slynne, Nana Shineflug, Jane Ganet-Sigel (Dance Therapy), Donna Sugarman, Richard Woodbury

ARTS AND ENTERTAINMENT MANAGEMENT

Paul Berger, Fred Fine, Dennis Rich, Irwin Steinberg, Charles Suber, Carol Yamamoto

ENGLISH AND FICTION WRITING

Randy Albers, Andy Allegretti, George Bailey, Sheila Baldwin, Steve Bozak, Fred Gardaphe, Gary Johnson, Phil Klukoff, Lynn McNulty, Tom Nawrocki, Sarah Odishoo, Paul Pekin, John Schultz, Betty Shiflett, Shawn Shiflett

POETRY

Gwendolyn Brooks, Maxine Chernoff, Eileen Cherry, David Hernandez, Paul Hoover, Angela Jackson, Joel Lipman, Haki Madhubuti, Caroline Rogers

LITERATURE

Hans Adler, Mark Benny, Paul Carroll, Peter Christenson, Jack Conroy, Ron Fair, Hoyt Fuller, Hoke Norris, Gene O'Hara, Harry Mark Petrakis

ADVERTISING AND MARKETING COMMUNICATION

Mort Kaplan, Philip Kaplan, Herb Kraus, Harold Lawrence, Dorothy LeFold, Don Nathanson, Margaret Sullivan, John Tarini, Al Weisman

LIBERAL EDUCATION: HISTORY, HUMANITIES, ANTHROPOLOGY, PHILOSOPHY, SOCIAL SCIENCE, AND CONTEMPORARY ISSUES

Ruth Adams, Harry Barnard, Heather Booth, Harry Bouras, Gene DeKovic, Elizabeth Edelson, Joan Erdman, Glennon Graham, William Hayashi, Rev. Jim Jones, Abbas Kessel, Ira Kipnis, Sidney Lens, Robin Lester, Albert Logan, Staughton Lynd, Rev. Richard Morrisroe, Sabi Shabtai, Louis Silverstein, Martin Sklar, Anderson Thompson, Les Van Marter, John Wabaunsee, Jon Wagner, Quentin Young

SCIENCE

Charles Cannon, Harvey Davis, Oscar Davis, Zafra Lerman, Jeffrey Lyon, Pan Papacosta, Ernest Sukowski, Louis Vacek

JOURNALISM

Jon Anderson, William Braden, William Brashler, Les Brownlee, Hank DeZutter,
Ron Dorfman, Daryl Feldmeir, Tom Fitzpatrick, Don Gold, Harry Golden,
William Granger, Lloyd Green, Nat Lerman, Eric Lund, Earl Moses, Charles Mouratides,
Eugene "Skip" Myslenski, Barbara Reynolds, Edmund Rooney, Nick Shuman,
C. Sumner Stone, Basil Talbot, Nicholas von Hoffman, Larry Weintraub, Howard Ziff

CONTEMPORARY MUSIC

Les Brown, Dom DeMichael, Charles Suber, Studs Terkel, Jack Tracy

SPEECH

Sue Ann Park, Hermia Serota

Also, a number of graduates returned as members of the faculty: Kazuo Ayukawa,
Bernie Caputo, Vandell Cobb, William Harder, Larry Heinemann, Brent Jones,
Ozier Muhammad, Pat Muldowney, Howard Shapiro, James Sheerin, Bruce Shuster,
Bob Sirott, Walter Topel, Ted Weber, and Ron Weiner.

The fundamental function of the board of trustees of an independent (private) college is to determine and monitor the main policies of the institution's life and welfare. Sensible boards stick to major policy decisions and leave the college's educational process to the president, college officers, and faculty. Sensible presidents carefully observe the board's expectation of being fully informed of important college happenings and allowed to exercise their policy prerogatives. In these respects, I was a very sensible college president.

Columbia, however, was unique. While I may speak of 1964 as the beginning of Columbia's renewal, to practical measure, a new college was beginning. I had an idea then with little real shape to it, and I had a small group of friends who were willing to help. They became Columbia's board, in name, at least. In actuality, they were my consultants, though I could never have purchased such competent, patient, supportive, and affectionate advice as I got from Phil Lewis, Seymour Gale, Bud Salk, Bud Perlman, Ira Kipnis, and Richard Mandel.

I continued for many years to depend on the board's counsel and forum. When the board's membership was enlarged to include a greater diversity of talents, the pattern of board service during Columbia's earliest years continued to guide members' participation in the college's life.

As said about Columbia's faculty, I cannot imagine a board more loyally and intensely committed to a college's welfare than the quality of effort exhibited by Columbia's board. In actively sharing responsibility for implementing Columbia's most critical decisions, members were far more than policy mavens. Despite endemic difficulties which frustrated fund-raising efforts, board members were personally very generous. They genuinely embraced and reflected Columbia's mission and consistently sought the best benefits for the college's students and personnel, while scrupulously preserving the independence of the college's officers, faculty, and staff in educational and operational decisions. The major business decisions which shaped Columbia's life were made in the board's forum; this may explain my narrative's emphasis on the board's role.

I was blessed with extraordinary board chairs. I often remember the enormous number of hours the chairs' job consumed and the extreme loyalty, patience, and skills they exercised in Columbia's service. I don't have enough words for appropriate compliment and gratitude toward Seymour Gale, Alfred Perlman, William Cobbs, Dwight Follett, Devorah Sherman, Charles Bane, Jay Fox, and Alton Harris, who still serves as the board's chair after fourteen years. Similar thanks go to board members William Wilkow, Sam Baskin, Steve Neumer, Sydney Gordon, Lerone Bennett, Barry Crown, Myron Hokin, Frank Anglin, Robert Rothschild, David Rubin, Milton Davis, Alan Saks, Sam Pfeffer, David Solomon, Louise Benton, Marjorie Benton, Patrick and Patti Crowley, Frank Fried, Ben Gould, Joel Henning, Albert Jenner, Don Mann, John Naisbitt, Don Nathanson, Stanton Leggett, Enid Long, Emmet O'Neill, Hope Samuels, Ron Williams, and Dori Wilson.

Inevitably, in any hierarchy, the generals get the credit, and lesser ranks and their troops do the soldiering. Columbia had a lot of great soldiers. In fact, those who managed and staffed the college's student, institutional, and instructional services performed essential work without which there would have been nobody to educate. Obviously, a college is a complex enterprise that requires a variety of functions to support the institution's educational project. However central to students' purpose, the classroom is only a part of students' college experience. Indeed, the road of students' college life is paved with potential hazards that require the attentive assistance of student service staff. It is they who are the face of the college most seen by students. Thus, these representatives are the greatest influence on students' regard for their college experience. Students are introduced to the college by field representatives and/or by the admissions staff, who in effect are the college's salespersons. Then continuing during the whole time of their enrollment, students remain dependent on the help of academic counselors, student-aid advisors, bursars, librarians, student life advocates, equipment specialists, and congeries of social and academic services, not to mention faculty.

If these services are performed inexpertly or indifferently, the whole college suffers the consequence of angry and frustrated students and inordinate withdrawals, and the college's elemental purpose to serve students is unforgivably violated. Students, after all, pay the college's freight, and as valuable customers, they deserve the best treatment.

In respect for this dictum, I once even entertained the notion that faculty and student service staff come to work "dressed for business" as a show of serious regard for students. I'll allow that that was a pretty laughable expectation, though to this day, I can't believe anyone is getting reliable counsel or instruction from someone dressed in jeans, T-shirt, and sneakers. Equally important to Columbia's life were those who provided essential institutional services and those who directed the college's cultural, civic, and community agencies. We had the best of these, too. The following is only a representative list over a long time:

Mary Schellhorn, Chief Librarian; Dennis Peacock, Dean, Institutional Research; Jack Wolfsohn, Director of Development; Keith Cleveland, Director of Graduate Education; Connie Zonka, Director, Public Relations; Horace Jimerson, Director, Instructional Services; Directors of Admissions, Edward Navakas and Debra McGrath. When registrars were also Directors of Admissions, Naomi Kellison, Nancy Sherbourne, and June Denham.

Marsha Reisser, Associate Director, Center for Black Music Research; Mary Badger, Manager, Theater-Music Center and Getz Theater. Jerry Gall and Mary Johnson, Directors of Graphic Arts and Publications; Steve Russell-Thomas, Director of Counseling Services; Peggy O'Grady, Bursar; Valjean Jones, Dean of Students; Comptrollers, Norma Calalang and Ann Kennedy; Bernadette McMahon, Supervisor of Administrative Computing. John Moore, Assistant Dean of Students.; Directors of Student Aid, Laura Day, Steve Bellin, Ray Pranske and John Olino. Jan Grekoff, Job Placement Director; Paula Epstein, Assistant Library Director; Edward Eddins, Director, Computer Operations; Carole Finder, Office Manager; Sheldon Siegel, Registrar; Millie Slavin, Bookkeeper; Patricia DeWitt, Secretary to the President; Susan Babyk, Assistant to the Provost/Executive Vice President; the master builder, Jacob Caref, Larry Dunn, the extraordinary Director of Building Services; Engineer, Jim Brady, who came with the 600 South Michigan building; Irv Meyer, who fixes everything and keeps the place running; and the incomparable Janice Booker, who for twenty years made the college work, from the reception offices to the telephone system to the mountainous paper flow.

I gratefully acknowledge the help and fraternity of my dear friends Ira Kipnis and Richard Mandel, who over many years gave Columbia the most expert legal counsel. And to all of those named and unnamed, I am profoundly grateful for having had the grand pleasure of your company.

Mike Alexandroff

The GI Bill

In concept and actuality, the GI Bill stands as the twentieth century's most enlightened, significant, and influential legislation. Only the constitutional amendment that granted women the right to vote, the Social Security Act, and the Civil Rights and Voting Rights Acts deserve equal rank. The GI Bill gave millions of young American men and women the unprecedented opportunity of education and job training and entitlement to psychological services on a scale previously unimagined. The GI Bill singularly changed postwar America. In previous generations, with small exception, a college education had been reserved for the elite, and job training was consigned usually to vocational schools where working-class young men might learn a trade. The GI Bill allowed millions of young Americans the opportunity to educate themselves for whatever professions they chose; similarly, it allowed great numbers to aspire to and qualify for a plethora of new jobs and occupations created by an expanding national economy in the years after World War II. The whole idea of student financial aid and job training, which students today regard as their entitlement, exists because of the unique precedent of the GI Bill. In essence, the GI Bill created the American middle class. With a little piece of the action, Columbia College was dramatically changed by the GI Bill too.

After the GI Bill was enacted in 1944, the Veterans Administration set up a giant apparatus to process claims and eligibilities for the variety of available veterans' benefits. These included education, low-interest loans to assist veterans in buying homes, medical benefits, prohibitions against job discrimination, and unemployment compensation, for nearly seventeen million U.S. veterans of World War II. By September 1945, the vast system was workably in place, though it would take more time for it to become efficient. In educational benefits, each veteran was entitled to a year's tuition at a trade school or college plus an additional month for every month of active duty service, to a maximum of four years of tuition subsidy, not to exceed $500 yearly. In addition to tuition benefits, each single veteran received a $65 per month "cost of living" payment ($75 monthly with one dependent and $105 with multiple dependents). To take advantage of liberal tuition subsidies, countless numbers of trade schools covering every conceivable trade and vocation quickly opened, which understandably occasioned unconscionable profiteering and gross exploitation of tens of thousands of veterans; and correspondingly, a sizable force of Veterans Association investigators and monitors. Inevitably, of course, some vets greeted monthly cash subsidies as "found money." But an overwhelming number of ex-service men and women took serious advantage of opportunities opened by the GI Bill.

Open Admissions

The subject of open admissions to a college education is full of contradictions which, even in the context of present realities, defy resolution. At issue are the core questions of education. Who shall be educated, and to what extent and social purpose? The principle of public education and universal access to the common schools has been settled, though the content of elementary and secondary school education and control of its process is still widely debated. Obviously, historical context shapes formal education and the societal imperatives that it is expected to satisfy. In the not-so-distant past, the education of many of the nation's children ended at the eighth grade, and those who went on to high school were usually divided into trade and vocational preparations and more intellectually demanding general education categories, the latter being college preparatory for the small numbers who graduated to higher education. This pattern largely persisted until the GI Bill after World War II gave impulse and opportunity to millions of young Americans and fertilized the democratic idea of universal access to a college education, a popular aspiration satisfied in part by government scholarships, financial aid, and a proliferation of junior colleges.

Unquestionably, the American economy has changed qualitatively in the last fifty years. It is clearly evident, however, that while the nation enjoys greater prosperity, it is unevenly distributed. Nowhere is the lag more prominent than in the living conditions of poor people and minorities isolated in America's inner cities or mired in rural poverty. I ignore a familiar catalog of sufferings and oppressions, except to contend that without qualitative remedy, no targeted inequities can be addressed successfully.

Education is linked inextricably to every national and human concern. Despite its paramount social function, the whole system of common school education is increasingly in philosophical and practical disorder, particularly in its service to children and young people in depressed and deprived communities where the quality of education is abysmal. Again, I avoid a litany of dismal statistics.

Colleges and universities have adapted more successfully to the radically changed state of American culture and the national economy than have the common schools, whose response is severely handicapped by their democratic mandate to educate everyone, and by the absence of a genuine national and local commitment to the welfare of the common schools.

As universally understood, formal education is a continuum that progresses from kindergarten to college. Appropriately, college is not simply an extension of high school. College enrollment is voluntary, and it requires skills and comprehension of previously learned material. It follows that if colleges are to perform their higher calling, they must expect students to be mature and intellectually competent. While under ideal circumstances the greatest number of high school graduates would be qualified for college study, the absence of anything even remotely ideal requires colleges to purify student ranks to preserve collegiate quality.

Hence, colleges have selective admissions policies, which are expedient and generally suited to present realities that treat as "natural" and inevitable the exclusion of masses of young people whose prior education did not prepare them for college. This, however, invokes the acutely undemocratic contradiction that those so excluded will suffer economic and social penalties, and however unintentionally, reinforces and validates inequity and contributes to public acceptance of its permanence.

It does not follow, however, that the institutions of higher education and their admissions policies bear primary responsibility for an inequitable society or the low state of elementary and secondary school education, though colleges do contribute, albeit subtly, to civic neutrality, and they are not without responsibility for the doubtful quality of teacher education. While the subject of college entitlement may be a derivative of larger national policy, some impulse of enrollment restriction traces to the elitism and discrimination once quite commonly practiced in American higher education. Current discussion of college admission policies seldom extends beyond conventional and convenient perceptions that the sanctity of the collegiate mission can only be satisfied by a selective student audience.

Collegiate exclusion is not some abstract penalty. In a more just and rational society, the greatest number of high school graduates, irrespective of life station, would have college qualifications, and "open admission" would not be an issue. That a college education is the route to a good life, that it gets you to where the money is, is a lesson pressed relentlessly on all American children. This is no less so among poor children, who despite their fragile expectations, are not spared witness to the better life enjoyed by the "haves" than the "have nots." Thus, the penalty of exclusion is compounded for vast numbers identified as unqualified for college opportunity.

When these innocents are sent off to schools, they accept the adult notion held by poor and privileged alike that they will be educated, except that poor adults are powerless, and the more privileged indifferent, to the quality of poor children's education and the cacophony of their lives. Indeed, at safe distance, the public believes that imposition of stricter educational standards will, of itself, compel learning, as it also believes that a draconian restriction of benefits will end welfare dependency.

The plain fact is that common school education in depressed communities is a grossly underfunded, failing system that cannot succeed in a context of racism and economic and social deprivation. Despite a bombardment of advertisements and persuasions to stay in school, 40 percent or so drop out because their school experience is unsatisfying and, more significantly, because education's promises are not believed.

Of those who successfully navigate a maze of obstacles to graduate from high school, some have college qualifications, acquired more as a result of stellar individual possessions and helpful life circumstances than from any unusual quality of high school education. But a "trick bag" awaits greater numbers, now separated from school affiliation, who are left to rummage about with the temporary myth that a high school diploma will get them something better than a lowly, minimal-paying, goes-nowhere job. Or they may hold on to college and career ambitions, though these are thorny alternatives, too. Predictably, they got a lousy education, although had they worked harder they could have seen different results. But nothing changes the fact that without lengthy and uncertain remediation, they are not college material. It takes a lot of personal motivation to repeat high school fundamentals at a city junior college, which seems awfully like another uninspiring high school.

Potential is primarily determined by impersonal standardized tests that intend to measure individual academic ability and possession of general information in comparison to a large universe of high school seniors. While tests of college aptitude are not intelligence tests, they are so interpreted. Students are ranked statistically by such measures without reference to their prior school records. Individual characteristics such as motivation, originality, personality, special talents and aptitudes, ways and rates of learning, and even test-taking are not considered because they cannot be measured and quantified by tests.

As the questions asked by college aptitude tests anticipate the academic intelligence required in freshman and sophomore college years, when individuality has least expression, the tests are reasonably predictive of initial college success, among highest scorers particularly, who also will be most likely to qualify for the most prestigious institutions. There is lesser correlation between test results and college success for those scoring in the midrange. Most test scores are gathered about the statistical mean, and gradations in these scores have questionable significance, as do gradations in the upper quartile, though slight statistical differences are often given undeserved significance. Those scoring below the fortieth percentile are usually marked as unqualified, though cut-offs go higher and higher as the prestige of the institution rises.

While most colleges attempt a broader view of an applicant's qualities, ACT or SAT scores remain the primary measure of qualification. High school grades and class rank have some influence, but these have much less currency for graduates of inner-city high schools, where academic competition is assumed to be minimal. If all, including those who "rank out," have only been incompletely measured, it follows that college aptitude testing is overemphasized in its use as the principal determinant of college qualification. Inescapably, a distinct and inequitable bias is present in the fact that college aptitude testing ignores the vast disparities in life quality and educational environment between privileged students and those of least privilege. The advantaged come to testing with the rewards of privilege, while the disadvantaged arrive with the educational baggage of poverty and racism. As test results for both groups are combined, the competition is clearly unequal, with the disadvantaged suffering the penalty of disqualification from college and eligibility for a good life. Indeed, the argument of distinguished professors of social policy Christopher Jencks and Meredith Phillips that "lower test scores by blacks are the largest single barrier to racial equality in this country," may express a grim truth.

I believe that if all students had the benefit of more comprehensive personalized assessment than tests presently allow, the added weight of missing factors might lead to more revealing judgments of individual potential. Undoubtedly, such comprehensive assessments would be very difficult on a large scale, but I submit that the human stakes are so high that a more universal effort is clearly warranted.

To varying extents, many institutions, particularly those where admission is highly competitive, now engage in comprehensive assessment of applicants, but the applicant pool is already carefully selected, in most instances from among those with high college-aptitude scores and glittering grades, usually from highly rated high schools. But this small-scale practice doesn't eliminate the need for a reorder of presently restricted methods of determining individual college potential and the myopic classification of students on a mass scale.

American education is presently stuck on the questionable assumption that, however imperfect tests are as measures of individual potential and predictors of college competence, more comprehensive assessment seems virtually impossible given the sheer number of student applicants and the infinite variations, subjectivity, and inconsistencies of assessors. Similarly, in the common schools, it is believed that standardized tests with universal norms are more dependable than sorting through teacher observations and examples of student work that could not be readily quantified. Consequently, at both elementary and high school levels, many school districts are adopting standardized achievement tests to qualify children for grade promotion and high school graduation. Indeed, there is wide demand to discard social promotion in the common schools and to give greater legitimacy to a high school diploma, which shows evidence that graduates have actually met reasonable standards of competence. Even if implementation of such policies does not accomplish universal improvement, a greater number of high school graduates may be better prepared for the rigors of college study, which could increase the success rate at colleges like Columbia that practice open admissions.

On the other hand, the imposition of stricter standards may narrow common school education to the specific expectations of achievement tests at the expense of encouraging intellectuality and may diminish the opportunity of instruction in subjects such as the arts that do not furnish the primary academic skills emphasized in achievement tests. Without improvement in the life quality of inner-city students and the scholastic attitudes it engenders, it may even be that stricter standards may result in greater numbers dropping out (though staying in school without learning is only a cosmetic benefit). It may also be that in the endemic absence of good entry-level jobs, the greater legitimacy of a high school diploma may confer little benefit on graduates without college interest.

However, imposing higher educational expectations for promotion in the common schools and for high school graduation could result in some students gaining greater intellectual competence. But this depends on a corresponding improvement in the quality of teaching and in the learning environment. If this was satisfied—a questionable prospect—inner-city high school graduates could have improved lives and better employment opportunities, and more would be qualified for college study. Surely these are valuable goals, even if the numbers do not change dramatically.

My discussion of the subject of open admissions is in some part after the fact, in that my present view represents an amalgam of ideas developed and refined over a long time. Consistent, however, has been the fact that a liberal admissions policy is an essential property of Columbia's educational and civic mission. Certainly, the issue of open enrollment is not confined to racial and ethnic minorities. In similar life circumstances, whites are as likely to have college handicaps as anyone else, though in institutions like Columbia that serve mainly urban societies, minorities tend to be disproportionately represented among those with questionable college qualificaions. But when, as in Columbia's instance, humane response to this reality incorporates a commitment to provide college and career opportunities to minorities among all others, open admissions cannot be separated from institutional purpose.

With some reservations, many public institutions and nearly all junior colleges have historically and do currently practice various forms of open admissions, usually at legislative mandate. The practice is less common among private colleges and universities whose admission policies historically have been determined independently with less impulse to reflect democratic themes, though mostly student selectivity is without deliberate social and racial bias.

In Columbia's past, unselective enrollment was unavoidably financially expedient and without social philosophy. Only later in the mid-1960s when the college began its quest for a distinctive identity and coherent mission did we begin to view open admissions in a larger social context. While a liberal admissions policy could open Columbia to a then-untapped student market largely ignored in college recruitment, such policy would also implement my and my colleagues' intense interest in democratizing employment in the arts, communications media, and entertainment professions, which Columbia's education served. And perhaps Columbia could even influence the extension of college opportunity more generally to the traditionally excluded. Despite such intentions, however, I recognized that Columbia's marketing effort among minorities had to be confined to prospective students who had expressed interest in the college's educational specialties, as others would not be motivated or sufficiently stimulated in an alien college environment.

In any discussion of Columbia's open admissions, it is important to understand that Columbia always required high school graduation or a formal equivalent as a fixed prerequisite to admission, and that our policy was fairly and sensibly modified in instances when prospective students were obviously incapable of successful college study. In not using college test results as instruments of exclusion, but only as diagnostic evidence of educational disabilities needing remedy, Columbia's open-admission policy attempted more comprehensive assessment of students' educational and life potentials. That pre-college tests were not required for admission to Columbia reflected the fact that many of Columbia's students had not even taken the tests because they had little confidence in doing well and/or because they were late comers to the decision to attend college.

It should also be emphasized that in the 1960s and 1970s, pre-college testing did not enlist the large numbers that it now does. Among racial minorities and poor people, going to college was not a usual expectation. Indeed, colleges then, except historically African-American colleges in the South, were quite accurately viewed as preserves of the elite. In sharp contrast, Columbia was at the same time one of a small number of private colleges to have no discriminatory barriers, and was nearly singular in asserting its open-admissions character. Moreover, this policy allowed college opportunity to those aspiring to careers in the arts and communications media who previously had no college route to these occupations.

The critical determinant of college and career success is the strength of an individual's motivation to succeed despite handicaps of life's circumstances, scholastic ineptness, insufficiencies of prior education, and discouraging college aptitude scores. Such students must be receptive to a college opportunity that encourages individual achievement and does not regard them as dumb and unresponsive in order to counter the "life sentence" levied at their high school graduation. They may be victims, but they are not necessarily unable to be helped. This was the premise of Columbia's open-admissions policy.

Undoubtedly, some students left Columbia because of academic discouragement, many of these discovering that while it was comparatively easy to get in, staying in required a more serious personal commitment than they were willing or able to make. Others left because they found they lacked the talent and intensity of interest to pursue careers in Columbia's specialties. A great number left because of personal and family distractions and financial difficulties. Many simply transferred to other colleges because Columbia had given them an opportunity to prove that collegiate competency.

Present emphasis on acquiring the credential of a college diploma has obscured inquiry about what may have been learned even if studies were incomplete. I never discovered evidence that anyone was hurt by an abbreviated college experience, or that the time spent impaired job opportunity. For recent high school graduates, it's hard to imagine that even a brief college time set them back in the job market. Unless individuals were entirely indifferent and unresponsive to anything experienced in college, something beneficial is learned in even a short time. In the course of the self-studies required by accreditation, we interviewed hundreds of students who had left Columbia. We discovered, surprisingly, that most had never intended to graduate, having chosen only to acquire specific professional skills in arts or communications and entertainment media where talent is more important than a degree. In fact, most of these ex-students were perfectly satisfied with their time at Columbia and, indeed, many were as successful as those who had graduated with similar skills. Such motives are not dissimilar from the great number of adults who attend college on a part-time or limited basis, whose intent is to learn more to earn more, to qualify for new job opportunities, or simply to furnish serious life or avocation interests. Even today when a bachelor's degree is only a little more useful than a high school diploma was some years ago, the degree may be initially helpful in getting a job. Afterward, actual work history is more important.

What is overridingly redeeming about Columbia's open-admissions policy is that many students who would have been disqualified by a selective admission policy—those who had previously failed in college, and those who rejected the elitism and societal role of traditional colleges—did make it at Columbia and went on to enjoy satisfying lives and careers. I was late to recognize an important implication of Columbia's effort to simultaneously educate two student constituencies: one, the largest, already exhibiting collegiate abilities; the other with less-developed academic skills. As the college deliberately accepts the very difficult challenge of such a mix, it follows that we have to accept the inevitability of lower graduation and retention-rate statistics for the college as a whole, which could invite, albeit unwarranted, doubts about Columbia's educational quality. It is absurd, I submit, that colleges are increasingly measured by their retention-to-graduation rates without regard to the numbers of at-risk students they enroll, and as if these colleges had not performed a critical, valuable educational and social service.

I readily admit that it was my intent to discard restrictive barriers whose effect was to exclude young people who were "screwed up" and "screwed over" by a world they never made. And I did mean to create a college that included students who sought to reverse their life course and have an opportunity to discover and reinvent themselves. Columbia's policy of open admissions was never some social sentimentality, the crude exercise of which created a minimally demanding college institution for least able students or a charity ward for the educationally inept. To the contrary, Columbia's quality of instruction and level of student expectation was and is of the highest order, and all of the college's departments of study enjoy distinguished reputation in the national educational community and in the professions they represent.

Though many colleges disguise their open-admissions policies with implications of selectivity, at Columbia open admissions is practiced as a result of a conviction that individual ability is not fixed nor unaffected by the opportunity of improvement, that disabilities can be overcome if students are strongly motivated, and that everyone can be educated to enjoy economic success and intelligently contribute to the commonweal. We deliberately intended an institution that embraces diversity and a wide range of ability evidenced at entry, including those who may fall short of an arbitrary measure of college potential. Correspondingly, we believe there is great value in giving students an opportunity to learn from and about one another. We contend, too, that students with the best academic credentials do not necessarily possess wisdom, special qualities of citizenship, or practical intelligence and creativity. We believe that student diversity, which includes a full range of ethnic and class identities and prior educational differences, fosters human exchange that can give learning great vitality.

Of course, colleges like Columbia have an unusual obligation to help students to correct their scholastic deficiencies. But it must also be observed that remedial programs sponsored by colleges and by private enterprises have largely failed to achieve large-scale success. This may reflect the dictum that learning is the responsibility of the learner. It may be, though, that remedial programs that center on scholastic skills and comprehension are not being conducted in a context that enlists individual purpose and self-motivation. Peculiarly, there may be something in customary remedial curricula, in teaching methods, or in instructors' attitudes that turns students off, despite their recognition that the acquisition of academic skills is essential to success. One might imagine that such recognition would be motive enough to engage in diligent study, but apparently it is not.

While Columbia's open-admissions policy and its centrality in the college's mission was firmly in place by the early 1970s, the national and local context in which it was exercised has changed significantly in the nearly thirty years since. During Columbia's renewal, race and class discrimination largely prevailed in college admissions, and the quality of common school education in depressed and segregated communities was not a prominent local or national priority. Correspondingly, college expectations by poor people and minorities were minimal. It was only after the compelling expression of African-American militancy in the 1960s and the succeeding anti-war ferment on American campuses had fueled advocacy of democratized college opportunities, that significant numbers of previously excluded young people could have realistic college and career aspirations.

Until that time, few local private colleges and not many public institutions made any significant effort to recruit students from Chicago's inner-city high schools. It was not primarily a democratic instinct that newly prompted college recruitment of minorities, though that may have been of some influence, as much as it was the result of a growing recognition by colleges, when enrollments were falling, that African-Americans, and later Latinos, represented an untapped student market with state and federal money in their pockets. Until then and for some years after, Columbia enjoyed a comfortably noncompetitive market among minority students of high ability with career interests in Columbia's specialties.

In the last twenty-five years, however, the depressed state of Chicago's inner-city communities has significantly worsened, class separations have become more acute, and neighborhoods more isolated and universally poor. African-Americans and Latinos presently constitute more than 75 percent of Chicago's public school enrollment. Most of them live below the poverty line. Many of the schools they attend are in serious disrepair. While the quality of teaching in inner-city schools is, at best, uneven, teachers are generally an embattled lot, cynically expected to teach productively despite chronic shortages of books, teaching supplements, and school supplies,

and despite poverty and racism, which contort the lives of their students.

Whether inner-city schools are worse today than they were thirty years ago is arguable. Undoubtedly, the local economies of the schools' neighborhoods have deteriorated, resulting in hostile environments for education. Many teachers, nonetheless, perform heroically, as indeed do many students who survive and graduate from high school. Of these, a distinct but impressive minority have good college potential and even more might if colleges had more insightful admissions policies, greater patience, and remedial ingenuity in dealing with at-risk students. In general, middle-class African-American and Latino students who have the advantage of economic and social stability, supportive families, and less disordered environments have college qualification and success similar to advantaged white students.

Virtually all colleges and universities today value student diversity and compete for the most academically gifted African-American and Latino students. That democracy has finally come to American higher education is no small signal of progress. The immediate effect of this new democracy on Columbia, however, is that what was once a noncompetitive student market is now fiercely competitive, not only because of the large number of college-bound students, but because minorities now have the opportunity of a full range of career and educational choices.

Where not many years ago Columbia's nondiscriminatory and open-admissions policies and educational focus attracted significant numbers of unusually able minority students, many of these now are attracted to more prominent institutions with generous scholarships and student aid. While the number of minority students at

Columbia has remained constant (though with the college's great growth they represent a lesser percentage of the total enrollment), the academic competence of the college's minority student population is lower because the number no longer includes as many students with high academic ability. At the same time, with Columbia's growth, white students have greatly increased both in numbers and as a percentage of the total student population, and this, too, adds greater numbers of students with deficient academic skills. The result of this is that a larger number and percentage of Columbia students have academic difficulties, and many Columbia classes have to contend with an increasingly difficult polarity of student abilities. Whereas the college once viewed scholastic differences as only one among other student diversities, the present scale of academic polarity may impair the college's educative process. Moreover, scholastic remediation for the sheer numbers involved is disproportionately expensive, and despite a proliferation and intensity of remedial efforts, effective remedy remains illusive. All this may explain why Columbia's "inviolate" premise of open admissions is presently at some issue and may need some modification that will nonetheless preserve the elemental intention of open admissions.

Excerpts from the 1973 Self-Study

The following is taken from the 1973 self-study, a comprehensive expression of Columbia's state and "mind" at that time. In effect, our report was a merger of statistical data and the social and educational philosophy that guided the college's life.

Current student enrollment is 1,041. Of these, 735 attend full time and 306 are enrolled part time. With few exceptions, full-time students are engaged in study leading to the bachelor of arts degree. Eighty-four part-time students have indicated a degree intention. The remaining part-time students are enrolled from term, to term and these mainly have limited interests or have not indicated an intent. The full-time equivalent population is 841 of 1041 enrolled.

All figures exclude irregular enrollments in community extensions, children's programs, etc. There is a variable enrollment in such projects that presently approximates 200 individuals. Also, the 1972 figure does not include twenty-five students whose enrollment is part of a cooperative arrangement with the School of the Art Institute of Chicago.

Two-thirds of Columbia's numbers are men. Women are a greater proportion of the part-time than the full-time population. Twenty-two percent of Columbia's students are African-Americans. Approximately four percent have Hispanic origin. Three percent are of other origin, mainly American Indian, Asian, and near-Eastern.

Fifty percent of the regular student population attended another college before coming to Columbia. These transfer students attended 102 colleges in 28 states. Thirty-four of this number are Illinois colleges. Previous colleges attended are divided between junior/community colleges and large universities. Fifty-seven percent of transfer students attended one college previously, 25 percent two, and 18 percent three or more prior to Columbia.

The financial characteristics of Columbia students probably have greater similarity to Chicago city and suburban public colleges (most are junior) than to local private colleges. Apportionment by family income shows:

Less than $6,000 annual	20%
$6,000 to $10,000	35%
$10,000 to $13,000	20%
$13,000 to $15,000	15%
over $15,000	10%

While Columbia's tuition is lowest among private colleges in the Chicago area, it is very high compared with public city colleges. Thus, it is understandable that large numbers of Columbia students require financial aid to attend Columbia.

45 percent qualify for and receive Illinois State Scholarship Grants and/or Federal Pell Grant awards

12 percent receive veterans' benefits

13 percent receive federal loans and other loan supports

3 percent receive other social-agency supports, state, federal, and private sources

5 percent receive Columbia College scholarship and work-study subsidies

Only 22 percent of students are entirely supported in the expenses of college by themselves and/or their families.

Columbia does not use media advertising to recruit students (too expensive). The admissions staff and some faculty and students visit city and suburban high schools to talk with prospective students. But, mainly, prospects write, telephone, or visit (in about equal numbers) to inquire about enrollment. These are largely the result of considerable college publicity and word-of-mouth advertisements, a special reputation among many young people, and the college's educational specializations.

Administration of scholarships, grants, and financial aid is a critical service and a large activity of the student-services office—particularly given the large proportion of students who depend on financial assistance. While state and federal subsidies are the main source of student aid, the college itself provides currently about $100,000 in various scholarship and work-study subsidies.

Over 70 percent of students reported an average of eighteen work hours weekly while attending college, but in many instances students worked more and, not infrequently, at full-time jobs. Full summer jobs, and jobs at other recesses were important to many students. Having a job is necessary to subscribing college costs above subsidy benefits and is very often crucial in providing for living costs. As an example of such difficulties, in recent months we recorded a number of students who qualified for state and federal aid but were unable consistently to afford transportation costs (home-school-home), which average in excess of a dollar a day and can easily exceed $200 in an ordinary school year.

Every inquiry affirmed that students come to Columbia because of their interest in one or several of the college's subjects and, less particularly, because they heard or sensed for themselves that Columbia is a good place. We don't know much about where their interest came from. Usually, it had a life's work ambition about it, however indefinite. Also, and we think importantly, the student's interest often identified a good way to spend college time. Many students began with a hope that their interest would lead them to a satisfying time now and opportunity later. The interests among Columbia students were strong, often intensely so. Few students in high school, in early college or otherwise, had a serious opportunity to exercise an interest that would shape an ambition that would lead them to Columbia. Certainly, popular culture encourages artistic activity among young people, and vocational interest in this has grown. Where the arts and their careers formerly were elite and difficult, popular media arts are more accessible to audience and ambition. In fact, these suggest vocation. Photography, motion pictures, and television stand in point.

Among Columbia students, job preparation was a strong expectation of their education. This is not confined to students of least privilege; though, understandably, it is, at least initially, a more prominent guide for those who have learned the world in hard economic terms, some in racist terms, and some in both. Most of these students came from schools and milieus where a sense of their self-worth was little cultivated, and self-satisfaction rewarded less than in satisfying others. For many students, the job remains a rigid guide. But many, too, learn to add "my work" and "myself" to their job perceptions.

Students gave high value to the ability to do something well. Skills are thought secure possessions that may be used however an individual chooses. These are available to opportunity. All faculty and student-service staff agreed that students were very serious about this.

Surely, Columbia is rare among colleges having interest (however atypical) in the arts, to which students of uncertain qualification and unpossessing of social, economic, cultural, and educational advantage are freely admitted. Many Columbia students are trying themselves out. Understandably, they are fragile, hesitant, and unsure. In the report of Columbia students, there is a sense evident that Columbia is a safe place to try oneself. It doesn't look very much like a college, some say to mean it isn't a hard, unfriendly, impersonal place. Some seem comforted that "Columbia's sort of poor, like us," that "It and we are trying to get ahead." But, also, some feel (even at the same time) an inferiority about being at Columbia. "It and we are outcasts. Others won't think I've been to college, so what good will it have done?" Being accredited is very important, even among those who seem not to care. And also, we think it is important that Columbia doesn't get the look of a big winner about it, another hard place of slick surfaces. This is understood in our building plans.

Obviously, not all Columbia students are poor. But, as shown, there are large numbers who are. The many ways in which not having money affects individuals and their lives are the most common and influential student characteristics. It is the overriding reason students leave. Sometimes it is simply an inability to subscribe college costs. These are difficult even with aid and subsidy. But often it is the cost of living or the dues that poverty's culture exacts of individuals that count for more. Many students have to work an inordinate time at jobs, and the time and energy for school is too greatly lessened. Others cannot afford advanced individual projects (such as motion pictures) that have costs beyond ordinary college supports.

There is an unusual quality of liberality—in fact radical ideas—within the college community. But the expression of this ordinarily occurs in association with the city community and its political agencies. Moreover, there have been no occasions when the college itself could be fairly held to represent conditions to which a national student complaint was directed or when its students or faculty have had major contest with the college or with particulars of its practice. While life issues are one of the college's vital signs, generally, it has been reserved as a place of work and study.

In convenient terms, Columbia is a college of the arts (albeit not typical fine arts) and media studies. Its student population is not one that evidences much prior ability or definite ambition in these, nor are the college's subjects mainly those in which the student might have had large past experience. Moreover, these students do not have the class reassurances that are helpful to arts and media ambitions. Thus, a great amount of a Columbia student's enrollment is, in a sense, exploratory. At Columbia the student finds that arts and media subjects are terribly hard. There are many discouragements, and success is a doubtful promise. That many discover it's not for them, succumb to doubts, have not the energy to sacrifice for its tasks—and drop out—is not surprising. More surprising, perhaps, is the fact that so many remain.

As the largest number of the college's students begin as comparative novices, the great accomplishment of so many of them in so short a time, put against even very sophisticated and competitive measures, is legitimate evidence of dramatic progress. This is perhaps even more significant when one considers the barriers to releasing themselves to arts and media ambitions and the education required to achieve them.

In the matter of the college's effect on the student, there is a paramount assumption in Columbia's process. It is that a college (in fact, any school) is not simply a preparation for the next school grade or time after it. But more, college is an important time of life in itself which should be happy and satisfying. A self-knowing time. A time to feel worthwhile. A time when individuals can find out and enjoy what they can do and be asked to do it well.

We believe this more after we have looked at ourselves, because many students, alumni, and their parents have told us that at Columbia they got themselves together, found themselves, got confidence, straightened out, felt they could amount to something.

Columbia is not in the therapy business. It wants instead to be a place where, as our faculty colleague, dancer Shirley Mordine, said, "Students can be returned to themselves." We attend to this because we believe (not uniquely, of course) that individuals who are not wrapped in hurtful threads and binds, in fact are helped to loosen themselves from these, can live more humanely healthy lives. Such individuals will realize themselves and reach out. And they will better take in education and use it more. We see it happening.

There is a recurring theme in student interviews. It is that many have a strong sense of the college's having affected their attitudes of self-regard and their social role.

Self-confidence usually comes when individuals know they are doing a task right and well. In time students learn to know when they are doing something to their own and other's expectations. The ability to do, to know that one has some mastery of a difficult task: to write stories and poetry, to make photographs and films, to perform in plays, to dance, to weave, to print a poster, to direct a television show—to know oneself and have confirmed believably that one is doing these things well is a very important feeling. Many students have never done anything or known anything like that before. Columbia gives them the opportunity and the ability to do other things and gain a sense of how to go about it. They find out they can create. And they begin to have an instrument, a reference that helps them define themselves and through which the world can be seen.

Self-confidence, of course, is an important part of an individual's self-esteem. Columbia appears to effect this in other ways, too. How is known only inexactly. No one puts down someone else's effort. Students are willing to try what they want instead of merely meeting assignments without mistakes (an independence essential in creative artists). Perhaps, because there is only a small fear of failing marks, many students discover the alternative is that they must do well for themselves, to merit their colleagues' approval, to engage the teacher's respected professionalism, and, in many instances, to satisfy a public audience. In succeeding in these, there is self-respect.

Columbia students, at least a large number of them, learn to write much more successfully than they did when they began college. This is often evidenced by the quality of writing in published student work. Many of these students had impaired English skills at entry, giving them no expectation that they were capable of respected writing. Some students do not ever learn to write well. Many of these can do something else well that does not stress writing. Most Columbia subjects require mature reading. Reading is a cardinal requirement of some subjects, such as theater. Many students learn to read in these. Obviously, many "doing subjects" do not emphasize extensive reading assignments, but often serious reading is important to expert performance. Then, reading is tested by its usefulness. Apart from immediate utility, Columbia tries to give the student a personal reason for reading. Partly, of course, this may grow from its requirement, but lifetime reading does not often have such origins. Often the teaching of literature has been exceptional. Many students who have done little except required reading confirm that they now read extensively on their own.

Obviously, the satisfaction of this is a first measure of a college's effect on the student. While there are many reasons students come to Columbia, they come mainly because it advertises subjects related to arts and media occupations that appeal to them. Thus, Columbia's education is in large part specific to the student's life's-work ambitions, though these may be only vaguely perceived.

Most Columbia students take subjects in a number of arts other than those on which they concentrate. The arts, of course, have a common aesthetic, and there are similarities among their practices. We considered employment to be related to the alumnus' educational preparation, irrespective of emphasis, when a job was related to Columbia's subjects. Most graduates reported that their jobs involved elements of several arts and media expressions and that their success on the job (and in many instances their success at getting it) was related to their versatility. Such value of a Columbia graduate is confirmed by many employers. We have had many confirmations of the benefits of a school of many arts and media subjects among which students may freely choose, as compared with conservatories that are confined to single specialties and with those university arts and media departments that have little relation with one another and largely restrict the student to a department's interest.

Columbia students do not have majors in the usual sense. They often heavily emphasize particular subjects. Whether this is because the college experience of these is more satisfying or this represents definite occupational choice or expectation is not known. Actually, while students do tend strongly to seek and work at jobs that follow their largest college interests, this is not a uniform pattern. Part of this has to do with job opportunities. But, also, this suggests that students view the education-job relation differently. Columbia allows students the opportunity of educating themselves as generally or as specifically as they choose.

The practical nature of the curriculum has a major effect on students. They feel that they are not merely in school, but that their work at Columbia is realistic preparation for, indeed is actually a part of, their anticipated lives. This attitude is variously true of the whole college. The result of this stress on doing leads to the realiza-tion that a student is not merely learning about subjects but is actually doing them. Students often express the idea that going to Columbia is like a job—you go to do something to get the skills to go someplace else to use them. The influential aspect of this is the students' realization that the skills learned and the skills used are the same, and that these are learned in conditions approximating those in the professional world.

Professional quality was cited by students in their interviews. The basic feeling is that because of the established professional-artistic ability of the instructors, students are imbued with a sense of excellence and the importance of quality in their work. This has significant implications for students' attitude toward their own work. Students gain standards of comparison reinforced by respect for the faculty member's stature in a nonschool community, and thereby assimilate an appreciably high level of quality as a minimal standard for schoolwork. Students are also aware that those who do well in the eyes of these teachers have, sometimes, an important helper in finding work in their field after college. This, too, functions to reinforce the sense of apprenticeship in the students and, indeed, in at least one case (the Cameraman's Union Scholarship), a student's final year was given union credit as an apprenticeship year. In actuality, Columbia students have jobs in remarkable numbers, particularly when one considers what occupations they aspired and educated themselves to. Most of them do very well. Much more so, indeed, than many believed they would when they came to Columbia. A successful occupational consequence to its education is a prime matter of Columbia's purpose. It is a purpose, we believe, impressively served by the record of graduate and other student employment in jobs for which their education was a practical preparation.

Measures of students' improvement are meant to help the college guide them, to give students a self-guide, and to inspire them to go ahead. Measures are not used to purify the ranks and keep survivors on their toes. The scares of failure do not have a large presence at Columbia. In fact, students may fail at a particular subject without cruel result. It signals that they must try again or go on to something else instead. They can even abandon the grade. It appears that a lessening of the oppressive quality of failure and noncompetitiveness is the most basic of the college's effects that lets students know that they are working for themselves and that they may try themselves out without risking severe penalty. In effect, the student has time and opportunity and is without nervous pressures to achieve.

Students who have earned a bachelor's degree obtain a diploma that verifies their completion of its requirements. The diploma does not certify that the graduate is a photographer, an actor, a writer, a television director, or whatever. Such identity is in the show of their art and of themselves at what they will do. Most Columbia students have a main interest. Ordinarily, this has an occupational relation. But the college's education intends much more than a narrow job preparation, and it does not mean to qualify or screen students for an industry. All degrees rank the same. Graduates differ at the finish as they did at the start, but they do not finish in their starting order. Students are openly admitted to the college, and they are not held to an elite measure to graduate. None's benefit or ability is lessened by comparison with another's. Columbia's largest benefit to a student may have been a specific or an aggregate of influences. Five courses in a subject may be good for a student and five more not necessarily better. As giving students an opportunity to find themselves is important to the college, and as this cannot be scheduled, students are not held to any fixed number of subjects. They may try themselves and be as uncommitted as they choose to the end of their time as students. Those who change their minds are not made to fulfill a new major to graduate. Surely, their education need not end at commencement.

The more ordinary students, i.e., those among the majority who have educational and other handicaps (in which sense the Columbia student is representative) often attend colleges where general education is a miscellany of area-survey requirements—a largely impersonal experience in large, often indifferently taught classes, whose benefit to students (apart from getting them past a requirement) and relation to individual purpose (or enlistment of it) are hardly known at all, an estimate widely confirmed by college students generally and explicitly by Columbia students coming from other colleges.

What is cardinal to the student's want is the need to feel strongly, to know because knowing makes one feel better and better able to cope, to feel more alive, more active, and more part of life, to be known individually, to have one's voice, one's perceptions valued and respected. And, necessarily, this personal, affective relevance is the prior need of the learner that must be satisfied if the abstraction of deferred relevance is not to be a barrier to education.

Particularly, because the old answers are in disrepair, the fundamental question renews. To what purpose do we educate? Broadly, still, of course, to abet the survival, self-realization, and socialization of the individual. What is difficult is deciding what information, quality of experience, and emphasis is appropriate to the needs of contemporary and succeeding individuals. What do our individuals need to know and experience for healthy survival and humanity? What study will help them relieve inhibitions to their self-realization and socialization?

More than anything else, Columbia is an assembly of talented teachers. It is a faculty whose members are impressively qualified artists, scholars, and professionals. Many have leading reputation. All work at what they teach. The result is a classroom with the real world in it.

The college makes scholarly demand of its faculty but holds significant concern for the human relation, the rapport between student and teacher. It believes that this human connection is the source of inspiration. The genuinely good teacher has special gifts of human quality. Columbia has sought the gifted human being as a teacher, a person having genuine accomplishment in an art, occupation, or scholarship.

Finally when we had finished with the data of our self-perception, had found and sifted and weighed it, strung it together and given importances, we came back again to the omnipresent fact that the special human being, the magic-maker as teacher, paled the importance of all other educational influences, however ingenious.

And so we knew again that the space we occupy, our buildings, our fiscal systems, our plans and schemes, our instruments, our curricula, and the order of our education were all comparatively small parts of what our college is and ought to be. For what we are is a place where students can come together with gifted individuals called teachers, among whom are some who have a magic that lets them affect other people significantly.

It changes student lives more than anything else that happens at schools. Not simply psychological changes (though these are not of small consequence), but the changes in individuals that occur because education (the knowledge, the skills, the new world learned about) really works for them. They are opened up. They take in. They search for more and take in more. And so they have much more to do with. Their lives are improved.

Others learn to do something or learn about something that gives them strength, confidence, and joy, and afterwards they are able to go on with it and to other things. Students who have had this happen to them remember that it began with a teacher.

While it is generally agreed that the teacher and the students are the main stuff of the educative process, respect for the importance of the teacher is often lessened by emphasis on curriculum, method, physical surrounding, etc. Perhaps this is because the teacher-student relationship is subtle, individual, and hard to identify, whereas the other substances, being more precisely known, are more comfortably handled. As it is also hard to weigh the magic spells woven between good teachers and their students, credentials and grades for other things are often wrongly used to determine who the magic-makers are.

None of this says much that is really new. So why do we say it? We do so because a renewed appreciation of the teacher's importance is an outcome, perhaps most cardinal, of our effort to investigate our present state and project ourselves to the time ahead. Columbia has a high proportion of unique, talented individuals as its teachers. It means more now to assemble a faculty, certainly among new additions and particularly in liberal education, who possess special qualities that can more dependably put students in vital motion. And so it becomes important to us to know better what are the constituents—of personality and intelligence—of those individuals who have a quality of magic-making about their teaching. In asking this and trying answers, we know that no precise, predictive catalog of such qualities can be obtained. But some impressions were confirmed.

There needs to be an evident human optimism (impressively so). A quality of loving and caring about students as individuals and the value of life generally. A passion about one's subject, an enjoyment that beckons the student to feel and know as he does, or who says, "Know and feel this, and the bigger mystery may be revealed." In opening up the student, the teacher's digressions are often as important as central expositions. Lively, knowledgeable, desirably intense interest in many things, most significantly in the arts. Dramatic, animated, humorous. These are appropriate identities.

Undergraduate education is largely begun in a classroom. Thus, the excitement made there is usually critical. Moreover, given that students have had in television and in the shrillness of their lives a staggering dramatic experience, they could hardly be expected to respond to individuals or situations that have an absence of strong dramatic quality. A teacher needs to be genuinely wise about life. Or, indeed, very innocent; an innocence so without guile that students feel protective and affectionate.

In short, the magic in teachers is probably largely a matter of the special quality of their personalities, and teachers ought to be sought who possess it. A college seriously needs to have, in a prominent role in teacher selection, some self-secure persons who have a high appreciation of these qualities of personality and intelligence, and some good intuition about recognizing them. (Columbia has this.)

Excerpts from the Accreditation Report

Columbia College cannot be approached with the traditional assumptions or measured by the usual standards. With the exception of one building, it owns no plant. Its spaces are rented and scattered around Chicago, and to ask about maintenance—some of the buildings are in bad shape—is less pertinent than to ask how people relate to each other in these spaces—there being no administration building, no classroom building, and no student union, people work together in a fluid community relatively free of the usual hierarchies. Just as there is no one place that is the college, there is hardly a sharply defined student body. Some students are part-time and some are full-time, and a jazz band at the music center will be only partly Columbia College students and partly high school students or post-college-age people from the neighborhood, and to ask about student profiles is less pertinent than to ask what is learned in this unusual mix. Clearly, a great deal is, both subject matter and, beyond that, the intangibles all liberal-arts colleges aim for. Again, Columbia College does not teach primarily through the printed word or lectures, but visually, tactilely, and audio-orally, all reinforcing each other. It therefore becomes less pertinent to ask about the library—it actually is more than adequate—than whether these ways of teaching really do supplement each other. They do.

The visiting team therefore found itself needing new approaches. It built its visit primarily upon a great many interviews with students, staff, faculty, and trustees. While we did everything possible to give a sense of ease and informality, we framed the questions carefully and reviewed findings as a whole team.

The commission and the committee by type will be helped by the team's assurance that Columbia College's Self-study is a most reliable picture of the college. There may be a great deal of philosophy in it, but Columbia College is held together around a solid philosophy. There are no factual inaccuracies in the Self-study, or in other data submitted, and no pretense. What the college claims to have accomplished, it has. Neither is there false humility; the problems frankly recognized in Self-study are really there.

As far as ability is concerned, the students who attend Columbia College are a typical cross-section of American college students. As far as motivation is concerned, they appear to be more serious and involved. They have a sophistication that comes from living in the city, but they are open to new ideas, people, and places. Of the 334 transfer students who enrolled this fall, only fifteen came with averages below a two-point in their previous colleges. Clearly, the college is a place that attracts not failures so much as those who come seeking the unusual curriculum and teaching it offers. They come to Columbia knowing what they want, and they find it. Many have found their high school and other college experiences disappointing. They have been impatient with education that was largely a matter of acquiring heterogeneous information, most of which spoke little to their curiosities and interests, and much of which could only be acquired via the passive activities of reading and listening to lectures. At Columbia they find—many for the first time—a happy blend of the connotative, the cognitive, and the affective. They immediately begin doing what interests them, and in the doing they begin to acquire the skills they seek, and to conceptualize from their experiences.

"You don't have to do the technical stuff very long before you realize you need a vision."

"No one can write without contemplating."

"The textbooks for my course were sold out the first day. Many of my students have not read much, but they have had real-life experiences. They are in the middle of things. From these things have developed curiosities. They are a joy to teach."

"Here I'm treated like an adult and encouraged to do what I can as well as possible. There's plenty of help – if I want it. If I blow it, that's my choice."

"We are graded on how much we have grown; not on how we compare with others."

"Expectations are high, and we work hard, but not against one another."

"I'm exhausted when I leave here."

Fostering maximum individual development rings out as a goal throughout the institution. It is accomplished by treating every student as an individual and helping them be what they are. "I was always different; I had different thoughts and always spoke them—at school and at home. People never understood me. I began to think I was a freak. But here it is different. I'm accepted. I know more people. They have a publication, and they tell me a couple of my pieces may be in it . . . yeah, I have less depressing days than I used to." Clearly, such students are learning to engage their full powers, to reach out, to discover their own voices, to respect themselves, all of which are goals of the college. And these observations are the rule rather than the exception.

As has been suggested, students begin with experiencing, go on to a new level of awareness, then to understanding, and finally to integrating and behaving in new ways. In this process there is much interaction in and out of class and a great deal of immediate feedback. Reading comes second and yields concepts to add to the students' own as they go through the stages of understanding and integrating. That the learning opportunities so well match the developmental needs and patterns of these students is indeed remarkable. *While there is good reason to believe that a sizable segment of the population learns better by doing than by reading and through oral expression rather than by writing, Columbia is one of the rare colleges that has been truly willing to recognize the needs of such people and honor them as students.*

Students readily articulate the view that public arts are for all the people; not for an elite few. "Art is about people and for people—not for a special segment." "The media are for the public, and it is for us to bring the best we can to the media—to inform the people, or to bring about changes or to lift the spirit and bring joy and awareness." These are the feelings echoed by many.

Students learn from practicing artists, newspaper writers, TV professionals, and composers, as well as others involved in professional careers. There are few colleges where students can learn from the managing editor of the best-known black daily newspaper in the world, or from a woman deeply involved in the women's liberation movement in Chicago, or a vice president of a management consultant firm. At Columbia the students can. And they learn something also about the world from these persons who are a part of it. "I've got a talent but no tools. I come here to get the tools so I can share the treasures of the street and help other cats who dropped out after the fourth grade like me know that they can do it. I attend two classes and haven't missed a meeting yet. They're good. I don't spend no more time here than that."

Many factors contribute to the learning atmosphere:

In addition to being competent and vital, teachers care about students and spend a good deal of time with them during and after classes. "Even the part-time teachers give you their home and business numbers."

Teachers treat students as "dignified individuals," as one student put it. They are accepting, and students are not afraid to express themselves or to fail; "You can try again."

Teachers try to relate the subject matter to student interests and concerns when making assignments. They build on their students' curiosities.

There is much interaction between students and between students and teachers. Many teachers give immediate feedback during class and immediately after, both in the classrooms and in the hallways and lounges.

The college recognizes that students can be liberated through areas in which they have interests as well as (perhaps better than) through exposure to standard courses in the traditional fields.

A prevailing attitude among students is: If you are interested, you do it and people are here to help. Our observations revealed help with a full sense of commitment.

There is much group effort. Students count on and learn to cooperate with one another.

It is a classless place; there are varied ages, experiences, and races. People accept the individual and relate to one another accordingly. "The place is very friendly. There is sort of a brotherhood in creativity. There are no bored people here; people are happy. We come from common backgrounds in that we all were fed up with our past education."

Many students indicated that the college really does encourage them to follow their own ways, but in the process to come out a better person. They feel that mediocrity is frowned upon; there is a strong feeling that "you have to give your full effort to get a full return."

Whereas some students enroll at Columbia to learn such vocational or professional skills as photography, journalism, radio announcing, or television production, the performing arts have a somewhat different appeal. The three separate centers for dance, music, and theater are community centers as well as arts centers. Programs for children and adults, in classes and in production, mix people from the larger Chicago community with Columbia students. While performance is very important in these centers, the processes of teaching and learning are even more so, as are assumptions made about students and their capabilities. Students aren't excluded from dance because they don't have "dancers' bodies" or many years of dance training behind them. They speak with considerable distaste about "elitist dance" and "arty" dance. Students have made serious efforts to discover how they can use "movement" to help people in the immediate neighborhood understand themselves. The striking thing about this is that the study of dance takes on components of liberal arts. A student who had become very much involved with social action through dance described how she had come to understand the relationship of art to society better in the experience than in any formal course she had ever taken.

A component of liberal arts is equally evident in the program of the Music Center, which focuses on the performance of rock operas. The director of the program uses Euripides, Brecht, Aesop, and contemporary social issues as texts for the operas, and the students are expected to study the originals carefully. One recent graduate composed a cantata made up of several Brecht poems and in the process read all of Brecht's poems and lyrics. And, as in dance, students in the music program need not come to Columbia with "a voice," with musical expertise or experience, or even knowing how to read notes. Through a series of brilliantly conceived and executed exercises, students learn how to improvise vocally and instrumentally, how to improvise lyrics to tones, how to compose and then how to theorize or analyze. The productions at the Music Center utilize visual projections, movement, amplified and traditional instruments, and large numbers of performers from the college and from the Chicago area.

The members of the board are clearly dedicated to the welfare of Columbia College and to preserving its unique qualities.

Columbia College functions with remarkably little central administration—both in the sense that it uses for its entire operation no more people than might be found in an admissions office in many other colleges of 1,000 students. On second thought, however, Columbia is doing as much with a half dozen administrators as many colleges manage to accomplish with three or four times that many, so it can hardly be charged with inefficiency, and what we are really talking about is style, our stance toward the people we work with. Colleges that run tight ships generally imply by their style that people work for the administration. Columbia's style says that the administration works for the faculty and students, and Columbia would not want it changed.

Until very recently, at least, the president's role has been less to interpret the institution to the public than to personify for students and faculty (never to preach, apparently) the ethos, the marrow-of-the-bone assumption about society and people and how they learn what makes the college what it is.

In spite of its spareness, the administration gets things done—partly because everyone on it puts in a good deal of time. The college is open from about eight in the morning until ten at night—as busy after supper as before—and administrators don't go home at five. They don't think of staying on as "overtime," however. It is just their way of doing things, unconsciously in harmony with a younger generation whose diurnal cycles really come to life late in the afternoon.

Columbia's faculty are professionals in the sense that they practice what they profess. Professional competence and a driving desire to develop it in others are the chief requirements for membership in the faculty, and this is one reason the majority are part-time. It should be noted, however, that at Columbia part-time does not mean "on campus only to teach." Students again and again attested to the availability of part-time faculty. Indeed, most did not know who was part-time and who was full-time, being unaware, until asked, of the distinction.

The Southeast Chicago Historical Project

While Columbia's labor education venture was unsuccessful in measures of student numbers, it unexpectedly gave life to "The Southeast Chicago Historical Project," a novel enterprise of far greater magnitude than anything we had imagined for labor education. The project began in a gloomy conversation I had in a South Chicago saloon with Paul Johnson and Ed Sadlowski. It was obvious to us that with the irreversible loss of jobs and union membership in the steel industry and a corresponding deterioration of Southeast Chicago's neighborhoods and economy, labor education would have no priority in the United Steel Workers Union or likelihood of attracting serious interest among its members. We agreed that what was far more compelling than a parochial interest in labor education was the grim actuality that Southeast Chicago's whole way of life was ending without historical record and with little effort to bring together the district's disparate memberships to confront the dissolution of their lives, jobs, and communities.

Historically, Southeast Chicago existed like a distant colony of a powerful nation. Politically exploited, people were foreign and unseen, their fates decided by alien managers. Throughout the twentieth century, the steel mills had shaped the life of Southeast Chicago. One hundred thousand people were bound to the pulse and requisites of Big Steel's work places. Hard times of strikes and layoffs, everything was made to fit work-shift schedules. A kaleidoscope of ethnic groups, Southeast Chicago has been for generations a big company-town isolated from metropolitan Chicago. The Chicago Skyway looks down through a smoky haze at a vast mosaic of giant industrial shapes and smokestacks, acres of discarded, rubbled company land, massive grain elevators, railroad yards, and great networks of pipelines and high voltage towers. Up close you can see scattered, crowded neighborhoods of frame houses with names like "Slag Valley," "Irondale," and "Millgate," a worn-out central business district, and ubiquitous churches and saloons.

Our discussion gave rise to the notion of engaging the residents of Southeast Chicago in a big-scale effort to recover the histories of their families, neighborhoods, and union locals; and in the process, to renew community pride, identity, and sense of fraternity. What we projected was not a typical scholarly study, which ordinarily holds no benefit for those used as grist for academic mills. Nor did we intend an inquiry in which a community is scoped and probed by outside experts whose findings get brief media attention or burial in esoteric journals. We wanted instead to organize the community's people to study and reveal themselves, recover their traditions, and improve their lives. "Make no small plans," Burnham said.

In October of 1979, I wrote a proposal to the National Endowment for the Humanities (NEH) seeking a $25,000 grant to plan and organize the project. I asked the Illinois Humanities Council for an additional $10,000, and cautioned both agencies to expect much bigger hits if we developed a viable and dependable plan.

I scurried the Washington corridors of the NEH, selling the proposition to officials. Though the project's ultimate ambitions must have sorely strained their credulity, they bought the package.

The project's focus on Southeast Chicago invoked many contradictions. Without precedents or proven guides and with limited staff, few, even among friendly colleagues, believed we'd be able to organize large-scale community and individual participation, given the customary difficulty of energizing large numbers of people and the great ethnic and cultural diversity and neighborhood separations of Southeast Chicago. And undoubtedly, it would take years and the involvement of powerful economic and political interests to renew the district, even if the strong fraternity of citizens the project vaguely envisioned actually happened.

In contrast, it was also possible that some perceived handicaps might function as strengths. This was confirmed during the first weeks of formal planning. It became evident that the district's life was already highly structured and articulated around ethnic, racial, cultural, religious, neighborhood, labor, and family identities. While organizing and energizing these affinities would still be formidable, having to create them would not, as expected, be the project's biggest challenge.

The project's plan and organizational design was shaped by a committee of community representatives, academics, and Columbia faculty and staff. There was a remarkable amalgam of creative talents, organizing skills, political insights, socially engaged scholarship, artistic abilities, and enthusiastic commitment that contributed to the project's idea.

I appointed Jim Martin, a member of Columbia's film faculty and experienced urban documentary filmmaker and photographer, as the project's director. The committee's community representatives included James Fitzgibbons, a retired U.S. Steel supervisor and an Irish old-timer, who was the chronicler of the history of the "East Side," one of the district's four main communities; Michael Pavich, a Chicago policeman for twenty-seven years, then the director of the South Chicago Chamber of Commerce, who was part of an extended Serbian family and a leading parishioner of St. Michael's Serbian Church; George Stranich, president of Steel Workers Local 5201; John Chico, president of Local 65; Rita Hernandez, a bilingual high school teacher; Esther Turner, a community-based social worker; and Ed Sadlowski. Also, though he had no direct participation, as alderman of Chicago's tenth ward, Edward Vrdolyak's cooperation was essential to the project's life.

The committee's academic contingent included the project's demographer, Dr. Betty Balanoff, a professor of history at Roosevelt University and director of an oral history project which studied labor and immigration issues; Dr. Howard Becker, professor of sociology at Northwestern University, whose research emphasized photography as a social document; social psychologist Tom Cottle, who had directed a major study of the psychological effect of unemployment on children and families; Dr. Mark Friedberger, director of the Newberry Library's Center for Community and Social History; Dr. Sol Tax, a social anthropologist and authority on community research; and as the Planning Committee's chairman, Dr. William Kornblum, chairman of the Graduate Department of Sociology, City University of New York and the author of *The Blue Collar Community*, a classic seven-year study of Southeast Chicago. My Columbia colleagues were Paul Johnson, the project's co-founder; Dr. Amy Horton, the director of Columbia's community extensions, whose experience at the Highlander Folk School and with many other community organizations was invaluable to the project; and Judy McLaughlin Gall, the director of Columbia's Southern Regional Culture Center in Chicago's Uptown community.

The obvious emphasis of the planning committee's work was to design ways to generate and organize large-scale community and individual participation in the project. While this was an easy recognition, implementing it would be very difficult. Had this been conventional research, its organization, personnel, and perceptions of its ultimate utility would be superimposed on the community to be studied and its members would have no role except as respondents to inquiry.

The Southeast Chicago project had first to effectively publicize its intent, then enlist and organize many of the district's people in a unique effort to study and renew themselves. Indeed, we had to convince a lot of folks that doing it would be genuinely worthwhile and personally rewarding. Moreover, we were asking them to join in an unfamiliar collective enterprise, despite the fact that the lives of most were traditionally separated into ethnic, religious, racial, family, and fraternal associations, and joined only in the workplace, union halls, and neighborhood schools.

Disquieting also was the committee's recognition that while the planning process might be privately regarded as a separate and uncertain precursor to the project itself, once we had begun to organize it, recruit participants, and stir up the community, we were committed inescapably to go the project's whole course, with no proof that the National Endowment for the Humanities would fund the project's final design.

It followed that mobilization of the college's resources and enlistment of student, faculty, and departmental participation was the reason for the project, however motivating its social purpose. It was widely publicized within the college and discussed in many classrooms and faculty meetings. As in initial organizing efforts in Southeast Chicago, such preliminaries within the college had to assume similarly that the project would be fully funded and actually happen. Again, there was no turning back.

In Jim Martin's regular sessions with department chairs and faculty, it was agreed that Columbia faculty and students would be responsible for the project's training workshops and for the continuing counsel of neighborhood historians. This commitment, however, only involved faculty expert in workshop specialties. Enlistment of greater faculty and student numbers could only be expected as the project developed and when its opportunities became more evident.

Realistically, it was enough that the faculty recognized the project as an exceptional opportunity for theater, music, dance, art, and media students to become involved in the study of the community's ethnic arts and cultural survival, and in helping the community express and exhibit its artistic traditions. Indeed, the college's engagement with Southeast Chicago was viewed as offering students and faculty a chance to exercise the greatest range of scholarly, professional, and liberal education interests and offered a wealth of individual study and creative options, within the context of a unique educational, social, and cultural experiment. Among many evidences of the project's appeal, more than three hundred students came to the first public orientation session, and a great number volunteered for project assignments, even before they had been charted.

With confidence undaunted, the committee plunged ahead, leaving me and my intimates, Paul Johnson and Jim Martin, to our private reservations. Despite these, the community's response to the project's initial publicity was astonishing, and the pieces of the committee's organizational plan fell easily in place, though we had only NEH's $25,000 planning grant and the college's contributed service to spend on the project's preliminaries. Nonetheless, an extraordinary amount and quality of work got done in a short time.

With so many unknowns, the committee sensibly expressed the project's public goals in modest terms. These were to give the district's people the tools and techniques to act as historians of their own past; to organize and counsel this inquiry; to create opportunity for sharing the richness of the community's ethnic and cultural diversity; to provide active, accessible archives of historical materials; and to use film, video, photography, audio recording, and narrative to document the project's events and process.

The committee identified the workplace, neighborhoods, community organizations, ethnic ties, and the family as the main agencies of Southeast Chicago's life and history. In organizational terms, the project's work would focus on the district's neighborhoods and community organizations. Southeast Chicago had four traditional subdivisions: South Chicago, East Side, South Deering, and Hegewisch, and these incorporated sixteen distinct neighborhoods. "Community organizations" included trade unions (principally the Steel Workers), political, religious, fraternal, and business organizations, social and recreational agencies, libraries, and public and parochial schools.

A key component of the committee's plan was to organize a comprehensive training program to give the project's many volunteers an opportunity to get the skills and information necessary to perform their historical inquiries. Everyone would be expected to participate in a five-session workshop, which would explore the project's ideas and the use of photographs, oral histories, and personal narrative as historical documentation. All participants would be trained in interviewing techniques and in the use of tape recorders and other audio-visual equipment.

Depending on individual interest, participants would have the opportunity to educate themselves in union history, photographic and film-video techniques, narrative writing, oral history methods, and archival records. Workshops in these subjects would be offered at various locations within the district and repeated as often as new members joined the project. Additionally, project staff and consultants would be regularly available to counsel individual's work and what was being produced in neighborhood and organizational settings. An important implementation of the project would be its active presence in the district's schools and libraries. Work with Southeast Chicago schools would be a primary focus of the project's coordinators and consultants.

While the raw ideas of a community-inspired history of Southeast Chicago enjoyed the district's interest, getting individuals to make a personal commitment to the actual work of the project often required a one-on-one effort and the persuasion of an experienced hands-on community historian. It was evident that such an expert at what was then a comparatively rare academic specialty had to be added to the project's organizing staff. We found an ideal person in Dr. Dominic Pacyga who was appointed as the project's assistant director. A skilled grass-roots scholar, persuasive interpreter, workshop organizer, and counsel to family and neighborhood "historians," Pacyga has since earned first rank distinction as an American historian and scholar of urban life and metropolitan communities. He remains today a much-honored member of Columbia's faculty.

In the course of the project's planning, which spanned nearly five months, Jim Martin, Bill Kornblum, Ed Sadlowski, Dominic Pacyga, and their planning committee colleagues met with more than one thousand people individually and in small groups, to organize the project's participation and to solicit community views. The *Daily Calumet*, with a regional circulation of 100,000 readers, gave a weekly page of the newspaper to project news, events, and announcements, a regular column by Jim Martin, and a feature story about a community old-timer. The Container Corporation of America's celebrated designers volunteered a series of brilliant posters and graphics to advertise the project.

At an early meeting of the planning committee, all had agreed that if the project expected community participation and sustained enthusiasm, first priority had to be given to developing forums and routes of expression that genuinely evidenced a careful and timely effort to keep the community well informed about the project and its sincere intent to incorporate community views and local leadership. Only in this way would the community gain confidence that the history of Southeast Chicago was a community possession. At the end of the second month of the planning effort, Martin and his colleagues made their first report to the district's community at a meeting in a union auditorium. More than four hundred local people representing seventy community and recently formed project committees attended.

The meeting was a remarkable expression of community fraternity and common purpose. Everyone spoke and the hall was full of ideas and the vitalities of earnest discussion. Everyone insisted that the district's diversity had to be included and that the project's leadership had to be representative of that diversity. Consistent with these themes, the meeting elected an African-American minister, Reverend Gary Osburn, as the chairman of the community council that would guide the project's implementation. Also, the meeting elected, among others, an African-American woman, Esther Turner; Ambino Vasquez, a retired steelworker; and Carlos Toralero, a high school teacher. This was no small signal of the project's democratic influence in a district that had traditionally brokered power on the basis of familiar white ethnic identities.

The meeting's most valuable reward came with the attendance of several NEH officials who shared the meeting's enthusiasms and later told me that they would strongly recommend the agency's funding of the project when its planning was completed. What a relieving endorsement that was.

In June of 1980, we submitted a comprehensive proposal to the NEH that budgeted a two-year engagement with the caveat that if the plan was performed successfully the project's potential could not be realized in the two-year span. This was in anticipation of submitting a succeeding proposal. When the project's planning was begun, among other underestimations, we had not contemplated the project's ultimate scale or the complexity of its structure and personnel requirements.

Reflecting the scholarly talent and creative organizing skills recruited to the planning process, the proposal identified a wealth of subjects and methods that would be part of the project. It also described an inventive plan for mobilizing, training, and sustaining community participation and detailed myriad project activities. These included neighborhood and district fairs, festivals, exhibits, involvement of local schools, social events, performances, archival collections, and a summary feature-length documentary film that would represent the district's history and the work of the project.

The proposal projected a total cost of $352,000 to be subscribed by an NEH grant of $192,000, $120,000 in Columbia services, and $40,000 in anticipated project revenues.

While in preparing the budget we consulted closely with NEH program officers and reasonably expected their support, as Yogi said, "It ain't over 'til it's over." But it was quickly done. The NEH said yes. The Southeast Chicago Historical project was in business. The good news made the front page of the *Daily Calumet* and got prominent mention in the metropolitan press.

The first implementation was to rent space in Southeast Chicago's central business district for the project's headquarters. This included a suite of offices, meeting rooms, exhibit and work spaces, and a place to catalog and store historical records. Though most of the project's staff had been identified during the project's planning, their actual engagement had been deferred until funding was assured.

Without official signal, historical inquiry had already begun in the district's neighborhoods and union locals and schools. Training workshops were ready to go, needing only locations and starting dates. When these were announced, more than three hundred neighborhood and union people quickly filled the project's initial training workshops and new sections had to be organized.

While the basic workshop subject, "Oral and Community History," enrolled the largest numbers and usually followed a five-session pattern, many of the individuals enrolled in "Union History," "Photography," "Film/Video," "Writing," and "Archives" wanted to go beyond fundamentals, and undoubtedly many wanted to extend the camaraderie enjoyed in their "classrooms." To satisfy this interest, advanced classes in workshop subjects were also offered, some even continuing informally for the whole of the project's life. Many students in these became quite expert in the work of their subjects and were among the project's most valuable cadres. As example, writing workshops had a continuing life and unusually serious students. With the inspiration of Paul Rubenstein, novelist, screenwriter, and Columbia faculty member, the writing workshops published an anthology of original narratives, poems, letters, diaries, stories, and articles authored by workshop members and other project respondents.

Enrollment in "Film/Video" workshops was comparatively small and instruction confined to elementary film and video skills by equipment limitations and the five-session format. Despite this handicap, many "Film/Video" workshop participants were invaluable in creating a filmed record of the project's life and events, and as "foot soldiers" in more sophisticated filmmaking.

Those who volunteered for "archival" workshops had a busy engagement that prevailed over the life of the project and even beyond. Together with expert consultants, project staff, and Columbia faculty and students, "community archivists" were closely involved in every project activity. Literally everything, every piece of paper, every collection of photographs, narratives, and oral histories that exhibited or recorded the district's history had to be identified, sorted, preserved, and cataloged. Creating a comprehensive historical archive was a difficult task, particularly because we had utterly underestimated the sheer quantity of historical evidence that would be generated.

Steel was the *raison d'être* of Southeast Chicago, and the district's labor and industrial history was a central theme of the project, and appropriately, the Steel Workers Union a main project concentration. While gathering oral histories and personal documents was a main emphasis, unlike other project subjects, the union's effort had the benefit of a wealth of accessible materials—books, articles, studies, and records to document Southeast Chicago's often dramatic industrial and labor history.

It is impossible in the limited space of this narrative to detail the project's activity over the first two years (Phase I) of its formal and funded four-year life span. There were thirty-five regularly functioning history committees and a number of related ad hoc organizations in Southeast Chicago neighborhoods, trade union locals, cultural and fraternal organizations, and local schools. While numbers are inexact, the best estimate is that more than 2,000 community individuals were continuously active in the project and that 20,000 participated in various ways within families, neighborhoods, labor, fraternal, and commercial organizations and in project events and school settings. Understandably, given the project's historical theme, the greatest number of participants were older adults, though a wide range of ages were well represented. More than 2,000 community people enrolled in training workshops, and many individuals in more than one.

Photography was a main instrument of the project's inquiry, a rich source of the district's historical record and an important incorporation of the project's permanent archives. Indeed, the project was awash in photographs. Virtually everyone had an album of family photographs, and every agency of the community's life was similarly documented. Five thousand photographs and 3,000 slides were selected for the project's archival collection from thousands submitted and retained by individuals and local history committees. Additionally, 3,000 contemporary photographs, 1,000 slides, and more than fifty hours of documentary film and video footage of the district's life were produced by Columbia students and faculty.

The whole history of Southeast Chicago was recorded in thousands of hours of individual oral histories. The most historically significant of these were reserved for the project's permanent archives, but the greatest number were incorporated in family and neighborhood histories. Many of these personal reminiscences were the only records of important events in the district's history, and in some instances, like the labor strife of the 1930s, were important documents of American history.

At Dr. Sol Tax's design and with the support of the Illinois Humanities Council, neighborhood and district festivals were a prominent part of the project's life. In addition to annual district-wide festivals, each of the four principal neighborhood divisions—South Chicago, South Deering, the East Side, and Hegewisch—had annual festivals, too, which included exhibits of family photographs, all sorts of local records, music, dance, folk arts, and an endless variety of ethnic foods. Remarkably intergenerational, festival audiences were literally in the thousands.

In addition to the project's weekly page in the *Daily Calumet*, the newspaper published the project's record of Southeast Chicago's history in a special forty-page edition issued to celebrate the *Daily Calumet*'s one-hundred-year anniversary. This special history edition went to every home in Southeast Chicago and was distributed to all the children in local schools. This served for years as the textbook for study of the district's history.

A large part of the project's sustained success was its faithful observance of the need for community control and possession of the district's history. The main instrument of this was the project's Community Council, which included representatives of the United Steel Workers, neighborhood divisions, fraternal, church, and business organizations, local schools, and community citizens. The council met every three months with the project's leading staff and various consultants, and a record of meetings was circulated to all project participants and published in the *Daily Calumet* and in bulletins and newsletters of local organizations. Two to three hundred community people usually attended the council's meetings.

A forty-five-page bibliography of representative documents, books, newspaper and magazine articles, and scholarly references about Southeast Chicago and important exhibits of the district's history collected in the course of the project were compiled by consultant historians and library specialists and widely distributed in the academic community. The signal event of the project's first two years was a multimedia exhibit of Southeast Chicago's history at the Chicago Museum of Science and Industry. This exhibit, which employed the most sophisticated audio-visual technology, occupied 3,000 square feet of museum space, ran for five months (November 1982 to March 1983), and was viewed and experienced by hundreds of thousands of museum visitors. The exhibit's budget of more than $100,000 was funded by a special NEH grant, the support of the Illinois Humanities Council, Columbia College, and voluntary community contributions. The exhibit's beautiful forty-five-page catalog was published by the *Daily Calumet,* and the newspaper contributed all of its costs. More than 1,000 prominent members of the local community, the history project's leaders, and Chicago business, civic, and political luminaries celebrated the exhibit's opening at a dinner sponsored by the South Chicago Bank. The Museum exhibit also occasioned impressive media coverage—from local television to the *New York Times*—and a number of major newspaper and magazine features. The project's first phase ended with a big bang!

As the end of the project's second year and funding term neared, a new proposal was submitted to the National Endowment for the Humanities that sought support for a two-year extension and for production of a feature-length film documenting

Southeast Chicago's history and the life of the project.

While extension of the history-gathering effort increased community participation, and support for a great variety of associated activities remained the project's emphasis, we proposed a number of new initiatives. These included organizing one hundred lecture/discussion sessions in the district's neighborhoods; assisting local groups in creating their own archives; locating and developing a central, accessible, and permanent repository for the vast amount of historical material collected; production of a feature-length film documenting Southeast Chicago's history and the life and lesson of the project; and compiling a book on the project's methodology and process that could serve as a model and manual for similar projects in other American cities.

The budget for the project's second two-year span (Phase II) was fixed at $352,000. Of this, Columbia would fund $120,000 in contributed services; community contributions and project income would supply $40,000. A grant of $192,000 was requested from the National Endowment for the Humanities, a portion of which amount would be sought from the Illinois Humanities Council, which had given critical support to the project from its beginning. Undoubtedly, the Illinois Council's advocacy was valuably influential in securing NEH's support. Particularly, the Council's director and his colleagues were most thoughtful and dependable allies, though it would be hard to imagine that the project's remarkable record was anything less than perfectly convincing. Whatever, NEH approved the grant, and the project had two more years of life.

That was a busy time. In every instance, the goals of the project's second two years were more than surpassed. Virtually all of the community individuals who enlisted in the project during its initial years remained for the duration, and hundreds of new folk joined in the project's final two years. Indeed, many history committees had life for years after the project was done.

While neighborhood history committees, prominent agencies of the district's cultural, religious, fraternal, and commercial life, and the Steel Workers union established archives that told their own histories, the most important archival question was the choice of a permanent and accessible place to house and maintain the project's main collection of the documents of Southeast Chicago's history. There were impressive offers from the Chicago Historical Society and other Chicago repositories, but none of these satisfied the project's pledge to preserve the community's possession and use of its own history. This intent was admirably implemented by the South Chicago library's decision to provide and maintain a repository for the project's documents and to develop a program to maximize the use of its materials and accessibility to the district's schools and the scholarly community.

As told, film and video were important instruments of the project, used to visualize Southeast Chicago: to document contemporary events and cultural exhibits; as vehicles for recording oral histories and other historical reports; and to create a filmed record of project activity. The project's summary document was a feature film, *Wrapped in Steel,* which traced the district's history and reviewed the life of the project. The production of such a comprehensive film had been Jim Martin's intention since the project's inception, and while thousands of hours of film and video had been accumulated during the project's life span, Martin had carefully filmed many episodes to fully professional standards using selected student film crews and independent filmmakers, who were employed in filming *Wrapped in Steel*'s deliberate sequences. Martin spent nearly a year in assembling and editing the film, whose preview occasion marked the end of the project's formal life. The preview had about it the celebratory quality of an alumni gathering, having brought together an audience of more than eight hundred people who had participated in the project: community folk representing the district's neighborhoods and fraternal, religious, cultural, business, and union organizations; Columbia faculty and students; the project's staff and principal consultants; the Community Council and members of the original planning committee; prominent representatives of the media, the NEH, the Illinois Humanities Council, academic and arts communities, the district's schools, and state political leaders.

Wrapped in Steel was a splendid documentary film that won many local and national awards, was broadcast repeatedly on the stations of the public television network and enjoyed wide local and national distribution to schools, colleges, universities, and scholarly agencies. When the film's audience is tallied together with the hundreds of thousands who viewed the project's Museum of Science and Industry exhibit and the district's numbers, it is said fairly that the product of the Southeast Chicago Historical Project was known to millions of people—an astonishing result, apart from the impressive credential Columbia earned in its sponsorship.

There are, of course, no precise measures of the project's effect on the people of Southeast Chicago. In an isolated mill town that for generations had suffered the low regard of the mighty city at its border, it is no small accomplishment to have contributed to a restoration of personal self-esteem and community pride in the revealed history of its individuals, families, cultures, and institutions, and in its record of resistance to endemic economic hardship and struggle to organize and dignify its labor. The project performed a valuable human service. Unquestionably, the project's extraordinary publicity gave Southeast Chicago a respected place in the sun. And surely, the project gave Columbia students and faculty a unique opportunity to practice their arts and media crafts in an intensely real-life setting and to relate their education to humane purpose.

A paramount goal of the project was to create a permanent, comprehensive, easily accessible archive of Southeast Chicago's history that would serve the community's succeeding generations. That this legacy continues to be fulfilled was documented fifteen years later, in 1998, by Dominic Pacyga, the project's associate director, in the book, *Chicago's Southeast Side*, published in November 1998 by Arcadia Press as part of its "Images of America" series. Pacyga's book included 235 historical photographs collected by the project.

Pacyga reports that the project's archives are now housed in the James P. Fitzgibbons Museum in a wing of the Calumet Park fieldhouse and administered by the Southeast Chicago Historical Society, though the collection has grown in size and use to such an extent that a new location will have to be chosen. It is hoped that this will be in a new library being constructed in the district's East Side neighborhood. In addition to the archive's use by professional historians, college students, and particularly by large numbers of district residents, Southeast Chicago's public elementary and high schools are closely involved with the Museum's collections. High school students work with community volunteers to help sort, file, preserve, and catalog archival materials, and the archive is the source of scores of student projects and history fair submissions. The museum is appropriately named for James P. Fitzgibbons, who was the project's main community organizer and principal guide to the district's history.

Most importantly, the result of the Southeast Chicago Historical Project is the continuing recovery of the district's history by local people, and most rewarding, by young people who were not even born when Columbia's project flourished. That this has happened is surely a tribute to Jim Martin's extraordinary leadership and intuitive organizational abilities and to Dominic Pacyga's immense talent as a historian and organizer.

I and others who had given shape and implement to the project's invention saw it as a rare opportunity to put Columbia's unique collegiate focus on arts, communication, and liberal education to important social purpose. Indeed, the project was an exemplar of the main themes of the college's mission. We did not intend it as an independent exercise in social philosophy, nor did we believe that it was Columbia's role to found and foster an agency of Southeast Chicago's welfare and enlightenment, without fixing the college's authority and benefit. Otherwise, there would be no justification for a large commitment of the college's resources. In short, the Southeast Chicago Historical Project was "our thing."

I have never figured out why I believed it would be possible to enlist large numbers of the people of Southeast Chicago in an abstract engagement that offered them no profitable or visible benefit. Nor do I have any good explanation why so many people and agencies of the community's life actually became involved; certainly, the Southeast Chicago Historical Project satisfied no political or economic motive nor did it have roots in a common public issue. Indeed, nothing about the project offered a remedy for the acute economic crisis that gripped the district, and it would have been thought that immediate life preoccupations would discourage serious interest in something as unpromising and comparatively insignificant as the community's history. Moreover, the project seemed absent of the sort of constituency grievances that customarily fuel successful organizing campaigns. The enthusiasms of the project's academic, and even NEH funders, are more easily explained by the fact that the project's idea was intensely interesting and gave academics a unique opportunity to do what they do. It's fair to observe, too, that while many Columbia folk were genuinely intrigued by the project, it was, after all, my baby, and I did have the rank to rally the troops, though it should be recorded that project interest within the college was hardly universal, and in not developing a more convincing rationale and creative curriculum, I failed to inspire the participation of even greater student and faculty numbers.

The only thing I can observe safely is that Southeast Chicago was a unique place that included many people who were peculiarly responsive to the project's advertisement that gathering a record of their roots, traditions, and life experiences was an enlisting proposition.

In retrospect, I regretfully observe that Columbia did not attempt an encore to our four-year engagement in Southeast Chicago. I regret, too, that the project's benefit to the community was ultimately muted by the irreparable social and economic dislocations that accompanied the decline of Big Steel in the national economy. Although as a college institution Columbia had no legitimacy as an agent or organizer of social, economic, or political change, we had validated the main tenets of Columbia's idea of education, even in my inexplicable failure to influence an incorporation of this discovery in the college's succeeding institutional and educative process.

Chicago Artists Abroad

Jane invented this unique agency, which drew on her knowledge of foreign arts venues and the performance and exhibit of world artists in the United States. Her ingenious plan reversed the familiar flow of artists from there to here to concentrate on sending Chicago artists to perform and exhibit in foreign countries. These artists were not to be the few arts stars who enjoyed usual commercial opportunities, but instead, local artists representing all the arts disciplines, most of whom never contemplated performance or exhibit in foreign countries. Jane believed that such exposure would give Chicago artists a sense of their artistic worth and dignity, enhance their careers, and encourage their professionalism. Obviously, Jane's plan would require large funding, a discouragingly difficult prospect. She unsuccessfully solicited a number of corporations, foundations, and local and national government agencies. And then by the rarest coincidence, two sisters, Edith and Madge Rosenbaum, one living in New York and the other in Philadelphia, who had grown up in Chicago where the family had a very successful business, met with Fred Fine, then the Commissioner of Cultural Affairs. They told him of their interest in contributing money to a Chicago arts agency that supported a large range of artistic activity. He suggested they meet with Jane, who he said had a great idea that seemed a perfect fit with the Rosenbaums' interests. A few days later, Jane and Fred had a long lunch with the sisters where Jane described her project with convincing enthusiasm and Fred's endorsement. The Rosenbaums were seriously interested, with the ultimate result that they would give $250,000 to fund the first year of the project's life with reasonable expectation of a similar contribution in succeeding years if Columbia would contribute offices and support services. Within weeks, the agreement was assured by contract, and Jane's descriptive shorthand Chicago Artists Abroad (CAA) became the project's official title.

Jane would serve as the director, and Fred Fine would be the project's unpaid advisor. Together, they organized a panel of leading representatives of the city's arts disciplines who would choose the recipients of CAA grants, subject to final approval by Jane, Fred, and the Rosenbaum donors.

The project's announcement got exceptional coverage by all the local media and national arts publications, and widest circulation among Chicago arts organizations and individual artists. Indeed, the announcement was sent wherever arts activity of any sort was happening in Chicago and immediate suburbs. Grants would be made to individuals or groups whose artistic quality was demonstrable and who had a verifiable invitation by an established venue to perform or exhibit in a foreign country. Later, some invitations would be initiated by Jane or at the suggestion of panel members. Grants would be limited to $35,000, scaled according to budgets submitted and approved by CAA staff, and were mainly confined to travel costs, modest living expenses, and the cost of shipping art work, musical instruments, or stage props. Grant recipients were not allowed any personal compensation. There were two granting periods a year at each of which $100,000 was distributed, usually to fifteen to twenty individual artists or groups.

To say the least, CAA's initial announcement struck a responsive chord.

There were more than two hundred applications, which represented the greatest range of arts activity—dance troupes, theater casts, artists, and performers of every style, musical groups, individual musicians, singers, even an ornamental iron worker and a Ukrainian egg painter. Many, of course, were artistically unqualified, and others proposed undependable exhibit and performance sites. Some applicants were disqualified by unrealistic budgets, and some were already too established or commercially successful to warrant CAA's support. Of initial applicants, however, sixty-five merited serious consideration. In most instances, some member of the advisory panel knew the work of an applicant, or if unknown, panel members went to view the work.

Among the first Chicago artists to go abroad were two impressive dance troupes to Europe, and another to Australia; a pianist to England; an outstanding classical guitarist to Africa; a jazz ensemble to Germany; four artists to their own exhibits in France, Holland, England, and Sweden; two improvisational theater ensembles to perform "on the fringe" of the Edinburgh Festival; and a weaver to exhibit in Japan.

In a four-year span to 1991, CAA supported the performance and exhibit of nine hundred Chicago artists in the countries of Europe, Asia, Africa, South America, Central America, the Caribbean, Australia, New Zealand, and Canada, and Mexico. Muralists went to Russia; a South Side African-American church gospel choir toured Sicily and sang for the Pope in Rome; Chicago jazz ensembles played at music festivals in Europe, Japan, Africa, and Australia; and Chicago's dance companies enjoyed a world stage.

A number of American and world cities sought to model arts programs to CAA's example, and Jane and Fred Fine were engaged as special consultants to the governments of Singapore, Thailand, and Hong Kong to assist them in forming national arts councils. Jane was awarded the Ruth Page Medal for her contribution to the Chicago dance community. Certainly, none of this would have been possible without the extraordinary generosity of the Rosenbaums, who gave more than a million dollars to CAA's project. Regrettably, it ended with Jane's and my retirement, though undoubtedly, the unique benefit Chicago Artists Abroad gave to the artistic life of the city lives on.

Columbia and Educational Associations

In the late 1960s, well before Columbia was accredited, as a way to publicize Columbia as a real college, I seized every opportunity to put Columbia in the company of other more established institutions. As told earlier, this effort got a big boost when Columbia was accepted as a member of Council for the Advancement of Small Colleges (CASC). For the first time, Columbia was able to enjoy publicity as part of a respected college organization and the benefit of membership in an agency promoting the welfare of similar institutions. It was not until 1971 when Columbia was granted "candidate status" by the North Central Association, that the college became eligible for associate membership in the Federation of Independent Illinois Colleges and Universities (FIICU) and in major national organizations of higher education.

As with all agencies promoting special interests, the paramount interest of the associations of higher education was mainly to get government benefits for member institutions and to protect them from hostile legislation and restrictive regulations. Given crucial dependence on federal student-aid funds and on program and research grants from a wide range of government agencies, vigorous representation in Washington was a cardinal interest of the independent sector, and as much so in Springfield, which was an even greater source of student-aid funds and institutional benefits.

The National Association of Independent Colleges and Universities (NAICU), which included most of America's private institutions, conducted an influential Washington-based lobbying effort. FIICU's membership represented more than fifty

Illinois private colleges and universities, and it, too, engaged in a high energy lobby focused on the governor's office, the state legislature, and the Illinois Board of Higher Education. NAICU had a large paid staff of lobbyists, publicitors, and research specialists, and for special campaigns could readily mobilize scores of presidents and other representatives of member institutions to testify before House and Senate committees and to lobby the members of Congress.

FIICU, with only a small staff, was more dependent on the political representations of its president, chairpersons of its boards of directors, and presidents of member institutions, who worked Springfield during sessions of the legislature, and otherwise solicited support from legislators who represented their college's district.

For many years, FIICU's president was Alban "Stormy" Weber, a retired navy admiral and once a Chicago alderman. A big craggy figure, Stormy was an exceptional politician and lobbyist. Both the state's public and private sectors enjoyed talented advocacy and fair-minded treatment from a succession of directors of the Illinois Board of Higher Education, particularly from the enlightened ministrations of Richard Wagner, who served that office for many years, and from Larry Matejka, who directed the state's student-aid program. More importantly, Illinois's governors, Jim Thompson particularly, were sympathetic to the state's higher education community and distinctly fair-minded in apportioning benefit to the independent sector.

Though all independent Illinois colleges and universities shared in the benefit of the state's largess, political participation by member presidents was unevenly performed, and efforts to enlist influential members of the boards of FIICU institutions in lobbying work were only minimally productive. Even when the cause is virtuous, its communication requires zeal, persistence, and skill, and few seem so inclined or comfortable with its rigors.

Over a twenty-year span, Admiral Weber and his successor Donald Fouts were zealous and skillful representatives of FIICU's cause. Memorable, too, was the leadership of that effort given by federation chairmen, particularly Donald Mundinger, president of Illinois College; Richard Stephens, president of Greenville College; and DePaul University's president, Rev. John Richardson, though other presidents of Illinois colleges and universities had distinguished terms as federation chairs: for example, the very influential advocacy of Illinois independent colleges and universities performed by Raymond Baumhart, president of Loyola University, and by John Cortelyou, an earlier president of DePaul University.

Columbia was a very important player in FIICU's political work, and I was a prominent advocate of the independent sector's interest and of the general welfare of higher education in Illinois and nationally. Unquestionably, Columbia fielded a formidable political team. I was an experienced political hand and so was Don Canar, the retired president of the Central YMCA Community College, who I had hired to represent Columbia's legislative interests. Don was a splendidly capable and persuasive man with a great store of political ingenuity. In the late 1980s, we also had the important benefit of Sidney Ordower's ties to the African-American community and to minority legislators.

In last analysis, Columbia's political effort was motivated by institutional self-interest, which reflected a clear recognition that a critical part of Columbia's success stemmed from legislated benefits, student-aid funds particularly. I believe, however, that Columbia's political effort and my role were regarded suspiciously by a number of FIICU presidents because of Columbia's recentness, unprecedented quick success, advocacy of questionably collegiate admission policies, and my bold passions, which may have discomforted some of my federation colleagues. But I was disturbed, too, by NAICU's and FIICU's emphasis on strategies for increasing and protecting government benefits to the near exclusion of discussion of contemporary social issues and matters of educational substance.

This generalization, however, is not meant to include the remarkably progressive sisters who were presidents of Catholic women's colleges in Illinois. All were intensely committed to humane service, and while active participants in the strategies of government benefit, the motives of their calling were never out of mind. Sisters Candida Lund, President of Rosary College; Ann Ida Gannon, President of Mundelein College; Margaret Burke, President of Barat College; Irenaeus Chekouras, President of St. Xavier College; Marjorie Noterman, President of Malinkrodt College; and Jean Murray, a later president of Rosary College were all educators in the fullest sense of its meaning. Whatever, I diligently worked the Washington scene in testifying before House and Senate committees and in lobbying the members of Congress and officials of federal agencies on behalf of higher education's agenda, its independent sector particularly. And I similarly worked Springfield, the state legislature and Illinois officials.

Not all of Columbia's associations were as immediately political as the college's NAICU and FIICU affiliations, though all served, at least indirectly, to extend Columbia's public identity and educational and civic influence.

In the early 1980s, my dear friend Ron Williams, then president of Chicago's Northeastern University and widely regarded as one of the most influential African-American leaders in American higher education, asked me to join a small group of local public university presidents constituted as the "Chicago Metropolitan Higher Education Council." The main purpose of this agency then was to secure state funding for TV Channel 20, which intended service to the Chicago region's educational community, both common schools, colleges, and universities. CMHEC's membership included Don Riddle, the Chancellor of the University of Illinois at Chicago; Benjamin Alexander, President of Chicago State University; Leo Goodman Malamuth, President of Governor's State University; Oscar Shabat, Chancellor of the Chicago City Colleges system; and Dr. Presley Holmes, who had been chosen as the intended TV station's president; Ron Williams; and myself.

The Chicago Board of Education had abandoned Channel 20's license as too costly, and the Federal Communications Commission reassigned it to the CMHEC consortium. When I joined CMHEC, the consortium had already developed an unusual program for the project's implementation when expected state funding was secure. What happened instead was a maddening series of legislative and official misadventures that extended over more than three years. Somewhere in the course of that time, I became CMHEC's chair. The station venture needed an appropriation of millions of dollars. It was voted and vetoed and voted again and lost in some inexplicable confusion, until the funding measure just fell out of the governor's and the legislature's agenda. While our effort to put the station on the air was exhausted, CMHEC still owned the rights to Channel 20. As it was potentially a very valuable property, we were reluctant to turn it back to the FCC, though there was no likelihood that the consortium had or could find money to launch and operate the station. The only known alternative was to transfer the rights to Channel 20 to WTTW, who were most anxious to get the channel to expand their programming. But our negotiations with WTTW were unsatisfactory, mostly because of our insistence that the station be used primarily for instructional purposes, which was probably not an economical option for WTTW. After some weeks of intense talk, the WTTW proposition collapsed, but by that time, Oscar Shabat had gotten the board of the City Colleges system to agree to equip and fund the station's operation. Their support continues today.

CMHEC's negotiations with WTTW had a déjà vu quality for me. In 1955, with then Senator Mark Tobey's leadership, Congress passed an act reserving two TV channels in every state for educational and public service broadcasting. The FCC received a much smaller number of applications than expected and the allotted time period for making applications was about to expire. I read some reference to the issue that led me to make a casual inquiry of Senator Tobey's office. Surprisingly, I got a phone call from Senator Tobey who said no application had been made from Chicago. He urged me to quickly make an application on Columbia's behalf. It was really a preposterous notion; Columbia didn't remotely have the resources for such a venture. But it didn't cost anything but a bit of time to put Columbia's oar in the water. I spent a weekend composing an application for an educational TV channel, which described a station which would emphasize news and public affairs. While I've no memory of what it said, I got something back which implied that Columbia might be awarded the Chicago channel.

Fortunately, before I choked on that, the application deadline was extended, allowing time for Edward Ryerson, a prominent industrialist, and other Chicago luminaries to organize a Chicago Educational TV Committee and to submit a more realistic application; though I think my emphasis on news and public affairs was a superior concept. Columbia's application, however, remained in play, at least to the extent that I was invited to participate in the Ryerson committee's discussions. In time, however, my ideas and I were put on a back bench, and after a gaggle of futilities, I retired, a TV mogul no more.

Stripped of its original motive, CMHEC decided to organize an enlarged consortium of metropolitan Chicago's public and independent colleges and universities who embraced an urban mission. No common agency of the city's urban institutions had ever existed before. I was reelected as chairman of the new CMHEC, which would focus on marshaling the energy and resources of Chicago's higher education community to better serve the city's elementary and secondary schools and on developing a collective role in Chicago's affairs for local colleges and universities. In this effort, we meant initially only to create a forum for regular dialogue between the region's collegiate institutions and to begin the design of an agenda of common interests. There were to be no organizational formalities nor dues expected, and we would avoid any effort to enlist institutions like the University of Chicago, Northwestern, and Loyola, which viewed themselves as national universities and did not emphasize a local urban mission. Nor would there be any effort to recruit small denominational colleges, which also did not identify themselves as urban institutions. We did, however enlist a number of city and suburban institutions. Among these were DePaul, Roosevelt, Governors State, and Illinois Benedictine College.

Lively discussion began immediately, and the new CMHEC's agenda was quickly crowded with issues. We chose several initial activities: a research project to reveal the relations between African-American and Latino students in Chicago public high schools; a collective effort of CMHEC institutions to recruit tutors to help students in Chicago's schools; and an exploratory effort to involved CMHEC institutions in the city's economic development. As our consortium had no staff or independent funds, these efforts depended entirely on implementations of member institutions. Understandably, success was a mixed bag. We did complete a perceptive study of a number of high schools that were acutely troubled by hostilities between African-American and Latino students, though unlike other CMHEC projects, this was funded by a grant I had secured from the Chicago Community Trust. While our institutions did recruit nearly one thousand tutors, the Chicago School System mostly bungled their benefit. In contrast, Mayor Washington's department of Economic Development welcomed cooperation with Chicago colleges and universities.

A bit earlier, when Chicago's schools were in customary crisis, Mayor Jane Byrne was responsive to an idea proposed by Oscar Shabat and me that a committee be formed with us as representatives of Chicago's urban institutions, Mayor Byrne, and a prominent business representative of her choice to advise Ruth Love, Chicago's school superintendent. Dr. Love was adamant in her rejection of the idea and since a squabble with the school superintendent was the last thing Mayor Byrne needed on the eve of a primary election, the proposition was abandoned, though we found Jane Byrne to be very thoughtful and sensitive to school issues.

Most regrettably, after four years, the whole CMHEC project collapsed with the death of Ron Williams, a most noble and talented man, the inexplicable replacements of Don Riddle as chancellor of the University of Illinois at Chicago, and Oscar Shabat as chancellor of the City Colleges system, and the resignation of Ben Alexander as president of Chicago State University. Like the Bulls, CMHEC's team was too diminished to go on. And regrettably, an organization of Chicago's urban public and independent colleges and universities has never since been reformed.

While FIICU's and NAICU's focus on government benefits for the independent sector addressed issues of paramount concern to Columbia, the Association of Urban Universities (AUU) better represented Columbia's commitment to an urban constituency. Again, Ron Williams was the agent of the college's membership in AUU, as he had similarly facilitated Columbia's membership in the Chicago Metropolitan Higher Education Council. Later, I would have the honor of succeeding him as chairman of both organizations. AUU had been founded by a number of public universities in major cities who contended that the national associations of public higher education failed to represent the special interests of big-city institutions. Their contentions were similarly valid in describing the indifference of NAICU to urban institutions in the independent sector.

Unlike NAICU or the national associations of public higher education, AUU intended to be an association with membership that would represent both public and independent urban institutions and transcend traditional public and independent separations. Though AUU's membership included only fifty or so institutions, these, including the University of Minnesota, the New York City University system, the University of Massachusetts, and New York University, the nation's largest independent university, represented a sizable percentage of America's college student population. AUU's Washington lobby was responsible for many Congressional enactments and representations to government agencies, which benefited all urban colleges and universities and their city communities.

AUU had a miniscule staff, and its lobbying effort depended on the commitment and zeal of the presidents of its member institutions. But it did have in its president, Jim Harrison, a wizard of congressional influence, and the indefatigable services of its legal counsel, Mike Goldstein, who served AUU and its membership with extraordinary talent. Harrison had spent many years as the administrative director of the House Committee on Higher Education and as the principal aide to Congressman William Ford who, with Senator Pell, authored and managed the passage of the main provisions of student aid legislation. Mike Goldstein perfectly deserved his reputation as the dean of higher education's legal counsels.

Prominent Alumni*

Leonard Amato, Producer

Daniel Asma, Editor

Kaz Ayukawa, Artist, Film Director and Cinematographer

Julie Badel, Lawyer, Partner; *McDermott, Will, and Emery*

Mark Ballogg, Architectural Photographer

Reginald Benjamin, Singer/Songwriter

Peter Berkos, Academy Award–winner for Special Effects, *The Hindenberg*

Ronit Bezalel, Documentary Filmmaker

Lee Bey, Deputy Chief of Staff, *Chicago Mayor's Office*

Peter Biagi, Cinematographer

Michael Black, Writer

Jay Bonansinga, Writer

Christopher "Spike" Brandt, Animator/Creator, *Duck Dodgers*

Suzanne Burge, Vice President of Marketing, *Elektra Records*

Charles Carner, President, *Southside Films*

Mary Carrol, Poet

Anthony Cervone, Animator, *Duck Dodgers*

Nick Charles, CNN Sports Anchor

Eileen Cherry, Professor, *DePaul University*

Vandell Cobb, Chief Photographer, *Ebony Magazine*

Karen Lee Copeland, TV Executive and Producer

Chet Coppock, TV/Radio Sportscaster

Anthony DeCavitch, Director of Marketing, *JAG Sports Management*

Denis Dimitreas, Songwriter, Entertainer, Writer and Restaurateur

Don De Grazia, Novelist, *American Skin,* Scribners

Andy Dick, Actor, *NBC-TV, News Radio*

David Drizner, President, *Data for Development*

Bruce DuMont, President, *Museum of Broadcast Communications*

Wolfram Dochterman, President, *Uniworld Communications, TV Stations*

Robert Enrietto, Director, *Sila*

Elaine Equi, Poet

Katherine Ernst, Associate Producer, *Dateline, NBC-TV*

Craig Fry, President, *Gould, Van Huis and Fry Marketing*

F. Gary Gray, Director

Vince Garrity, President, *Fansteel Corp.*

Yan Geling, Prizewinning Chinese Novelist and Screenwriter

Michael Goi, Cinematographer

Laura Good, Singer

Steven Gross, Photographer

Charyl Hallman-Manning, Executive Producer, *Manning Productions*

Michael Hecht, President, *Hecht Realty Group*

Larry Heinemann, Novelist, *National Book Award* recipient, *Paco's Story*

Buzz Hirsch, Film Director, *Academy Award* recipient, *Silkwood*

Isabella Hoffman, featured TV and Film actress, *Homicide*

Michael Inglesh, Emmy Award-winning cameraman, *Jenny Jones Show*

Sandra Jackson-Opoku, Writer/Poet

Rashid Johnson, Photographer

Jeff Jur, Film director, *Last Seduction* and *Dirty Dancing*

Robert Kaden, President, *The Kaden Company*

Janusz Kaminski, cinematographer, *Academy Award* recipient for *Shindler's List* and *Saving Private Ryan*

Jon Kass, Columnist, *Chicago Tribune*

Justin Kaufmann, WBEZ, *Schadenfreude* cast member

Jennifer Kelliher, CEO, *Market Strategies Inc.*

Stephen Kmetko, Co-host, *Entertainment Daily*

William W. Leff, Radio Personality, *WNND*

Tod Lending, *Oscar-winning* Documentarian

Martin Lennartz, *WXRT Radio*

Josh Liss, Anchor/Reporter, *WBBM News Radio*

Donald Mann, Sales Manager, *WBBM/CBS Radio*

Robert McNamara, Senior Correspondent, *CBS News*

Joseph Meno, Novelist, *Tender As Hellfire*, St. Martin's Press

Mary Mitchell, Columnist/Editorial Board, *Chicago Sun-Times*

Ozier Muhammad, Photographer, *New York Times, Pulitzer Prize*

Patrick Muldowney, Network TV News Anchor

Nancy Mattel, Executive Director, *Mercy Hospital and Medical Center*

Franklin McCarthy, radio personality, *McCarthy's Circle*

Michael McCarthy, Senior Vice President, *Cineplex Odeon*

John McNaughton, film director, *Mad Dog and Glory*

Kenneth McReynolds, Sportscaster, *Comcast Network*

Janine Nolan, children's book writer, *Harvey Potter's Amazing Balloon Farm*

Ivory Ocean, TV actor, *Fox TV*, Key West

Anita Padilla, Correspondent, *NBC 5 News*

Harry Parrish, Vice President, *Howard Johnson, Inc.*

Joseph Peyronnin, Executive Vice President, *Telemundo*

Tonya Pinkins, Singer/Actress

Mark Protosevich, Screenwriter, *The Cell, Batman*

Declan Quinn, Cinematographer, *Leaving Las Vegas*

Alan Rafalson, President, *Rafalson Public Relations*

Robert Renzetti, Animator/Creator, *My Life as a Teenage Robot*

Melinda Roenisch, Filmmaker

Andy Richter, cohost, *Late Night with Conan O'Brien*

Charles Rudnick, Creative Director; *Foote, Cone, and Belding Advertising*

Edward Russell, Executive Vice President, *Tristar Pictures*

Patrick Sajack, Host, *Wheel of Fortune*

Lindsey Schwartz, Associate Producer, *Dateline, NBC*

Howard Shapiro, TV Director, *ABC 7*

Bob Sirott, Host, *Chicago Tonight*

Hollis Sigler, Painter

Joe Sikora, Actor

Peter Schlesinger, Former Governor of *Academy of Arts and Sciences*

Nancy Stern, Film Producer, *Across the Moon*

Paul Tarini, Director, Public Affairs, *Johnson Foundation*

Genndy Tartakovsky, Animator/Creator, *Dexter's Lab, Samurai Jack*

Robert Teitel, Producer, *Soul Food, Men of Honor, Barbershop I/II*

Kirkland Tibbels, Producer, Founder, *Funny Boy Films*

George Tillman, Director, *Soul Food, Men of Honor, Barbershop I/II*

Walter Topel, TV and Film Director, *Theater Producer*

Rosalyn Varon, Traffic and Entertainment Reporter, *ABC 7, Chicago*

Frank Vascellero, News Anchor, *KARE-TV, Minneapolis, Minnesota*

Sam Weller, Author, *Secret Chicago, The Authorized Biography of Ray Bradbury*

Jonathan Wellner, Actor

Marlon West, Animation Supervisor, *Walt Disney*

Albert Williams, Writer/Critic

Jim Williams, Reporter, *WBBM-TV News*

Ron Wise, Vice President of Public Affairs, *Cedars-Sinai Hospital, Los Angeles*

Theodore Witcher, Film Director, *Love Jones*

★In some instances, employment affiliations may not be current.

PHOTOGRAPHY

Steven D. Arazmus
PhotoChicago Associates

Chappell Studio

Randy Donofrio

Eric Futran

Larry Glatt

Sydney Harris

Janie Hutchison

Joseph Janowicz

Lynn Manuell

James Newberry

Michael Tropea

ILLUSTRATIONS & DRAWINGS

John Fischetti

Jeff MacNelly

Hollis Sigler